THE STRANGE A

ROY FULLER was born in 19
Oldham and Manchester. For [illegible] was a solicitor with the Woolwich Equitable Building Society, from which he retired as a Director in 1987. He has also been (during the Second World War) a radar mechanic, the Oxford Professor of Poetry 1968–73 and a Governor of the BBC 1972–79. His many books of verse include *New and Collected Poems 1934–84*, *Consolations* and, most recently, *Available for Dreams*, together with nine novels. *The Strange and the Good*, his collected memoirs, follows his life until demobilization at the end of the war.

By the same author

Poems

NEW AND COLLECTED POEMS 1934–84

THE INDIVIDUAL AND HIS TIMES: SELECTED POEMS

SUBSEQUENT TO SUMMER

CONSOLATIONS

AVAILABLE FOR DREAMS

Novels

WITH MY LITTLE EYE

THE SECOND CURTAIN

FANTASY AND FUGUE

IMAGE OF A SOCIETY

THE RUINED BOYS

THE FATHER'S COMEDY

THE PERFECT FOOL

MY CHILD, MY SISTER

THE CARNAL ISLAND

Criticism

OWLS AND ARTIFICERS

PROFESSORS AND GODS

For Children

SAVAGE GOLD

CATSPAW

THE WORLD THROUGH THE WINDOW:
COLLECTED POEMS FOR CHILDREN

Anthology

FELLOW MORTALS

Roy Fuller

THE STRANGE AND THE GOOD

Collected Memoirs

COLLINS HARVILL
8 Grafton Street, London W1
1989

COLLINS HARVILL
William Collins Sons and Co Ltd
London · Glasgow · Sydney · Auckland
Toronto · Johannesburg

BRITISH LIBRARY CATALOGUING IN PUBLICATION DATA

Fuller, Roy *1912–*
The strange and the good: collected memoirs
1. Poetry in English. Fuller, Roy. Biographies
I. Title
821'.912

ISBN 0-00-272029-9

Souvenirs first published by London Magazine Editions 1980
Vamp Till Ready first published by London Magazine Editions 1982
Home and Dry first published by London Magazine Editions 1984
This revised and abridged one-volume edition first published by Collins Harvill 1989

© Roy Fuller 1980, 1982, 1984, 1989

All rights reserved. This book is sold subject to the condition that it shall not, by way of trade or otherwise, be lent, re-sold, hired out or otherwise circulated without the publisher's prior consent in any form of binding or cover other than that in which it is published and without a similar condition including this condition being imposed on the subsequent purchaser.

Printed and bound in Great Britain by
Hartnolls Limited, Bodmin, Cornwall

To my brother John
who should have written some of it

AUTHOR'S NOTE

A somewhat extended version of these memoirs was published by London Magazine Editions in three hardback volumes – *Souvenirs* (1980), *Vamp Till Ready* (1982), and *Home and Dry* (1984). But for the critical and practical encouragement of Alan Ross I should not have proceeded beyond *Souvenirs*. I am thankful I did.

The generic title comes from the late Glyn Daniel's fine autobiography, *Some Small Harvest*, where he recounts that Sir James Wordie, Master of St John's, Cambridge, "used to classify the world into strange men and good men".

Contents

I

SOUVENIRS

I *Jeux*

As I start an explanatory note about the genesis of these memoirs of my childhood and youth, thinking that so truncated a life and brief a narrative ought to be thus prefaced, I remember that the table in the dining-room of my grandparents' house, soon to be mentioned, was on one occasion an operating table. I believe I was twelve when my mother decided I should undergo a tonsillectomy and this for some reason I cannot fathom was to take place while we were staying at the house in Hollins Road, Oldham, though we had lived for some years in Blackpool. My mother may have had knowledge from the past about the doctor concerned, or perhaps my grandfather urged his claims, possibly as a pillar of the Conservative Club. I had stayed in bed, breakfastless, on the morning in question, but when at last I was summoned for the ordeal I saw that the green table-cloth had been removed, as though I was going to use my water-colours or indian ink, and a sheet substituted.

I had a general anaesthetic and when I woke found myself on the sofa under the dining-room window from which, kneeling, I used on normal days to watch people going in and out of the little park, likely catching a glimpse of Ernest's lean, almost ragged figure. Probably I had been carried there by the doctor and the anaesthetist, if there was one. I felt terribly sick and was sick: tonsillectomy is (or was) messy, and for minor surgery comparatively risky, because of the impossibility of staunching the blood. But later in the day, and despite the soreness, I ate a boiled egg. Though set in the mid-Twenties the scene seems Victorian; some Academy picture: "A Young Life Preserved".

This was actually my second tonsillectomy. The then-considered harmful appendages had been removed in infancy but had grown again. The doctor of the second operation was critical of the first: unless the *roots* of tonsils were thoroughly excised these twin foci of infection *would* re-establish themselves. He himself would ensure that this time the knife, so to speak, plunged deep enough. An additional eradication was to be performed. An eye-tooth, seemingly surplus to requirements, had grown out of the gum above existing teeth. Though I realized something would eventually have to be done about this, cowardice stopped me from initiating any action; indeed, I had developed a habit of smiling, even laughing, with my lips closed (an accomplishment that would have been useful at the theatrical treat later bestowed by the Boss), to prevent my mother being reminded to take me to the dentist. However, I think it was she who mentioned the tooth to the doctor. I was greatly impressed by his confident promise to remove it on his way to the tonsils – that he should have the skills and implements for the job. Again, how antediluvian seems the absence of orthodontics in the life of the middle class, albeit rather lower middle class.

The book that follows grew from the chapter "Long Time a Child", which in its original form was commissioned by a magazine for a series on writers' family life. Some time after writing the piece it seemed to me I might, and ought to, continue a little further. A pattern of introspection, comedy, and the ills that flesh is heir to, had already been set, so that though there is chronological progression, the book (for the continuation itself continued) essentially partakes of the nature of a set of variations. This may be seen in the tonsillectomy episode just related, which (in a couple of senses)had its roots in infancy, involved boyhood and then went on into adolescence and beyond – for after I left school I suffered severe attacks of tonsillitis, at least one occasion bordering on quinsies, if not actually reaching that torture, and the doctor of those later days wanted to remove my tonsils for the third time, a course by then I had enough status to resist. Luckily it was not the school doctor who was involved, a big, moustached, masterful Scot who once, looking at a boil on my cheek, said: "Aye, I'll just ease that", fumbling in his waistcoat pocket and producing what proved to be a portable scalpel, the unscrewable blade being reversed and fitted into the handle when carried. The ensuing scar is visible to this day: the absence of hygiene had no ill effect, however.

I seem to think Dr MacFarland lived and had his surgery in the very street in which the school was situated: certainly my friend Leslie and his mother's house was there, a house they shared at that time with the uncle who later drew Bartók from the air. And as to that carbuncular epoch, I have somehow had to omit mention of another boy who became a friend, though less close than Leslie, called Charles Edward Emanuel Fahmy. I have changed the surname as I have done throughout where an actual name might cause pain or embarrassment. Fahmy arrived at school when already fifteen or sixteen, typical of the exotic boarder the school would catch in greater numbers in its palmier days. Though he was an Egyptian – or at any rate lived there: the clash of forenames with surname rather mysterious – his English was first class and he was contumelious about the ability in that sphere of the headmaster of his previous school in Alexandria, whose notion of idiomatic English was to say as rapidly as my grandfather repeating the ice cream recipe given anon: "Very nice, very good, very nice for the bally vater-closet." Thinking of the impregnable Boss, this ignorant folly on the part of a headmaster struck me as strange indeed.

I refer subsequently to one's personal sense of the significant autobiographical detail, and the misgivings about trying to share it. In certain instances there is an historical or archeological element, slight reminders or revelations of the past which have intrinsic interest. I might have written, for example, with not much guilt about the risk of boring, of Jack Hylton, who in very early days starred in the pierrots in Happy Valley; his father, also on view, being the impresario of the troupe. Later "Jack Hylton and His Band" appeared at the "Palace Varieties", famous enough to take up the whole of the "second half". The big band sound of special timbre was to be heard for some seconds before the foot-lighted curtain rose, causing my Uncle Freddy (visiting us at the time) to remark justly on the formicating frisson these aural and visual effects induced. Later Jack Hylton himself became an impresario, but on a scale far beyond his father, though by then he had strangely come to resemble the elderly man who used to mooch about Happy Valley. I could also have expanded experiences in the theatre. My paternal grandmother was said to have been a Spanish dancer, but perhaps everyone lays claim to some romantic forebear. In any case, as will be seen, I inherited a sufficient taste for the boards from my mother's side. I wonder how many remember as vividly as I do Cora Goffin (marvellous Jamesian name, now overlain by the distinguished but more commonplace cognomen Lady Littler): an extremely pretty girl, excellent dancer on excellent legs, with a more than passable voice, usually taking the lead in

Number One touring companies of Twenties musical comedies like *Princess Charming*.

But this is degenerating into an old buffer's chain of consciousness. One or two links more must be added, however, though the last thing one wants to do is to impose a method of reading the book or give away such game as it possesses. Certain musical compositions have been made out of wisps of themes, fitted together simply where practicable (as it appears) and scarcely repeated. One says "compositions" but perhaps a single work is in mind, *Jeux*. Not for the first time one thinks apropos of creativity: if only one had been a composer! As in life, the scenario of the ballet has its strong elements of the commonplace not to say ludicrous – "a park, a game of tennis, the chance encounter of two girls and a young man in pursuit of a lost tennis ball" (as Debussy in part described it) – yet the music's final effect is enigmatic and elusive. During the writing of my later pages I read for the first time *The Education of Henry Adams*, with increasing dismay at the grasp the author shows of his life, particularly of its broad intellectual turns and advances. Here, that side of things is more or less confined to such discoveries as that the title of the sad song "Vale", often sung in the drawing-rooms of childhood, was not pronounced like "veil", an item of women's attire still quite popular at the time – and the subject of a joke I think told by Fred Walmsley which I found memorably funny. Two women are eating tripe in a restaurant and one remarks: "This tripe's tough." Says the other: "You wouldn't find it so tough, dear, if you pushed your veil up."

During my life various kinds of enigmas or conundrums have come into fashion, been worked to death, and then forgotten. "There's no Owen Nares," I used solemnly to say to grown-ups, he being a celebrated matinée idol of the time. When this was challenged as contrary to reality (the challenger nevertheless uneasily feeling in a dotty kind of way that one so handsome might possibly be a waxwork or automaton), the explanation followed that indeed there was no "o" in Nares. Rather later, the catch took the form of a question about a popular song, such as "Do you know the big horse song?" "No, what's that?" "*Because I Love You.*" Coincidentally it comes to mind that this number was in the repertoire of Layton and Johnstone, favourites of Auntie Vi.

Recalling, or trying to recall, riddles – that not too badly describes the autobiographical process, conducted as it is in my case with the most meagre of source material. Nor, of course, is the past frozen in the mind, to be dug out in lumps like ice, some fragmented in the doing. Rather, it goes on changing until the end of life. Only the other day did I read that 1911 was Coronation Year, with a summer of exceptional heat. In that season I was conceived (my young parents' first child) in circumstances – perhaps of *al fresco* curiousness – no one can ever know.

2 *Long Time A Child*

My father and his sister were brought up in Caithness in circumstances that have never been made clear to me. They were "remittance children", probably illegitimate, destined for a life far above the station of the family that looked after them. Early photographs show them prosperously, even ornately, dressed, looking out with aplomb. Then the remittances stopped, perhaps in their early teens, and they came south to Manchester or its immediate environs where there was a business connection with the family that had reared them. Both children proved extremely capable. My aunt, Minnie, became Matron (or possibly merely Assistant Matron) of the Manchester Royal Infirmary at, I should judge, a remarkably early age. My father, Leopold, twenty-seven or twenty-eight at the date of my birth in 1912, was then assistant works manager of a rubber-proofing mill just outside Manchester. Later he became a director. Both children must, in their late teens and early twenties, have addressed themselves energetically to making a way in the world, rather as if they were native small-town Scots of the epoch. Minnie's career speaks for itself. I have a copy of *Vanity Fair* awarded to my father "for success in Practical Inorganic Chemistry" during the 1904–05 session by the Manchester School of Technology which presumably he attended out of working hours. I have also (in a sparse collection of relics) a notebook he kept as a young man, in his elegant and masterful hand, of stock exchange speculations mostly in options and for comically small sums, obviously all he could afford to risk. His interest in rubber plantation shares persisted, for I recall them being discussed when I was a boy: they were low-priced and highly speculative, and presumably he knew something about the demand for and price of the product – ideal subjects for a flutter.

At every age his photographs show him to have possessed quite startlingly good looks. Blond as a child, his hair later turned dark and wavy; his complexion as an adult was of the olive kind; nose straight, lips well-formed; eyes light rather than dark. This appearance was often thought to be "foreign": it caused consternation to my maternal grandfather when my mother introduced her fiancé or intended fiancé to her family. My grandfather was always greatly suspicious of anything alien to his own way of life or at any rate the way of life of the English provincial establishment. It must have been as late as the time of the first Labour administration that I heard him grudgingly admit that the gang of Labour politicians in local government owned at least a simian cleverness.

At the time of my mother's marriage in 1910 my grandfather, Fred Broadbent, must already have been Superintendent Registrar of Births, Marriages and Deaths for Oldham, the industrial town seven miles to the north-east of Manchester. He had previously been Master of Oldham Workhouse, before that Clerk to the Master, and a good while before that a schoolmaster, though I guess his academic qualifications were minimal. The story goes that a qualification for the initial workhouse post was the ability to play for the services in the workhouse chapel, an accomplishment he falsely claimed. When it was put to the test he played a few elementary chords on the organ (probably with the restricted fingers to be hereafter mentioned), my grandmother diverting attention with her expert voice. My mother used sometimes to surprise people momentarily by observing that she had been born in the workhouse, as was literally the case. She had a repertoire of stories of those days, some scatological: the effect of the sudden richness of the beer and plum pudding served for Christmas dinner on the internal economy of the geriatric inmates, the simpleton who used to collect the ordure from the lavatories upsetting his wheeled bin and interspersing his bare-handed scooping-up with bites from a piece of bread.

There were a few books in my grandparents' house (notably,

from my point of view, Austin Freeman's *The Singing Bone*) and my grandfather probably borrowed from the public library, for he was once heard to say that he liked a good novel (which he pronounced "nuvvle"), instancing Donn Byrne (a middle-brow writer who may now be forgotten) as a purveyor of that commodity. He was a Justice of the Peace, active in local politics, a Tory Councillor, later an Alderman, and in 1924–25 Mayor of the Borough. Yet he was essentially an indolent man, though plainly not lacking application and ability in areas of life that interested him. Perhaps his talent was for "play" rather than work. He was, for instance, very keen on bridge which he played both at home and at the local Conservative club. At home at least he would punctuate the game with remarks, often quotations (as were not a few of his remarks in general conversation). When playing an obviously losing hand and his opponents got the lead, trumps exhausted, he might, for example, say: "The curse never fell upon our nation until now." He showed in other contexts familiarity with the text of *The Merchant of Venice*, very likely a hangover from his pedagogical days.

I know my brother will not mind my saying that he and I often recognize in ourselves these and other characteristics of our maternal grandfather. (In my case I feel I have become more and more like him in physique and habits as the years have gone by, though even as boys we imitated him – sometimes to the extent of tucking the two outer fingers of each hand into the palm when playing cards or raising a glass, for he suffered from the shrinking of the tissues known as Dupuytrin's Contracture.) I would include a certain recklessness about gaining personal advantage. And about personal dignity. Both my grandparents had catarrh (Oldham is high, cold and damp: good for cotton-spinning, bad for human respiration). When in the mornings of 1924–25 the mayoral limousine arrived to take my grandfather to his duties he might not immediately enter the door held open by the chauffeur but go behind the car to expectorate into the gutter the phlegm raised by the sudden influx of outside air to his chest. There may well have been a conscious element of self-deflation in this: his accent always became very broad when encountering proletarian characters and being so well known in his various avatars his progress in the street was a succession of such encounters: " 'Ow do, Fred?" " 'Ow do, Albert?") Though two of his brothers, James and Newton, did well for themselves, he never had any more money than his salary and pension, and lived in simple circumstances. As time went on I think he grew fond of my father and certainly appreciated aspects of the latter's rapidly changing life-style. "Leo spoilt my taste for cheap cigars," he once said. He lit and smoked an occasional cigarette almost as carefully and daintily as a cigar, the mode accentuated by the limited number of fingers available.

Emily Jenkins (her maiden name), my maternal grandmother, had a background even humbler than my grandfather's. Her father had been a regular soldier, had served in the Crimean War, had ended up as Sergeant. At one time, presumably as a pensioner, he had had a newspaper round, my grandmother acting as delivery girl – shoeless and stockingless, according to tradition (though that would not have been uncommon at the epoch in question: I myself as a boy saw barefoot children in Oldham). Later she worked as a mill-girl, probably in a cotton-spinning factory. She had an outstanding singing voice, was in a church choir at the age of eight and as a young teenager was invited to join a small paid church choir as leader. She had acting ability, too, and before she was married rejected, on the advice of the old stick-in-the-mud parson at her church, the chance of a stage career. After bringing up five children and playing her part in public and charitable affairs, in old age she took up drawing and painting, mostly of the "automatic" kind. Her talent in this line was not great but the facility had blossomed in two of her sons, who were adroit amateur technicians in the graphic arts. Most of her children could sing and act. My mother inherited "a good voice", as they used to say – a mezzo-soprano, as I imagine my grandmother's to have initially been – but in the years after her marriage employed it only for occasional domestic purposes.

My grandparents owned an HMV gramophone whose beautifully made oak horn probably indicated that it was a good machine of its epoch, which may, however, have been somewhat remote. Though I remember my youngest uncle bringing home Luigini's *Ballet Egyptien* as a hair-raising sample of the new technique of "electrical" recording, I do not recall records at an earlier date other than of band music and such things as Harry Lauder's song and monologue called "When I Was Twenty-one", occupying a single-sided black-label HMV record, most of which I still have off by heart, or had a few years ago. (Lauder, in the role of a boozy Scot, accounted for his high colour by what even in those remote days I thought of as a remarkably poetic trope: "I ate too much red cabbage and the vinegar never left ma face.") However, I suppose the restricted repertoire I remember may have been the result of my own reiterated selection from the available discs. I was at least fourteen (probably fifteen) before I listened properly to classical music, but I did quite soon become attuned to what may be termed "pier-end" music, having regard to the limited modes of dissemination of the times.

The first house my parents took and in which I was born I had imagined to be of the terrace kind, opening straight on to the street. When my son was teaching at Manchester University I went to find this and other houses in the district I had known as a child. I had more than half expected my birthplace in Timpson Street, Failsworth (an urban district between Manchester and Oldham), to have disappeared in some slum clearance scheme. Not a bit of it: the house proved to be well built, of red brick, semidetached, with a little front garden – small but perfectly respectable. How odd to stand there, a middle-aged man, with the far memories of my infantile life in the house, notably of being under the dining table with a neighbour's female child, hidden by the tablecloth (in style similar to my grandparents' but with a blue pile), the feeling-tone being of excited love. But the house stayed strange, brought no additional recall.

My father was quick to make his material surroundings reflect his progress in his career. By the time my surviving brother was born in 1916 we had moved into Oldham itself, to a bigger house in a "better" neighbourhood – a long road called Frederick Street. Opposite was an open space where the terrain fell, giving a good view of the smoking factory and huddled domestic chimneys of the area, a few miles away, from which we had elevated ourselves.

Quite impossible to recover what immediately emotional or more enduring effects the 1914–18 war had on a small child. Naturally I was well aware of the war's existence, wondering, as my father read the paper at breakfast, how it would find enough news to fill its pages when the war was over. One of my uncles, a mere lad, was in the Army, but I do not recall the family anxiety. Nor do I remember anything of the second son, born to my parents in 1914, who died when a few weeks old through an undiagnosed genetic defect in the pylorus, preventing the natural emptying of the stomach into the intestine – a defect curable by a quite simple operation. Surely there were effects in the little outliver. The birth of my surviving brother, my parents' third son, I do have a memory of – my mother still in bed in a front bedroom of the Frederick Street house, the new infant in a cot with a muslin canopy, my mother reading to me from a paperback volume of fairy tales, a regularly-published series often bought for me. I would have been almost four years and four months old. I suspect that the occasion was the result of my demand for attention or, more likely, my mother's way of indicating my continuing importance – and remembered because of this. Indeed, I am convinced I could read for myself before my surviving brother was born: surely I was alone with my father and mother (in the front seat of the family motor car) when I read my first word – OXO – from an advertisement hoarding, a feat which surprised me almost as much as my parents.

The rubber-proofing mill did well during the war, with government contracts for groundsheets and the like. My father became a shareholder in and a director of the private company that owned it. It was probably in 1919 (though it could have been 1918) that we moved to a house in Waterhead, on the extreme outskirts of Oldham, in fact just over the Lancashire border with Yorkshire. Beyond lay the moorland of the Pennines: my bedroom looked out on its vivid green and the black dry-stone walls that ran over it and I recall lugging a crimson-bound volume of *Chums* up to that window to catch the last light as I read illegally after going to bed. The road the house was in led through the moorland to tiny grey-black manufacturing towns in the steep valleys, a landscape that still seems to me mysterious and haunting – just as the mill-dominated streets of urban east Lancashire, so long quitted, remain, as the phrase goes, my spiritual home.

The Waterhead house struck me at the time as being very grand. It stood high above the road and had a name and no number. I was proud of being seen proprietorially opening the front gate on which the name was painted. It was in fact, as I saw on the pilgrimage already mentioned, a mock-Tudor house typical of many built in Edwardian times or slightly later for the professional class. It was commodious enough for my brother and me to have a day nursery, with a cupboard each for books and toys, which gave me strangely keen pleasure. Into my cupboard went *Tales from Sir Walter Scott*, a present from my Aunt Minnie, hangover from her Caithness upbringing. My father had had the floor laid with a patent green material which I remember him proclaiming was as hard-wearing as linoleum yet warm and quite resilient to the touch: ideal for bare knees, as a foundation for Lotts' bricks and Hornby train lines. There were two maids but I do not think both of them lived in. The chauffeur certainly did not live in.

I wonder if the chauffeur were not acquired only after my father's illness, when the strain must have been great of driving the now not inconsiderable distance from home to work and back. My father made a will on 9 April 1920, and that may have immediately preceded the colostomy he underwent to alleviate the bowel cancer he had been found to have. I remember the day he went for the operation and I do not think he was driven by Smith. After great suffering my father died on 18 December, 1920. He was thirty-six, my mother thirty-two. I think my mother was pregnant with her fourth son before my father's illness was diagnosed: at any rate, the child was born not long before my father's death. Like my first brother, it suffered from the pyloric defect and died after a few weeks' unhappy life. I remember it being said later, probably by my mother, that they tried to take as little account as possible of the baby's death because of my father's desperate condition.

Of course, my father's appearance changed devastatingly during his illness. I have been told he was extremely courageous in his final months, for a time continuing to play bridge – a great passion – though afterwards he might have to go on hands and knees upstairs to bed. It was a source of sadness to him that towards the end I was afraid of him. I wonder whether that was the emotion or whether it was not, already at that age, compassion so extreme as to amount to cowardice. I was certainly afraid of him after his death, seeing the closed door of what had doubtless become a dreaded bedroom, wondering if the body were still there. There was no full disclosure to the boy of eight and three-quarters of the appearance and facts of death, as presumably there would have been in Victorian times. I was sent to stay with friends for some days, covering the period of the funeral. One evening, while there, I messed my pants, an indication, as I see now, of the troubled state beneath the pleasure at sharing the play of the two little girls of the family, but then a wholly enigmatic event, causing me immense embarrassment. It seems clear that I was already an introverted character, whose tender heart went frustratingly with a distaste for displays of emotion, indeed for anything much disturbing the commonplace routines of life. Apart from being a "bad" boy I suppose I could not have had a nature less helpful to my mother in the ruins of her life.

My father had been fond of the Fylde coast – accustomed to the sea in his Scottish boyhood – and for several years had taken a furnished house in Blackpool (then, certainly at its "North Shore", still possessing a degree of "tone") for a month or so in the summer, he himself commuting when his own holiday period had expired. It was to live in "rooms" in one of those houses that we (my mother, my surviving brother and myself) went initially following my father's death, after the house and furniture were sold, the maids and chauffeur dismissed. The landlady, Mrs Vero, and her son were of course in residence with us (we had not the whole house as for one of the previous summer holidays) and they were the first I recall of the Dickensian characters encountered in my mother's wanderings during the rest of my life with her. The son, perhaps in his early twenties, played Rachmaninov's notorious piano prelude so assiduously that I still refer to the piece as "Willie Vero". He frequently did dialogues in assumed bass and falsetto voices (a talent also possessed by Dickens's Sloppy), usually with persecutory Pinterish undertones. One dialogue began on the following lines:

Bass voice: "Where are the papers?"
Falsetto voice: "What papers?"
Bass voice: "Those secret papers." Etc.

The characters seem Dickensian not only because of the essential truth in Dickens's vision but also because of our forced and usually fleeting relationship with them, sometimes as fleetingly renewed. At a later epoch we lived in a Blackpool private hotel where the passing show was concentratedly thronged, swift and varied. My sense of the ludicrous in human character and action is possessed by my brother even more sharply, perhaps because his power of observation is keener.

We left the Vero household to return to Oldham to a house

my mother bought not far from my grandparents. I guess she was encouraged in this move by them. The house was not even up to Frederick Street standards, as I think my mother was morbidly aware.

My father's share in the rubber-proofing mill, and other possessions, eventually realized sufficient for my mother to live on without working and to educate my brother and me. Our way of life was modest and my mother, without being at all specific in the matter, always made me conscious of the limits of her resources, so that my possibly native parsimony was reinforced by a real fear of the money running out. At the end of my schooldays, for example, when I was sixteen, what was presented was the opportunity to qualify as a professional man, so I was articled to a solicitor. The job in journalism or training in art (either of which would then have met my own wishes) would not have fulfilled my mother's plan to manage her money so as to launch both her sons safely into adult life. As it happened, this cautious view – sustained by consultations with equally unimaginative or ignorant friends – could scarcely have been more ill-suited to the talents possessed by her children. Though my brother and I both made successful careers (mine slightly more conventional than his), only when we have moved into spheres somewhat away from them have we begun to show our true abilities. In my case at least, such movement has almost always been at the behest of others. My father's death shattered my mother's existence: it also caused his children to lead lives that were for many years divided and too narrow in scope.

One psychologizes about oneself in this way with apparent confidence but may be wide of the mark. Possibly no amount of lift-off which public school, university and money – and a standard English accent and *savoir faire* – would have provided could have changed the dominating part of my personality: shy, intellectual, naïve to the point of gormlessness (archetypally poetic, one might say) and not badly summed up in the well-known phrase by Hartley Coleridge I happened to light on while writing this: "Long time a child and still a child."

I must also make it clear that the petty bourgeois life – carless, servantless, seats in the pit rather than the dress circle – to which we were suddenly returned was far from uncongenial to me. Many of my most enjoyable hours were spent at my grandparents' house where in the front room already mentioned, nominally the dining room but used as a living room, the square table with a scrubbed top existed, normally covered by a green plush cloth with a fringe. This latter would be replaced by a white cloth for meals; and after a lunch of, say, hotpot (baked best-end of neck chops, sliced potatoes and onions) and apple pie (with Lancashire cheese – prize, of course) the white cloth would be removed and a newspaper laid down so that I could draw or paint. At a later epoch I might be joined in this by my grandmother: she with her free style, me probably copying something I had squared up from *Chatterbox* or a coloured postcard. My mother's siblings and their spouses and children also gave pleasure, providing social life without too many accompanying pangs of shyness.

A good few catch phrases and memories, perhaps setting the whole tone of one's attitude to everyday existence, predominantly comic as it must be, have survived from that period. I think of the only child of my mother's elder sister, slightly younger than me, who was a proverbial source. At the (silent) cinema she would say out loud, as much because of her infantile incomprehension of plot as innocence about sexual mores: "What's that man doing to that lady?" – an annoying phrase then but useful today when confronted by the narrative obfuscations of modern film and television drama.

I should emphasize that these memories of my grandparents' house are not confined to the time of my mother's return to Oldham. That come-back was so unsuccessful that with phenomenal rapidity she sold the house and we went back to rooms in Blackpool. It could be that she was less pleased than I was to be close to her parents, (it was some time before the penny dropped and I saw her as an attractive widow who despite her fidelity to her children and to my father's memory was capable of fresh personal attachments). There were other relatives at hand near her own age but the friends of Waterhead days had largely fallen off, not to be wondered at in the utterly changed circumstances. She had acquired friendships in Blackpool during the annual visits there and I daresay they seemed more congenial and, potentially at least, more accessible. Was my own particular area of unhappiness taken into account by her? During our short return stay in Oldham I attended the local board school whose great bleak playgrounds, vast numbers and strange routines (as they all seemed to me) were purgatory after my previous experience of genteel dames' schools. Back in Blackpool I returned happily to a girls' school where boys were taken in the lower forms – until I was too old for it and went to a private boarding school. Strangely enough I should almost certainly have been better off in the local authority system: I was a good examinee but my private school never entered boys for university scholarships. Moreover, though it is nice to be coddled, I have got along quite well at various epochs as an unprivileged member of society.

Our accommodation in Blackpool was not in the Vero household, though nearby. (Perhaps the Vero rooms were not available or my mother had wearied of the Prelude in C sharp minor.) We occupied the new place for what seems in retrospect – and seemed then – a long time, though was probably no more than a couple of years. Our landlady, Miss Barraclough, was a gigantically fat woman who slept in her kitchen and never bathed. I still often repeat (and not now wholly in jest) a phrase of idiomatic construction employed by her to indicate her sense of the woes of the world pressing down on her: "Dearie me today." In the side part of the garden, adjoining the street, was a small billboard that showed the weekly attractions of a local cinema, called "The Imperial". This display entitled her to two seats gratis at Monday matinées, to which, during school holidays, I often accompanied her; Miss Barraclough's "free pass" seeming to me an astonishing bounty. Strange pair. I think she invariably wore a navy-blue "costume" of thin, shiny serge, through which the projecting upper rim of her corset was almost as visible as when she was without a jacket indoors. Thus, and at others of Blackpool's numerous cinemas, was sustained – developed, rather – my passion for that art.

It was only to be expected that my mother's health should have declined during all these events. She was by no means a chronic complainer but I was aware of her "nerves" (the term in *The Waste Land* was in common use, perhaps still is) and later of her "palpitations". Concern about her physical well-being grew to be as nagging as the concern that we were not drawing on capital. Rentier's worries, communicating themselves in classic manner even to the younger members of the family – they would get no sympathy today, but were real and painful. Later my mother's symptoms assumed rather more obvious physical forms and very belatedly she was diagnosed as having Graves' Disease

– hyperthyroidism – and underwent, just before the Second World War, a partial thyroidectomy, then a perilous operation.

She died in 1949. A good many years after her death I became more and more troubled by irregular beating of the heart. The electrocardiograph and other tests showed no organic cardiac trouble. A consultant soon diagnosed Graves' Disease. "Are you nervous?" was one question asked. Almost without hesitation, rapidly reviewing my ancestry, character and behaviour, I said: "Yes" – though at the time I was at the broadest stretch of my scope and responsibility as a lawyer. In fact my "nerves" were doubtless efficiently concealed behind the mask by then perfected for presentation to the ordinary encounters of life.

Defects are inescapably inherited: it is more difficult to see or appreciate the compensations that accompany them. Some sort of soft centre, such as my mother possessed (and I should add that she was totally unintellectual), is surely almost essential to a poet: he must also have intelligent ability, the quality my father seemed to own in abundance. I dare say he was also not without imaginative insight. One of my few memories of him is of his taking me to the dentist for an extraction or extractions – in those days, in that place, a far from painless procedure. Afterwards we went to a stationer's shop, where he bought me a large black-japanned tin of watercolour paints. On another occasion when we were out together he announced that we would go to see the pictures. My spirits rose, anticipating the entertainment later offered by the Imperial. To my initial disappointment we went into the Oldham Municipal Art Gallery. Could it have been on that early visit that the enormous and then famous canvas of Cleopatra applying the asp to her bosom made its mark on me? Perhaps its sensuous splendours were something my father particularly wanted to see, following the line indicated by his acquisition of the illustrated Macaulay I will refer to again.

I am slightly surprised to recall that my father also took me to Watersheddings and Boundary Park, the respective homes of the Oldham rugby league and association football clubs – surprised only because of the brief time I seem in retrospect to have spent with him, for I have inherited his broad interest in watching sport. I see us approaching the Watersheddings ground over some well-trodden cindered "tips", yet any tone and details of the relations between us have dropped completely away. I hope

I concentrated on and responded to the proceedings to the best of my puerile ability, giving him a bit of confidence about my future nous. Would we ever have seriously clashed had he survived into my adolescence and beyond? Or would he simply have had to put up with my withdrawn evasiveness, like many another? His own character is to me essentially elusive. Presumably his talent for management and decision-taking was not, like mine, vitiated by a species of pusillanimity – too great a facility for seeing another's point of view, an almost morbid concern for another's feelings; qualities which assort oddly with ruthlessness in sticking to unpopular positions and resolves.

I might put a word in here about my father's great attachment to his home, a trait almost on the exaggerated lines of that of Mr Woodhouse, and appearing again in my brother and myself. In my father's case the cause may have been his parentless upbringing: in his sons the cause perhaps his own early death. The patterns over the generations may be somewhat mystical, however. A few years after my father died I had a septic right index finger as a result of which the nail came off. The new nail, when grown, appeared down one side as though detached from the circumambient flesh. My mother said that this nail was exactly like that on my father's right index finger.

Apart from the chemistry prize already mentioned, my father's books (of no vast number) were disposed of immediately after his death (my mother was the reverse of a hoarder). Among them I recall John Buchan's *Greenmantle* – a title that seemed strange and reverberant to me as a boy of seven or eight – and Macaulay's *Lays of Ancient Rome*. These two works may well have indicated the parameters of his literary taste. Indeed, the Macaulay seems not altogether in character – more like the taste of early enforced reading by my grandfather, whose sayings included a number of quotations from the poet Thomas Campbell, who I put in the Macaulay class. The *Lays*, as mentioned, had line illustrations of an occasional anatomical explicitness, a bit like the work of Flaxman, and that perhaps accounted for its presence in my father's bureau.

I had a fair number of books of my own in the Waterhead days and do not remember poaching on any of my father's. It might have surprised him (and surely would have pleased him) to have discovered, had he lived, the eventual maturing of my taste in that area. To translate my lust for reading into the practical terms of buying books would have been just up his alley (and as I write this I am reminded that my brother has been a book-accumulator all his life, and in his own field a notable collector). How pure (if tedious for others) is pride in one's children! I deeply regret that my mother died before such honours and positions as I possess came, almost inevitably, to me: she would have seen them as justification of her care and application – and educational policy – during those early years.

I ought not to omit adding that the puzzlement to me of the Caithness childhood was not helped by my Aunt Minnie, I feel sure even before my father died, marrying an Australian (I believe a patient in her hospital) and moving to what was thought of as the outback and possibly was. She never returned. After bearing two or three children she died prematurely of cancer like my father. But even had I met her again in my later life would I have catechised her about the past? I doubt it. I see now that even my mother might have illuminated many questions had she been asked. The character I possessed, that soft-pedalled interrogation, will sufficiently emerge.

3 *Comics*

It must have been in 1923, when I was eleven, that I went to boarding school in Blackpool. What could have been in my mother's mind? (It would have been easy for me to be a dayboy because the house where we had "rooms" was no more than three or four miles from the school.) It could scarcely have been to free her for some amatory relationship, for my brother remained at home (though it is true he was four years younger than I.) I feel that it was simply for my social and educational amelioration – perhaps my father had in his lifetime spoken of "boarding school" as desirable for his children, though the school chosen by my mother was far from what he might have had in mind, conscious as he always seemed to have been of the importance of solid quality in what he got for his growing income. If some friend had recommended the placc to her the advice was not far-sighted. There were two sizeable boys' "private" schools in the town: the one I went to was shortly to be on the downgrade; the other eventually became a public school, of however minor an example.

The nature of the school I joined (and stayed with until the end of my schooldays) will likely be unfamiliar fifty years on. On arrival I was put in Form 2b, so that there must have been boys of only nine or ten in Form 1. At the other end of the school were boys of sixteen, possibly seventeen. At first there were about seventy dayboys and thirty boarders. The numbers declined but the school always ranged beyond prep school scope. One could stay to take matriculation (as the leaving examination then was), though no boy in my time proceeded to university. Undoubtedly the school traded on the gentility principle: in those days it conferred a higher social status (if only temporarily) than the state schools, and in the case of dayboys for a modest cost. It probably also took boys who had failed to pass into grammar schools. No exaggerated social snobbery was involved, however. Thinking at random, one of my contemporaries became a woman's hairdresser, another a coalman (though both were self-employed).

Why the boarders came is a more complex question. A few were foreign or the sons of parents abroad. One or two were so gormless that their parents were no doubt glad to have them taken off their hands and somehow made literate that the agency was unimportant. But as to the majority of boarders I expect the school was trading on past glories, my mother's hearing of it evidence of that. One of the first things that struck me was some photographs on the dining room walls (photographs already slightly yellowed and old-fashioned) of a school production of *Les Fourberies de Scapin*. That boys porting rapiers, in plumed hats and tights (however wrinkled), should give a play in French, to me denoted a past of great enterprise and intellect.

However, it must be said that during my time I judge the standard of teaching to have remained remarkably high. The standard was set by the Headmaster himself who never allowed any boy, however dull, to evade participation in his classes. This he achieved by *ad hominem* interrogation and, not infrequently, some kind of dramatic action. "If I were a Zulu I'd do a war dance," he said once at a boy's crass answer, later going behind the blackboard (for some obscure but strangely effective reason) to fulfil the terpsichorean side of the proposition. Another time he took a boy out of the classroom and ran him round the playground "to wake him up". During his absence the class was in awestruck silence, straining to catch any sound of the two ill-assorted pairs of feet. Effective teaching was actually helped as a result of the school's decline, classes getting smaller and smaller as one progressed through the school, the highest consisting, when I was in it, of no more than a dozen boys, if that.

My mother and I went to the school for a preliminary interview (doing the journey by tram along the promenade), though I guess my admission was not in doubt. The building was undistinguished, consisting of a pair of large semi-detached houses in a street at right angles to the promenade. The pair had been altered so as to communicate in what always remained for me a somewhat mysterious manner. On the ground floor, from the noise and I daresay squalor of the boarders' dining room, common room and coat lobby one could reach the quiet gloom and relative opulence of the Headmaster's family quarters. The first room one came to was the Headmaster's study. Across the hall was the drawing room, entered only on two or three curious occasions, one being prior to the interview referred to. The rest was virtually unknown territory, as was the first floor. Did this also intercommunicate? I do not remember, perhaps never knew. One or two masters slept and had their ablutions on "the boys' side" of this floor: at the time it would have struck me as strange indeed if they could have penetrated the intimate quarters of the Headmaster and his family – though now the notion seems less outré. On the second floor, to get from one house to the other you simply walked through one of the dormitories.

The classrooms were at the rear of these two houses, in a single-storey building erected where the property was bounded by a back street. The building was extended during my early days at the school to make a science laboratory, perhaps the school's last gesture of prosperity and expansion. All the back land (not of any great extent) was eventually asphalted over as a playground, except for a small walled garden appurtenant to the Headmaster's side of the pair of houses and the "bogs", redolent during all my time at the school of one particular brand of disinfectant.

The interview took place in the Headmaster's study, my mother and I facing him across a substantial desk. He was a handsome man, though after I had left school (perhaps on the strange occasion described later) I discovered he was not, as I had always thought, tall. His acquiline features were surmounted by thick grey hair, neatly parted and brushed, the large head carried slightly on one side, as though perpetually considering some matter of grave consequence, his own virtue and right judgement being unquestionable. I and my brother (who eventually joined me at the school) have laughed a great deal recalling the character and habits of the Headmaster, but at the time I was afraid of him. He was one of those individuals whose absence from the scene greatly lightens the spirits of more flippant beings. His nickname was (anticipating the gangster films of the coming "talkies") "the Boss", the hissed syllable indicating with sickening menace his impending arrival, even though one's occupation might be innocent. He had a deep knowledge of the weakness of boys and at this first meeting plumbed my ignorance and foolishness with one simple question. He asked me to spell "cupboard", which I failed to do.

Later in the interview my mother remarked that I was "a terrible reader". Having assessed my spelling, the Headmaster naturally did not take this colloquially and said that I should have extra lessons or special attention in this field. Though my mother explained that she merely meant that I always had my nose in a book, the Headmaster's scepticism about my literacy was not removed and, as stated, condemned me to 2b where the school's younger dunces spent a good deal of time. However, after one term in 2b I went straight to Form 3.

I really did read a lot, mostly rubbish, perhaps almost entirely "comics" (innocent term in those days), novellas published in such series as the Nelson Lee and Sexton Blake "Libraries", and the children's "annuals". My mother borrowed books from a local twopenny library – popular novels of the romantic kind in the main. That I did not choose any books for myself from this source shows how unenterprising I was, for it surely contained such authors as E. Phillips Oppenheim who had me under a spell a little later on. The public library was a facility that, with typical conservativism (fear of dirt and germs possibly also playing a part), it never occurred to my mother to take advantage of for either of us. In later schooldays I joined under my own steam and was stunned at the riches open access revealed.

Going to boarding school enlarged my range of reading matter through both what was called the "boarders' library" (merely a restrictive term, for there was no similar facility for dayboys, though it is true each form had a small collection of books) and books brought to the school by boys. For some books in early days I formed a passion: for instance, Richmal Crompton's "William" stories, then starting to come out. My enthusiasm was usually for works that especially ingratiated themselves with the reader, through cosy ideology or intense readableness or both. After a time a master must have seen that I was a "terrible reader" and offered books from his own collection, the first being by Ian Hay and O. Henry. He asked which I'd liked better. I said the Ian Hay (it was *Pip and Pipette*), speaking the truth though conscious that O. Henry was the more considerable literary artist. Surely all this was indicative of a lack of application and seriousness – lack of genius, it might be said – that has dogged me all my life and prevented great achievements.

A new boarder with me was a boy called Hamlet. As I write I cannot recall his Christian name but in any case I always think of him in the cigar or Shakespearean mode. Through our newness we became friendly though he was a year (or perhaps more) younger than I. He was a serious boy with a scientific bent: in adolescence he treated his pimples by injecting them with a pin with Euthymol toothpaste, a strong concoction. Despite the pimples he was not unattractive, humour lurking under the solemn style. When my brother (over four years younger than I) came to the school he got to know Hamlet quite well. It was probably my brother who observed the Euthymol experiments. They would have greatly appealed to him. In any case, my brother had a wide range of Hamletiana, for many years after school Hamlet got in touch with him. In the interim Hamlet had lived abroad as a missionary in a leper colony. Perhaps he entirely lacked friends after coming back to England (he had been the sole child of a widower or grass widower). At any rate, on Hamlet's initiative the two husbands and wives met on a number of occasions. Hamlet had married only on his return and his domestic happiness was short-lived for he very soon died of a heart attack.

After a few terms Hamlet and I drifted apart – he was below me in the school and in a different dormitory. Strange epoch of life, the immediate pre-adolescent years. Had a record been kept, no doubt some sort of progress or attitude could be discerned.

As it is, the period seems merely to have continued the pleasures and worries of earlier childhood, intellectual growth confined to the utterly puerile, even reading tinged with the lower activity of collecting. "The Feats of Dormitory Three" I remember entitling a holograph magazine (perhaps of no more than one number), my cover drawing being the end view of iron bedsteads with bare feet protruding. Most of the contents – probably all – were written and illustrated by me, and what is certain is that nothing in it would have shown the slightest talent. My taste for puns was carried into my conversation, much of which was designed to amuse – as ever, though I wonder whether it was as obstipated as it certainly became in adolescence and after. One boy at least in Dormitory Three was an alert audience, a mischievous fellow (in fact, his appearance not unsimian) I will call Byng, though I rather think he was killed in the war and cannot be hurt or defamed. His butt was Ames, whose aspect strangely enough also inclined to the simian, though whereas Byng resembled one of those narrow-faced monkeys with large hairless upper lips and lower jaw, Ames had been modelled on the great anthropoids – bullet head, back humped with muscle, small puzzled eyes, dangling arms, shortish bowed legs. At one time his nickname was "Gorill", the word accented as a trochee. He never used his strength to discourage Byng and his other tormentors (including me, I am sorry to say). His protest merely took the form of a verbal appeal, which in time became stylised and unvarying – "Chuck it, you rotten beggar, Byng. I wish you wo-ould. You rotten beggar." Down the years this whining litany has been shortened in my family to the first phrase of it, to be used in addressing anyone exercising oppression.

Ames was a boy of limited intellectual attainments. Today in the State system such a one might well leave school unable to read or write. As it was, the small classes plus the all-seeing eye and academic energy of the Headmaster enabled Ames to keep up, in some way and to some passable degree, with the current of school work. The exercise book containing his essays was sometimes procured by Byng for the purpose of reading aloud the literary efforts there painfully put down. It must be admitted that like Caliban Ames had a power of memorable expression exceeding what might have been expected. In a story (set as essay prep) some action of the protagonist was described in succinct but mysteriously Joycean manner: "He stooped. He stoped. He stopped." Another essay (if half or three quarters of a page can be so dignified) ended with the *jeu d'esprit*: "All done by kindness. A. P. Ames." These words, too, are still useful today, marking completion of some satisfying and satisfactory job.

Byng left prematurely and Ames's life became much more ordinary. In the end, he and I were the two fullbacks (as they were then called) in the school's soccer XI, his dogged strength making up for my deficiencies, since my speed made me an "attacking" defender, not always reliable. But this must have been in the last year of my school life when the school's shrinkage was beginning to be apparent (I was even in the cricket XI, though having a meagre talent for the game), not least in the staff. Mr Tregenza had become senior master, a promotion that could scarcely have been foreseen. He was short, stout, as uncommunicative as I later became, possibly in his mid-forties. When accompanying the boarders on their Sunday walk he sometimes held his walking stick upright behind his back, the crook hooked on to the brim of his trilby to stop it being blown off in the stiff wind usually prevalent at Blackpool. I think originally he had taught only French but in my latter time took History as well and perhaps English also. I was never on easy terms with him but then in those days, at such a school, the wall of reserve between masters and boys was rarely breached. Strange that a master would so seldom try to gain affection as well as respect; try for perspectives other than those, such as they were, running from the curriculum. Still, the boys (coming, as almost all of them did, from thoroughly petty-bourgeois seaside town backgrounds) must have lacked the social *savoir faire* to enable them to respond to other than utterly conventional approaches, in my own case the thing aggravated by shyness and respect for rules.

Mr Tregenza was an able pianist. Two "pieces" of his that I recall were Chopin's *Fantaisie Impromptu* and the "Andaluza" of Granados, which indicate his technical proficiency. In the evenings he often used to come across to the classrooms building to play on the piano used for the morning hymn. I suppose these recitals made their mark about the time I was conscious of losing arguments with two dayboy pianists in which I foolishly maintained that compared with "pier-end" music (such things as the *Ballet Egyptien*, familiar through the Stokowski records bought by Uncle Freddy in the first days of electrical recording) classical music lacked the essential ingredient of tunes. It seemed greatly daring when at last I ventured into the actual classroom where Mr Tregenza was playing, to sit and listen (the music was audible elsewhere, for most of the classrooms were formed by ingeniously mobile wood and glass partitions on rails, duty of the monitors to slide into place before and after morning assembly). I expect some further time elapsed before I had a few, probably laconic, conversations with him about music. I remember only two of his remarks: one that he was fed up with the *Fantaisie Impromptu* (which I had daringly requested), the other (in response to my question) that Busoni was the best pianist he had ever heard. These replies, when I ponder them, perhaps indicate a somewhat greater depth of relationship than I recall. I mean I did not initially know the name of the Chopin piece, so must have hummed its haunting central theme or otherwise with some particularity identified it. The name of Busoni stuck with me (helped by Busoni's Beethovenian head being on the cover of a piece of Mr Tregenza's music, probably a Busonian arrangement) and many years later, coming to him again through *Music Ho!* and Bernard Van Dieren's *Down Among the Dead Men*, I wrote a longish poem about him, justly unpublished; also, he lies behind the title of my first novel for adults, *The Second Curtain*. A theme of Constant Lambert's book is the desirability of a continuous tradition in music of the modern epoch – the fingerprinting and almost unconscious changing of the old forms being sufficient "progress" in the art, a notion (though I put it crudely) that has always greatly attracted me in the arts generally. Curious that the origins of this lie so far in one's past. It strikes me, too, as I write this, that I have acquired four or five discs of Granados' piano music, currently being recorded complete by the excellent pianist Thomas Rajna and still, to me, appealing. I have written a poem about that composer, also, though the non-musical interest of his being torpedoed during the 1914–18 war and perishing through needlessly trying to rescue his already-rescued wife played some part in that. I might even today remark to my wife "Mr Tregenza used to play that" when a Chopin Scherzo, say, comes over the wireless but I must not exaggerate his repertoire and influence, for one of the two dayboy pianists referred to became a special friend, and listening to *him* play and to his gramophone records (for a boy most discriminatingly chosen) went on after we had left school.

In literature I progressed from Ian Hay and O. Henry pretty well without guidance. It was a time when good writers were famous. Perhaps G. B. Shaw, mainly because of his ideological iconoclasm, was the first contemporary to get my devotion (I see the date 1927 on the flyleaf of my copy of *Androcles*, bought some time after the enthusiasm began), but before I left school at sixteen I had read Aldous Huxley and ploughed through *The Dynasts* (to indicate a range of some kind). Though I also read, for instance, the nineteenth-century Russians, it now seems incredible that writers of the past did not attract me more. I quite enjoyed the set books for various examinations but do not recall exploring much further – *Silas Marner* did not lead on to *Middlemarch* – though it must be said that the classics of English literature were sparse in the boarders' library and, indeed, elsewhere in the school. So I got to know a few books pretty thoroughly, rather like my grandfather with *The Merchant of Venice* (and in this connection, having recently refreshed my memory through my elder surviving uncle's letters, I may say that he apparently varied his Lancastrian greeting of " 'ow do?" with the somewhat more baffling "How now Tubal! what news from Genoa?").

I enjoyed without reservation the organized visits made by the school to the Shakespearean touring companies that regularly took in Blackpool. An element of a "night out", rare enough in the monastic life led by the boarders, plainly enhanced the enjoyment, but I was absorbed in the plays in the manner of their original audiences, with little or no compulsion to read the texts. It was still the epoch of Sir Frank Benson, spry enough as Caliban to climb a palm tree on the magic island and come down it head first. But he was indubitably ancient and though I saw him play Mark Antony in *Julius Caesar* and, even more incongruously, Hamlet, he later resigned himself in the latter play to the part of the Ghost. Edentulousness had made even more esoteric his mannered diction, of which I can still do a fair imitation. In his company was Robert Donat, extremely funny as Aguecheek and memorable in previous visits in smaller roles because of his fine but already asthmatic voice, wide-legged stance, and slightly Lancashire diction. Plays like *The Rivals* and *She Stoops to Conquer* were also sometimes done: they seemed of almost guilty lightness to form part, as it were, of the Boss' curriculum. However, all this intellectual taste and development now seems to me, again, characteristically unthorough, second-rate, non-critical.

In my earlier days Shakespeare did not much enter the programming of the "concerts" given by the school, of which there were two a year – one in a nearby church hall, the other unofficial (though pretty well rehearsed under one of the masters) and given by the boarders on the last day of the autumn term in the classrooms building (the partitions drawn back) the audience being merely the staff, the boarders not taking part, and those dayboys who chose to come. However, in my middle years in the school the boarders did put on the play scene in the last act of *A Midsummer Night's Dream*. By some unlikely stroke Gorill played Hippolyta. The Wall would surely have been more appropriate – though come to think of it Hippolyta had, to be sure, once been Queen of the Amazons, a physically robust past the master casting the scene may have had in mind. Gorill eventually learnt his part, though words and sense suffered lapses. "He hath played on his prologue like a child on a receiver," he persisted in saying, it being long before the time when the recorder was a familiar article of school apparatus and Gorill possibly having the wireless in mind, just about coming into general use. "I am weary of this moon; would he would change": Gorill in turn laid emphasis on every word of the second clause of this, except the right one. "Would he would change – on a receiver," I used to tease Gorill by singing, fitting the words to a song of the day called "Shepherd of the Hills".

A more serious episode in the works of the Bard came to be done later. Just after my brother joined the school the Headmaster enlisted a visiting master to give elocution lessons as an "extra". They could with advantage have been an unoptional part of the curriculum: the Headmaster (who himself came from Oxfordshire) often complained at morning assembly about his pupils' characteristically Fylde lack of aspirates and articulatory lip movements. "Let it come *out*, boys," he would say, opening and shutting his fingers at the side of his mouth to indicate the sort of action required. "Don't mumble" – enunciating the last word with special clarity. A phrase, perhaps a quotation, he often used to illustrate the lamentable sort of speech to be heard was: "Two men sat in a light'ouse, rubbing their 'orny 'ands."

Now I have pondered the matter, it may have been through the Headmaster's alarming use of the formal prefix "Master" that I first became aware that I myself used the short "a" and before I left school changed my usage, for in my last year I now recall imitating one of the maids saying at supper time: " 'ere's yer coker (cocoa), Măster Fuller." The visiting elocution specialist also lent a hand with the official concert. He had been an actor, Shakespearean it was said (perhaps a Bensonian), now retired or "resting" in the vicinity. His name was Rider Boys; his unromantic rotundity counteracted to some degree by a black velvet jacket and silvery curling hair worn long for those days of the Twenties.

Tickets for the concert were printed and cost half-a-crown, a tidy sum at the time. Boys were encouraged to sell tickets, boarders being limited in this activity since they were only let out of school premises on Saturday evenings, a couple of hours devoted mainly to consuming and stocking up with food. A favoured nearby sweetshop was run by Mr and Mrs Waddicor. I believe it was my brother himself who tried to involve Mr Waddicor in buying a ticket, perhaps two. Mr Waddicor read the offered pasteboard:

THE BOYS OF SEAFOLDE HOUSE
ASSISTED BY RIDER BOYS . . .

"Who are the *rider* boys?" he asked quite interestedly, probably envisaging a turn of juvenile cyclists or even horsemen.

Under Rider Boys' coaching, and I expect at his suggestion, the potion scene from *Romeo and Juliet* was included in the concert for which Mr Waddicor's patronage had been sought. My brother, who despite his immature age had already made his mark on the school, played the Apothecary: the Romeo was a boy I shall call Matley, the name of the character founded on his in *The Ruined Boys.* The elocutionist himself produced, also undertaking a solo item, one of Belloc's "Cautionary Tales" which he announced as being by Hilaire Bellòc – a pronunciation whose eccentricity caught my and my brother's fancy, though I suppose it may have had authority in view of the poet's Frog ancestry.

Matley was not in doubt that his destiny was to be a member of the Anglican clergy, High Church wing, but he was also greatly taken with acting, perhaps visualizing moving from one career to the other like the Rector of Stiffkey, quite soon to become notorious. At school he was able to combine these two strands of his ambition by dressing as a priest in the dormitory and administering the Sacrament to himself at an altar mainly ornamented by a brass crucifix which could then be bought at Woolworths, possibly still for the sixpence that originally was the price limit ruling in the store. Bespectacled (small oval lenses, gold-rimmed), with stiff, blond, rather frizzy hair (not awfully manageable even with the quantities of Pears' or Californian Poppy solid brilliantine fashionable among the boarders and which the exertions of Saturday evening shopping caused to run in a green veil down their foreheads, particularly the villainously low one of Ames), a pale soft skin and somewhat deficient in chin, he was not the ideal Romeo. And when he removed his spectacles (as he did, of course, to play the part), the naked eye sockets gave him the air of a white mouse – perhaps the whites of the light-blue eyes were pinkish. However, on the night of the concert make-up offset some of these deficiencies and his success was generally admitted, though some thought he overacted insufferably. Certainly my brother was a notable, if dwarfish, apothecary.

After the war, my brother stayed on in the forces for several years, seduced by the promise of rapid promotion in a branch relevant to his pre-war career. On a station to which he was appointed, in a far part of the shrinking Empire, the C of E chaplain turned out to be – who else? – the Reverend David Matley. The character presented was far from the precociously devout dormitory friar, even the unwarrantably narcissistic juvenile lead – much more a one-of-the-boys padre, with a liking for gin-and-tonics, and exuding the raffish tone of some services character from Waugh or Powell. My brother saw quite a bit of him, delighted, as in the case of Hamlet, to find a bizarre but not wholly unpredictable development of personality; confirmatory, too, of my brother's concept of humanity. Alas, again like Hamlet, Matley died at quite an early age.

In the latter years of my time at boarding school my mother, brother and I lived in a "private hotel". I do not know whether, besides my mother's restlessness, there was any reason for our moving from the "rooms" in Miss Barraclough's house, though it is true the accommodation and service provided there were by no means top notch. My mother bought our food, so that little could go wrong with such things as cold ham or even breakfast bacon. I cannot recall the standard of the more elaborate parts of the cuisine: possibly tasty enough, despite the pungent aroma of the kitchen quarters, caused by Miss Barraclough never bathing and intensified by her sleeping there, habits previously referred to. She was helped by the maid, Amy, who had a glide in her eye, her spectacles steel-rimmed and round (anticipating a fashion of today), frizzy-haired (not, like Matley, blonde, but black, slightly grizzled). Yet Amy was attractive because of expressive features and a truly kind nature. In those days I thought of myself as a cartoonist in embryo and I especially admired Tom Webster of the *Daily Mail* both for his draughtsmanship and creation of character, human and equine. Buying a comic one evening, I spied the new issue of *Tom Webster's Annual* and craved it. Back at Miss Barraclough's I told Amy of this desirable collection and at once she forked out a shilling (or more likely one and three) so that I could buy it, which I did at once. Even then I felt guilty at using her money, so hard-earned and (I guess) so meagre in amount; nor did the pretence stand up that she too would get a graphic frisson from the booklet. As I write this it comes to me for the first time that not only was Amy a sterling soul: possibly she also loved me, a benefaction that throughout life my character has not counted on. I wonder as well whether my mother learned of the incident (I seem to think she did) and if so very probably she refunded the one and thruppence – for in those days my mother had a reputation for being "soft" (though simple justice rather than sentimental generosity would have seen Amy right).

The private hotel was called Seacliffe and though in that part of the town cliffs had long since given way to concrete it actually overlooked the sea and also Blackpool's then premier hotel, the Metropole. It was owned and run by a lady (whether a widow or *femme sole* perhaps I never knew) with three nubile daughters whose agreeable looks added to the establishment's attractions. Their characters were as contrasted as Chekhov's three girls, but their yearnings were not in the least intellectual or towards the metropolis. Our family life, particularly my mother's and particularly in winter when we might be the only guests, became bound up in theirs; and in the season we were involved with a succession of holiday makers, some making departures and reappearances also reminiscent of Chekhov. My brother and I naturally identified, discussed and imitated the more Chekhovian visitors (if degrees are possible with such an epithet). The invariable remark of Mr Heaton, an elderly valetudinarian, I still come out with at appropriate times: "I like a bit of sweet cake with my cup of tea." His liking was in despite of a digestion which incessantly generated wind, expelled through almost closed lips with a noise that began with the labial tenuis and ended with a hiss, no doubt in the hope of disguising its eructatory origin. The reproduction by my brother and me of this curious sound became somewhat obsessive.

The Metropole came to play a part in our lives, albeit for its time and place rather expensive and chic. On the side of it away from the sea was a row of shops, one selling sweets having a notice above it which read: "Princess Marie-Louise, staying at the Hotel Metropole in 1904, said 'Higgins & Co's rock is very good' " – or words to that effect, the notice and Higgins & Co having vanished long since. The hotel lounge, large and of Moorish décor, was available for anyone's use for the price of a drink or a pot of coffee. A small band played there for *thé dansants* as well as background effect in the evenings. On one occasion I recall having pointed out to me the celebrated Dr Barton, of advanced years but still erect and lean – indeed, skeletal – and an indefatigable dancer, whose habit it was to "stop" the tune being played on his partner's spine as though it were the fingerboard of a cello, not neglecting to induce an imaginary vibrato. The grillroom, to which access could be gained not only through the hotel but also from the street where stood the emporium of Higgins & Co (not twenty yards from Seacliffe), served excellent food in a discreet atmosphere of dark wood and starched napery. Probably we got to know Miss Paine through visiting the Metropole lounge. She had a dominating character and a white wig arranged in the close-curled style of Princess Marie-Louise's relative, Queen Mary. I surmise that, for her, living permanently at the Metropole was not achieved without financial difficulty and that this could have been at the root of her running battle with the manager. "Frish" was how Miss Paine pronounced his name (though as my intellectual snobbery developed I imagined it to be really "Frisch"), not prefixing it with "Herr" or even "Mr". More frequently she referred to him as "the Prussian" (memories of the atrocious role, alleged or actual, of that nationality in the late war still vivid), but I do not think he was German – probably, as will appear later, Czech. Sometimes, as I sat over a soft drink among the exotic arches of the lounge with my mother and Miss Paine, "Frish" would be glimpsed in the distance, wearing a "marlborough" outfit such as I wore to dancing class, his short light hair and blunt features (Miss Paine's tales of his oppression adding to whatever air of menace he naturally possessed) conforming to one's notions of the essential Germanic nature. (And it is possibly worth recording that during the 1914–18 war I must have overheard, perhaps read in the newspapers, of German sexual atrocities, for I remember thinking, as an infant, that to have one's bottom – the most sexual part I could conjure up – cut off by a bayonet would inflict utterly unendurable pain as well as present problems of butchery). Yet I divined that Miss Paine was not guiltless in the affairs that set them at daggers drawn. Her part of the grand dame, though plausibly sustained by the wig and a broadly regal style of dress, was threatened by the lack of cash already mentioned and also, I guess, a native closeness. She would sometimes take my brother and me to an early dinner in the Metropole grillroom where, either at her bidding or, more likely, through some subtle appeal to our consciences (mine at least already tenderized by long knowledge of my mother's limited resources after my father's early death) to let her purse down lightly, we almost invariably chose sausages and chips, by far the cheapest dish on the menu. She called the waiters by their first names, especially favouring one with a distinguished grey moustache called John, a refugee from the Bolsheviks according to her: all were deferential though receiving poor monetary benefit, sixpence being about the size of the tips dispensed by her. I seem to remember that on these occasions she herself did not eat or drink: perhaps she had the table d'hôte dinner later in the dining room, entitled to it as a "resident" under a package deal negotiated with the Prussian, a contract often the subject of complaints from one party or the other. Or maybe her money did not run to a formal evening meal for herself.

What did we talk about over the sausages and chips (usually followed by a vanilla ice, also, by comparison, modestly priced)? Why did Miss Paine entertain those two young boys? Could (it comes to me) my mother have lent her money? Though not lacking a certain zest for experience, I spent much of my childhood (and later life) missing connections in human affairs obvious to others. Possibly such connections embarrassed me or failed to arouse interest, and now time or some censor has deleted them from my memory. At Seacliffe in the early days there stayed a stoutish dapper man of late middle age called Mr Wheatcroft. The vee of his waistcoat was edged with white as a result of buttoning in, underneath, two starched linen strips – effective but even then a rare and old-fashioned enhancement of the masculine turnout. He managed the premier wine merchants of the town, was a friend of Miss Barraclough's brother, was interested in my mother. I see that he could have been overfond of the bottle, that his marriage might have broken up or his wife been dead, and that it could have been him who had introduced us to Seacliffe. At the time I would have put from my mind the question of our precise relations with him (it would have embarrassed me to have discovered anything non-superficial), just as I would have taken avoiding action, if at all possible, on seeing any family acquaintance in the street.

Writing these pages the strange question has arisen of motivation in pre-adolescent days, the sources of the strength of one's hold on life. Thinking of animal parallels (coming back to my desk after throwing bread to garden birds, some familiar individuals having been patiently watching me through the study window), one turns, of course, to food. At once I remember, following my father's death – indeed, soon after that cataclysm, for we had still not moved from the house in Waterhead – burst pipes revealed by a thaw, water actually coming down the stairs, myself having a kitchen tea with the servants and, left alone in the confusion, cutting more bread and butter and loading it extravagantly with Tate & Lyle's golden syrup – death, burst pipes, damaged carpets of less consequence than the good bread and my greed. The bread was probably home-baked, as in my maternal grandparents' house, though shop bread (a matter of apology for my grandmother to have to send out for) could also be excellent in those days, and continued to be for years, for I remember well the cylindrical milk loaves, and the small cottage loaves we called "cobs", that were bought from the bakers' shop actually in the same street as Miss Barraclough's house.

I daresay at Seacliffe the food, though of greater formality, was essentially no better than at Miss Barraclough's. The sausages and chips of the Metropole certainly stand out in that epoch. And the only specific memory I have of Seacliffe food is a pudding, regularly on the menu, that pleased me aesthetically as well as being decently edible – half a tinned apricot on a slice of sponge cake, cream poured over. The simulation was of an egg on toast, though it always bothered me that the cream had to be scraped off the fruit before the similitude was fully apparent, in my experience an operation rarely performed by Seacliffe guests.

Food played a great part in life at school, as already implied. There was never enough, except at Sunday lunchtime when one's teeth were furred and appetite jaded through eating, after church, the remains of the sweets bought the previous evening at Waddicor's and elsewhere. Mutton and cabbage and even roast potatoes, almost invariably on the Sunday luncheon menu, I was put off for years after, for under the Headmaster's moral scheme food could not be left on the plate and one had to swallow the nauseating stuff unless it could be hidden in envelope or handkerchief, as narrated in *The Ruined Boys*. Had I to write that book now I would not give it the confident ethics it possesses. The overall plan of the novel is the young hero's gradual discovery during a school year of the moral truth of the school he newly joins (and, incidentally, of the outside world), a truth the reverse of what he first imagines. I would now be more indulgent to the school's deficiencies. To take a small instance: the insufficiency of bread and butter and jam at tea time, the jam spread ludicrously thin, may have played its part in the modesty of the boarding fee. The values the Headmaster tried to inculcate and the teaching he so ably undertook have lost some of their hypocritical or irrelevant undertones during the decline in public and private standards since the novel was written in the Fifties; and my own testy reactionariness has grown. Bullying caused Gorill unhappiness for a time (and I myself suffered similarly) but at least the school made him literate. The order and direction imposed in some respects now seem remarkable: my own tastes were superficially literary, yet under the Headmaster, who took the Fifth and Sixth Forms in the subject, I matriculated with distinction in both Mathematics and Additional Mathematics. He owns only a small part of the blame for my entering a profession which called for talents I possessed neither by nature, nor by education thus far. Strangely enough, though the headmaster of *The Ruined Boys* is the villain of the piece, some readers have found him sympathetic, even faintly tragically so.

I left school and was articled to a firm of solicitors when I was sixteen. In preparation for this new life my mother took a flat. One evening, not long after the end of my final term, the doorbell rang and I found the Headmaster standing outside. It was only then, away from the school or school occasions for the first time, that I saw he was shorter than I. Fear or at least unease seized me, though I realized at once I had moved almost entirely out of his power. As a matter of fact there had been an affair in my last or penultimate term that had put me in his bad books and it struck me that he had come to report about that to my mother, belatedness not making this dread speculation much less likely to be true having regard to his measured and steadfast character.

It turned out eventually, after he had chatted to my mother for a while implausibly seated in one of our easy chairs, that he was inviting me to accompany him to the "Palace Varieties", using my Christian name in making known his intention. For this and other obvious reasons the outing had no connotations of enjoyment, though the theatre, thus colloquially known, usually provided excellent entertainment. It was plainly among the last places one could have associated with the Boss. One sees now that he had acquired two complimentary tickets and lit upon me as (probably last-minute) guest because our flat was near the theatre. I cannot think there might have been anything more devious in his great brain. We sat in the dress circle and must have conversed but I recall nothing of what was said.

Top of the bill was Joe Jackson, I suppose one of the funniest music-hall mimes ever; I believe Viennese in origin, of Anglo-Austrian parentage, former cycling champion of Austria. In his silent act called, I think, "Stealing a Bicycle" (it would have commended itself to Mr Waddicor) a dark-chinned tramp in rags came on a woodland stage. A gleaming bicycle is leaning against a tree. After much timid hesitation the tramp tries, with elaborate variations, to ride it away – the rags catch on the cycle, the tyro is also entangled, he and it fall, the machine gradually disintegrates, is wrongly reassembled, and so forth. The deformed vehicle is eventually brilliantly ridden. The Boss did not laugh as the resourceful and hilarious spectacle unfolded, and so I followed suit. In any event I think I would have supposed laughter from me quite *de trop*. I sank my nails into the palms of my hands to suppress the cachinnations that filled my interior like some *question* of the age of torture. Awful pain accompanied incongruously the complete recognition of comic genius. At long last the Headmaster said: "Foolish fellow" and I myself allowed a giggle or two to emerge, as some frightfully strictured patient is blessed by the relief of even a few drops.

4 *Happy Valley*

While I was a solicitor's articled clerk I met the girl who became my wife. It turned out that she lived quite near Mrs Vero's and Miss Barraclough's, overlooking an enclosed area of sunken ground near the sea, which perhaps because of subsidence or bog had never been built on and belonged, eventually at any rate, to the municipality. In later days most of it had been laid out as a putting course but in childhod it was known as "Happy Valley", its main feature being a wooden stage, deckchairs ranged in front, where a pierrot troupe performed. Even when we were only summer visitors to Blackpool I regularly attended this entertainment. So also had my future wife, of course unknown to me – though one speculates as to whether one had not in fact clapped eyes already captivated on the pretty child whose photographs were later examined with Larkinesque interest and emotion.

Children were allowed – encouraged – to squat in front of the deckchairs, there being in any case no charge except for the hire of the deckchair, the performers rewarded by a collection and the profits on the sale of copies of the music they sang. So close to the action, so faithful in support, one saw deep into the appearance and characters of the performers as well as learning by heart dialogue spoken, jokes cracked, songs rendered. The make-up on the faces of the actors embrowned the white ruffs they wore, fairly grubby anyway. The soubrette for several seasons was called Lila Dale, a not wholly natural blonde, a little past the first flush of youth, somewhat resembling Alice Faye (to become famous in a few years through the "talkies"). Part of her role in the scheme of things was to get the better of the comedian, whose response to teasing (not utterly unlike

Gorill's) was a catch phrase employable in one's own affairs – "Oh you are awful, Lila Dale" – which I still speak with idiosyncratic emphases precisely echoing those used by the oppressed comic. What strange songs became fixed in the mind, sometimes involuntarily returning even sixty years later:

> Avalon, Avalon, nightly I pray:
> Bring back my loved one some day.

Any Arthurian connotation was not grasped by me: I thought of Avalon as being like Dixie – an American place of nostalgic significance. Perhaps I was right. Other pastoral themes did not always concern places: I have already mentioned in Gorillian connection a song that started with the Arnoldian apostrophe "Shepherd of the hills, I hear you calling." And did one really regularly utter, with no sense of the grotesqueness of the claim, "I'm the Sheik of Araby"? – the required pronunciation being "Aŕr-ă-bée" (also "sheik" was then not "shake" but "sheek", conjuring up a less dignified figure). Of course, incongruity of song and singer is inherent in the art form. Byng would sometimes command Gorill to sing for him. Despite the hefty body the voice was thin, uncertain in pitch, strangely high; the song, well known in a much earlier day, always the same, the tune just discernible:

> Sweetheart, I want to tell you,
> Tell you how much I love you.
> That is the story . . .
> That's all I know now.

The last line, though not part of the song, Gorill fitted to the melody with his Calibanesque lyricism.

I marvel now at the culture with which my mind was stuffed: characters such as Marzipan the Magician from a comic called *The Rainbow*; the vigorous pen and ink illustrations to the serials in *Chums*; silent films with actors now almost forgotten like George K. Arthur and Lya de Putti, the latter, as he confessed, touching even my grandfather's libido; and songs from drawing rooms as well as Happy Valley, my mother still being asked to use her mezzo-soprano:

> Dearest, our day is over,
> Ended the dream divine.

You must go back to your life,
I must go back to mine.

– a characteristic song of hers, by Tosti, and which for my benefit Anthony Powell makes Moreland quote in *A Dance to the Music of Time*. A wonder that a little later on there was any room for the *Fantaisie Impromptu*, *The Dynasts* and so forth.

I also played in a not large, railed-in, public space over the road from Happy Valley, mostly grass but with a few flower-beds, which my wife told me later was known to her as "Sparrow Park". For a reason now seeming obscure but presumably ornamental, a tall mast had been erected in the middle of it, sustained by steel hawsers up which one often tried to climb, though atrociously rough on the hands. At a certain epoch Sparrow Park was a not negligible feature of my boyhood, its sparse, indeed boring, features being of great physical immediacy – hawsers, rocks in the rockery surrounding the mast with a peculiarly intense whiteness and sharpness, veronicas in beds dwarfed by the sea winds, the terminal semicircles on the just-climbable iron railings, and a worm from its sandy soil, which some larger boy once tried to make me eat, of predominantly gritty effect. Most of those I played with there, mainly at a time before I went to boarding school, would need, to be intelligible, explanations too tedious to embark on; the complexity of even simple lives being an inevitable result of the lavish time scale involved. Besides, as noted by Anthony Powell's X. Trapnell, only fiction can be truthful in such matters – memory is too defective and distorting.

Mr Fraser, the man who had been my father's partner (to use the term loosely, for the organization in the end was that of a private limited liability company) in the rubber-proofing mill between Manchester and Oldham, lived near Sparrow Park, commuting to the mill by train. His presence in Blackpool could well have been an additional reason for my mother coming to live there. For a few years I was friendly with his five children – until their removal to a grander and more distant house, which more or less coincided with my own removal to boarding school. I will say nothing of this relationship except to recall, by way of introducing a theme possibly felt to be somewhat muted so far, playing with the four sons, perhaps the daughter, too, a fortune-telling game using playing cards, the object being to ascertain one's matrimonial destiny. First, the cards enabled in some way the girl concerned to be chosen, though restrictions prevailed and one was excited at managing to get a beauty of the neighbourhood, a fragile blonde called Joan Eastwood being greatly in demand; also Cynthia Hall, and in her case the euphonious name alone might have been for me sufficient attraction, for I do not remember her appearance and may well never have seen her. Such was the domination of what Moreland called the "*princesse lointaine* complex" that it did not seem to matter that the girl was known to the chooser merely by sight or reputation. Needless to say, the cards did not reveal my true fate, doubtless at the time in Sparrow Park or Happy Valley, not five hundred yards away.

Other indications of the conjugal ceremony and subsequent life were gained by reciting certain lists to the extent demanded by the card turned up, for example "coach, carriage, something or other, dustcart." I remember pointing out with what seemed masterly sophistry, to alleviate the ill-luck of driving from church in the dustcart, that such a vehicle could be cleaned out and tastefully draped. Freud's childhood "latency period" by no means precludes foolish amatory preoccupations, though true anguish in such areas is reserved for adolescence.

A married sister of Mr Fraser also lived close to Sparrow Park and I occasionally played with her son, too. Mr Fraser's paternal aunt, who had brought up my father and *his* sister as "remittance children" in Caithness, never, so far as I know, came to Blackpool, nor did she marry. She was called Margaret and was known in my family – had probably been thus known to the two siblings in her charge – as "Aunt Maggie". I remember her first at our Waterhead house, to which she paid several visits, presumably from Scotland, my father probably feeling a continuing debt owed to her, for her presence gave him no apparent pleasure, indeed was a source of irritation. She would usually make white puddings during the course of her visit, a delicacy my father was fond of, but their manufacture disordered the house: the operation prolonged, oatmeal and sheep guts everywhere. There was also a smelly process, perhaps that of boiling the sheep guts prior to them being used for the pudding skins. I think, too, they presented a problem of procurement, though the oatmeal would come from the sack imported by my father from Scotland and normally used for oatcakes, dipping herrings in before frying or grilling, and his porridge, the last named eaten with the milk in a separate bowl, a sensible habit adopted by me at that time, later in desuetude.

That Aunt Maggie doted on my father I expect added to her power of exacerbating him. Even my earliest memories of her involve wildish hair, old-fashioned garb, feyness if not precisely at times being a bit M. She was staying with us when the 1920 Derby was run. The matter was discussed, my father liking a bet as much as speculating in options on the Stock Exchange. Aunt Maggie ignored the favoured horses, pronouncing with visionary power that the winner would be Spion Kop. My father, though scornful of the selection, told her to back it if she was so sure. I do not know whether this was done: unlikely, since she was the last person to be involved in vulgar pleasures or material gain. Spion Kop won at odds of 33–1.

In a very short time after my father's death feyness had become paranoia. The last time I saw her was during a stay with my grandparents in Oldham, very likely during the year of my grandfather's mayoralty, 1924–25. One day, after visiting my father's grave in Failsworth Cemetery, we called on Aunt Maggie in her lodgings not very far from the cemetery, nor indeed from the house where I had been born. An allowance was paid to her by Mr Fraser and at some date she had come permanently down from Scotland. Her lodgings (in fact, one ground-floor room) were also within easy reach of the rubber-proofing mill and hence of her nephew. A brass bedstead dominated the room and Aunt Maggie was in the bed, in grubby white nightgown. Could she even then have been suffering from her terminal illness? I do not know. She had on occasion to get out of bed, for one thing to serve us, from the bag, with shop cakes of a garish kind, utterly despised in my mother's scheme of things and afterwards educed by her as evidence of Aunt Maggie's characteristic improvidence. Aunt Maggie must have been warned of our coming, though neither plates nor beverages were supplied. I was struck by her dirty feet; perhaps as much as by her constantly returning to the theme of being watched by detectives through the window which, where not masked by a dressing table, looked out on the shabby street. She referred openly and often to my father's death, especially distressing to me who even at that early age wanted such things swept under the carpet, dominated as I was by self-consciousness, an inability to comfort even by a formula of words, a general desire for cosy happiness to reign. "Och, the dear," was a Doric phrase of her lament, still vividly remembered, as is her emphasizing the loss of his physical beauty and embarrassingly demonstrating her recognition of its inheritance by my brother and me. Not long after this she died of the malady that had killed him. The undoubtedly painful and squalid circumstances of her end I tried not to dwell on.

Even in the couple of years or so since we had left Oldham my father's grave had, to my mother's distress, become wildly overgrown, despite her having paid for its upkeep. She had had it marked by a large dark-grey marble gravestone, which referred to its containing also the bodies of my infant siblings George and Eric. That they were already there probably accounted for my father being buried in Failsworth, quite a distance from the house in Waterhead where he died. The legend of these deaths, incised so permanently and publicly, impressed me greatly. I saw the marble only once more, though I do not entirely rule out the possibility of again seeking it out, despite the growing toughness, even cynicism, in such areas since those days of loss. I think, too, of the miniature and more commonplace tablet marking my mother in the gardens of a Yorkshire crematorium, never revisited. "Why does my pen not drop from my hand on approaching the infinite pity and tragedy of all the past? It does, poor helpless pen, with what it meets of the ineffable, what it meets of the cold Medusa-face of life, of all the life *lived*, on every side." The conclusion of that wonderful cemeterial passage in Henry James's *Notebooks* comes to mind, but I transcribe it only to underline how far short of what I wished, in art as well as in feeling, I have fallen in life.

I now regret a little that I took so much of my memory of my mother's family for my novel *The Perfect Fool*, not a satisfactory work. It might have been more effective as unadorned autobiography but it would not be sensible to filter out all the actuality from its considerable fictionalizing. Something may be said, however, about the greater complications of reality in the matter of my grandparents' children, especially since my fiction has avoided difficulty in such matters, often conveniently positing the orphan or the only child.

My mother's eldest brother, Herbert, died as a young man in the influenza epidemic at the end of the First World War. He had a harelip, partly hidden by a moustache with waxed ends on the lines of my grandfather's as I knew it in earliest days (the wax and some of the Nietszchean luxuriance subsequently disappeared in my grandfather's case). At his death Uncle Herbert was married, with an infant daughter: his young widow (who bore the same Christian name as my mother) had to go back to mill work. But even when Herbert was alive the family was poor. My grandmother's singing voice (my mother, too, had a strong true mezzo-soprano) had descended to Herbert in full measure. He had been a boy chorister at Ripon Cathedral, and returned later as a bass. In the interim he worked as a journeyman painter and decorator; had no better job when he returned to Oldham after his second spell at Ripon (a post which presumably could not support a family). What a waste of talent! My mother sometimes spoke with regret of the loss, also, of his intelligence and sweet nature. The contrasting widowhoods of the two Nellies struck me even as a small boy: my mother, not rich but never in peril of having to try to earn a living; Herbert's widow bringing up my cousin, Kathleen, in a small terrace house which perhaps was her parents' house to which she had been forced to return. Besides singing, Herbert's leisure was occupied with painting of a different kind. A respectable oil of his of tall grey tree trunks always hung in my grandparents' dining room, though Herbert's initials were followed by an acknowledgement to some other painter. I was in my grandparents' house when two or three days before his death in 1918 he called on his way home from work saying he wouldn't come in because of a cold. Kathleen, in her turn, inherited the voice. She sang as a soprano with the Halle choir, and in 1955 was presented with its long-service medal by Sir John Barbirolli.

Two daughters came next in line to Herbert: Edith and my mother. Edith, the elder, was known in the family as "Keck", indicating her bossiness as a child. The word is dialect, probably obsolescent even in Edith's youth. Smaller and fairer than my mother, she had inherited more of my grandfather's characteristics. (My grandmother I see now as a saintly person – not at all pious or lacking in the critical faculty, but simply "good". In my mother the critical side was more apparent, especially in later life, but the "goodness" was not lost and I detect it among my own descendants.) Keck was married to the manager of a gas-works and they had a house or flat on the premises. I remember looking down on a courtyard, its cobbles glistening with the dampness common in Oldham, scene of the rats that infested the gasworks marching in military formation in one of their frequent anabases, as sensationally narrated by Uncle Tom, Keck's husband. A somewhat Victorian deathrate persisted in places like Oldham: Keck, too, became a youngish widow. The means she inherited were between my mother's and the other Nellie's, but in some way she eventually met a musician and married him. I say "in some way" because I think Keck was the only one of my maternal uncles and aunts not impressing my youthful mind as musical – though as I write that a memory rises of her "dressing up" in male attire with my mother, presumably to sing a comic duet. My mother dressed up (the character sometimes favoured being Charlie Chaplin) as late as Seacliffe days: the occasions were rare, the clothes and make-up quite elaborate, the effect successful to others, to me, typically, more or less embarrassing. I suppose my mother's slimness ensured an appeal to the taste prevalent in that ambiguous area; the counterpart of Violet, a character soon to be touched on.

Keck's new husband, youngish, quiet and charming, with the Wodehousian name of Archie Gladman, was really a trombonist but because of a tendency to TB was forced in the end to play his second instrument, the double bass, for which there was less demand in the theatre and cinema bands he played in. The coming of the talkies also caused difficulties. Around that epoch he died of the disease mentioned, and once more Keck and her cinema-baffled daughter by Uncle Tom were left in far from easy circumstances.

One must be struck, setting down such brief lives, by their suitability for the fiction of, say, Arnold Bennett's best period – their illustration of the petty bourgeoisie's social mobility coupled with its immersion in the more or less sordid details of human existence, yet with a readiness to cope with life's material side and in many ways – some the ways of art – to rise above it. John, the sibling immediately following my mother, spent most of his Army service in the First World War in a concert party. He was then extremely young, blond, blue-eyed, slender, and, among other roles, was a "female impersonator", apparently celebrated, for I have a printed postcard of him in drag, signed by him with his sobriquet "Violet". He brought back from the Near East an inscribed cigarette case presented to him by some local potentate appreciative of his performance. Nothing untoward need be read into this: soon after the war Uncle John married a girl called Edith – I think in fact a sweetheart before he went off to play Violet for the soldiers and the "sheeks" – and lived happily ever after. Never rounded, Edith after bearing her first child lost a fair amount of weight and so was known ever after as "Bone", a nickname deriving from the communist medico Dr Edith Bone, at that time, as she was much later, prominent in the news. This also helped to distinguish her, in conversational reference, from "Keck".

Uncle John worked on the administrative side of the cotton trade but as the years went by he did more and more acting for the BBC, appearing, for instance, in a long-running radio series with Wilfred Pickles, and in more serious productions by Norman Swallow and D. G. Bridson. When I was a boy I had seen and admired him in amateur dramatics. In private life he had a professional's power of mimicry and assuming accents; also he could make one laugh. He was close to my grandmother and, like her, "good". He retained remarkably the appearance that had made his personation as Violet so effective. I say this though I did not see him during the last twenty years of his life. In his latter days, after Bone had died and he was permanently in a guesthouse aptly, one hopes, called "The Anchorage", on the Fylde coast only a few miles from my school of former times, we corresponded, perhaps his first letter prompted by my election as Oxford's Professor of Poetry. He told me that one of his fellow "guests" at The Anchorage was a Miss Kenworthy, aged eighty-five, who as a young woman had lived in my birthplace, Failsworth, and was acquainted with my father before he was married.

Miss Kenworthy apparently knew my work as a writer before Uncle John tied up at The Anchorage and so was somewhat staggered by the perspectives opened up by his relating his history. He asked me to write to her as an action that would give her pleasure, and a letter came in reply which I will reproduce with certain omissions and explanations – not, however, distorting the facts. I should emphasize that the mystery of my father's origins were pervasive, the veil lifted only in a few accidental ways. For instance, after he had left school my brother went to teach in a prep school while brooding over possible careers and found that the matron had come from Lybster, where Aunt Maggie had reared my father and his sister, and was able to shed some light, also cast a few more shadows. The enigma was deepened by my father's looks and ability. Miss Kenworthy told Uncle John that when he arrived in Failsworth they thought him the scion of Spanish nobility, though it must be said that rickets and poverty made it easy to stand out physically in those days, and later, among the indigenous population of the Manchester conurbation. However, Uncle John confirmed that he looked the hidalgo part, was one of the handsomest men he had known.

Your letter [wrote Miss Kenworthy on 28 January 1970] revived a lot of old memories. Days spent in my youth in Hollinwood [where the rubber-proofing mill was situated] and Failsworth. I remember Mr Fraser bringing your father and his sister Minnie, who became a nurse, from Scotland to stay with him in Failsworth. Your father entered the business during the [First] War and evidently made good. I was sorry to hear of his death, also your mother's. I have lost touch with the Frasers, except Mr Fraser's sister, who is living near Windsor where her younger son lives. She was engaged to my cousin, Dr Lomas, when they were young, but he died at twenty-six. Afterwards she married Dr Buckley, but it ended in divorce. They had two sons, the elder killed in the [Second, of course] War. It is a small world. I never thought I should know your uncle. I believe Mr Fraser's father was gamekeeper on some estate in Scotland. Mr Fraser used to talk about the boy and girl with whom he and his sister played when young. Well it certainly has revived old memories. I am not much good at writing. I am past it. Wishing you every success.

There was already something amiss with Mrs Buckley's marriage in the days when I played in Sparrow Park with her elder little boy (so unlucky in the war in which I myself had a comparative joy ride). And was death rather than desertion put about as the reason for Dr Buckley's absence? Perhaps that is exaggerating the horror of scandal still prevalent in that society at that time: more likely that, as ever, my understanding was deficient.

I have left in simplified form the mechanics of my father's business association with Mr Fraser and indeed many details necessarily remain obscure. I will not say more except that the firm name originally included that of an elderly Jew who I think had died or retired by the time my father had achieved partnership (more properly by then, directorial) status. I mention this for several reasons. My father was sometimes thought to look not Spanish but Jewish, an expected presence in a trade in which in Manchester Jews played a great part. This may well have been the cause of my grandfather's initial prejudice against him as a suitor for his younger daughter, especially having regard to my grandfather's familiarity with *The Merchant of Venice*. Some of my father and mother's friends were comfortably-off Jews and I daresay that bore upon the increasing luxury and sophistication of my parents' houses and possessions. The truly intellectual side of Jewish life I suspect did not exist among the Weinbergs and the Gotliffs, friends whose names seem utterly familiar sixty years on, and so was not communicated, but whisky and good cigars, solid furniture, a love of the theatre and of motor cars, an excellent tailor in Manchester memorably called Macbeth, serious bridge – many such things were probably rooted in my father through his Jewish contacts, though the native ground was obviously fertile. I should add also, for there is some evidence for it, that my father's mysterious father may in truth have been Jewish.

My mother, whose cultural background was small-town Tory politics, low Church of England, church choir, parlour music and a general life style of enforced modesty, had some adjustments to make. She once told me of her astonishment, threat of uncontrollable giggles, when first dining with the Weinbergs (or the Gotliffs) and a preliminary prayer was said, at my father, not having a skullcap (yarmulke) like the other males, putting his folded napkin on his head. After his death she more or less slowly regressed to the styles and prejudices of her upbringing, though she was always lavish about her clothes and saw that my first suit with long trousers was made to measure, also finding a decent tailors and outfitters in Blackpool called Southworths, who supplied my suits and overcoats until I left the town when I was twenty-three or twenty-four.

My father's pleasure in going to the theatre may well have been useful common ground during any sticky times with my grandfather during his courtship of my mother. I believe I myself saw the comedian Wilkie Bard in a pantomime to which I was taken by my parents in extreme youth, but I cannot be sure, so rapidly and vividly did a passage from the production in question become a part of what Carlyle in his *Reminiscences* reminds us the Germans call (or used to call) *Coterie-sprache* – family-circle dialect. Wilkie Bard in the person of Simple Simon is granted three wishes by the Fairy Godmother. When she is gone he expresses his desire – in his eagerness to test out his good fortune, a modest but eccentric one: "I wish I was a hard-boiled egg." His eyes tight shut, he asks the audience: "Is it doing it?" Both phrases came to be applied in a variety of family contexts. Wilkie Bard also originated one of my grandfather's sayings, plainly at a much earlier stage of the comedian's career, and I remember my grandfather once explaining the ambient theatrical circumstances. Wilkie Bard has quarrelled with his stooge and they are to fight. Bard lays down the rules: "When I say 'Begin', begin. When I say 'Leave off', leave off." They face up. Bard says "Begin", strikes a blow, then immediately says "Leave off." *Da capo.* Possibly Wilkie Bard is not much remembered today. His most famous song ended "I'd like to sing in opera, sing in opera, sing in op-pop-pop-pop-era."

I called Mr Fraser "Uncle Alf", in the manner of the North. His mode of life may too have caught something from Jewish business associates. After he had moved from the Happy Valley area we were only very occasional visitors. In the drawing room of the new house was a grand piano, a pianola of such sophistication that as indications came round on the roll – "*p*", say, or "*rall*" – a row of levers in front of the keyboard enabled one to add the required expressiveness. The piano rolls available included classical pieces, so one temporarily became a Tregenza of the instrument. Typical of my lack of enterprise that I never even attempted to learn the piano. I decided at an early age that it was something I could not do, just as having established myself as open sprint champion as early as my penultimate year at school I never tried to win the half-mile or mile.

On one visit to the Frasers' I accidentally came across Uncle Alf in a room lit only by a lamp that threw illumination on his open book, a drink at his side. The comfort and purpose of the scene caught my admiration. Perhaps he was turning a page with the hand on which, from a cause never revealed, one finger lacked its top joint. The minaciousness of this feature was recalled later by the sudden staggering close-up of the hand of the Godfrey Tearle character in Hitchcock's *The Thirty-nine Steps*. The rubber-proofing mill had obviously continued to prosper. It was sometimes said in my family that my mother's shares had been acquired by Uncle Alf too cheaply. Was it a trace of guilt or mere respect for culture that prompted him at the end of my schooldays to enquire about my taste in gramophone records apropos of a birthday present? More probably my fascination with the pianola had tickled him, glad to have an enthusiast for his extravagance – though I expect I was too green ever to have discussed music with him. A list was sent and to my amazement he bought everything on it. Included were Bax's *Tintagel* and some Bach violin sonatas played by Isolde Menges and Harold Samuel, somewhat odd indication of breadth of taste, still persisting. Jewish generosity and ostentation unfortunately played little part in my own life, the petty-bourgeois anal-erotic character pretty well taking over.

A Gentile friendship, however, best survived the crisis of my father's death; a couple addressed by my brother and me as Uncle Fred and Auntie Vi, the titles again honorific. Uncle Fred had been a business associate, a drysalter; and he also took his family for holidays on the Fylde coast, eventually retiring there. I remember him from my father's lifetime: he owned an unusual car – a Ford with an English body, however that had come about. I was in it once when he drove in the tram track leading from Blackpool to St Annes (where The Anchorage was situated in later times) and took the speedometer up to what seemed then the dashing speed of 30 mph. He called to my father, also driving an open car nearby (could it have been his first car, the Yankee Overland?): "I'm a tram." It comes to me that Uncle Fred, small, sandy, humorous, was no stranger to the bottle, certainly in retirement, though that epoch was sadly truncated for I judge him to have been no more than fiftyish when he died – leaving £30,000, a tidy sum for the Twenties.

His ménage in the house on the front at Lytham where he ended his days had a good few features regarded by my brother and me as bizarre. It included at one time both Vi's parents, the father already decrepit. I once came into a room where he was sitting with eyes closed, head forward, a thread of saliva hanging from his open mouth, and with a lurch of the stomach thought he was dead. On that occasion he had merely fallen asleep. Vi's mother survived him but most of the time I knew her was suffering from the effects of a stroke, though capable of being inserted into the large, chauffeured limousine Uncle Fred possessed at that period, for a "drive". She was troubled by one of her toes, which gradually stuck up to such an extent as to stop her getting a shoe on. The solution adopted, striking as it seemed to me, was to have the toe amputated. I would guess this proposed and arranged by Auntie Vi, always sweepingly direct and practical. My mother told me of being with her when buying gramophone records. "Yes, I'll have that," she would repeatedly say after a few revolutions of the disc played by the shop assistant, carrying into everyday occasions Uncle Alf's birthday lavishness.

This was the heyday of the coloured duetists, Layton and Johnstone (the former only recently dead, well into his eighties), a liking for whose records Vi passed on to my mother. From these, as from Lila Dale and her confrères, I got to know many songs including one I sang then as incongruously as "The Sheik of Araby" but which today becomes more and more apt:

> There's nothing left for me,
> Of days that used to be,
> They're just a memory among my souvenirs.

From my mother, herself an excellent if limited cook, I inherited a notebook of recipes, unfortunately sparse and unsystematic. However, it includes some of Auntie Vi's recipes which in their generous proportions of rich to plain ingredients reflect her nature, and fondness for what she conceived to be the good things of life, e.g:

PLUM CAKE (VI)

6 oz butter, 2 oz syrup, 6 oz caster sugar.
Beat these to a cream, add 3 eggs and ¼pt warm milk, and beat again.
Add ½lb [plain?] flour, ½ teaspoon baking powder, 1lb currants, ¼lb. candied peel, 3 oz. ground almonds. [No oven temperature or baking time given, but presumably lowish and prolonged respectively.]

Discussion among Fred and Vi's friends was caused by the rise in the household of a Rasputin figure – the comparison is purely metaphorical – called Mr Marple who I believe began as the person in charge of Uncle Fred's motor yacht. When I was aboard, this commodious vessel merely chugged about the Ribble estuary – to my relief, for I feared the open sea, with its twin threat of sickness and death by drowning. But longer voyages were undertaken, though these did not satisfy Mr Marple's capabilities, and gradually he came to participate in most family affairs, even appearing in the drawing room at tea time, and probably giving advice over such problems as the vertical toe. He was certainly useful in getting the great bulk of Vi's mother into the back of the limousine, but the attractions of his physique and conversation seemed minimal, complacency and dogma ruling in the latter area.

Who can tell from the outside what forces operate within a family, particularly where cash or infatuation play a covert part? When Uncle Fred died some thought that Mr Marple would succeed in marrying Auntie Vi, but both the yacht and its Palinurus were got rid of (with what complexities I do not know) and she settled down to widowhood. She would have been an attractive catch and not only for her money: pretty, blonde, plumpish, with fine pale skin, she was always enclosed in a cloud of Caron's Sweet Pea, and she managed her household with controlled lavishness. Perhaps she had gone along too easily with Fred's whims and eccentricities: once on a country drive their little daughter, an only child, had coveted a lamb seen on a farm. This was bought for her more or less on the spot and actually kept in the house until its droppings became too copious to tolerate. But to have stood out against Fred in such matters would have implied an element of feminine nagging quite alien to her nature. Indeed, who knows but that she was the prime mover in the lamb affair?

All these older people mentioned are dead to my knowledge or must surely be dead, but as I write this in the spring of 1978 my grandparents' youngest child, called Fred after his father, lives still. We exchange an occasional letter but I have not seen him for a great many years. He is not all that much older than me: when I was born he went off to school gleefully repeating "I'm an uncle." He was still living with my grandparents well on into my boyhood, the source of a few miscellaneous precepts in the conduct of life I would never have thought to challenge though incapable of following them myself; for example, that in hand-writing the movement of the pen must be guided by the whole hand not just the fingers. Though at the time of this pronouncement he was studying for some technical qualification in the grocery trade, in the end he succeeded my grandfather as Superintendent Registrar of Births, Marriages and Deaths where penmanship was more to the point – at any rate in the time of my grandfather who I remember making the register entries and writing the certificates in his copperplate hand (two fingers extended on top of the pen, the other two, victims of the contracture previously mentioned, tucked neatly away). The boxes of fine pen-nibs, capable of meticulous thickening of the down-strokes nonetheless; the miniature pair of clogs; the wooden bas-relief by some primitive artist of a Milletesque man with a wheelbarrow – such memorabilia of visits to my grandfather's office must have descended to Uncle Freddy with the job. The office was near Tommyfield, Oldham's ancient open marketplace where once were to be found such figures in my grandfather's lore as the man standing there (as he would say on 31 December) with as many noses as there are days in the year, and the vendor of ice cream who called: "It's made from milk, sugar and eggs; highly flavoured with the juice of the pine; frozen into consistency by the power of ice, assisted by muriated soda. Only one half-penny a glass." Those, of course, were the days when the results of even Auntie Vi's kind of recipes might be found in the market.

Perhaps from Uncle Freddy came my admiration for pier-end music, to be undermined at school though perhaps never entirely deleted – composers such as Luigini and Eric Coates played by him on my grandparents' gramophone, exotically single-horned like a fabulous beast. I must add, however, that all his life he has sung more serious music with choral societies, including that of the BBC. Alas, the Broadbentian vocal powers were not part of my inheritance: "Avalon" and "Shepherd of the Hills" and "Parted" have down the years been warbled by me more in Gorill's style.

5 *The Metropole*

For a reason I never knew or have forgotten, the proprietress and her three daughters left Seacliffe. Perhaps the lease was up or she sold the business. We went with them to a like establishment farther north in the town, only obliquely overlooking the sea, the house smaller, more elegant, only recently – possibly at that moment – having changed from use as a private residence. Here I passed the holidays of my later schooldays: dim period, scarcely worth trying in the least to depict, as it seems to me now. Where were the inspiriting forces that worked on other poets in their youth? "Ugliness be thou my beauty," I might have said to myself at almost every stage of my life, but in Blackpool I had lost the scenes of early childhood, meaningful however banal – the mill chimneys, red brick both newish and grimy, muddy cobbles wisped with cotton escaped from great sacks on horse-drawn carts, winter days whose atmosphere was so heavily yellowish-grey that they never really grew light, shawled women and girls, trams redolent of workers' dinners carried in white basins closed with white-spotted red cotton handkerchiefs and where one sat on yellow-varnished, hole-ventilated wooden seats facing passengers often bow-legged, usually pale. This was a spiritual loss, felt quite early (no doubt subconsciously connected with my lost father), and therefore significant to me as the writer I wanted from the age of fifteen or so to become. The Pennine green fields and small dark-grey valley towns, mostly known from our tragically few years at Waterhead, came rather into the category of dream landscapes – desirable things theoretically available yet never satisfactorily appreciated let alone possessed. Some imp of the perverse has kept me from what I know I would have responded to warmly in this area, just as I never fulfilled my love of billiards and snooker nor, like Proust, got to Venice. Not until 1955 did I even have a garden of my own. As a youth I was only exiguously attended by a vision splendid.

I also seemed handicapped as a novelist by leaving the speech and social life of industrial east Lancashire at so early an age. The whining, frozen-lipped tones of Blackpool which the Boss tried to eradicate in his pupils were perhaps the dilute result of various Lancashire and Yorkshire accents brought by those who had come to the holiday town in retirement or to make their modest piles in catering or entertainment. The social strata were simplified; the population much reduced out of season, of course, and to a degree culturally stagnant. In time I did conceive that a broadish novel might be written, possibly on the lines of those American novels located in small towns delineating the old founder families, the smart set, the judge, the bootlegger, and so forth, but I was never quite sufficiently impelled to try to write it. Except insofar as I feel guilty about all books left unwritten, I do not regret the absence of the seaside resort novel, but I believe, given a decade more of Oldham life, I might have attempted a fiction about the work, politics and classes of a northern manufacturing town (which my *Image of a Society* does not aspire to).

I suppose what Blackpool had to offer in the realm of the Wordsworthian made its mark: seabirds, ribbed sand, rugeous sunsets – all appearing at the end of the short street, Wilton Parade, in which the new private hotel was situate. An early poem ends:

> They watch a portion of the slaty sea
> detach itself, flutter and become a gull,
> rise wheeling, crying, over the dissolving pier
> whose minarets are charcoaled on the sky.

I say "early" but the poem was probably written in 1932, "they" being poor and exploited fishermen, required type of dramatis personae for poetry of the time. Before that epoch I wrote a fair amount of muck, perhaps some still to be found in one of the trunks in the loft: I doubt if it would contain much as accurate as the image implied by "dissolving" for the pier at high tide (and for its rusting legs), somewhat surprising and pleasing now. In my last year at school, 1928, or possibly earlier, a typewriter became available (by what mysterious means I do not recall) and I typed out some short stories in the manner of H. G. Wells and Aldous Huxley and sent them to periodicals, never neglecting to add in the covering letter some such smarm as "The fact that I am sixteen may be useful for publicity purposes", rather in the manner of "E. J. Thribb (17)". My tyro's one-finger typing in single spacing would have helped to ensure rejection, though very early on I was excited to get instead of a rejection slip a letter from the then editor of *John o' London's Weekly*, Wilfred Whitten, in which he conferred a word of praise, adding that I must read authors like Galsworthy for all I was worth so that I would learn both what to include and what to reject in my fiction. Kind action, though at the time I did not see the rejection point, it being difficult enough to get material *in*.

I doubt if my really early work could now be found – a minuscule play, for instance, called *Barabbas*, giving some twist to the crucifixion story that escapes me; and another drama, more appropriately skeletal because in the manner of Maeterlinck. Both in prose. Even these were written at an age which for some writers would be considered advanced, fourteen or perhaps early fifteen (almost every month counted in those days). The latter age I judge to be when I wrote for some purpose not of self-expression (perhaps humour or parody) a short piece of blank verse. As soon as I showed it to a friend I realized it was not blank verse at all but syllabic verse: that is, I had misapprehended until then the stress element in English poetry; or even more gormlessly had known perfectly well what blank verse sounded like but failed to *compris* the method of getting that effect. All the same, my "ear" was plainly never a strong point in my poetic equipment: at any rate an odd gap existed between ear and pen.

Apart from a mock Elizabethan song composed as a show-off soon after the blank verse episode I did not write any verse at school, unless some beneficent censor has operated on my recall. I wanted to write prose drama and fiction, mainly the latter. My turning into a poet seems slightly mysterious, out of character: even now, especially with novels behind me, I feel unease at seeing myself referred to as "the poet".

Where precisely did I write *Barabbas* and the like? I kept the MSS in the pockets of those wallet affairs – "compendiums" of stationary, as they were called – conveniently containing writing pad and envelopes, and used by my mother. I remember having these things at my grandparents' house in holiday time but the recollection is lost of sitting down to write in Seacliffe or the house in Wilton Parade. Not that I would have sat down for long. Like some early machine gun, I have always operated in rapid, short, unreliable bursts. Only in fairly recent years have I ever sufficiently re-drafted. The small lined pads are typical of the feeble materials I used, at any rate for many years. In other words my habits of literary work were – have never really ceased to be – thoroughly bad. When we went on holiday in the later Thirties with Julian Symons, actually younger than me, I observed with guilt and awe his professional industry and equipment: knuckling down to work after an arduous evening of paper games; using green paper in the manner (wasn't it?) of Dumas *père*. It is the only advice one can give to the young: work regularly; rewrite; keep a journal, a commonplace book; indulge yourself with pens, notebook, paper, typewriter, for they will inspire when life has failed.

Though at Wilton Parade we spent a good deal of time in the proprietress' sitting room, it is unlikely I wrote anything there, what with the daughters and the pursuing young men, and so forth. In a corner on a card table was a portable gramophone. The only classical record was of Paderewski playing Liszt's Second Hungarian Rhapsody which I put on a lot, for at school I was entering the Tregenza era. We did not have our own gramophone either there or at Seacliffe: it must have been sold or given away, together with the stock of records accumulated at Miss Barraclough's during the time of Auntie Vi's musical influence. My mother bought me an HMV portable after we had moved from Wilton Parade to the flat she took when I left school (to which, in our earliest days there, the Boss paid his memorable visit) and I began to accumulate records far from the Layton and Johnstone category. I carried on with a friendship formed at school with a dayboy, one of the two pianists already mentioned, who already had a record collection, from which I learnt such sacred and reverberant names as Otto Klemperer and Karl Muck. Because Leslie greatly admired Cortot he possessed César Franck's *Variations Symphoniques* played by that pianist but his taste was really more severely classical. I nervously revealed to him my purchase of an album of Ignaz Friedman's performance of the Grieg piano concerto on dark-blue label Columbia discs, the work to a tyro of those days seeming almost modern and possibly ephemeral. A little later I was even more nervous about Ravel's *Introduction and Allegro*, on plum label HMVs, the colour again indicating cheapness. But I must not waffle on about gramophone records, my interest in which has gone on, no less coloured by collector's crankiness.

It was an odd flat for my mother to have rented (though she was not then quite so conventional as she later became). She complained that it was somewhat beyond her means, but in reality she guarded her capital and income rather too carefully, and less for herself than for her sons. The flat, on the second floor of a building whose ground floor was shops, looked out from its sitting room and main bedroom over the promenade to the sea. It was actually just closer to the centre of the town than the Hotel Metropole, the entrance to which – at the other end to the grillroom meagrely patronized by Miss Paine – could be seen by us diagonally across the road. The flat's bathroom and second bedroom were not behind the, so to speak, front door, but across the access staircase; and the cooking arrangements hidden by a partition and screen in the dining room. This bohemian layout had given my mother food for thought before she signed on the dotted line.

In the couple of years or so that had elapsed since Seacliffe days Miss Paine had disappeared from our lives, possibly dead, but the Prussian was still in charge over the road and seen when I went to the chamber concerts held there a little later which attracted the Blackpool musical élite, such as it was, and gave me a bit of needed practice in small talk with the posh.

Strangely, at a time when I no longer frequented the Metropole lounge, in house-that-Jack-built fashion I got to know the leader of the tiny hotel orchestra through its pianist, who had married the girl who had been the inseparable friend of my wife-to-be in her schooldays and after. So I never heard the band when it included these two excellent players, but I sometimes listened to them at the pianist's flat, probably playing the Max Bruch No 1, whose strains even today recall the fiddler, a big shambling fellow who had it not been for his tender phrasing of the Bruch melodies and his committing suicide after his wife's death one would have thought utterly commonplace. Len, the pianist, told me that Frish was no Prussian but a Czech (possibly Sudeten German, soon to become a direly familiar phrase), who regularly requested the orchestra to play the overture to Smetana's most celebrated opera, which he pronounced *The Battered Bride*.

So a fresh set of characters appeared on the scene. Naturally the most vivid were those working in the office of the solicitors, T. & F. Wylie Kay, where I was to serve my five years' articles. I had left school at Christmas 1928 but had to wait until the following February or March to start my service, for the firm chosen was in the upset of moving from long-occupied offices in the town's main professional street to a larger building, in fact opposite the entrance to our new flat, diagonally across a modest-sized square. For this brief journey I remember putting on, certainly at first, a newly-acquired trilby hat, strange symbol of emancipation from the Boss. The overcoat I wore with the hat I must surely have had at school, bought from the ready-made department of the tailors already mentioned, Southworths. But the next overcoat I had, quite soon, was certainly bespoke from them: it was black, with a lighter fleck, and I instructed them to make it long, with a half-belt at the back. With this I wore a black snap-brim trilby. The effect intended was of a literary man; the result more like the spiv character Slasher Green, portrayed by the comedian Sid Field after the Second War. I may add that the last overcoat made to my specification by Southworths, just before I got a job in Kent in 1935 or early 1936, was a complete contrast. The material was expensive: substantial, smooth, camel-coloured. I changed to an all-round belt and the pleats it enclosed were smaller and more numerous than in the Slasher Green article – gathers, almost. It was double-breasted, long, very warm. By 1940 it had seen better days according to the high standards of non-shabbiness inherited from my mother, and I lent it to Giles Romilly when he was sent by his newspaper, the *Express*, to cover the Norwegian operations. Unfortunately he was captured by the Germans in that fiasco and being Winston Churchill's nephew was sent to Colditz with other VIP prisoners, so the loan was permanent. Typical of me that I cannot remember asking him, when we met again after the War, if he had found it useful in the rigours of that now well-known fortress.

My brother also patronized Southworths. The man we used to see in the ready-to-wear department was one of two Southworth brothers, extremely lean, hair parted in the middle, greased perhaps with Pears' Solidified, vertical lines in his cheeks through (or causing) a constricted manner of speech, the lips tight at the corners, the words emerging from some minimum labial movement at the centre. He would expertly button the jacket one was trying on, run his finger under the lapels to ensure they were sitting properly, and more often than not remark: "Very tony, Mr Fuller. Extremely nutty." My brother's imitation was good, perhaps facilitated by his past experience as the Apothecary in *Romeo and Juliet*. Both he and I had a fetish for having jackets and overcoats made to fit over-snugly. I had a brown and cream houndstooth Harris tweed jacket I was very fond of: it lasted so long that even I came to see that it should have been cut more generously. Besides, it embodied another quirk of mine that I eventually realized was aesthetically insupportable – double-breasted style lapels on a single-breasted jacket. More successful aesthetically was a pair of dark grey, almost black, flannel trousers I ordered after seeing Charles Sweeney playing in a similar pair in the amateur golf championship at Royal Lytham St Annes. Before then flannel trousers had been light grey, the lighter the better. The last garments made for me by Southworths were two suits, just before my marriage in 1936, one of which I wore at the ceremony. Both were light brown – the two materials had been so attractive I could not choose between them and had them both. One cost £3 10s., the other three guineas.

I was articled to Eric Wylie Kay. He and his uncle, Tom, were the only partners at that time. It was a sound and flourishing family firm. Both Mr Eric and Mr Tom were nutty, Eric also handsome in the teeth and toothbrush moustache style of a subaltern of the First War, somewhat later made famous by Anthony Eden. A man from Savile Row used to come and measure Mr Tom for his suits, which were said to cost fourteen guineas apiece, putting Southworths in proper perspective. T. & F. Wylie Kay was not the right sort of firm to train me in the practice of the law, as will appear. But a harder furrow was of my own rejecting. My mother had been put on to a much smaller firm in Preston where there was a vacancy for an articled clerk – Whittle & Co, the "Co" being then a fiction – and we had gone for an interview. The waiting room was separated from a clerks' office merely by an obscure-glass partition. From behind this, as we waited to see Mr Whittle, came the severe Lancashire tones of a buxom, middle-aged, woman managing-clerk, letting some smaller fry have it in no uncertain terms. My blood ran cold at the prospect of a régime as repressive as that of the Boss. Nor was I warmed by Mr Whittle, a fairly diminutive cripple with a rubber-tipped stick and incisive voice, who possibly simply to emphasize value for money (in those days a premium had normally to be paid for articles, with no return by way of salary) spoke of the hard and thorough training his office would afford, especially in the unappealing litigation field. Afterwards my mother immediately agreed as to Whittle & Co's unsuitability, for she was as "soft" as I was in such matters. The avoidance of the crunches in life is often within one's own power; but the benefit may be questionable. In the end my career in the law was outwardly more successful than my career in letters, though I was in middle age before I found scope for such legal talents as I possessed. An early shake-up by Mr Whittle might have brought that about far earlier. It was even the same in the Navy. An instinct for self-preservation made me put my name down for a mysterious long course while I was still at my initial training establishment. The result was I diverted myself from an executive commission to being an NCO in the mechanics of radar, and it was not until 1944, eventually commissioned and at the Admiralty, that I had (as Technical Assistant to the Director of Naval Air Radio) any sustained usefulness or relief from excruciating boredom.

At T. & F. Wylie Kay's I was put into a topmost room with another articled clerk (who happened to have the same name as Gorill's tormentor, Byng) and the engrossing clerk. The latter worked on a stool at a high sloping "desk" fitted along one wall and evidently brought from the old premises. All the deeds turned out by the firm were still "engrossed" by hand, rather than typed, though "parchment substitute" was sometimes used instead of parchment. The engrossing clerk was a young man called Norman Lees (who later kept me posted about Blackpool), shortish, with a large intelligent head and lively features. I shall refer to him by his surname, as was customary in those times. He had done well at his late school and it was an indication of current economic conditions and educational opportunity that he stuck at the soul-destroying job of copying out in copperplate handwriting the typewritten drafts brought into him by the managing clerks and occasionally the partners. One says "copperplate" but though Lees threw off the engrossing clerk's various arts ("texting" the gothic lettering where that was required; "pouncing" the parchment; erasing errors with a penknife or razor blade and rubbing the erasure smooth with the tip of a (cow?) horn to enable it to be written over; sewing sheets together with green "ferret"; affixing the wax seals with their attendant ribbons; and so forth) compared say with my grandfather he was not a good calligraphist. His finished work had a superficial air of authenticity but closer inspection might reveal letters unjoined or ill-formed, even ambiguous, especially when he had been trying, always in vain, to catch up with his backlog of drafts. The engrossed deeds were sometimes complained about by the conveyancing managing clerk, J. T. Ogden – who was the first of that alas obsolescent breed I got to know and by no means the last I came to regard with respect and admiration, tinged with fear. Not that JTO was ever other than the kindest of men but one's work often failed (and one knew it was going to fail) to measure up to his standards. I greatly admired his fluent handwriting evolved from a time when he was an engrossing clerk, and his draft deeds, founded on the most traditional of the conveyancing precedent books, *Prideaux*. It was only conscientiousness brought to the point of exacerbation that caused him so often to burst into the attic room, look with angry despair at the draft deeds ranged to Lees's right on the sloping desk, groan, and bring a few of his most urgent ones to the front of the row – a ploy often frustrated by others doing the same.

Lees relished a good many things in life; some surprising, having regard to a background which today might almost be conceived of as "deprived". His mother had died when he and his sister were young: his father, in a by no means lucrative job, had never remarried. He had a good memory for the comic side of his schooldays. Some things he told me I used in novels years afterwards: others I wished I could have worked in, like the parody of Tennyson's "The Revenge", one brilliant line only of which remains with me now:

> And a pinnace, like a buttered turd, came sliding
> from far away.

I soon discovered that he had a taste for reading as individual as most elements in his make-up. He liked particularly Arnold Bennett's novels and even more the journal that I think began to be published about this time. The latter would appeal partly because of its depiction of a provincial breaking into the world of high politics, art and large yachts, without that provincial ceasing to see through the flummery. Above all, Lees had the sharpest sense of the absurd and the fallible in human behaviour, although his life was conventional, his pleasures largely orthodox. His Saturday nights, for instance, were at this epoch always spent drinking with male companions. But his Monday morning reports rarely failed to single out some strangely memorable features of what might seem invincibly tedious hours. One of his friends, weary of being repetitively interrogated during the evening about a facial wound, pinned to his lapel a notice:

I HAVE CUT MYSELF WHILE SHAVING
WITH A POM-POM PENNY BLADE

The resonance of this (apart from its being a "fourteener", as I am sure Lees also appreciated) was the fact that the penny razor blade, competing with Gillette's product at threepence, was an article whose dubiety (and danger) was significantly reflected in a brand name such as "Pom-pom". Lees' analysis of all at Wylie Kay's was devastating and led to many running gags between us. There was, too, a deep quirkiness and reticence about him which made him, especially in later life, agreeably unpredictable, forcing one on the *qui vive*.

His power of looking with detachment at the kind of life and culture he had inherited, and which in his engrossing clerk days he still more or less moved in, was remarkable. I remember his once pointing out the grammatical curiousness of the idiom (I think a wholly North of England one) "partly what", and then moving on to a kind of Empsonian discussion (the occasion must have been in a pub) of the difference between saying a glass was "partly what full" and "partly what empty".

Looking back, I see that he in his turn was influenced, possibly his life transformed, by being put in with the articled clerks, passing his days on terms of intellectual equality with them. He was greatly taken by an overcoat belonging to Byng. It should be said that the latter was an Oxbridge graduate and therefore older than me and serving only three years' articles. The overcoat in question, a lightweight tweed, single-breasted with raglan sleeves – a far cry from the Slasher Green garment later made for me – had been built for Byng by obviously excellent tailors in his university town. Lees saw "Raglan", as he always called the coat, as evidence of some superior style in life, not necessarily the result of affluence, more a tradition or *modus operandi* which it was a provincial's (or any supposed inferior's) highest duty to acquire, the end result being a satisfactory, indeed beautiful, conquest of the grosser side of existence. He speculated as to whether the material of which Raglan was made could not be classed as "ratcatcher", a term he had picked up in his reading, maybe apropos of Edward VII or George V (the earliest slang usage of the word in the Supplement to the OED – the *Field* in 1930 – is surely too late and too esoteric). It was some time, I think after my days at Wylie Kay's, before Lees' own turnout reflected any notion of mastering life, and then merely in the shape of good dark suits or, for leisure, neat tweed jackets and flannel trousers. I remember once battling with him to the trams on the Promenade in one of Blackpool's characteristic squalls of wind and rain – and this must have been well into my articles for we were both bound for South Shore where he lived and where my mother had once more taken "rooms". He wore a bowler hat, necessarily large but of antique block, and his far from new, drab garbardine raincoat was buttoned to the throat. I said fondly to this Dickensian (or, rather, Gissingesque) figure: "The seedy clerk." The phrase as applied, and in such weather, struck me as funny but the reality was not so funny, Lees and his family at that time far from comfortably off.

We were eventually joined in the attic room by a third articled clerk whose purchase of an expensive trilby hat made by Stetson (could it actually have been imported from the States?) and other would-be grandiose gestures failed to impress Lees, whose mind as ever was fixed on some style beyond the fashionable or showy. His destiny may be briefly told. After my articles expired and I left Wylie Kay's, the post of engrossing clerk was seen to be anachronistic and Lees became a conveyancing clerk. The job presented no difficulties: quite apart from his ability, he had engrossed and read aloud (to check against the drafts) so many deeds of various kinds he was a walking encyclopaedia of precedents. Later he was given his articles, passed his examinations and qualified as a solicitor, eventually setting up on his own. He became quite famous in the local police and county courts, and his practice prospered. He had married one of the shorthand typists at Wylie Kay's, the courtship typically kept dark. His two daughters did well educationally, one of them publishing a book with the OUP on A. C. Bradley, a stroke of unobvious gamesmanship Lees no doubt much appreciated: later she was the author of an excellent book on Coleridge. In a strange way everything he achieved, though of conventional success, took on an element of the good or ideal life, the provincial's dream fulfilled. The beer he drank, cigarettes smoked, bridge played, the mass-produced car he drove, golf club eventually joined: on all these he conferred some proper value of his own; everything to do with the car, for example, carried off in a competent but offhand manner, as though to demonstrate its useful but essentially unBennettesque nature. The first time he visited us in London by car I gave him directions. He told me later that a phrase of these had become a useful family saying: "Eschew all side roads." Who knows what even more ludicrous traits of one's persona he had anatomized?

The articled clerks were idle beyond belief. No wonder Lees lagged in his engrossing. When the third articled clerk arrived we had a bridge four, and with a system of safeguards such as laying dummy out in a desk drawer which could be shut when Ogden *et al* were heard approaching, rubbers were more or less peacefully played. Byng had played at Oxbridge: he was a competent performer. I am not sure about Lees' expertise in the initial stages: he would have rapidly improved, anyway. As for myself, I had watched from an infantile age my parents and grandparents (and possibly even the Weinbergs and Gotliffes) play what was then merely auction bridge. In our Waterhead house when I must have been no more than seven or eight one of a serious four was called from the table and I offered with trepidation to take the hand, successfully carrying off this first excursion into actual play. I have already referred to my father's and grandfather's devotion to the game, the latter playing pretty well every night of his later life at the Conservative Club in Oldham. The underground family complaint was that whisky and bridge losses reduced his always modest income but this can scarcely have been true in any serious sense, though perhaps his rate of saving suffered, was extinguished even. I wonder whether at the club he came out with the patter indulged in at the family bridge table – the tags from *The Merchant of Venice*; the sharp startling snore, or cry of "That's it!", as one fingered alternative cards in one's hand; such maxims as "There's many a man walking the streets of London with his shirt hanging out of his britches through not drawing trumps."

I cannot remember when I first played contract bridge. Certainly at Wilton Parade, where a fellow "permanent" called

Mrs Laycock, a woman of immense ugliness and charm, was a demon addict. The epoch of playing at Wylie Kay's coincided with Culbertson's great influence on the game. I studied his "Blue Book" with rather more assiduity than the four blue-bound volumes of Stephen's *Commentaries on the Laws of England*, the set book for the Law Society's Intermediate examination. The Wittgensteinian title was apt, for Culbertson's system was intellectually rigorous and in parts odd. The "honour trick" count, the originating and responsive forcing bids, the points evaluation of a purely supporting bid – to mention a few elementary features – would seem stiff to players today, I suppose. But I was already adroit at the play of the cards at a decent family bridge level, and Culbertson showed the way to more scientific things – a way not taken, for I never played the game competitively nor at all in latter times.

A more orthodox form of dissipation for articled clerks also went on: betting on horses. One episode included an elaborate charade about the bookie welshing after a winning week of joint wagering, designed to cause temporary despondency to the third articled clerk, not, I seem to think, permanent loss. Despite his hat by Stetson and his playing in the pack for the Fylde RUFC Second XV, this colleague, nicknamed by Lees rather unjustly but not unconvincingly "Fatty", became something of a butt, though far from the Gorill class. The betting was extremely modest though at one epoch acquired an unpleasant momentum. The uniformed commissionaire, Dalton, an old sweat by definition, had bought or otherwise acquired a betting system called "The 220". From the flat racing calendar 220 races had been chosen, all stakes or plates, no handicaps. The winners of these races were to be backed the next time they ran. If winners again they were dropped from the list. If losers, they were backed once more on their next appearance and then dropped win or lose. At the start of the season in question the system was startlingly successful, the highlight being a 20–1 winner at Yarmouth. Foolishly we increased our stakes. Needless to say, the system fell on evil days, until only Lees and I persevered. At one time no winners at all came up and Lees likened the situation to that of a constipated man. "If we could just expel the hard nut . . ." Eventually Lees, too, dropped out, and I was left losing money alone, forced secretly to cash in my only asset, £10 worth of National Savings Certificates – typical of my stubborn support, in several of life's affairs, of dotty logic over common sense. Indeed, I still can't help thinking that with an adequate bank and a staking method (the stake perhaps doubled on a required second bet on any one horse) the system might have been profitable over a number of seasons.

With more resilience Dalton himself acquired a new system, up to a point as rational and plausible as the "220", weights and so forth taken into account. But the final selection depended on the phase of the moon ruling when the race was run, a factor reminiscent of Aunt Maggie's lighting on Spion Kop but by no means so successful. Dalton must be long dead. In the days of my articles we completed property sales and purchases in cash, strange to say; the acceptance in the profession of the banker's draft being in its infancy. Dalton used to be sent to the bank to get the cash required for the day's transactions and on one occasion, as he crossed the windy square near our flat on his way back to the office, some hundreds of pounds in fivers and tenners blew out of his grasp or whatever he was carrying them in. Such was the morality of the times little or no loss was suffered by the firm, people returning the banknotes to Dalton or handing them in to the police. He himself in their position might have been tempted to do otherwise having regard to the depredations of the 220 and moon systems. He bequeathed to me a few words of (presumably) sergeant's Hindi, useful when indicating the direction required in a journey by lift.

Over the long years one inevitably picked up some knowledge of probate work and the simpler conveyancing as well as of bridge and betting. I rather think it was I myself rather than Eric Wylie Kay who felt that this would be a meagre result in the light of the premium paid and time served. Yet as I write this it comes to me that he might have been intent on breaking up that focus of office corruption, the bridge four. At any rate, I moved for a spell down to the litigation section to be instructed in their mysteries. The section was small in relation to the size of the practice as a whole, consisting merely of two men and two rooms on the first floor. There may also have been a girl in the typists' room downstairs. In the section's outer office was a clerk, quite young; tall, thin and pallid, invariably dressed in a dark suit. The name Docking had supplanted his real surname. J. W. Docking & Son were leading undertakers in the town, familiar in the articled clerks' attic through our entering funeral expenses in a schedule to the affidavits required by the Inland Revenue for estate duty assessment.

One had to go through Docking's office to reach Mr Ianson's room, overlooking the back street. Harry Ianson was not a partner in the firm though comparatively an elderly solicitor. He had white hair, a red face, big ears, a scattering of fangs, and a voice so loud that on the telephone some claimed he could be clearly heard in the back street. He was a masterly telephoner: initially genial, somewhat vulgar ("the green end of a duck's turd" I once heard him say in a metaphorical context that now escapes me), and liking to employ the machine to try to settle actions or otherwise gain some advantage in them. I think he did not much care to appear in court himself, preferring, if the case could stand it, to brief counsel, usually a stout junior called Edmund Rowson (later a silk) who often visited the office on Saturday mornings to exchange jokes in a voice rivalling Mr Ianson's in penetration and probably to report on or pick up a brief or two. Occasionally, in actions trivial and by their nature incapable of settlement, Mr Ianson would have to appear in court himself, and here he used almost exclusively the ingratiating side of his talent, taking up a position on the solicitors' benches close to the box in which his witnesses would appear and then, when addressing the court, working himself by some gradual flanking movement closer to the judge than might seem theoretically possible, all to gain persuasive intimacy.

Though always amiable to me, he lacked the interest (and probably the time) to teach an articled clerk anything much about litigation. Docking, with whom I sat, was like all litigation clerks I have known, incapable (or unwilling, the occupation itself encouraging caginess and obduracy) of lucidly and systematically imparting the principles and practice of his job. One of the first things I was put on to was a case where we were acting for an insolvent trader intending to present his own petition in bankruptcy. The steps to be taken remained almost wholly enigmatic, though evidently arranged in Docking's mind in some sort of rational and effective order. It seemed to me he was not displeased to find me lacking in gumption in such matters, far short of understanding his Kafka world.

In the middle of my articles Mr Ianson left to become a partner in a firm in a nearby town. Ogden also left: he was given his articles by a solicitor in Blackpool with a view to a partnership when he had qualified, which duly came to pass. Both moves were surprising, prompted somewhat by internal tensions in T. & F. Wylie Kay. For one thing, both moves took place after the death, virtually on the operating table, of Tom Wylie Kay, a shock and grief to all. Despite his tony turn-out he had never really come to terms with "the new Act", as we still called it – the Law of Property Act, 1925, which had come into effect on 1 January 1926 with the other statutes revolutionizing the law of real property and conveyancing practice. Nor did the internal telephone system, a novelty of the new offices, appeal to him: he preferred to come out of his first-floor room and call or send messages fluttering down to the outer office on the ground floor. He left a good deal of money, even more than came to Auntie Vi, but except for the practice I believe I am right in saying that it was not inherited by Mr Eric. TWK's death revealed an unsuspected division between uncle and nephew, or perhaps more generally in the family, for the solicitors who acted in the administration of the estate were not T. & F. Wylie Kay but a firm in Manchester.

All this caused a stir in the attic room, not lessened by the additional news that under TWK's will the firm's clerks were to have suits of mourning. A deep question of interpretation arose. Did the term include articled clerks? The question was resolved in a generous manner, though the rather Victorian bounty was diluted by the decision that the suits were to be made by a client of the firm, a tailor not noted for raglan or ratcatcher or anything to go with a hat by Stetson. "Suits of mourning" was a phrase generally thought to imply black jackets and striped trousers (as worn by me not awfully long before at dancing class and Matins) but Lees, and one or two others infected by his enterprise, ordered a dark lounge suit and so fared better, though I think the jackets were without exception cut without chest seams, like blazers, and hung vilely. With my usual thriftiness I persevered with my outfit until the trousers were impossibly shiny which, because of the initial stiffness of the material, they fortunately very soon became. It was at this epoch that Docking acquired his sobriquet, the occasion being when the bridge four were waiting in the upper room for TWK's funeral carriages, looking out over the square – across which the litigation clerk was observed hurrying to the office in his new black and stripes, complete with bowler and umbrella. Lees asserts that on seeing this apparition I said: "We shan't be long now – here's Docking."

TWK's death, coupled with the defections of Ogden and Ianson, was the start of a hecatomb at the firm, both metaphorical and actual. Byng left when he qualified, as afterwards did I, and eventually Fatty. The litigation managing clerk who replaced Mr Ianson committed suicide. I have referred to Lees' going. Eric Wylie Kay brought in as a partner his brother-in-law, already in practice in the town, who, however, died quite soon after. Mr Eric's demise, too, was premature. Driving his car along the promenade, he had a heart attack and ran into the Hotel Metropole at a spot I always imagine to be by the Grill Room entrance, opposite Seacliffe.

By then I had gone from the town. The practice remained a good one, the senior partner a man who like Lees had been given his articles but in my day had been merely the probate managing clerk. As I write this in May 1978 I see in *The Law Society's Gazette* the news of his retirement after sixty-four years with the firm. Had I stayed on after being admitted a solicitor, as Mr Eric asked me to, how could I have avoided becoming the senior or next senior partner, with strange consequences? How should I have run respectable prosperity along with radical friends and beliefs? What should I have written out of a continuing provincial life?

During the War my wife and son went to Blackpool to escape the London bombing. The Metropole was closed or requisitioned, though a bar under its management, of superior kind, remained open. The entrance to it was near where Higgins & Co had sold the rock praised by royalty and the jeweller's shop patronized by the Peele girls. In May 1941, on leave from the former boys' shore establishment at Shotley, *HMS Ganges*, where I had done my initial training, my wife and I went into this bar, perhaps on our way to some such entertainment as the nearby Palace Varieties. I was in matelot's garb, bronzed and fit, and embarrassed to be bought a drink by some civilian who made it clear he thought me engaged in active service. What had happened to Frish, I wonder? Perhaps interned with the British fascists and enemy aliens in the Isle of Man – whose outline on some clear evenings one had seen from Wilton Parade against the sunset, bringing thoughts of my brother listening to Amy

Woodforde-Finden's piano – safe evenings of only a few years before.

6 *The Little Railway*

In the passage outside the dining room door at school was a table, normally used only for boarders to pick up their incoming letters. One morning, as we went in to breakfast, instead of letters (or perhaps the letters were overlain) it contained the recumbent form of Ettaboo. He held on his plump stomach (a height convenient for most of the passing boys, though a good few of them, instead of reading the message, committed some physical assault on its bearer) a piece of paper on which was written the voting in the Blackpool constituency in the General Election of the previous day. I think this must have been the election of December 1923, for surely Major Malloy, the Liberal candidate, was shown on Ettaboo's abdomen as victorious over his Tory opponent, and I see from the twenty-sixth edition of *Pears' Cyclopaedia*, itself a relic of those days, in the "Dictionary of Events", that what happened on the third of that month was "Mr Baldwin's policy defeated, 259 Conservatives elected, 191 Labour, 165 Liberals and others". A Liberal voted in in Blackpool denoted deep radicalism elsewhere.

Possibly on this occasion my emotions were not much engaged, though presumably I was surprised at the Tory candidate's defeat. He may well have been the elegant Sir Walter de Freece, who had married the famous music-hall male impersonator Vesta Tilley. The arrival of the Labour party into second place in Parliament prefigured my Conservative alderman grandfather's acknowledgement of the chimpanzees' tea-party quality of the breed. During my later years at school I became convinced of the justice and feasibility of socialism and at the General Election of 1927 (the local result of which was not, as I recall, announced to the boys by Ettaboo) I proclaimed my allegiance to Labour, a position still highly unrespectable for the provincial middle classes. I arrived at the belief through reading the polemical side of Wells and Shaw, after being captivated by their imaginative work. One or two experiences in this line of the hero of *The Ruined Boys* incline to the autobiographical so I will not go into details of conversion. Because of the name I was deceived into feeling chuffed at the size of the German National Socialist election vote (could that have been as early as 1924 or as late as 1928?) and though I quickly tumbled to the party's real nature I was not introduced to Marxism-Leninism until I had been left school for two or three years. In any case I was sidetracked from politics by coming across D. H. Lawrence I suppose just about the time I did leave school, and was greatly taken with his adolescent notions of society being changed by men paying more regard to the instinctual side of life. Even his most cockeyed notions, like the value of wearing tight red trousers (the relevant piece may be found in his journalism and I believe in *Lady Chatterley*), appealed to me – and to Leslie, the pianist friend I had made at school.

I see now when I try to shock by uttering reactionary views as I once achieved a similar effect by leftism, that being part of a minority has always been for me a natural role. Of course, in serious art the position has been inevitable in my time; and in politics I must not discount the hope given by the principles of international socialism even as late as 1931, a hope quite aside from any rather perverse pleasure in feeling oneself the repository of some more or less esoteric or unobvious truth. Why one should always want to ally oneself with the underdog is not altogether clear. One is tempted to discount utterly any virtue in the matter: I mean why should trying to see that a certain one-clawed pigeon gets more than its fair share of bread on the lawn, as has been a concern for some months, reflect creditably on the bread-scatterer? More likely, as a great horror of violence is said to mask a sadistic nature, the conscientious underdog-lover is demonstrating the depth of his self-pity and self-love.

I cannot remember whether Ettaboo was the nickname under which the Headmaster's son was generally known among his school fellows or merely a nickname invented and used only by my brother and me. It was intended to indicate Kennie's way of talking (he had some impediment, or infantile speech hangover), perhaps his way of pronouncing his own surname. He was nearer my brother's age than mine and so my brother, staying on at the school for a while after I had left, was able to amplify Ettaboo's legendary character and exploits. Poor Ettaboo: neither boarder nor dayboy, his position must have been difficult, though at the time one saw him only as some privileged and therefore detested heir, especially favoured in the matter of diet, as seemed evidenced by his embonpoint. Besides, the imagination boggles at being under the Boss' eye pretty well at all times. Still, I have no doubt he was blessed with proper paternal love. He was often addressed or referred to by the Headmaster as "Master Kenneth", even as "Master Kennie", an extension of the various magisterial uses of name and that title, mainly indicating the respect and formality owed by third parties to a scion of the ruling family – much as a monarch might as a matter of course prefix in conversation his son's name with "Prince", not excluding the affectionate diminutive.

Ettaboo had succeeded to his father's great cranium but the distinguished good looks were lacking, certainly at pre-pubertal age. On top of the cranium Ettaboo wore what seemed a curiously small school cap, though perhaps it was the largest available. Yet I seem to think that the Boss was not dissatisfied with his son's appearance, even approving of his ample figure, in the manner of Squeers's fond observation of young Wackford: "Here's flesh . . . Why, you couldn't shut a bit of him in a door, when he's had his dinner." I daresay, though, the Boss may have regretted that his son was still unable to follow his constant enjoinder to the school to speak out.

I doubt if I shared such things as the uniqueness of Ettaboo with Leslie. Our friendship, though not utterly solemn, was sustained by music and books. It was marked from the start with his selflessness. For mid-morning "lunch" he always brought to school bacon sandwiches, his mother's dab hand at cooking revealed even by these, for he fell into the habit of sharing them with me; eventually, after I had met his mother and she had seen that I was "a nice boy", bringing an extra supply especially for me. What a delicacy compared with the school cuisine! Even Ettaboo did not fare so well: well-buttered new white bread, the fat of the bacon crisp, even slightly burnt, for Leslie's mother's culinary style inclined to the successfully reckless and lavish.

Leslie was slender and not tall, long straight nose and smallish chin lending him a starling-like appearance. His intellectual interests and physical slightness did not prevent him from being the school's very effective centre forward. His adroit style of play, particularly his heading – indeed, his general appearance – was recalled many years later by Charlie Vaughan, a centre forward who played for Charlton Athletic and far too seldom for representative elevens. As to his being bitten by the Lawrentian bug, I remember after we had left school quite accidentally seeing and being impressed by a line of verse he had written: "If you call, I shall come" – very Look We Have Come Throughish. But he was utterly secretive about his literary work, and I do not recall showing him mine, though very likely I did. We were ardent pursuers of what we thought vital in culture, the opportunities of exercising such a role in the provinces of the late Twenties being restricted beyond today's conception. On one occasion we realized neither of us had ever heard Beethoven's *Fifth Symphony*. The enormity of the omission made me with Vi-like extravagance then and there ask my mother to fund the purchase of the records. We went straight to the shop and bought the album of four black label HMV records conducted by Sir Landon Ronald, the cost twenty-four shillings, a tidy sum. The discs were already elderly but I hadn't yet become fastidious about recordings. A lot of music then had a shock effect. I remember playing the first movement of Mozart's late G minor symphony, recently acquired, one summer afternoon by the open window of the flat overlooking the Metropole, the opening subject, except for its final cadence, sounding to me staggeringly modern. I expect I was also conscious that a few of the holiday-makers perambulating below, including some beautiful and intelligent girl, might well hear the strains and think that in the unusually chic and convenient premises high above dwelt an appropriately lofty intelligence. Insane intellectual and amatory fantasies of adolescence, unspeakable yearnings and frustrations of that epoch, so prolonged, seemingly unassuagable! I would not like to have to write about them again, as either reality or fiction, let alone relive them.

Leslie's uncle by marriage was a radio buff, his apparatus complicated, unreliable, low fidelity, bits of it actually being changed during reception – bits that when I became a compulsory buff during the war I realized had been inductances. We went to his house to hear a broadcast of Bartók quartets (or, more likely, a concert which included one of them). The music, dimly heard through shared earphones, was a revelation. "Another Beethoven" I pronounced. One year, almost certainly 1929, we holidayed together in London with our respective mothers and my brother. On arrival, after a testing journey by charabanc, Leslie and I beat it to the Queen's Hall to a Promenade Concert, standing stoically in the "promenade". Sir Henry Wood usually left the last item in the second half to be conducted by the orchestra's leader, Charles Woodhouse. By then the promenade had become less congested and one might be lucky enough to see Sir Henry look in for a minute or two – perhaps curious about the orchestra's sound or Woodhouse's ability – wearing a soft black hat, on his way home to that domesticity later revealed to be so unhappy for him.

Needless to say, the leader of the Queen's Hall Orchestra did not conduct with his bow, violin in the other hand, as was the practice of Mons. Spiro, a noted Blackpool musical figure – indeed, an exponent of that pier-end music from which Leslie helped to wean me. Balding, short, with full lips and pince-nez, Mons. Spiro looked like a plumper Stravinsky. The latter would probably not have approved of the Spiro style – joining in the tuttis only at climaxes, frequently inserting a gratuitous solo violin part, and playing during the interval in the ray of a spotlight. The intervals in question were at the Palace Cinema, in the same building as the Palace Varieties where Joe Jackson had failed to make the Boss laugh. Mons. Spiro's orchestra was easily big enough to have included Archie Gladman's double bass. It was eventually displaced at the Palace by the talkies but I seem to think Mons. Spiro returned to or took up an appointment on the North Pier.

I cannot remember if Leslie and I glimpsed Sir Henry on that first night. When we returned to the Regent Palace Hotel my mother told me that she and Leslie's mother, with my brother, had strolled out after dinner to find a likely cinema, which they did in the Haymarket. The ladies had been baffled by the film on show, though my brother's laughter had dislodged him from his seat. But even he found difficulty in describing what he had seen. Despite the pleasures of the concert I felt jealous, for after a brief spell of resistance to the shocking American voices and general vulgarity I had succumbed to the talkies as I had to silent pictures. The film had been *The Cocoanuts*.

The fresh cast of characters my life recruited after I left school was partly formed from the shops and business establishments by which the new flat was surrounded. Among these personages was Mr Meng or, rather, M. Meng, for despite his oriental name he was French, though not proclaiming the fact as ostentatiously as Mons. Spiro. He had a ladies' hairdressing salon and was said to be not at all frustrated in his romantic ambitions. His son, also M. Meng (for such was his initial), did look more Chinese (of the giant kind exhibited in Victorian times like Chang, "the tall man of Fychow"), and had been at school with me and my brother, who was delighted with the characters, appearance, name, and possibility of observation of both father and son. The owner of a furniture shop and his wife became friendly with my mother, who in fact in much later days went to live with the wife, by then widowed, as a paying guest, and through that met my step-father. Moreover, my brother was at one time engaged to the attractive daughter; but of course this again lay pretty far into a future to be strangely unfolded. Below our flat was a flat and workroom belonging to Madame Pym and below that, on the promenade, the milliner's shop she owned. Madame Pym was not a compatriot of Mons. Spiro, despite her title – that being assumed to better her trade image. At one period she had staying with her and working in the shop an extremely good-looking niece with whom I had a brief, innocent, unsatisfactory affair, conducted mainly in an unsatisfactory place, namely the access staircase referred to previously which petered out so curiously between the two parts of our flat. There had been a boy at school appropriately called P. King, for like Meng *fils* his aspect was somewhat Chinese. At the flat his aunt, if aunt she was, came into our lives, I think initially because she was in the nursing profession and she gave therapy of some sort to my mother. I was dashed when she expressed herself weary of *The Ring* because of my repeated playing of a couple of records of the start of *Rhinegold*. She was not young but on the other hand by no means too old for exchanges of an unofficial kind, a point I may well have taken on board. But my desires were for unattainable nieces rather than skittish aunts.

About this time my appearance changed considerably. I grew my hair longer and gave up my devotion to Pears' Solidified Brilliantine (though to be strictly accurate, fashion in the anointing of hair had changed shortly before I left school, a fluid called "Anzora" – or its greasy sister, "Anzora Viola" – coming into favour. It kept the hair in place, even retaining the corrugations of the comb, but lent it the feel of cardboard, as though one were wearing some helmet designed for children to "dress up" in. No doubt it was this I gave up.) My hair, previously straight, became wavy. It was still the days of shirts and separate collars but I liked as far as possible to wear my old cricket shirts (plus tie) so as to get a desirable low-cut Byronic effect, a style I fear Mr Southworth would have thought the reverse of nutty. These arrangements clashed with the sartorial image I had evolved for myself immediately I had left school, and for some time I went hatless, eschewing the pre-Slasher Green overcoat, favouring instead a mackintosh cut rather long that had been made for me from traditional biscuit-hued material supplied by Mr Fraser from the rubber-proofing mill.

This was a time, too, when I got to know the heart of Manchester, previously only a fragmentary memory from childhood. A recent requirement had made it necessary for a solicitor's articled clerk to attend a year's law school. The nearest place where the statutory lectures were held was Manchester University. On Mondays and Thursdays in term time I travelled to Manchester for the day. On one of the days I got up very early to go to some lectures on contract and tort, part of the ordinary law degree course, which articled clerks were entitled but not obliged to attend. In winter I rose in the dark and walked through the dark along the promenade to the station, the moon perhaps over the sea, the dawn just breaking in the opposite sky, only one or two other pedestrians challenged in the waning dusk. The wind would blow the shutters, if any, of the Metropole (quitted as I started off) and my abundant, ungreasy unanzoraed locks, and twine the skirts of my mackintosh about my shins. In my stomach (prematurely, the stomach sensed) were two boiled eggs. I persuaded my mother that she at least need not appear at such an ungodly hour, so I had the alarm clock. That I should make my own breakfast was not at all part of my mother's conception of the feminine role, and that I should start the day other than by eating bacon and egg seemed to her gravely disadvantageous (though she did not concede that I was capable of or would have time for preparing that dish). She even put the water in the egg pan the night before.

I would sway through the yellow winter gloom on the upper deck of the rather well-designed Manchester trams, probably sitting in the ship-like enclosed stern or prow, overconcerned at getting out down Oxford Road at the right stop for the University. I cannot exaggerate my seriousness about the trivialities of life, lack of know-how, nervousness, shyness – coupled, though of course it is hard to judge how effectively, with masks designed to hide my deficiencies. As to the right tram-stop syndrome, a recurring anxiety dream to this day concerns the last hour in a foreign hotel; the bill not paid, traveller's cheques not cashed, next destination unfixed but a vital train time imminent, the room where the luggage is still not packed unable to be found. As to masks assumed, these may often have been mistaken for conscious superiority of one kind or another, so I judge in the light of impressions conveyed to others which have leaked to me in later life. A strange penalty for shyness is to be completely misunderstood.

Most of the time until the afternoon lectures, the compulsory part for articled clerks, I would spend going round the bookshops. Through parsimony (really, as in my mother's case, to preserve the family fortune, not my own pocket) I missed a good many desirable acquisitions, though I was never a serious collector nor willing to risk more than a few bob. On the other hand, as with the 220 System, I occasionally foolishly plunged. In this category I would put a first edition of David Garnett's *The Sailor's Return*, the author then widely accounted an exceptional young novelist; even the first American edition of *The Captain's Doll*, though that might now recoup the six shillings expended, if only through inflation. The winter in question would be that of 1929–30, for I see that my copy of *Dubliners*, which I certainly bought on one of those spendthrift occasions for two shillings, is inscribed "March 1930" under my signature on the flyleaf. The edition is the second edition published by the Egoist Press in 1922, which opposite the title page announced: "In preparation *Ulysses*". (At the time I am writing about the latter work was banned and remained so for a number of years, more tantalizing for those, like me, who wanted to copy its fictional techniques than possible corruptees. When I met John Davenport, I rather think in the summer following this very winter, he told me of two or three Charing Cross Road booksellers who might well supply me with the illegal article on mentioning his name. But when this ploy was tried, doubtless with guilt and trepidation, it did not work, and one had to be content with extracts from the novel that appeared in critical works and the memory of Gorill's story in similar style). It was in 1930 that in the train back from Manchester (with typical thriftiness overlooking someone's evening paper) I read of D. H. Lawrence's death, shocking as the death of Byron in a former day, and probably helping me and others to turn from follies concerning the personal life to political involvement, more appropriate to the age but also not lacking in wacky illusions.

Thursday nights were Hallé concerts nights, for which I often stayed, journeying back to Blackpool by the last train. The seats I favoured in the old Free Trade Hall were under the side balcony, cheap but near. What arrived as novelties in those days must be marvelled at again: I need only instance a first hearing of *Eine Kleine Nachtmusik*, which left one with a sense of a commonplace genre transcended with amazing resourcefulness, and a set of marvellous melodies just beyond recall. The permanent conductor was Hamilton Harty, florid of face, not much in my line then with his practical advocacy of Berlioz and his own typically British compositions – do I dream that I actually heard his tone poem "With the Wild Geese" and the scherzo from his "Irish" symphony? But now I see more clearly than in those days of yore that he was not unenterprizing as a programme builder and also did quite a bit for modern music. When the fine records of Constant Lambert's *The Rio Grande* came out, the Hallé was conducted by the composer and, astonishing me, the piano part brilliantly played by Harty.

It was in the year I first went to boarding school that the curious entertainment *Façade* was offered to a London audience. Behind a curtain in the Aeolian Hall were six instrumentalists, the composer W. T. Walton and the poet Edith Sitwell. A feature of the painted curtain was a head with an open mouth, the latter being the outlet of a patent megaphone through which the poet read some of her poems while the instrumentalists played musical numbers under the composer's direction. Osbert Sitwell was MC; Sacheverell Sitwell had discovered the megaphone. The Sitwell siblings were, of course, notorious members of the post-war avant garde: their work influenced me quite a bit when I started seriously to write verse. Their friend Walton was a young man from Oldham whose music when *Façade* was first performed had never been before the public. He later revised and expanded the numbers from *Façade* and the work was enterprisingly recorded by Decca, the poet joined as reader by Constant Lambert. Leslie bought these records and I can still attempt an impression of Edith Sitwell's rendering: in timbre and enunciation the voice greatly resembled that of Nellie Wallace, a music-hall comic of a just-past day (of whom, indeed, Edith Sitwell was an admirer).

I myself bought the Decca recording of Walton's overture *Portsmouth Point*. It is a congested piece and sounded even more so on a ten-inch 78 of the epoch. It was no more to my mother's taste than *Rhinegold* to Miss King's. Moreover, she off-handedly claimed a familiar acquaintance with the composer: as a girl or young woman she had taken singing lessons from Mr Walton and had often passed his son Willie playing on the pavement outside the house. This amazing revelation probably came after I had seen the young composer conduct the Hallé in the orchestral suite he had made out of *Façade*. He was tall, pallid, awkward, and when conducting carried his left arm as though in a sling, plainly obeying the precept that in the conductor's art the batonless arm has no proper function. I may add that my mother's brother John told me in a letter in the last years of his life that his music master at Hulme Grammar School had been William Walton's brother Noel, especially remembered for his enthusiasm for the part-song "Nymphs and Shepherds, Come Away."

The Hallé also performed on Mondays in a series of a more popular kind called the "Municipal" concerts. I stayed for one of these, then found to my extreme horror, at the station, that the late train to Blackpool did not run on Mondays. I was marooned. I managed to get a message by telephone to my mother, then set off to stay the night in Oldham with my grandparents. This solution seemed resourceful (the notion of a hotel in Manchester was presumably rejected through lack of cash or, conceivably, thriftiness) but I could not give forewarning. I changed terminuses in Manchester and took the Oldham train.

There was no real reason why the order and nomenclature of the stations between Manchester and Oldham should be greatly familiar or have Proustian undertones, for in my father's day the journey would be made by motor car and later our visits to Oldham from Blackpool were not awfully frequent, and indeed were latterly made again by car, my mother going in for one in the very early Thirties. Yet the names had significance for me such as the poet W. J. Turner found in Chimborazo and

Cotopaxi; and of course the places themselves had some associations and physical features that memory retained. I have not looked them up. The line may even have been lopped by the Beeching axe. I will guess that the stations were Miles Platting, Newton Heath, Failsworth, Hollinwood, Werneth, Mumps.

Newton Heath must not be taken to indicate any countryside, however exiguous, between Manchester and Oldham: the urban brick was unbroken. Failsworth being the place of my parents' first house was also the home of childhood friends, most forgotten, a few recalled. How did we come to know the Richardsons? He was an actor or, more accurately, music-hall performer, perhaps best known in pantomime where he had been the King figure to Little Tich's Dame. My mother cared for the art neither of Little Tich nor of Arnold Richardson but since she must surely have been wrong about Little Tich she may also have erred in the other case. However, I remember a postcard, printed for propaganda purposes like the photograph of Uncle John as "Violet", depicting Mr Richardson as a square-faced man of middle age wearing a crown, seemingly of no great individuality or humour. Like many husbands of the era he died prematurely, so I never myself saw him perform. We continued to be friendly with the widow and her child of my own age, the former famous for plucking whiskers from her chin behind a guarding hand, tweezers hidden in the other, chatting nonchalantly, a slight jerk of the head, like a nervous tic, indicating occasional success.

In Failsworth, too, lived the Peeles, our closest friends when my father was alive and to whose house, somewhat impressively set back in the main Manchester to Oldham Road, I was sent – I have said following my father's death until after his funeral but I wonder if this was so and whether the time might not have been that of the birth and early death of my youngest sibling Eric, which occurred during my father's terminal illness. Certainly I have no memories of Eric's brief life, though I am almost certain his death occurred in hospital. The doubt here is perhaps characteristic of the misunderstandings of childhood but surely has been augmented by self-centred obtuseness. Mr Peele was a well-to-do mill manager, dark, quiet, good-looking. His wife was an incongruous mate, it now seems: plump, jolly and, as it turned out, a secret drinker. Their two daughters were older than me, the younger by not so much. They were allowed – seemed, to my envy, to have the right – to go every Tuesday to the cinema almost opposite their house, thus keeping up with the serials which in those days came on before the 'big picture', a stroke of lifemanship marvellous to me. They were taken by the maid, Annie Fleury, who came from the Channel Islands and whose younger sister Emily had come to work for us.

The Peeles, like us when my father was alive, used to take a furnished house for a month in the summer. One year (probably more than one) they rented Mrs Vero's house: hence my mother taking rooms there at a later and sadder date. We rented the next-door house. The Veros would not be in a residence, of course, so I do not know whether in those days the grave chords of "Willie Vero" were yet to be heard. I played with the Peele girls in the back gardens of the adjoining houses, sometimes making "brooches" out of leaves, flowers and berries in competition for the most beautiful. They had ample pocket money: once I went with them to the jeweller's near Higgins & Co in the row of Metropole shops where the older girl bought a little gilt egg which could be opened to reveal tiny opal eggs in a nest of cotton wool. The aesthetic sense shown impressed me, though I was worried by the inutility of the object. Plainly the elder girl must have been the instigator of the brooches game. She was like her father in disposition and looks. Mr Peele inscribed a bible "with fondest love" from himself and his wife to my father, dating it "Christmas 1920". Whether my father derived any comfort from it or even saw it must be doubtful, because he died exactly a week before Christmas Day. The inscription is in Mr Peele's somewhat conventional but extremely graceful hand, carefully done, probably on pencilled guide lines, subsequently erased. The compassion involved may be imagined.

Mrs Peele was the sort of person who might well have introduced us to the Richardsons and also to Mrs Gee, a friend of very early days who gave my brother and me napkin rings at our christenings, still in daily use. Mine, even in 1912, was William Morrisy in its engraved decoration. My brother's, four years later, was quite "modern" in its plainness: just one more example of my luck in life, as I used to think. I only dimly recall Mrs Gee – imperious, enormous, seated in a drawing room full of knick-knacks like a sinister character in a story by Walter de la Mare. It was said she ate half a dozen eggs for breakfast; other dietetic details, now forgotten, were equally sensational. It comes to me that she lived at Newton Heath, which may have had its salubrious parts after all.

Hollinwood was, of course, the place of the rubber-proofing mill; also the nearest station to my grandparents' house in Hollins Road. Perhaps it was the dark Monday night, peering anxiously out from the carriage window, that the successive station names were finally imprinted. How did I find my way so late from the station to the bottom of Hollins Road to catch the appropriate tram? The route was not straightforward and I doubt whether I had ever taken it alone before. Even at seventeen or eighteen I would be apprehensive about missing the way, asking directions.

When I got off the tram I would have a short walk up the quite steep road to the house, passing Frederick Street, where my brother had been born and my father had read newspapers full of the First World War. The house was in darkness when I rang the bell. My grandmother appeared in night attire, eventually reassured to find my presence portending no more than a missed train. I do not recall my grandfather being on the scene. Perhaps he was still playing bridge at the Conservative Club. Indeed, virtually nothing remains in my memory of the occasion beyond a sense (which I may be retrospectively importing), through that late encounter, of my grandmother's eventual widowhood which was prolonged into the period of the Second War; amazingly and inappropriately, as it seems to me now, experiencing some of those awful days. My grandfather retired in 1933, died, I think, in 1937. Who knows whether what he achieved, as mayor, alderman, justice of the peace, and so forth, enabling my grandmother to play her largely supporting role with dignity and humour, compensated her for characterstics of his she may have found too eccentric or insensitive, to say nothing of the inevitable stifling of her own talents? Certainly he left her in reduced circumstances, as they say. Among my mother's few surviving papers was a notebook in my grandmother's writing recording the periodical sums (usually thirty shillings a week) received from my mother for living expenses (recouped after my grandmother's death from the proceeds of sale of the Hollins Road house, which I imagine to have been my grandparents' only asset of any substance).

In my grandfather's presence, in his latter days, I expect I kept dark my socialist beliefs and literary tastes. In my penultimate year at school, on a visit to Blackpool, he had taken me to buy a pair of spiked running shoes, which probably were decisive in my victory in the 100 and 220 yards in the first of my two successive victorious years, to say nothing of breaking the school long jump record with 19 ft. 5½ ins. in my last year. His trouble and generosity were not characteristic but pride in heredity was tapped: he had once been amateur sprint champion of Lancashire. His finding a shop that stocked the things and his knowledge of the type and fit required impressed me a lot. His concern with the practicalities of life was usually strictly limited: the buying of prize cheese, for instance, or washing the small change he had been given in shops or on the tram. He may have been disappointed that I had dropped athletics – all sport – after leaving school. As to literature, he had once picked up a slim volume of W. H. Davies brought into the house by me, read it in about twenty minutes, and remarked: "Not much in that." That would have been in my *John o' London*'s epoch, when Georgians were still OK, but the galling thing was I felt his judgement fundamentally justified. On the other hand, Lawrence would have had little more appeal.

That night I expect I slept in the room that in my childhood I had known as Uncle Freddy's. Being at the front of the house it was well situated to hear the trams as they rattled down Copster Hill Road and ground round the sharp corner into Hollins Road as though about to run into the house itself, which was fairly high above the road but separated from it by only a small front garden. The view was of the modest park where as a boy I had played bowls on the two crown greens and talked to Ernest, the park keeper, who, my mother maintained, with only faint exaggeration, had teeth to match the colour of his bowling arenas. There was no back garden, just a tiny concreted yard, bounded by coalplace, WC, and wash-house, places of some interest on boyhood visits – even the WC, dark in spite of its whitewashed walls. It had a scrubbed unpainted seat and was equipped not with a roll but squares of newspaper hanging by a string from a hook, good enough for my grandparents' servant (who I suppose was the principal user) faithful and loved though she was. In the wash-house was a mangle with a wheel and cogs of high capitalistic substantiality, the wooden rollers fraying slightly in the middle with decades of use. On the shelves were a few substances appealing to the instincts later so developed by the Boss that I matriculated in Inorganic Chemistry with a high mark – among them linseed oil and whiting which I had read somewhere (perhaps in a bound volume of *The Scout*) were the ingredients of putty, as I pleasurably proved.

Messing about in the back yard (also in the lane running along the side of the house where, opposite, a chicken-run was fenced by planks containing, for a reason never discovered, an occasional tiny ceramic cylinder which could be prised out and acquired) one was in touch with the kitchen, equipped with a coal-fired "range" as solid as the mangle and in which bread was made, the process ending with muffins (thin, holey, the outside faintly leathery) evolved on a baking-stone on the cooling oven floor. I was impressed by my mother sometimes efficiently taking the lead in this, though at Waterhead insulated from such chores by Emily Fleury, Nellie Straw and the like, vigorously kneading the dough which when risen might be compared by some family vulgarian to a pale, fat, nude bottom.

I do not believe I ever alighted at Werneth Station. Just before the War I wrote with Julian Symons a never-performed play, a political satire set in an imaginary Europe, a genre sufficiently indicated by the prose parts of the Auden-Isherwood *On the Frontier*. Two characters I christened Mr Failsworth and General Werneth, right-wing union leader and politico respectively, the names seeming of sufficient ambiguity for a non-specific nationality – "Failsworth" typing the character in ancient dramatic tradition; "Werneth" possibly being imagined to have the pronunciation "Vairnet". (After writing this I found in *A Centenary History of Oldham* by Hartley Bateson that the old form of Werneth was Vernet). I went to my first school in Werneth, not far short of a mile walk from the Frederick Street house. Beyond a dim vision of a flight of steps up to the school door, my only memory of my brief attendance is an instance of early odiousness. A member of a group who walked to school my way became top of the class, a place I coveted. After school I encouraged the rest of the group to run off and leave him in the lurch, calling out with vile antagonism: "We never had anything to do with the last top-of-the-class." Such a phrase sounds stilted and sophisticated for a six-year-old but I do not doubt it is close to the *ipsissima verba*. I was secretly and immediately ashamed of them once uttered, for no age is too young to be aware of ill conduct.

Even a denizen of Oldham must be conscious of the strange nomenclature of the locality Mumps. A lowish railway bridge across the main road; perhaps greater damp and dark than elsewhere; a nadir reached – such features reinforced the connotations of depression and disease. When we moved from Frederick Street to Waterhead I had to go to Mumps to attend a dame's school, though by tram not rail, Waterhead being on Mumps's farther side. I used to call for a neighbour's child, Marjorie Marsland, on the way to the tram. On leaving the house she made her long black stockings simulacra of a boy's "golf" stockings by pulling her thin elastic garters below her knees and turning the stockings down. She may also have got rid of other trappings of femininity: certainly she used to slip the constraining elastic of her hat from under her chin and tuck it into the crown. All this evidence of a strong character and a wish to be liberated (an additional and more fundamental aspect of which is given in *The Perfect Fool*) did not make her any the less attractive as a companion. Though I recall an occasion in our nursery when my bare leg rested against hers (perhaps she always turned her stockings down away from home), I do not think feelings went much beyond friendship. She was already a pupil at the school and like Vergil guided me through the initial purgatories of its routines and the journey to them.

A week or two before I wrote the foregoing paragraph, Marjorie Yates, the widow of the Metropole pianist who had helped to oblige the Prussian with Smetana's overture, came for lunch bringing a book of reproductions of paintings by the Lancashire primitive, Helen Bradley. It had been bought by Marjorie's daughter, brought up in Blackpool but married to an American lawyer, and stunned to see in a Washington bookshop a dust jacket of a Blackpool railway station, albeit depicting it as it was in 1908, she had sent the book to her mother. I opened it at random. The page showed Buckley & Proctor's drapers shop at Mumps in the same epoch. Near the shop an arrow on a public lavatory wall indicated the direction of Mumps Station. I doubt if I had seen or heard "Buckley & Proctor" for almost sixty years, yet the names were as familiar as Debenham & Freebody. The other Marjorie and I had passed the shop every time we got off the tram from Waterhead.

Some forgotten actress or other heroine of the masses may have made popular the name Marjorie for girls who grew up with me. Even the niece of the bogus "little French milliner" was called Marjorie. I felt a lack of consistency when the girl I was to marry proved to be called Kathleen but reassurance came when she told me that her parents nearly had her christened Marjorie. "Joan" ran Marjorie close. Skeltonic and Shakespearean names: even now when their possessors are in their mid-sixties – Joan Eastwood perhaps seventy! – they trail romance.

One publication I did buy in Manchester without miserly qualms during my law-school year was Lawrence's *Nettles*, published in Faber & Faber's "Criterion Miscellany" at a shilling. I took it to the afternoon lectures in the statutory series and had it in front of me on the desk, no doubt from the same motive that had prompted me to play Mozart near an open window. The lecturer picked up the bright red pamphlet with a grin. Lawrence's name was generally known, I expect through the recent publication of *Lady Chatterley's Lover*, though perhaps it had had significance ever since the banning of *The Rainbow*. I seem to think the lecturer was a bright fellow who went to the Bar and was eventually elevated to the Bench: he read out a few lines at random and genially asked me if I thought it was poetry. The idea of Lawrence being vulnerable in that way seemed to me very *vieux chapeau*. The poem may have been one called "The British Workman and the Government":

> Hold my hand, Auntie, Auntie,
> Auntie hold my hand!
> I feel I'm going to be naughty, Auntie
> and you don't seem to understand.

The poem later contains a passage reminiscent of Stephen Spender's "Now You've No Work, Like a Rich Man", which was in the *Oxford Poetry* of the year of *Nettles* and I think had earlier appeared in the *Criterion*. Though one did not quite realize it yet, for the young writer the world of David Garnett and the Sitwells and Major Malloy and Sir Walter de Freece had ceased to have significance.

A Portrait of the Artist, the cheap edition of *Point Counter Point*, both bought in the year I bought *Dubliners*; and imitations of the techniques of *Ulysses* – such as these brought a new aim to my writing of fiction, on the whole disastrous. Certainly not until round about the start of the war was I able actually to finish a novel and that has rightly stayed unpublished. The worst aspects of experimentalism usually attract the bad or novice writer, and I was no exception. I recall seriously outlining to Leslie the scheme of a projected fiction: it would begin quite normally (and by that, in those days, I would mean fixedly inside the protagonist's head, *à la* Dalloway) and gradually get more and more boring, ending with long Latin quotations. Presumably this was to depict some adolescent or provincial agony. Any consideration for the reader's enlightenment let alone pleasure, or any ingratiatory quality in the author, was not allowed for, such was the pervasiveness of "modernism", still not exhausted today and by no means emanating solely from survivors of the epoch like Samuel Beckett.

The new or, rather, renewed impulse to write prose fiction seemed particularly associated with my bi-weekly journeys to Manchester, even with the fresh glimpse of the little railway. The navy-blue, black-sleeved waistcoats worn by porters in those days; the pungency of station urinals; the noise and bitter smell of steam exuded like some sudden excretory relief from under locomotives; the compartments' dusty upholstery, of idiosyncratic texture and pattern; dawn breaking or dusk falling beyond shaded yellow station lights; above all, the chance of amatory adventure among fellow travellers and at the end of journeys – I expect such things could be found in all my botched fiction of the time. As would what Peter Quennell in his volume of autobiography, *The Marble Foot*, has well described as the "single terrifying or disgusting image" – images from reality I collected as I collected the titles of those rare novels (*The Old Wives' Tale*, for instance, and *A Passage to India*) which I considered gave a true sensation of the detailed length yet swift passage of life, and the meaning of its lack of meaning. Both images and titles have now been largely dispersed in my mind. As to the former, an example would be of an anthropoid masturbating in its cage at a zoo, eating the semen; but the collection was by no means exclusively sexual.

Such fiction was far from the rational and comprehensive novel envisaged some years after the War, anatomizing small town society, which would have delineated elements that in what for me were my student days (when in a quite real sense everyday life seemed poetic life) I took little artistic account of: for instance, the smart social events of the year, the Spinsters' and Benedicts' Balls, Mr Eric himself being on the organizing committee of the latter; the remnants of the families of fishing village days, enriched by the rise in land values or involvement in the entertainment business, major shareholders in the companies running such things as the Palace; the seasonal workers in winter, as idle as articled clerks but rather more impoverished; and the tribe of various landladies, the Barracloughs, Veros and Sideys. Strange that modern English fiction (and films, come to that) has never quite contrived to give its provincial settings the universality and sophistication captured by transatlantic counterparts. No sense of depression, however slight, comes over one when one realizes that an American novel or movie is set in a provincial city or even small town. My own novel of provincial life would set out to do at least that. But it never got written: for one reason I found I came to shirk the labour of writing novels which scarcely earned their modest advances and failed to go into paperback or appear in the United States – strange admission, for even through middle age I did not imagine I was affected in the enterprise of writing by lack of critical or commercial success.

But I must add, apropos of the foregoing, that I suppose for me everyday life has never ceased to seem poetic life, except, of course, for those recurring periods when all poets lose their power of observing, comparing, and writing rhythmically. It could be said that the poetic sense has been too easily satisfied by the life I slipped into; but then, thinking back on the poetry produced, a good part of it is of, say, Baudelairean strangeness. Much could be quoted from Wallace Stevens' letters on this baffling subject of the artist leading a "rather routine life" (as he once phrased it), for example: "While one is never sure that it makes much difference, one is equally never sure that it doesn't."

7 *Beauty*

Like those of war service, memories from childhood incline to be unrepresentatively funny. My brother once wrote home that he had been caned by the Boss for carrying sage. That my mother, though puzzled, did nothing about this harshness over a practice as apparently unvenal as warding off vampires with garlic is not only evidence of her trust in the school but also of her profound acceptance of the *status quo*. It should be said that the orthography of the letter may have been faulty. Sage was the name of a boy, quite in the Little Tich class, and for ever being lifted by other boys as though he were an engaging doll, so much so that the Boss had issued an edict against the practice. Hilarity ensued when my mother's misunderstanding was subsequently removed but my brother would scarcely have found the episode amusing.

In spite of my schoolboy socialism, later evolving into something more extreme, I inherited my mother's resignation. It never crossed my mind that with sufficient will I could have opted out of the law – abandoned the daily journeys across the square to the offices of T. & F. Wylie Kay; the prescribed books for the Law Society's Intermediate examination, the four volumes of Stephen's *Commentaries on the Laws of England*, plus works on trust accounts and book-keeping; and the positively uncongenial side of a solicitor's practice represented by Docking's world. I went on accepting what I had chosen in ignorance at sixteen. About my mother's affairs I was also peculiarly passive (dread combination of diffidence and narcissism), not least her health. I worried about it, yet helped her not at all, even convinced sometimes that "nerves" and "palpitations" were merely hypochondriacal, little thinking I should myself be a victim of their reality in later years. Her hyperthyroidism remained undiagnosed, and worsened, and the flat on the promenade became too great a burden for her. Once more we moved into "rooms". Whether if I had done more myself in the domestic line or insisted on help from the outside the move could have been avoided I do not know. In any case, perhaps it is looking back from my sessile sixties that makes the change seem more regrettable. My mother's restlessness was not always altogether forced by events and possibly met some inner need.

The rooms were in Blackpool's South Shore, far from T. & F. Wylie Kay's office, past my old school, well on the way, in fact, to the school's playing fields, scene of my athletics triumphs and partnering Gorill at fullback. The accommodation may have been found or recommended by Leslie's mother, who then lived nearby. I accepted the inconvenient tram journey to the office, actually coming home for lunch, and the return of Barracloughian conditions. The house or rather "semi-bungalow" was owned by Mrs Sidey, presumably a widow. She had a son, Victor, and a Pekinese bitch called Beauty. We added our African grey parrot to the household, the only pet we ever had, brought from the Gold Coast (as it then was) by Leslie's father who was a railway official there. I say "pet" but the bird was of uncertain temper. Even with me, who was the most emotionally involved (as in the case of all actually or metaphorically incarcerated), its moods were variable, sometimes when on my shoulder taking an earlobe in its beak and increasing the pressure until one was convinced that injury was about to be done. But this was only some Gold Coast tribal test, as it were, and if one stood firm the grip was relaxed in due course. The same rule applied when one scratched its head through the bars of the cage: the bird had to be allowed to snatch at the intruding finger, attempted withdrawal likely to be disastrous.

Beauty had no great appeal, her bad temper more consistent than Polly's and shown in both looks and behaviour, though like many female characters it may be that her worst features stick in the memory. She was certainly a good house dog, the mere utterance of the words "Send them off, Beauty" causing her to rush to the nearest window in a cascade of yapping, though the lurking miscreants had no more reality than Aunt Maggie's detectives. My brother and I sometimes tested her prowess by introducing the triggering words into conversations about quite other matters and with no change of tone: she was rarely, if ever, caught out. Did I count among my stock of "single terrifying or disgusting" images that of finding, late at night in the bathroom (where oddly enough she slept), Beauty assuming with her sleeping cushion what was then generally regarded as the male sexual role, having myself returned from similar preoccupations on a level conceived to be altogether more elevated? It could be so, for one's notions generally were extravagantly romantic, so much so that though I have usually hoarded such things I quite soon destroyed a journal-notebook of the period as seen even then to be too embarrassing, in some entries Leslie and I figuring under names I imagined to be more apt than our real ones.

Mrs Sidey's son Victor was in age between my brother and myself – long-nosed, sallow, old-fashioned. He was as taken with the parrot as his zest for life allowed, standing in front of the cage watching the bird preening, juggling a sunflower seed with beak and tongue, clambering laboriously about the wire enclosure, pursuing other psittacine occupations. Sometimes Victor would utter the single syllable "warks" which more often than not the bird echoed, but whether Victor taught the parrot this enigmatic word or vice versa was uncertain. Actually it was quite capable of coherent English speech, its longest phrase being "Polly Fuller lives at Blackpool", the banality of this being accounted for if not excused by Leslie's family parrot, of the same breed, from the same source, having (save for the different surname) the same words on its black tongue.

I confuse Mrs Sidey somewhat with a later landlady of my own, in the digs I had when I went south in the mid-Thirties, so I could not be sure which lady had some artificial addition – in bulk or colouring or both – to her hair. It was from his mother that Victor had inherited those traits of his already mentioned (except that of limited discourse with parrots). But really all that has stuck firmly in the mind is her theological defence of a fly-blown piece of gammon, left over from breakfast, brought on for my lunch.

We were not awfully long at Mrs Sidey's, yet enough happened during that time to fill a lustrum of old age: like some weak monarch she gave her name to the epoch, remaining herself unmemorable. It was while we were there that I introduced my wife-to-be to my mother and brother, awkwardness lessened by the meeting taking place at a cinema – the Palace, as I recall, where Mons. Spiro could not have long ceased to be – to which the two brace of us had made separate ways. I think mutual awe attended the first encounter of future brother- and sister-in-law. By then (he would be fifteen or sixteen) my brother's character and appearance had altered from childhood rather more than might have been expected from the natural effects of time and biology.

The childhood character "Jack" Fuller was impish, verging on the irresponsible; the round face alert, blue eyes merry; figure not to be called plump, but by no means exiguous. My mother used to say that playing out of doors he would lie on the pavement as though it were as clean and comfortable as her own sofas but this may have had the touch of exaggeration characteristic of her pronouncements about matters that particularly offended her, such as household dirt or personal shabbiness, just as in a similar context she may have played up the scruffiness of the young Willie Walton on the pavement outside his father's house. Jack always had a good many friends or acquaintances. At Miss Barraclough's I would be sent to look for him when he failed to turn up at his notional bedtime. There were half a dozen pavements he might be prostrate on, to say nothing of more *recherché* locations like Albert Griffiths's hut, this being at the rear of a butcher's shop kept by Griffiths *père*. In the hut, meat stolen by Albert or donated by his father was cooked in dripping that usually smelt as though not far from rancidity. Here perhaps were laid the foundations of my brother's notable future career in hotel and catering education, studies certainly needed by Albert Griffiths. At this epoch Jack went to the kindergarten I myself had attended, situated in a hall attached to a "Baptist Tabernacle", near the offices to which T. & F. Wylie Kay later moved.

Northlands High School – a girls' junior school as well as a kindergarten – was run with great efficiency by the proprietress, Miss Moorhouse, assisted by three able mistresses, Miss Arnott, Miss Proctor and Miss Schooler. Like the Boss, Miss Moorhouse had come from a region or class where Blackpool speech habits were alien. She was tall, gracious, slightly stooping, her bun of grey hair with a faint threat of disintegration. When her pupils at the end of the school day had changed back into boots and shoes from the plimsolls compulsory in school, and were in their outdoor clothes ready to depart, Miss Moorhouse was always at the exit to say au revoir. "Goodbye, shrimps!" she used to cry to the youngest groups. My brother, already conscious of a proper, non-native style of speech and for once deviating from irresponsibility through the force of Miss Moorhouse's personality, would respond with a gentility hard to indicate phonetically: "Gudbye, Miss Meurherse!"

As to shrimps, after he had joined me at Seafolde House and I had become head house prefect, I beat him for eating that delicacy at a stall on the promenade. The incident encapsulates much of its epoch: the tradition of behaviour for boys wearing the school uniform; my dotty and priggish devotion to authority; my brother's early enterprise and gourmandism, the latter eventually international. It hardly needs saying that in later life I had to have the occasion recalled to me: the censor had expunged the memory.

After lingering a little with the Boss and Ettaboo and such as Meng junior and Sage, my brother went on to King William's College, in the Isle of Man, his educational milieu during the Sidey era. Spartan, games-orientated, it was not his cup of tea really but it opened up more vistas than could have been found at Seafolde House in its declining days. For instance, he had a housemaster and in the housemaster's study was the piano on which his relation Amy Woodforde-Finden had composed the "Indian Love Lyrics", familiar to us from parlour performances in Oldham, to say nothing of those in the Metropole lounge or on the North Pier. The drastic change of schools at an awkward age did nothing to settle him academically and he emerged at the end of his schooldays lacking both foundations and impulse for a conventional career. Like me, he needed the breathing space and contacts with a wider world a university would surely have given. He had been a precocious reader of prose fiction, changing Christmas and birthday presents of children's books for the Russian classics, and the taste continued and widened. The boy encountered that night at the Palace Cinema was tall, handsome, with a flair for dressing well, far from the rancid-fat fryer of Albert Griffith's hut. He was becoming, probably had already become, the Jekyll character "John Fuller".

I suppose a school in the Isle of Man being chosen for him to escape the decline and fall of Seafolde House was not totally divorced from our having previously holidayed on the island, initially prompted by a family connection. Sam Mills, the father of "Bone" (the girl my Uncle John married), was a stockbroker's clerk who lived in Oldham, in a house in Hollins Road, perhaps half a mile nearer Hollinwood than my grandparents' house. I went there as a boy with my uncle, probably to pick up my aunt-to-be for a Sunday afternoon walk preceding "tea" at my grandparents' (where the cheese and onions dish that was my grandfather's speciality might well be on the menu), a courtship ritual then common, perhaps still so. Though Sam Mills' house was a small old terrace house, the living room reached directly by a step down from the street door, it was said that he had done well in the cotton share boom. Whether he was caught in the dire slump that followed I do not know, but he had enough money to retire eventually to the Isle of Man. His house there was more commodious and we stayed in it at least once, perhaps as paying guests. He had become an obsessive vegetable grower.

When boiled, his potatoes were like "balls of flour", the last word in his Oldham pronunciation strongly two-syllabled and the phrase permanently taking our fancy. The house was drained to a septic tank which he raided to manure his tomatoes. Or so tradition goes. Perhaps this was why on a subsequent holiday on the island we stayed elsewhere.

I missed two months of life with Mrs Sidey and Victor through going to Gibson & Weldon's law classes in London immediately before my Intermediate. A like period was similarly spent before the Final (when, however, we had long left the semi-bungalow). To try to disentangle the two occasions, give some account of the good many extraordinary incidents and characters involved, seems at the moment beyond my will. I believe at the time I was wholly conscious that much of what was happening to me was fundamentally antipathetic, yet such is youth's vigorous acceptance of existence I adopted the life style of others without much protest or attempted avoidance. But possibly even in this area a weakness, a wish not to offend, a fatal concern for third parties – cowardice of a kind – was operative and partly accounted for the strange life of sitting late in Soho cafés, fitfully but intensely getting to know enough law to qualify as a solicitor (the Intermediate in particular having a high casualty rate), not to mention follies into which one was led by friends overbearing, slightly insane. I think, for instance, of removing collar and tie for pathetic effect (the separate collar surely dates the occasion as the earlier one), collecting for a friend singing in the gutter near the Angel rather more from daring than penury.

As I write, I remember that still in the house are the letters I wrote to my future wife during both London absences, never perused since sent, which would probably allow a reasonably accurate narrative to be constructed, pinpointing my meetings with the then youthful writer Paul Potts, hearing the then Lady Mosley speak at a New Party mass meeting, to say nothing of more self-revelatory occasions. That would be an exercise of literary art a deal different from what has so far been attempted – the inaccuracy of which I feel I must labour. I know from this and a little previous biographical writing, through checking references and through consultation with others, how staggeringly at fault my memory can be, a matter I will briefly return to later. Some matters here have been corrected, some not checked: what can be said in favour of things set down is that I believe them to be true – though occasionally it has struck me that I may well have misjudged mood, injecting into the past feelings I hold now. I mean, for instance, was I not possibly unhappier in early days about a life far from fulfilling its deepest and truest desires and gifts? Later, some sort of compromise was achieved and endured.

Apropos of the acceptance of quotidian existence, it hardly needs saying that a vital ingredient was literary ambition, albeit singularly ungratified. Time rolled by without periodical or any other kind of publication. I believe the first appearance of a poem of mine, the "dissolving pier" piece already sufficiently resuscitated, was in the *Sunday Referee*'s Poets' Corner, the name of the feature a sufficient indication of its dubiety, reinforced by the reward I received, namely a penknife. The thing has got into literary annals, however, through having published early work by Pamela Hansford Johnson, Julian Symons and Dylan Thomas. But the poem referred to could not have appeared before 1933. At various stages I hawked round collections of poems, in one of which Macmillans seemed genuinely if languidly interested. Still, the years from sixteen to twenty-two were pretty well a complete wash-out. Nor did the rest of the Thirties bring any really measurable success. It never occurred to me I was in the wrong ball game, though once, sending poems not for the first time to a decent but now forgotten paper called *Everyman*, I burst out in my covering letter: "Are these any good at all?" From the literary editor I had a sympathetic note – and the poems back.

I never stopped writing prose and verse, and trying to market it, but when recognition of a kind eventually arrived – far from that hoped for when my heroes were such as Wells and Chesterton – I was amazed by it nevertheless, as I would be now should a substantial readership or critical acclaim be suddenly bestowed. I was amazed at appearing in due course in *New Verse*, having admiringly witnessed its birth, just as after the War I was amazed at the evolution of my first novel into print. As was hoped for in the 220 System, when the hard nut of utter failure was expelled a series of modest successes followed, due really to the sympathy of editors, especially John Lehmann over many years, but also Julian Symons, J. R. Ackerley, Alan Ross, Anthony Thwaite, Karl Miller . . . I will not try to complete the list, for as I go on more names occur and to omit through forgetfulness would be unforgivable.

In a sense the wheel has already come full circle, since most of my books are now as though they had never been published – out of print, unlikely ever to be in print again, some novels indeed never achieving sales of more than two or three thousand copies, books of verse with circulations even more exiguous. Such a destiny for my ambitions would have been beyond contemplation in the pre-publication days – an irony of due Hardyesque proportions. Equally unforeseeable would have been the stoic or perhaps blasé attitude of old age to this odd state of affairs. Though the anxiety to write does not seem to fall off as one gets old, the notion hardens that one has proved a point simply by having in the end joined the ranks of the creators who engage the interest of some at least of those bound up in the strange pursuit of reading imaginative literature.

Bobby, the friend at whose suggestion I subscribed to the chamber concerts held in the Metropole lounge, was not of the race of truly devout readers, nor did his interest in me prove entirely intellectual. I suppose he was in his mid-thirties, which would make him, as I write this, less than likely to be still alive. There was a moment after the war when we could have met again, though we had been out of touch for – what? – fifteen years. The press must on some occasion have linked my literary and legal work and Bobby, being briefly in London, telephoned me at the office suggesting a meeting. Whatever the circumstances, no doubt militating against freeing myself at short notice, I ducked the invitation. I regret that. I would not have done it now, more adapted to dealing with such excessively non-routine occasions and, indeed, more capable of letting ordinary human feelings govern my actions, though that is not saying much.

When I wrote *The Perfect Fool* I assumed he was living, so the character in the novel who stands in for him is to a substantial degree invented. What I would say now is that though I had no interest in male friendships other than the "innocent" kind with Leslie, and at first obtusely imagined Bobby the same, his different affection was rarely and most tactfully indicated. I could not respond but that was the only embarrassment. And even had I possessed from the start more gumption, there was nothing to be done about the situation. Curious that in the three or four years that had elapsed since school, erotic activity with members of one's own sex had become unthinkable – not that at school it held any great attraction, simply that there a fairly uninhibited commerce existed at times at a certain age, not of the least emotional importance or complication.

I feel sure that Bobby sensed, as did I, some grave contradiction between his job and his persona. He was exceptionally well turned out and his manner *très comme il faut.* To the chamber concerts he used to bring an attractive widow, rather older than himself; and he holidayed abroad. But at other times, travelling for a firm of popular manufacturing chemists (a modern version of the character in the song, quoted later, often sung by my grandfather), he had to visit the little general shops of Lancashire, keeping them stocked up with acidosis remedies and the like, many such products being displayed on cards to which the phials of pills were attached on thin white-cotton-covered elastic. It may well have been that "Daisy" headache powders and "Lung Healers", specifics familiar from my infancy, were among those dealt with. He did not own a car so his itineraries were done by rail. Our first meeting was appropriately on the last train from Manchester, both bound from the Hallé concert, brought into contact through a troublesome drunk in the same compartment, though I do not doubt Bobby had engineered his own presence. At the time of that episode we were still living at the flat but strangely enough on moving to Mrs Sidey's I found myself quite near the house where he, too, lived in "rooms", to which I was occasionally invited. The house belonged to a member of his family and compared well in décor and comfort with Mrs Sidey's, a good piano in Bobby's sitting room notably impressing me, and I think photographs of antiquities on the walls.

Many years after the events narrated here the actress Jill Balcon brought home to me in conversation the utility of the curious, if not ludicrous, term "artiste" when discussing the theatrical profession (and even the appearance of poets in public, reading their own work; grisly entertainment) if employed with the right nuance. Fowler is correct in emphasizing that despite the terminal "e" the expression is applicable to either sex: he adds that its use should be confined to "professional singer, dancer, or other public performer", with no implication "that the performance is in fact artistic". All the same, I think sophisticated usage nowadays confines the term to performers of a slightly old-fashioned cast, perhaps with mild versatility and a tendency to sentiment – troupers with a wide appeal, guaranteed to cause no offence.

Muriel George was an artiste. I do not remember, if I was ever told, how Bobby got to know her. By then middle-aged, she became even better known later in life when she played parts, usually vignettes, in more than a few British films. As I wrote those last words it occurred to me, as it had never done before, to look her up in Halliwell's indispensible *Filmgoer's Companion*, where I find the usual accurate and succinct professional characterization: "Plump, motherly British character actress who often played charladies or landladies. Music-hall background." According to Halliwell her film début was in 1932, the year after I was introduced to her by Bobby, which confirms my notion of her career. The *Companion* says she was born in 1883, so the "music-hall background" could well have been shared with such as Little Tich and Arnold Richardson. In fact Halliwell is referring to the inter-war years: before the First World War she was in the sort of show of which that on the Blackpool Central Pier (and in Happy Valley) was a hardy descendant. Her first appearance was as a young girl in Pélissier's famous pierrot troupe, when apparently she was already married to someone called Robin George. In the same epoch that marriage had come to an end and she married her second husband and stage partner, Ernest Butcher.

It must be stressed that the person I met was far from the Miss Barraclough or Mrs Sidey type, despite the film parts she was about to play. In the past she must have been personable enough – not hard to imagine, though she could never have been a beauty – to contract two marriages and the possible union I shall refer to. Ernest Butcher was two or three years younger than her – a light comedian originally, I suppose – who in his songs and dialogue inclined to Mummerset. "British character actor who spent a lifetime playing mild little men" is the extent of Halliwell's characterization; unusually, a trifle lacking in precision, for Butcher had a long concert-party, if not music-hall, history, and I think his film career did not start until early in the Second World War.

My glimpse of this world was a result of Bobby taking me one evening to the summer show in the pavilion on the middle pier of Blackpool's three. Each had its individual entertainment, even class, character. The North Pier, befitting its position by the Metropole, had two pavilions: in the one on its head, Mons. Spiro (or his equivalent) conducted, as it might be, the Second Hungarian Rhapsody; at the end, before one descended to the jetty to fish for "dabs" or embark on a steamer that might ply round Morecambe Bay or even to the Isle of Man, there was a second pavilion where a fairly lavish summer show was mounted, the impresario being Lawrence Wright who under the famous *nom de plume* "Horatio Nicholls" (a name in the Blackpool parlance detested by the Boss coming out as "Oraysher Nittles") wrote many songs of the day, including "Souvenirs" and possibly "Shepherd of the Hills". At one time he lived conveniently at the Metropole, his riches presumably putting him on better terms than Miss Paine with the Prussian.

The pavilion on the southernmost pier, the Victoria Pier, was dominated in my time by an annual entertainment always starring Fred Walmsley, an elderly low comedian, funny, who in winter played pantomime dames and carried this side of his talent into the summer shows, a sketch particularly successful including a routine of undressing for bed, a voluminous nightdress being first put on and the day clothes taken off underneath it (a procedure not unrealistic, for I recall servants who used to do just that). Always good for a laugh was his giving himself, with sighs of satisfaction, after bringing out a pair of corsets from under the nightdress, a thorough scratch round the ribs. To digress further, when I was at boarding school Blackpool staged a carnival modelled on the one at Nice. The notion was to vivify the late spring so as to entice visitors before the crowded high season, but the municipality had not weighed the difference in climate at that time of year between Mediterranean and Irish Sea. The carnivals had their successes, possibly mainly of an unofficial saturnalian kind, but a *bataille des fleurs* on the exposed promenade I suppose did not attract great masses or give great pleasure. Even in the start of the official theme song of the second (and last) carnival might be detected, pondering the epithet and the indication of untimely repetition, a disillusioned or wearied undertone:

> Hello, hello, hello, breezy Blackpool,
> It's Blackpool carnival time again.

When war broke out at last in 1939 (and though I had then been agonizedly anti-fascist for a long time) I was quite shocked at the sudden appearance of vulgar broadsheets against Hitler. In a similar way the Blackpool carnivals released forces that the good taste and manners of the time had hitherto forbade public expression; one manifestation being the sale on the streets, among the carnival crowds, of a small paper called *Billy's Weekly Liar*. The title indicates a periodical nature but it had never come my way before and its surprising contents influenced my own publication, *The Feats of Dormitory Three*, previously referred to; though I did not dare to be as scatological. The literary genre exploited by *Billy's Weekly Liar* that I particularly admired was the cod library list, containing such books as *The Tiger's Revenge* by Claude R. Sole, *My Life in a Nudist Colony* by I. Seymour Cox and *The Passionate Lover* by E. Tudor Tittiov (the last-named a somewhat implausible Anglo-Russian *mélange*). After the publication of this instalment of my memoirs, the philosopher Anthony Quinton told me he had found it funny. I asked him if he had liked the book-titles. He said some were familiar; in past times had invented a few himself; and only the other day had heard a new one: *The Wild Party* by Segovia Carpet.

The grandparents of Byng, Gorill's tormentor, had a largish house on the promenade, not far from the school, and the boarders were invited to view the carnival procession from the front garden. The Carnival King (or, more likely, Queen) was none other than Fred Walmsley, and when the float bearing him and his consort passed, the comedian stood up, sceptre raised, and called: "Three cheers for Seafolde House!" The assembled boarders (though, if anything like me, stunned at this royal attention) responded heartily. How had Fred Walmsley been put on to doing it? The idea of the Boss sitting through the nightdress routine to go backstage afterwards to make a request for a commercial, so to speak, was not on the cards, despite his later attendance at the Palace Varieties. In fact, I guess that behind the business was Byng's family, who had music-hall connections, his uncle being Percy Honri, always billed as "A concert-in-a-turn", the subtitle cleverly alluding to both his principal instrument and musical prowess in general.

The entertainment on the Central Pier, though in the part of Blackpool appealing most to the proletarian holiday-makers of the summer Wakes weeks, was usually mid-way in tone between the other two pier shows. What Muriel George and Ernest Butcher were starring in was essentially a pierrot show or concert party, such as my Uncle John had figured in as the soubrette during the First World War. The convention still held that though the cast was in pierrot costume in the first half, in the second evening dress was *de rigueur*. The two stars did well in the sketches, as borne out by their later careers in the cinema, and their own "spot", late in the second half, rather surprisingly largely featuring folk songs, was put over well. Afterwards, Bobby took me to their dressing room, the journey itself giving an exciting sense of eminently exploitable literary material of a kind never before met. How typical, absurd and forgivable of him to introduce me to Muriel George as a slavish admirer to whom he would find it incongruous – impossible – because of the youthful charms that had helped to captivate me, to explain a stout figure lurking in the shadows of the dressing-room. It says a good deal for Bobby's social graces that all this was insinuated rather than laid on the line, which, however, did not make it much less embarrassing for me who at that time would be quite unpractised in dealing with drama (or flannel) imported without warning into small talk (even today relishing it not at all).

The figure on the dressing room's periphery was Muriel George's son, John Davenport. Who his father was I do not know. There was an Arthur Davenport who wrote the lyrics for Pélissier's songs but I fancy there is no more than coincidence in that. I heard it said that John's one-time affluence came from his father, who may well in fact have been Muriel George's first husband, John avoiding his mother's stage name. At this date he was or lately had been a Cambridge undergraduate. The uncertainty arises from his having appeared in and helped to edit *Cambridge Poetry 1929* which marks him as already having been up for three years. Of course, he may have been in for a fourth year, which would be consonant with his incongruously frittering away part of the Long Vacation in Blackpool. In later years he put on more weight but even when I first knew him he was notably solid, a stout man of the formidable rather than genial kind. His brown hair was cut and brushed in schoolboy style (and I mean without the oleaginous or adhesive auxiliaries used by such as Matley) above a flat face. Bulldog Drummond is introduced as ugly but attractive, a rather literary concept which John, however, could be said to embody. On me he made an impression hardly to be over-emphasized. I put him in an unfinished novel of the epoch and in a romanticized guise he even appears in a fiction I wrote some time after the war called *Fantasy and Fugue*. At that first encounter some literary talk was exchanged and a further meeting arranged. The initiative would have come from him, for, as already laboured, I was as green as grass. Almost certainly Bobby must have given warning that I was a budding writer, so John could not have looked forward to my introduction with any relish. But I can see that he was patient and kindly behind an exterior already tough, to grow more so over the years. On my side, exchanges with one of greater literary sophistication – indeed, vis-à-vis the new poetry perhaps less than a score of people of equal knowledge could at that time have been found – was remarkably decisive. I do not suppose we met more than half a dozen times that summer, nor do I recall much of what was said (probably did not hear a good deal of it, for he had a habit of speaking quietly or into open space or extremely allusively), yet my endeavours in art were permanently altered.

Four books I bought initially through his commending them: the *Cambridge Poetry* already mentioned; the *Oxford Poetry* of 1930, because it contained poems by Stephen Spender; Edgell Rickword's *Invocation to Angels*; and Auden's 1930 *Poems*. It says much for the standard of service of the day that all these, mostly cheap, mostly from small publishers, were ordered from and promptly supplied by Sweeten's, Blackpool's virtually sole bookshop. (F. P. Sweeten, tall, grey, stooping, giving personal attention to any customer not yet shelling out, was a character like the Boss, capable of inducing fear, though willing to do a financially advantageous deal with my brother over the *Greyfriars Holiday Annual* and Dostoevsky). The drama of coming across for the first time the work of Rickword, Empson, Spender, Auden, *et al*, though stirring, must not be exaggerated. The penny took a little time really to drop. John Davenport himself was remarkably open-minded about recent generations. For example, when I foolishly wrote off Flecker (whom I would then have thought it correct to regard as outworn compared with the Sitwells, say) he said he thought Flecker quite a good poet. I expect this would be a relief of a kind, for I had admired Flecker and having been thus reassured, went on reading him. I think I had a growing sense that I must write poetry whose aim was not "beauty" of the kind for which Flecker supplied notable touchstones, but the touchstones went on being touched:

> Then the grey square of wall should fade away,
>
> And glow again, and open, and disclose
> The shimmering lake in which the planets swim,
> And all that lake a dewdrop on a rose.

When I opened Rickword's marvellous book I found at once beauty pretty well of the kind accustomed to:

> Trees have been named and brutes with shining skins,
> and in pure darkness many a planet spins
> no living eyes have seen, yet men say *There*
> *Orion's gathering-in his massy hair* . . .

The same thing could be said about some of Spender's five poems in *Oxford Poetry 1930*:

> The trumpets were curled away, the drum beat no more.
> Only the Swan the Swan danced in my brain:
> All night she spun; drooped, lifted again;
> Bent and arched her arms; sunk on the frore
> Snow-brittle feathers skirting her . . .

But I suppose (though in the absence of documentation the *post hoc* rationalization may be already askew) that elsewhere Rickword's disillusion and Spender's poem about unemployment helped the concept of a poetry of direct social function, having to do with life in a wider and more down to earth way than the provision of stimulating or consolatory sounds and images. This was confirmed in a nevertheless somewhat baffling way by the Auden book. What on earth did one's uninstructed mind make of it in 1931? No doubt, as in so much of Auden, there was immediate recognition of a life one had lived oneself:

> On Sunday walks
> Past the shut gates of works

– recalling Mr Tregenza holding his hat on in the breeze, and a remoter past in Oldham. Many of my current preoccupations were expressed in startlingly-employed traditional forms:

Lawrence, Blake and Homer Lane, once healers in our English land;
These are dead as iron for ever; these can never hold our hand.

Still, I am sure I used the book to some extent as I had used books of poems in the past – to discover in them mottos for my own life, and those special bits of poetic poetry – though things like Lawrence's *Nettles* may already have convinced me that writing poetry was not a matter of trying to create beauty. Above all, the Auden book may have stressed the need for a new life, to come out of difficult, probably violent, struggle. I should add that Auden sanctioned in me, as in many, obscurity, so that even though he perhaps helped towards a verse of social and political directness, I had largely worked through that by the time my first collection of poems, published early in 1939, was made up. A good deal of that volume was "clotted" or "thick", the critical adjectives we often used for what nonetheless often seemed an inescapable style in the confused and doomed later years of the decade.

In my account of my initial relationship with John Davenport there will be as many gaps and as much dubious history as in what I have said of his introduction to me of my own generation of poets. I see us sitting at a table in a largish bar on the pier – a room of windows and cast-iron decorated pillars – at some hour when it was little patronized. I drank scarcely at all in those days: going into a bar would never have occurred to me. A dull companion I must have been for John, who liked a drink then, though I expect not so much as in later life. I remember, too, going one morning to the pier pavilion and finding him at one of the two pianos that on a lower level flanked the stage, the pianist of the show at the other, playing the solo (or perhaps the arrangement of the orchestral part) of a Bach keyboard concerto. I like to think that the troupe's excellent tenor was also knocking about, making some highbrow contribution to the proceedings, but cannot be sure: he was a young man called Webster Booth. I must have seen the show, or parts of it, several times, for I can recall some of the songs – concerted numbers from the whole cast and items from the repertoire of Muriel George and Ernest Butcher. I see from Halliwell that they both died in 1965, a mere coincidence, for their marriage had been dissolved during the

War and Ernest Butcher had a new wife, the sister of a famous ventriloquist of the epoch. John himself only outlived his mother by a year.

After the War I encountered him on a number of occasions. On the first I feel sure I referred to our meeting in bygone days in one of those Blackpool edifices "whose minarets were charcoaled on the sky". By this date he was bigger, more formidable, almost certain to have a few drinks on board. I did not press him when he failed, I think pretty well completely, to respond to this jogging of his memory. In the event we never discussed former times. I did not realize then that some are cagey about their past: it may fail ignominiously to correspond with a past they have created in their own or the public mind. In John's case, being up at Cambridge with Lehmann and Empson and Eberhart and James Reeves and Michael Redgrave and Hugh Sykes Davies and Basil Wright and Bronowski and Julian Bell, and putting their poems together in an anthology, may in retrospect have seemed real, while his mother taking part in the action song "One finger and thumb keep moving" not at all an actual part of his past. Thinking of the time he spent as a liver of the poetic life among Blackpool's insanities, who can blame him? Of course, it could well have been he had completely forgotten meeting the aspiring, near teetotal provincial poetaster.

Though by the time of these encounters of the second kind I had made a reputation which despite its modesty he would certainly have been aware of (for even as an undergraduate his knowledge of literary affairs was encyclopaedic) he did not refer to that either. Slightly surprising, then, when at a party he came quite amiably up to me. I was already talking to Stephen Spender and said something fatuous-sounding, such as: "You two know each other, of course." To John, Stephen said (I give an approximation of his words): "Yes, I know you and what you have been saying about my brother, my entire family." He was extremely cross. John immediately moved away, though quite capable, with far less prompting, of initiating a physical kerfuffle, as happened at Bernard Gutteridge's rather smart wedding reception. I think by way of palliation I told Stephen (or perhaps I merely wished I had) that even before he had published his first Faber collection John had been a propagandist for his poetry.

When *The Death of the King's Canary*, a cod detective story John had written with Dylan Thomas in 1940, was belatedly published in 1976, the writer of the introduction said that in the very early Thirties John was a poet compared by his contemporaries to Auden, Spender and Day Lewis, but this was not so. Some claimed to have prognosticated difficulties on seeing his long poem in *Cambridge Poetry 1929*, ominously subtitled "A Fragment". I must have recognized that it blatantly employed the styles of Rickword, Eliot and Sacheverell Sitwell, to name but three: nevertheless, I liked its knowing turns and references – and, truth to say, the lingering Nineties sense of verbal "beauty":

> Now that the year is shifting in its bed
> Adonis-like in petal-feathered sheen
> the boar, dark winter's domination ended,
> the earliest shoots of April can be seen;
> save in interminable pale ending streets
> where dazedly the poet now repeats –
> an atom before a tracery of steel
> cylinders, dynamoes, pistons, wheel on wheel –
> the names Picasso, Cocteau, Schoenberg . . .

To put the case crudely, over-sophistication was in those days John's trouble, the opposite of my own. He did not recover: at his death he was really known only for his *Observer* book reviews, though whether one will be remembered oneself for anything more weighty must be doubted. However, on our re-encounter he may have been embarrassed to be apparently overhauled in a contest in which he had seemed to start with such an advantage. On the other hand, and perhaps more likely, the thought may never have crossed his clever and obstreperous mind.

Characteristic of what was crammed into the relatively short sojourn at Mrs Sidey's was starting to smoke, a habit more gripping than booze and which lasted until my early sixties, invariable accompaniment of work, pleasure, hurt. I picked up one of my mother's "Craven A" cigarettes, then actually cork-tipped, without filter, and lighting it, as I had seen done, with an ember held in the fire tongs, remarked: "I think I'll start smoking." The action and phrase had been meditated. Characteristic that my mother's mild opposition should have been on the ground of expense but who at that time linked smoking directly with death?

After Mrs Sidey's, despite the continuance of memory's blanks and blunders, autobiographical material becomes more abundant, involving greater difficulties of selection, chronology, frankness. Would it be too simplistic to try to deal with it in the manner that has served so far? In any event I am sure my memory is morbidly defective. I used to say being a solicitor had trained me to forget facts and remember sources, practical and effective knowledge of the law being a nose for retrieval rather than a grasp of detail, the ability (to use a better metaphor) to hear faint bells ringing. Though that may have been my working method as a lawyer it does not explain the deficiency. Someone (I forget who!) once remarked that memory was self-justification. Again, that would not explain my case, for though the subconscious no doubt operates to allow a certain quota of guilt, gaffes, failures and wrong turnings to hide in oblivion, a good few are still vivid, often pondered, as will have been seen.

Perhaps a sharper memory (and additional stamina; the lack of that in a physical sense indicated by my jibbing at the mile) would have led me to write fiction incorporating more of the material reality of life, demanding to be densely and quite extensively delineated mainly in terms of character and social class. These are Dickensian categories, and whenever I read Dickens I am struck afresh by the apparent sureness of his knowledge of social traits – clothes, food, servants, the role in the family of its subsidiary members, money, reading matter, details of places of public resort. Mere caricature pertains, of course, when the aristocracy is offered to be depicted; and the sureness may falter in the ranks of the upper middle-class, but elsewhere all is copper-bottomed. Even in *Boz* and the early parts of *Pickwick* the knowledge is richly at work. It is the knowledge gained by the mobile petty-bourgeois, which I was from my earliest days. It implies a sensitivity to habits, behaviour and appearances in English society, things that have always played a large part in our literary art. George Orwell lacked it and some of those he has influenced, such as the new novelists of the fifties, recklessly disregarded it. TV drama, so susceptible of being an inferior art, goes on getting things wrong; regional accents and their consistency within a single piece, for example. And when my novel *Image of a Society* was dramatized for TV I was pained to see the second or third executive in a large provincial building society washing the dishes, and in an apron. In literature truth about life cannot be attempted without truth about society, which is where much post-war fiction and drama is shaky, though the deficiency may be common in feebler writers in all epochs.

8 *Kind Doddy*

Inevitably, in the course of writing, detached memories have arisen not easy to fit in their proper place; some in fact seeming to have a special right to appear as afterthoughts or in isolation. "Musical fruit" my grandfather called peas, even garden peas, the joke (when I had divined or, more likely, had explained to me its vulgar point) capable of effective repetition, like a line of poetry whose observation or trope, originally startling, remains operant when utterly familiar. As has been seen, my grandfather was not loathe to repeat sayings, quotations, actions, a trait I inherited, possibly have inadvertently exhibited here. I used in *The Perfect Fool* his complaint or boast about having to go to see Gandhi at a time when the Indian nationalist leader was especially troublesome, the person involved eventually proving, however, to live on the Fylde coast, by name Gandy and an executor with my grandfather for a mutual relative. My grandfather was alert to puns and alliteration and so forth – a sort of poetic sensitivity, so I must not think that side of my nature comes exclusively from my grandmother. He always liked to say the name of a friend of his, Corny (short for Cornelius) Kershaw; perhaps his bridge partner on that night of my unannounced visit. "She has a voice like a cinder under a door," I once heard him observe, I seem to think apropos Keck's singing prowess, though this notable simile may not have been original. Both here and in the novel referred to I have given the recipe for pineapple ice cream, which, like Constant Lambert in *Façade*, he used to deliver in a tempo of virtuoso rapidity, copied from the market-place. Another phrase of similar origin was "Pies or cakes or pop!" – also prestissimo. Interest in market hucksters perhaps helped to determine the siting of his office near Tommyfield. A song he sang about such a character must have come from the music-hall of an era long before he was Superintendent Registrar of Births, Marriages and Deaths, however:

Oh my eye, oh my eye!
Anyone ill, anyone ill?
Oh my eye!

For he's a jolly good chap, chap, chap,
And he carries a pack on his back.
He's plasters and pills to cure all ills
And they call him "Medicine Jack".

A line from another of his songs became fixed in my memory because of what I regarded as the brilliance of its literary allusion: "They call her 'Monkey Brand' because she won't wash clothes." I was familiar with the line before the proprietory article in question – which was a hardish oblong cake of cleansing material. Imagine my pleased astonishment, akin to opening *Hamlet* for the first time, when I found, on the paper wrapper that "Monkey Brand" came in, the legend "Won't wash clothes" – an implied boast of the article's utility in all other such affairs of life, which the lyric writer had adroitly turned to characterize a lazy housewife, whom my upbringing would anyway be more than ready to scorn.

For years I used a saying of my grandfather's when refusing a second (or third) helping: "No, thank you. I've had an elegant sufficiency." The epithet always bothered me by its seeming inappropriateness – until much later in life I found the words in Thomson's *The Seasons*. But I have never discovered the source of the phrase "lucky bargees" ("Come on, you lucky bargees," he used to call when offering chocolates to his grandchildren), though "bargee" appears in *Stalky & Co.* in an affectionate as well as a pejorative context. Also remaining mysterious is a sentence he employed to indicate any substance, usually food, either of a strangish nature or the name of which he could not immediately bring to mind. "I'll have some of that scanamanah, commonly known as lobjaw," he would say, confronted by a choice of pudding. Possibly the words, here necessarily indicated phonetically, were of his own invention. Almost equally esoteric was his crying "Ee, diddle, diddle" in a loud soprano voice in my grandmother's ear when he came down (unshaved, collarless, wearing a neckerchief) and kissed her, feigning to menace with his bristling chin, before sitting at the breakfast table. I used to wonder whether her annoyance was real or assumed, part of the act. The syllable "Ee", very much a feature of the speech of east Lancashire (pertaining, indeed, to Yorkshire) has also an enigmatic quality. At one time my brother and I had picked up and frequently used a phrase which my mother in the end characterized as near swearing and forbade. This was "Ee 'eck an' aye"; as broad in its expressive purposes as Miss Barraclough's "Dearie me today".

A joke not my grandfather's own which nevertheless pleased him concerned the subterranean public lavatories by the Oldham Theatre Royal, an amenity he worked long to bring into being and which immediately became known as Alderman Broadbent's two-valve receiver, the wireless allusion being prompted in regard to the technical specification by the feature of twin glazed domes above ground to admit the light. His occupation would confirm him in a temperament likely, as I think was the case, to take a Sweeneyesque view of human life.

My memory of the house at Waterhead, scene of so much distress (shared by my grandparents, who were there when my father's death was announced to me, probably when it occurred), is not so nebulous as may have been implied. The steep garden, though by no means large, was wooded on its lower levels, always somewhat mysterious, and leading to a side entrance. That would be the way my brother and I went out on to "the moors", where I would frighten him with a tale of a nearby boggart, and then run away. The yard at the back of the house my father had had asphalted and there I played with my scooter. I had coveted such a vehicle (probably Marjorie Marsland owned one) and my father had mine made by the carpenter at the rubber-proofing mill. The result was heavy, unhandy, with solid wooden wheels, perhaps even iron-shod. I see myself inexpertly battling with it in the yard but not for worlds would I have admitted its deficiencies, being then as now anxious through some species of embarrassment (for myself and for any vis-à-vis) to underplay disaster, even to find good in it. When my mother, in tears, embraced me on that Sunday morning of my father's death, I discovered something irrelevant to say or do – a message, or a sweet passed on to my brother, from my great-uncle Newton with whom I had been to church, being told about my father on returning, though aware before that because of a boy I knew saying on my way home that our blinds were down and asking if there had been a death – my reply characteristically a denial, advancing spring-cleaning as the cause, however unlikely a week before Christmas.

One fairly soon became conscious of being oneself a witness to change, if not yet acutely felt as bodily decay. While at Waterhead, the dressmaker measuring my mother pronounced that to fulfil fashion the skirt should be ten inches off the ground, a height that seemed as daring as the thirty miles an hour in the Ford with the English body later on. I remember being taken to the unveiling of a memorial, on a site towards Mumps, to the dead of the First War. When I first went to boarding school, the handyman, with a species of palsy we used to imitate, was said to have been reduced to such wreckage through shell shock. While we were at Mrs Sidey's a fresh cast was once more assembling: it would help me to act out the few years of ineffectual work for peace, employment and the downfall of fascism before I left for Kent, and, soon after, I was living in London, as long desired. But on the heels of that was the start of the Second World War: my wife and son came to Blackpool for refuge, and before hostilities had ended my son was attending Northlands High School, now conducted by Miss Arnott and Miss Proctor, Miss Moorhouse having some time before said a last farewell to her shrimps.

The fresh cast referred to might be described as a blend of Isherwood and Upward, the latter predominant – such as the communist snack-bar owner; the declassed intellectual who served in it, member of that strange, in many ways admirable, sect, the SPGB; the skilled worker, CPGB member, forced to take work digging trenches for the Corporation gas department; the young Trotskyist grammar-school master – variously to die of self-neglect; to go bonkers on and off; to go south and make armaments; to be killed in the Spanish Civil War; to decline into marriage and a species of respectability. Even I myself, sheltered from many evils, virtually joined the ranks of the unemployed before I left for the South-East; an apt irony, for in the latter days of my articles I watched with guilt from an office window some friends in a feeble procession I had helped the National Unemployed Workers Movement to organize but which it was tolerantly recognized I was in the wrong social position to join myself.

Ideological turns followed each other as did historical turns.

Psychoanalysis struck Seafolde House in 1927, when I heard two young masters discussing it, but though it plainly constituted a powerful and still more or less private key to the riddle of human existence I was not then tempted to look into it. I can still vaguely recall titles and authors mentioned (Freud and Jung not among them, the masters having already moved into esotericism), the word "id" familiar, though for years I should have been as stumped at defining it as spelling cupboard when I first met the Boss. One of the masters concerned was in fact his nephew. He it was whose genius had cast Gorill as Hippolyta, who had lent me Ian Hay and O. Henry and was to measure my record long jump, perhaps generously, for it was a leap so notable for those times as to earn a paragraph in the local paper. Having the same surname as the Boss he was always referred to by his first Christian name. Mr David was handsome and a good teacher, like his uncle, and with a facetiousness and sarcasm that despite being schoolmasterish was always good-humoured, going down well with me. "Stop exercising your prosimian propensities," he would say – to Byng as likely as not. Until recently the adjective had always been a slight puzzle: would not "simian" have sufficed? Then I looked up the word and found it described the order of lemurs, not apes. Presumably Mr David knew this and was identifying a particular type of restless and mischievous animality – unless he had uncomprehendingly taken over a rotund phrase invented by someone else, like "terminological inexactitude". As to simian, I heard mentioned the other day a district of Manchester called Whalley Range, which was where Byng's home was and which in my schooltime fantasies I took to be an area of bare hills like the Mappin Terrace at the Zoo, and perhaps similarly of artificial construction, where during the holidays Byng capered about with the rest of his monkey-faced family.

If my early life has seemed to consist mainly of surfaces, at least the reader has not had to suffer more nebulous speculations. When eventually I read him, Freud's account of the hidden life seemed to me strikingly plausible and illuminating. No doubt his models of the mind will seem medieval to subsequent generations but his connective insights and literary genius inspired me long into the post-Second War era. When we were very young, probably still at Waterhead, I used in bed to tell my brother John stories about a character called "Baby Bronco", a human baby not a foal of the Wild West. Where did the name come from? There is (or was) a lavatory paper with the brand name "Bronco": is it too fanciful to see in my choice of nomenclature an infantile confusion between babies and faeces, as in Freud's Little Hans case history? And was I, perhaps, to assuage some felt guilt, resurrecting my brother George, whose birth and death had occurred between my own and John's?

In the *TLS*, Maurice Richardson (soon afterwards to die, alas) once quoted a dictum by an early convert to psychoanalysis, Dr Eder: "We are born mad. We acquire morality and become stupid and unhappy. Then we die." It is an arguable view of life, not shared by me who believes, as these pages must have made plain, in the rule of the super-ego, mixed blessing though it may be. That is not to derogate from the power of the id which, indeed, some would see as the source of the renewals and developments of creativity which have sustained – helped to make not unhappy – my life. Soon after I first went to boarding-school I had a nightmare which sent me, crying out, running over the adjoining dormitory beds before I was fully awake and scurried back to my own where, when the light went on and some wakened boys discussed the bizarre event, I pretended to be asleep. In the morning I dared not face quizzing and mockery, and went on feigning sleep or a dozy illness as the others dressed, being eventually visited by the Headmaster's sister (who in those days was matron) as someone reported sick, perhaps dotty . . .

It has now come to me why "Uncle Alf" was so generous with gramophone records – and why, when I qualified as a solicitor, he bought me a gown, bands in a green leather case, and a barrister's blue bag to transport them in. An uneasy conscience about shares acquired too cheaply I doubt was in point. He was my godfather, a relationship then as meaningful as in the Mafia now, even for the irreligious; and which I see as of some account, like a good few vanished things bordering on the sentimental. In this and similar matters my grandfather's formula is relevant. If, he said often in the days of my childhood, watching the domestic disposal of his purchased prize specimen, when you cut yourself a piece of cheese you included a due proportion of the rind you were a conservative; if your helping was rindless you were a radical. He did not obtrude his own convictions of right and wrong in the matter, content with pronouncing after the event on the politics or cast of mind thus in Freudian manner revealed.

According to the cheese test I seemed at first to be a dyed in the wool radical. Yet soon some overmastering puritanical or parsimonious inclination turned me, in the realm of cheese, into a conservative, conscious of virtue in leaving for those to follow me neat right-angles and a proper share of sustenance. Darwin tells of his son, nicknamed Doddy, who "when two years and three months old . . . gave his last bit of gingerbread to his little sister, and then cried out, with high self-approbation 'Oh kind Doddy, kind Doddy.'" Thus perhaps was I at a similar age; only later my concern for others and desire to be thought good assuming, through shyness and so forth, chilly and convoluted forms.

The "detached memories" spoken of must be regarded as ever carried forward, part of the running total, but not always getting itemized. Thinking of Marjorie Marsland's dislike of long black stockings, for instance, reminded me of an almost pathological hatred I had at the same epoch for my "sou'wester" – a black mackintosh headgear, like that worn by the sailor holding the giant codfish on the label of the also detested "Scott's Emulsion". Were the weather too inclement to prevent me from getting out of wearing it, I was agonizingly embarrassed at being seen in it and, if alone, took it off, rolled it up, and put it in my pocket until I was back in sight of home. The misery conferred was equalled in later life, at Seafolde House, by a pair of shoes, always too small for me. In the shop I had deluded myself about this defect, for the shoes had been reduced in price and I wanted my mother to have the advantage of the bargain. The reason for the reduction was plain (though I also glossed over this at the time): the toe-caps were curiously (and unfashionably) blunt and bulbous – unbecoming as well as too short for my feet. Unlike the sou'wester, one needed no phobia to want to discard them. Being new, they came up from the school cellars on Sundays only, but even this hebdomadal wearing was torture enough since the day's programme included a march to church and the Sunday afternoon walk. Such sparse pleasures as that routine afforded crippledom diluted (and one event good for a suppressed laugh was, I may mention, spotting the arrival at church of a regular worshipper crudely but accurately christened "Big Conk", the very person later played bridge with at Wilton Parade, Mrs Laycock). Not for many weeks, perhaps a few terms even, did I have the enterprise to go illegally into the cellars on Sundays and get (and subsequently return) my weekday shoes from the rows laid out for cleaning by the shell-shocked handyman. I would have promptly sacrificed the sou'wester but the comedian's shoes I persevered with – surely a constriction of my character induced by the intervening events of life.

Far more tenuous than such remembered facts is one's sense of the disappearing perspectives of people known, experiences undergone – richness that doesn't know why it has faded. Sometimes we used to visit my (or, rather my mother's) Aunt Polly, a good tram-ride or car-ride from Hollins Road. Aunt Polly was my grandmother's (I think elder) sister; lived in pretty humble circumstances. Dimly I recall humorous interplay between them; and Aunt Polly's strong-charactered daughter, in whose life there was, or was to come, some such tragedy as an illegitimate child. But here memory is merging into something like dream. Was he from my grandmother's or grandfather's family the marbleless man who sat on the sofa in the front room at Hollins Road and occasionally ejaculated the word, or words, "Cat's-piss"? And was I there?

Analagous to the rediscovery of the Mumps drapers, Buckley & Proctor, was recently reading in the first volume of Dodie Smith's autobiography of the multiple grocers – multiple in the Manchester area – Seymour Meads, a name for me of perhaps greater antiquity and reconditeness, whose euphonious syllables possibly my grandfather took every opportunity of repeating as in the case of Corny Kershaw, and but for that chance reading surely lost to my mind for ever. But what is to remind me of blanks truly vital?

II

VAMP TILL READY

I *Vamp Till Ready*

Gilbert Waller joined Seafolde House as a dayboy at the same time as I went there as a boarder. Similarly to my own case, the Headmaster had underestimated his abilities, and after a term he moved up with me, skipping a form. When I think of him at this moment I am reminded of the start of *Madame Bovary*, though his character was far from that of Charles Bovary. But first encountering him then was, as with Bovary in Flaubert's novel, a memorable though oblique way into an entire story, in which, however, he came to play only a subsidiary and eventually off-stage part.

The chiming of his surname with my own struck me, at the age of eleven, as of significance in some mystico-coincidental way: his long head, and face narrow rather than otherwise, were also common possessions. But there was no deep physical resemblance: Waller presented an owlish aspect, the immobile-save-for-blinking characteristic being exaggerated in the face of authority or in stubborn or impudent mood. When, a little later, I visited his home in holiday time, his mother said to him, perhaps more than once: "Why can't you stand up straight, like Roy?" So I suppose the owlishness was accompanied by something of a stoop, though he could never be classed as really tall.

His interests were unscientific, in fact proved in a way to be literary. But, rather in the manner of Hamlet's injecting his spots with Euthymol, he once demonstrated, by swallowing and effortlessly regurgitating a largish fragment of apple, that the stomach (or, rather, the oesophagus) would reject anything not digestible. I was sufficiently impressed to have remembered the experiment for nearly sixty years, but was not convinced the theory was a sound one. There was something prestigious in the business, plausible at first blush but not withstanding reflection – journalistic, one might say. And a journalist was what Waller became.

For the foot in the door, picture-snatching side of the journalist's craft, Waller was plainly fitted from an early age. It must have been at the Boarders' Concert of our first year that he stood on a desk seat and sang "The Lass with a Delicate Air". Day-boys were encouraged to attend this evening function, though I do not recall any other instance of them otherwise participating, or, indeed, of any other impromptu or unsolicited contribution, which Waller's certainly was. His services were offered (probably to Mr David, the master always in charge of the affair) and the song begun, in determined fashion. The unhasty climbing on the desk seat so as to be properly seen and heard was a Wallerish touch added after the extra item had been allowed.

The performance was impressive if one cared for that sort of thing: a strong, tuneful treble issuing from the full lips, inclined to be pursed even when not in song – the gaze steady through the round spectacles, challenging ridicule, though promising complete indifference should catcalls come. My head full of Tosti and Amy Woodforde-Finden, Michael Arne's tune seemed recherché, even highbrow. Waller may well have learnt it not at his previous school but at home, where elements of an intellectual life style existed. His father was a commercial artist: his connections with the local newspaper probably helped Waller in due time to secure work on it as a cub reporter. His mother was a pretty woman, domestically capable; her moral fibre indicated by her approval of an upright stance.

Waller did not stay long at Seafolde House; was sent to be a boarder at some grammar school, I think with Quaker associations. Perhaps his parents had become rather more affluent, or had foreseen Seafolde House's decline, not an impossible piece of prognostication. My brother claims to know a precipitating reason. It seems that a senior boy called Wetton had punched Waller. Later, Waller's father came into the school playground and asked a boy to point Wetton out, which the boy was able to do, Wetton being a famous character, centre half in the school XI, a good off-spin bowler, a sharp dresser, and with sleeked-back yellow hair. Mr Waller then went over and punched Wetton, presumably with some words of explanation. The story need not be doubted, for Wetton was no stranger to violence, and Waller would certainly attract it.

During the rest of our mutual schooldays Waller and I were only tenuously in touch, yet when, after two years or so as a solicitor's articled clerk, I went to London for a couple of months at a law crammer's to prepare for the Law Society's Intermediate

Examination, I encountered Waller once more. His parents may well have recommended the digs in Guildford Street to which I went, for Waller was then, or had recently been, living in them – more likely the latter because of the feud to be mentioned later; also I do not remember being in the place with him. However, recall of the time is utterly patchy. As in the Blackpool boarding houses lived in during boyhood, I must have come across noteworthy characters in Guilford Street, but all have faded. My brother says I told him of a fellow lodger who at the time impressed himself on me. "There, can't you hear it?" he said to me. "What?" "The pigs' wireless." Enquiries as to my reception of this service took place on a few occasions, presumably over breakfast, the only communal activity; my answers always disappointing.

Waller's career as a provincial reporter had been interrupted to take a year's course in journalism at London University. Perhaps the first instance, in London at any rate, of his prevailing on me to do something foreign to my nature was his illegal invitation, knowing of my interest in the subject, to attend a lecture or seminar, part of the English Literature strand of his course, at University College. He had a proprietorial pride in the quality of these lectures; assured me I should without question be taken for a member of the course. The lecturer was J. Isaacs, later, if not then, a well-known academic. Discussion was encouraged after Isaacs' remarks: typical of my character that having gone into the lecture room with apprehension I should then argue, in the testy manner I already evinced on such collective occasions, with the lecturer. Our point of difference was my maintaining, against his dictum, that any worthwhile literary criticism was bound to be a matter of personal judgement not the application of formal principles. Needless to say, I did not appreciate the nuances of this controversy (which still goes on!); my stance being based on commonsense and the conviction, derived from D. H. Lawrence, of the primacy of gut feeling. Waller sat next to me with the smug satisfaction of one who, carrying a swordstick, sees an Alsatian dog making a leap for him; an image less outré than might at first appear. Also, he had the true journalist's delight in rows, however mild or minor, coupled with the power sometimes to foment them.

His Diploma in Journalism, or whatever it was, acquired, he never returned to the *West Lancashire Evening Gazette*, but got a job, perhaps the editor's, on a rag called *The Holborn Gazette*, and later lived perilously on linage (that is, being paid, per line, only for stories actually printed) for the *Daily Express*. With merely a touch or two the boy soprano had transformed himself into a somewhat transatlantic idea of a journalist: a trenchcoat almost invariably worn; either no hat or a trilby with a brim turned down all the way round; cigarette in a holder; a hint of sideburns. It must be added that in the end he did become a regular reporter on the *Express*, and in its palmiest days. He would not necessarily have awaited that status before behaving in the manner appropriate to it. He may well have still been merely on linage when he took me over to sit down to drink with the great foreign correspondent Sefton Delmer in the Fleet Street Henekey's. And in due time even the transatlantic manner was justified.

During my London sojourns as an articled clerk I saw a good deal of Waller. In retrospect, that seems strange. Intellectually we had little in common, but he did introduce me to the records of such as Duke Ellington, Louis Armstrong, Joe Venuti, some of which (mainly the more *cantible*, less frenetic parts) I liked a great deal. I think it wouldn't be unfair to say that his cultural grasp was journalistic – referring to Hemingway or Epstein, say, with plausible knowledgeableness. His way of life (though, as will be seen, the normality of his origins asserted itself in the end) had successive peaks of the bizarre, though the troughs of his existence were outlandish enough. In one of his bad economic spells, for instance – hanging on to Fleet Street, to a life in London at all, by his eyebrows – his main meal at the café in Marchmont Street we used a lot was almost invariably tea and an "individual" syrup sponge, a far cry from his mother's cuisine.

Probably it would be early evening. He would enter the café, trenchcoat open, the *Evening Standard* in hand (no doubt a walking stick as well), push his spectacles up with a forefinger, say to the man behind the counter: "Cupper tea and a golden pudding, Charley." The pronunciation thus of "cup of" seemed to acknowledge a life-giving or life-enhancing quality in the article referred to, something universal yet specially therapeutic – rather like the *Daily Express* of those days (the *Standard* was much more highbrow), which had a common enough touch to attract an enormous readership though its style was arguably a mere front for something almost sophisticated and cynical. A few of its contributors seemed self-consciously pastoral, like the cartoonist Strube with his character of the "Little Man", perhaps anticipating (though less odious than) Chaplin's use of the term "the Little Fellow" in the commentaries added to the reissue of his silent films.

Charley, the proprietor of the café was Spanish; provided good food at amazingly modest prices. The golden pudding was one of a number of concessions made in those pre-mass-foreign-travel days to English taste. The cheapness of the delicacy (probably 3d, not more) and its satisfying quality were sufficient reasons for Waller's choice, yet allied to the tea it reflected or symbolized something in his being, fundamental yet hard to put a name to.

But Waller often expressed himself in more spectacular ways. Once he bought sneezing powder from the joke-shop in New Oxford Street. The strategy for its use was that he and I should go separately into pubs and disseminate it to the discomfort of the drinkers – separately, so as to be less likely to fall under suspicion. Before our entries, the powder was sprinkled into the middle pages of Waller's *Evening Standard* and the newspaper then folded. At the bar, a half-pint ordered (usually mild, sometimes in public bars as cheap as 2½d), one or other of us would open the paper and, after a mock perusal of, say, Arnold Bennett's weekly books article, feign a sneeze, thus wafting the powder towards the nearby bar-flies.

The wheeze (the vocabulary of *The Magnet* or *The Gem*, magazines of our Seafolde House schooldays, comes appropriately to mind) actually worked, though a few hard looks were bent in our direction, perhaps our youth a tell-tale sign in those quiet pubs down the Gray's Inn Road which at that early time of evening were patronized only by a few lingering craftsmen and the elderly proletarians of the quarter. Leaving, after a staggered interval to put the sneezers off the scent, as it were, as well as to enable us to savour the jest, Waller would positively chortle on the way to the next pub. "Did you see his pipe actually fall out of his mouth?" I recall him saying, apropos one victim assailed by an unanticipated sternutation.

A final example of Waller's mania may be given. He had left the digs I was in, at enmity with the landlady and her spinster daughter. There is no reason to suppose he felt robbed or oppressed: more likely some louche behaviour of his promoted the antagonism. In any case, he had found a softer bed with a younger landlady, a grass widow, a few doors away. His entrée to his former digs possible through my own occupation, he conceived a campaign of revenge for real or imagined slights. On the penultimate day of my two-months' stay he hid a kipper behind one of the pictures in the dining-room; concealed, too, a depilatory substance called "Veet" which he claimed had also an objectionable smell. It was characteristic of his journalistic style, closely adapted to the requirements of the *Daily Express* of the time (perhaps perennially demanded of the popular journalist), that, as he told me, he later called at the digs on some pretext, maybe actually penetrating to the dining room – at any rate claiming to have experienced the miasma in the house resulting from his concealments, and reflected in what he alleged were the haggard, haunted looks of the landlady. Those able to hear the pigs' wireless may have believed that broadcasting authority responsible. I should say, speaking of mania, that the walking stick carried by Waller was a swordstick, bought from the famous walking stick and umbrella shop near the joke-shop he patronized, and with which, he said as confidently as he sang, he had once stabbed to the heart an Alsatian dog that had injudiciously sprung at him.

It would seem Waller had become a regular *Express* reporter by the time of my second London stay, for I accompanied him on two jaunts which would scarcely have been assigned to one merely on linage. The first was an attempt to interview Winston Churchill's daughter, Sarah, in the news because of her matrimonial affairs. She opened the door to her flat – we glimpsed Titian hair, a transparent complexion, a fine ankle – and smiled a couple of virtual "no comments", and closed it. When the story appeared I was astonished at Waller's resource in putting his own questions into the interviewee's mouth, as well as her own negatives, so enabling a few inches to be devoted to what had been an utter non-event.

On the other outing, Waller proposed to photograph a corpse, or, rather, have a corpse photographed by an *Express* photographer. The plot had been hatched before the evening in question. A young man had died in circumstances rumoured to be suspicious; perhaps poisoned by someone who wanted him out of the way. Even in those days, when some popular newspapers could assume a readership rather than a viewership, there was a premium on pictures, but one of the deceased did not seem to exist. Had Waller read in American journalistic annals – perhaps on his London University course – of the cadaver-photo ploy? It may well have been so. The mortuary keeper, or the relevant assistant (nominally a Shakespearean character, but his personality has not come down), had been squared (the amount of the bribe a mere two or three pounds), and we were admitted, out of office hours, so to speak, to institutional premises somewhere in North London. We had waited in a nearby pub till the time of assignation, and I at least had taken care to have a few whiskies to insulate me from any grisliness to come, rather like swallowing a seasickness remedy in a high wind at the quayside.

The nude corpse was wheeled out of refrigeration on a trolley, appropriately covered at first by the striped material of a butcher's apron. Emaciation emphasized the bony arch from which the pathetic genitals depended; red lines, like those indicating cuts of meat in a cookery book, showed the autopsy had already taken place. The eyelids were drooping but sufficiently open: Waller attempted to comb the tangled hair but it started to come out in the comb's teeth. My task was to prop up the head to enable the photograph to be taken. My brother remembers that I told him I used a hammer for the purpose. Slightly mysterious how it came to be available, but the idea that I would be too fearsome to touch the body must be right since even now I prefer to interpose a spade between my hands and a dead bird. The photograph was duly printed, I think with some faking of a collar and tie; not too bizarre to those who had no reason to imagine it as otherwise from life. Almost simultaneously, the inquest, or adjourned inquest, discovered the death had been due to natural causes, so the story also died.

For occasions such as these Waller introduced me, when necessary, as from "the AP", which he said was the American equivalent of the PA, the initials providing credentials difficult immediately to verify. Similarly on a later occasion, when showing us over the *Express*, he introduced my future wife as "the sob-sister" on the *West Lancashire Evening Gazette*, though in fact she was the editor's secretary. Thus was one drawn at a stroke into Waller's world of instant and enduring fancy.

In the early days Waller's great friend in London was Alec Marston. It may well have been Marston who put him on to such discs as Armstrong's "I'm a ding dong Daddy" and Ellington's "Hot and Bothered", a far cry from "The Lass with a Delicate Air". Marston played jazz piano and, I think, attempted the clarinet, though I am maybe confusing that instrument with the black, silver-knobbed walking stick he usually carried at this epoch. Marston was tallish, pale, hair brushed straight back; quite a look of the comedian Sid Field – eyes even at that early age slightly poached. The walking stick was a typical strand in his faintly seedy elegance, more than a touch of the Dick Swivellers – another being a black evening bowtie converted to day wear. He worked in an advertising agency: I think really was a copywriter though hardly out of his teens, if that. Jazz was an amateur pursuit, but after the war he wrote some numbers for revues presented in a more or less low dive in Irving Street.

I knew Marston already. The coincidence was not so great as might appear, for he was from Blackpool; must have come to be friendly with Waller through that connection, rather like the protagonists of "If You're Going Back to Dixie". My own contact with Marston arose in an even earlier epoch, at our kindergarten, in fact, Northlands High School, where he had stood out as a knowing and articulate infant, plump in the school's male uniform of white jersey, black-and-white horizontally-striped tie. After kindergarten our ways had parted, though my wife-to-be had known him in his later schooldays, also noting his confidence in worldly matters. Now the plumpness had vanished: the *savoir faire* and gift of the gab remained.

I fancy Marston, though his lifestyle was far from conventional, was less positively eccentric than Waller. He would have taken sneezing powder and concealed kippers as everyday matters, if not going so far as to deal in them himself. It may have been Marston rather than Waller who introduced me to a set of characters hanging about Soho cafés, particularly the Café Bleu in Old Compton Street, later to go up in the world but then a shabby establishment where a great swatch of time might be spent over a coffee without challenge from the management. Occasionally in those purlieus one brushed against the modestly known, the modestly notorious, though if pressed for instances of the latter I could come up only with Ironfoot Jack, recalled recently by Anthony Powell's autobiography where though not named, he is accurately described as:

> a man with a broadbrimmed black hat, long black coat, got up to look perhaps like The Sheriff in a Western. This effect,

> if aimed at, was diminished by one of his legs being shorter than the other, the short leg terminating in an appliance that looked rather like an iron door-scraper.

Anthony Powell goes on to give a good example of his characteristic permanent irascibility. He was the subject of an article in the *Evening Standard*, and later of a book, whether biography or autobiography I forget.

Though I liked Soho, I saw that those of its denizens I knew were failures, perhaps permanently in that category, in which I did not put myself despite utter lack of literary success. I used to wonder, as the hours slipped away in the Bleu, just when the painters painted and the writers wrote, though the same question applied to me with even greater point. A fair slice of my days was spent at lectures at the law tutors, and the rest of it (the evenings, too, come to that) should have been devoted to reading for them. But I studied as spasmodically as I wrote verse or fiction. I was blessed (or cursed) with a brain usually capable of rapid comprehension of the printed word, and a dislike of not getting to the bottom of anything imparted by way of instruction. Instead of laying the foundation for becoming a really learned lawyer or prolific littérateur, I would listen to Red Nichols on the portable gramophone borrowed from Waller, or play the pin-table in Charley's.

The pin-table, incidentally, was nothing like the light-flashing, bell-ringing, vulgarly decorated and high-scoring machines of later years: it resembled more the old-fashioned Corinthian bagatelle board, and accurately judging the amount of pull-back required on the spring-loaded propelling piston could lead not only to getting the balls in the holes but also to getting a ball in the hole of its own colour, which then doubled the score for that particular hole, a refinement that added much interest. Charley offered twenty Players (then priced 11½d) if a certain score were attained or exceeded, and since only 1d was required to release the balls for play the odds were generous to those sacrificing their careers to become adept at the game. "What you want now is the double yellow," one would remark, as Waller, trenchcoat open, swordstick handle hooked on the glass top of the pin-table, pushed up his spectacles, and cautiously inched back the piston, risking his golden pudding. I say that, but at one period we were warned off the table by Charley for, he said, winning so many packets of Players as to hazard its profitability. It seems to me now that this ban may have been imposed less for the reason given than from Charley's irritation at being called from his steaming urn and other occupations behind the counter to check at the pin-table face that a winning score had been achieved, a nuisance exacerbated by Waller's manner of doing it (and he would also summon Charley when I was successful). The blank, owlish stare was belied by the complacent chortle in some such cry as: "Charley, Charley – another packet."

My two periods in London during my five years' articles, each for a two months' spell at the law tutors, Gibson and Weldon in Chancery Lane, were immediately before the Law Society's Intermediate Examination held in March 1931 and the Final in November 1933. As already made plain, the two periods have become in some degree conflated in my memory, though as I think about them I see they could be pretty well sorted out, probably with more explanation than they could bear, however.

London had previously been only the subject of a few brief visits, but I was soon on terms with it in 1931, at least the Soho, Bloomsbury, Chancery Lane axis; using the Underground a good deal. One stepped off the escalator with studied nonchalance; rather less easy to do than nowadays, since many escalators terminated not in the stair intermeshing with the floor and parallel to it, but in an oblique arrangement that required a positive alighting from the moving part. Down the subways one followed the appropriate colour of the guiding lights out of the corner of one's eye so as to conceal unfamiliarity. The subterranean wind seemed stronger, grittier, hotter, more aromatic in those days. No doubt one's hair was more unkempt, garments looser, flesh more sensitive. At Russell Square, the home station, a lift brought you up to seasons always milder than those of the North-West, an effect enhanced by the frequent presence in the lift and the streets round about of studious Indians and Orientals. Doubling back along that curious part of Herbrand Street, almost a back alley (in which, nevertheless there was a pub, rather dim but occasionally visited), the straight macadam of Guilford Street was soon seen shining in the night rain. Or I might go direct to Charley's. Marchmont Street's modest shops and pubs (which in those days were still extant at the Bernard Street end, now ruined by foolish development), some of their habitués becoming familiar, offered almost a village ambience.

Of my remembered experiences, I expect the more naïve belong to the earlier stay, the more political to the later. As to the former, I once passed two respectable young girls in Southampton Row. Said one to the other, apropos an individual walking somewhat in front of me: "Just listen to that old man farting." The remark amended my innocent conception of the feminine. I often walked to Chancery Lane, usually via Lamb's Conduit Street and Red Lion Street, in the latter probably lingering at Charlie Lahr's bookshop. There were second-hand bookshops, too, in Chancery Lane, before one reached Gibson and Weldon's premises, No 27, though most were of the legal variety, regarded by me typically as boring.

Another axis (it just occurs to me) was partly formed by the Kingsway Tramway Subway, euphonious combination Marston, with his musical ear, liked to have on his lips. Did the tram come along Theobalds Road? Certainly it could be boarded at the top of Kingsway, and it then quite soon went below ground, emerging on the Embankment. There was at least one intermediate stop, round about Sardinia Street, involving (if, against the odds, one found it convenient to use) Piranesi-like staircases to the nether regions; regions now, of course, a one-way underpass for motor cars from Waterloo Bridge to Holborn.

Though I occasionally used the Kingsway Tramway Subway with Waller and Marston, I expect on some pub crawl, it was the mode of my getting, alone, to the Old Vic, where I was quite a regular patron of the gallery, less frequently the more expensive pit. Five pence (old money) was the price of the ordinary doors gallery seat, that being a not overgenerous length of backless, scrubbed, wooden bench, good preparation for the seating later normally supplied by the Navy. The early doors price, a few coppers more, usually ensured a seat on the front row or, preferably, the second, so as to avoid the brass rail along the gallery parapet spoiling one's line of sight. Opera and plays alternated, but whatever the programme the gallery held a fair proportion of local residents, some regulars, or otherwise known to each other, a few of proletarian eccentricity – an extension of the life of the market stalls in The Cut and Lower Marsh. The ambience, that quite short tram ride from the West End, took me back to Oldham days.

That the cultural aspirations of the poor, or not over well-off, paralleled what came more easily to the affluent seemed to me perfectly natural. Questions of élitism, of hating "bourgeois" culture, of a special brand of drama or poetry for the working class did not arise; and even in later, Marxist days I imagined culture being desirably broadened as much by increased mass leisure and prosperity as by new forms and attitudes. Cruder (indeed, sillier) art for the "community" would have been a complete puzzlement. In Oldham, passing Garside Fold, as I often did as a boy – a court or little square of terraced cottages (by then a slum) characteristic of the housing accompanying factory building, a sort of secular cloisters – seeing the bare-footed and pantsless children, the slatternly women, I thought merely jobs with decent wages were required to bring learning as well as cleanliness into the deprived lives so painfully on view. Though there was an enigma that if the children were to stand eating jam "butties" at unseasonable hours, their parents ought to be able also to afford a cake of soap – even of "Monkey Brand" – I never doubted toiling humanity's essential goodness, its innate wish for advancement. That the latter was widespread among the lower classes was demonstrated, one might add, by conversations had and overheard during the ensuing war.

To return to the anarchist bookseller and publisher Charlie Lahr, I was reminded of him not long ago by an excellent article by David Goodway in the *London Magazine* (Vol. 17, No. 2). Lahr's Red Lion Street shop had no glass on the outside, so that the books could be handled from the street. Putting a volume back on a shelf on one occasion, I accidentally pushed a few of its neighbours into the shop. Lahr, talking to a friend or customer inside, said in a voice I clearly heard: "What the hell's happening?" They were words that embarrassed me greatly, and whose impersonal complaint struck me as so effective that I have used the formula myself when the time might not have quite arrived for direct verbal attack on some trespasser to one's person or property. Lahr could see me through the gap between books and shelves, enlarged through my depredations, and I imagined myself for ever stigmatized in his view as a careless nitwit. In an instant he had picked up the dislodged books, so there was nothing remedial I could do. I related this incident in a letter printed in a succeeding number of the *London Magazine*, and placed it, because of the feeling involved, in 1931, when I was nineteen, and gave 1933 as the time when I submitted two essays to Lahr for publication in his Blue Moon booklet series. It seems to me now the book-pushing episode could quite well have happened in 1933, for it was many a long year into manhood before I was able to cover up my gaucheries with a decent degree of charm and apology. The essays, too, may have been of a vintage slightly later than originally given, for they were full of gobbets of raw Marxism. But a letter came back from Lahr in which he said: "I would publish them if I wasn't broke." Bitter-sweet words! I had published scarcely anything at that date, was madly keen to do so, and his response was one of the few positive ones I had ever had to my numerous submissions.

Like other characters quite often to be seen about, such as Ironfoot Jack and a young right-wing poet in a red cloak with hair down his back who called himself, possibly with justification, Count Geoffrey Potocki de Montalk, Charlie Lahr had achieved a degree of fame or notoriety. He used to pass on his bicycle, his feet in sandals in all weathers, a strange feature being that his big-toe nails were small and embedded in ample surrounding cushions of flesh. Not until I went to Africa during the war, and saw the big-toes on display there, did I realize that this was a result of going shoeless.

I had a strong wish to gaze on the admired and famous, no doubt a pretty universal trait, but surely most marked in the restless provincial. At this epoch I once saw Aldous Huxley in St James's Square (possibly coming from the London Library, I realize now), and followed him into Straker's, a stationer's in the Haymarket, long vanished. There he picked up from the counter, the more closely to examine it, a grotesquely large cardboard model of a lead-pencil tip, made for advertising display purposes. For some time after, I scanned his work for mention of this, a typical image of his earlier writing, not really kept up, alas. He was wearing a nice tweed suit, a plain orange tie (not then to be found in ordinary shops), and carrying a copy of the Phoenix Library edition (cheap hardback) of *Crome Yellow*, needless identification, for despite the absence of TV, still to be made available if not actually invented, he was immediately recognizable. I myself bought nothing in Straker's: probably, if accosted by an assistant, went out with some slight mime, convincing to myself, of having left my wallet at home or of being taken short – needless elaborations of the shy.

Of course, a different world was entered stepping into 27 Chancery Lane. Gibson and Weldon had started as an ordinary firm of solicitors, taken on law tutoring for articled clerks perhaps as an adjunct to its London agency work for provincial firms, then found the tutoring side grow to become virtually a separate enterprise. The cramming was carried on with great skill, the two-months' course a swift but intensive revision of the entire syllabus, culminating, just before the examination, in a test under examination conditions. The results of this were posted – dread proclamation! – the course members bracketed in such categories as "Will pass", "May pass", and ending with a few varying degrees of hopelessness, speculating on divine intervention and suchlike facetiae.

The lecturers were solicitors: most had been in ordinary practice; all were adept at forecasting the examination questions. One of them, L. Crispin Warmington, some elderly solicitors will still remember. Like Aldous Huxley, he wore tweeds and a soft collar, but was plump, not etiolated. He lectured on tort, perhaps contract as well, in a relaxed and extremely leisurely style, making a good few, funny jokes. "I am strolling in my garden in Esher before dinner," he would begin, retailing some circumstantial details not of strict relevance. Then a bough from a neighbour's tree falls on his head, or noxious fumes drift in from other property. The picture conjured up (particularly by the susurrating syllables "Esher", a place known by name but never visited, Warmington's utterance throwing new light on their pronunciation) was of a gracious way of life, far from that implied by a Blackpool clientèle of "spec" builders and boarding-house landladies. According to R. H. Kersley, a fellow lecturer, Warmington's humour became so elaborate in later years that additional lectures had to be squeezed in to fill the gaps.

Normally, the nomenclature of the land, in fictional examples illustrating the law relating to it, was Blackacre and Whiteacre (the connotation of great estates perhaps a hangover from days when small owners of freeholds were less common). Two names were usually enough – in relation to rights and obligations annexed to the property, for instance – though a Greenacre might sometimes have to be imported. I believe it was Warmington, moving away from his Surrey neighbours, who introduced such exotica as Purpleacre, a usage I took up eagerly in answering test questions, even examination questions; proceeding straight to such concepts as Puceacre without first exhausting the restrained palette, a good example of the pointless show-off side of my nature, also illustrated by my choice of pseudonyms for labelling test papers – Panurge, Stephen Dedalus, and the like. The American film actor, Edward Everett Horton, called his Californian estate Belly Acres, a jest I would certainly have taken as mine had I known of it then.

There had, of course, been more or less boring codifications, such as the Sale of Goods Act and the Bills of Exchange Act, but it seems in retrospect that the subjects of my student days were still dominated by the common law, the great leading cases about the escape from property of dangerous substances; snails in ginger-beer bottles; advertisements guaranteeing the efficacy of influenza remedies. Though I came into the law at an awkward moment so far as real property was concerned, the old law having to be learnt as well as the 1925 property statutes, by comparison with later developments I enjoyed the last glow of a golden age. Parliament had not yet become maniacal in its statute-making activities; the war had still to come that was to give such an amazing fillip to government by statutory rules and orders (already the subject of foreboding by some who had found sinister the comparatively modest effects in that area of the 1914–18 war). Before my call-up in April 1941, I was already used to a mass of law being contained in pages ever-changing (but ever-accumulating) between loose-leaf binders. For the Law Society's examinations in the early Thirties, books could be safely read in editions of leisurely obsolescence, and certain fluid topics, like tax law, were actually excluded from the syllabus. Nevertheless, the examinations were a burden, notorious obstacles, flooring quite a few who aspired to be solicitors, some of them condemned to an unqualified (and even embittered) life in the law. The failure rate in the Intermediate could exceed 40%; for the Final not greatly less – so even placed in the "Will pass" category, as I was on both occasions, anxiety persisted until the results came through. Towards the end of my articles I resolved never again to study for an examination, being cheesed-off with the unceasing routine that had started with the Oxford Junior Locals (the "O-levels" of the time) some seven years before. Little did I imagine that as I turned into my thirties I should once again spend long months being examined in fields of learning to which I was fundamentally indifferent.

The question arises here, like confining one's running prowess to contests over short distances (and as it might in some celestial school report), as to lack of energy, application, genius. For the Law Society's Final the Honours papers were separate, taken a week after the Pass examination. I had decided initially Honours were beyond the notch I was prepared to stretch myself to; had no enthusiasm, anyway, to sit for them: besides, I was reluctant to be longer parted, even for a week, from my wife-to-be. But it was borne in on me that most of the finalists studying at Gibson's were dimmer than I, a lesson somehow not carried over from the Intermediate course, or other events in my life where such comparisons were possible. Eventually I went to some authority at Gibson's (I expect with inward quaking and after much courage-screwing) to try to enter for the Honours examination after all, but it was too late, even to pay the late fee. Acquisition of Honours meant nothing in the business of being a solicitor, but might have told when it came to seeking jobs – and therefore changed my life.

Anxiety to reach another, happier state of existence (such as being united with the loved one) raises another perhaps more universal question; namely, the characteristic life possesses of compelling one to waste it. Or, if that is putting the thing in terms too extreme, the sense at almost every stage of life that the present is a mere preliminary to true happiness or fulfilment, a time to be passed, occasionally stoically endured or frittered away. I advanced this business in a poem once – man's squandering of his most precious substance – but have failed to turn up the lines. It was acutest during the war, as I shall come to again, but it showed its power during my two London sojourns. Indeed, it could be said that the purgatorial state of being an articled clerk (and a schoolboy, too, for that matter) was designed to keep one's eye on some Nirvana ahead, no doubt a ploy of the bourgeois ethic and the strategy of its dominance. The matter was well put in a song of the day, though the singer perhaps places the emphasis on his own misfortunes or deficiencies:

> My life is only a vamp till ready,
> I've played the long introduction thro'.
> How much longer must I wait
> For the orchestral leader to give me the cue?

This excellent song was made familiar to me, I think in the period immediately following my Final, by Marston, who sang it both away from and at the piano. The words were by Clark Gibson, a forgotten name now; the music by Fred Elizalde, a remarkable musician who needs, I believe I am right in saying, to be rediscovered. Marston may not have known that Elizalde was also a composer of "classical" works, including a violin concerto, but it would be unfair not to credit him with a considerable nose for the good and the unusual. It did not need him to introduce me to the music-hall, but he revealed that one could stand at the rear and sides of the stalls (probably the dress circle, too) at the Holborn Empire for half-a-crown, may have been two shillings. Obliquely across the great, gently sloping upland of heads and shoulders I see in my mind's eye the figure of Billy Bennett ("Almost a gentleman" the subtitle of his billing) in tails, with a dicky apt to curl up and escape from his low-cut waistcoat; hair in a quiff – perhaps not awfully unlike in appearance and attitudes his namesake Arnold, risen rather more convincingly from the petty bourgeoisie. I recently came across a specimen of the rhyming couplets recited by Billy Bennett as the climax of his act, and wish I had copied them out: still funny, they seemed to me, and anticipating by a few years the surrealism that was to appeal quite a lot to English intellectuals when it crossed the Channel. His patter usually had to do with physical deformities of family and friends, like that of the contemporary comedian Les Dawson. "He had a wart on the back of his neck," said Bennett, "so big he used to button his collar on it." After the war the fine comedian Jimmy Wheeler continued this appealing tradition, though his material also concerned human ailments, e.g. he goes to the doctor with a boil on his nose, which the doctor taps with a medical hammer. "Does that hurt?" "Yes." "I thought it would."

It was sometimes possible at the Holborn Empire, though having only paid the standing charge, surreptitiously to occupy a vacant seat, in my case with guilty unease. The trespass was safest after the main turn in the second half, when some seat-holders left for good. What probably remained to be seen in sudden comfort was an acrobatic or juggling act, perhaps two men who called themselves the Haekenschmidt Brothers (or Twins), the climax of whose performance was to wrestle in slow motion, the snail's pace of the convolutions involving enormous but unostentatious strength, the cinema illusion enhanced by the pair being lit only by a flickering spot. I sometimes wonder if I saw at that time two tap-dancers, man and wife, regulars at the Lewisham Hippodrome and New Cross Empire after the war, when certainly they were getting on in years. Come to think of it, though, they were more an opening than a closing turn. The climax of *their* act was the man assuming a succession of characters while still dancing. Truth to tell, the differentiation was not great, a drawback countered by the nature of the characterization being announced before being carried out. Some of these phrases became family sayings; one of them, "Old man crossing the road", once used when driving in the car, now getting fresh laughs through its personal pedestrian application.

Neither Marston nor Waller lasted the pace in London. (No boast is implied about my own toughness. I had one of my tonsillitis attacks, and my mother came down, worried about me. I had moved into an attic room, I think at Waller's suggestion as being a great bargain – perhaps it had been occupied by him before his feud with the landlady. The small saving in money was scarcely relevant, though probably the sloping ceilings, and commodiousness, appealed to me. On seeing it, my mother was appalled: far from finding it agreeably reminiscent of *La Bohème*, she described it to my brother as being like the *mise-en-scène* of *The Rat*, a play and film of the age in which Ivor Novello played the eponymous hero or villain, an Apache, in the hooligan of Paris sense). Waller contracted TB; Marston some less definable ailment. Against the odds, the latter returned to the family house in Blackpool, worked in his father's business.

Councillor Marston was a genial man, steel-grey hair greased and brushed back, a cigarette ever between his lips – which nevertheless did not prevent him from being as talkative as his younger son. The elder son had already married, left home, though I got to know him slightly, even playing bridge with him, as did my brother. He lacked his brother's self-confidence, his character indicated by words he often employed when embarking on trying to make his contract at the bridge table, as my brother soon pointed out to me: "This is insuperably difficult, partner" – another phrase that passed into *coterie-sprache*. His wife was good-looking, though (to be ungallant) not so good-looking as her younger sister, chiselled-featured, pale-blue-eyed, with whom Marston himelf was then involved. This girl had long been noted by the articled clerks at Wylie Kay's, for she worked nearby. On meeting Marston again, in his Blackpool milieu, it was initially an agreeable if tantalizing frisson, rather like standing next to Aldous Huxley in Straker's, to find myself cutting the cards for her.

The Marston house was an ordinary modern suburban house, though commodious, even running to a room that housed a half-size billiards table. The passage to the room was impeded by a number of large cardboard cartons, which proved to contain packets of Kensitas cigarettes, bought by Councillor Marston wholesale, though I suspect his motivation was less the saving of money than having at hand a store of fuel for his inordinate consumption, plus the pleasure of accumulating, in advance thereof, the gift coupons then to be found in Kensitas packets. I sometimes accepted a Kensitas from Councillor Marston, but marvelled at anyone smoking the things, even allowing for the gifts. My own taste, moving from my mother's Craven A through such exotica as Abdulla brownpaper Russian blend and Wills's oval, though Virginia, Passing Cloud, had probably already settled down with Player's Gold Leaf, then untipped, sold in tin boxes containing twenty-four cigarettes at 1s. 5d., coffin nails of real excellence.

There was a free and easy air in the Marston house, despite the domestic bind to be mentioned. Marston's quick, if not profound, grasp of public issues enabled him to trade opinions with his father on local as well as national affairs. The Councillor was by no means averse to skirting the cartons and having a game of fifty up, a performer in the adroit family class – a Gaev. Pots of tea, sometimes food, were to be had at irregular times, and late hours were kept – a bridge four of Marston and his girl, me and my future wife, once going on, at Marston's persuasion, till dawn; debauched life for our kind of provincial society, though only tea was drunk. Marston's mother occasionally appeared, to be typically treated by him with ostentatious endearments (not precluding genuine affection, however), disarming (though not necessarily designed to do so) any outsider suspecting strains in the household. Was Mrs Marston on the bottle, or a touch like the receiver of the pigs' broadcasts? At any rate, her vagueness and largely off-stage existence were useful years later when I had to invent a wife for the villain of *The Second Curtain*.

It was not unknown in the town that Councillor Marston was

involved with another lady; visited her at her house. One evening, a good deal later than the marathon bridge-playing period, I saw him across a hotel lounge, too far away to be obliged to greet him. He was sitting at a table with a person in a fur coat. My companion told me this was the lady of the long-standing liaison. In those days of my still essentially romantic view of life, I was amazed: the lady was far from young, and less superficially attractive than Mrs Marston. Going from wife to mistress – it was like the gag of the comedian Michael Bentine when his black hair was particularly upstanding. "Don't worry about my hair," he would advise the audience, "it's only a wig." And to prove it he would indeed remove a wig, only to reveal his own equally, if not more, abundant hair beneath.

Waller's TB merely punctuated his London life: he returned to Blackpool to live not until some years after the war; an even more surprising example of the Dixie syndrome. I had the details of his illness only in retrospect, being out of touch with him at the critical time. The case was grave, involving at one stage an artificial pneumothorax, which nevertheless did not allow the infected lung to heal. Needless to say, Waller personalized the disease in characteristic manner. He said once he woke out of a doze in hospital to find a clergyman at his bedside, perhaps even muttering some *nunc dimittis* over him. For the first time, he realized his death was anticipated, resolved there and then to postpone that fate; as an initial step telling the cleric to bugger off. A quack remedy for consumption called UMKALAOBO had been achieving publicity for its efficiency, perhaps in the *Daily Express*, despite the connotation of witch-doctoring in its name. It was the invention of Major C. H. Stevens, who inspired the creation by H. G. Wells of Tono-Bungay and its originator in the eponymous novel. Waller commanded his parents to obtain a supply, took it as directed, and was quite rapidly cured. It may be that his old faith in the power of the human body to dispel unsuitable invaders helped the process.

2 *The Loose Group*

In the train on my way back to Blackpool after my first spell at Gibson and Weldon's in 1931, passing along the side corridor, I saw in a compartment some prominent members of the New Party, then recently founded by Sir Oswald Mosley after his break from the Labour Party, that being prompted by frustration at the impotence of its policies about unemployment and so forth. I lingered outside the compartment, in the manner of my sleuthing of Aldous Huxley. Eventually, Harold Nicolson emerged. Somehow the opportunity came for me to tell him I had been at the Party's big meeting of a few days before, when Lady Cynthia Mosley (as I had written in a letter or lost journal: the awful phrase unforgotten) had "bared her bosom to the mob", a reference to the slightly low-cut black dress worn by the attractive speaker and the heckling by the left-wing slice of the audience. The meeting could well have been that actually launching the New Party, which Sir Oswald could not attend through illness, and from which W. J. Brown apparently ratted.

In the first volume of Harold Nicolson's *Diaries and Letters* there is an entry about his going by train to Manchester on 27 April, but I feel my brief encounter was earlier than this, some time in March. I can't recall what, if any, item of political news or wisdom was imparted by Nicolson, but he did momentarily pinch my sleeveless pullover (worn under a jacket) between finger and thumb, and say: "I like your sweater." It was in fact unusual for those days, being red – a nineteenth birthday present from my wife-to-be, who had searched for it long and far. Of course, I knew Nicolson was married to Victoria Sackville-West and guessed of his preferred sexual proclivities no more than any other member of the public, even after his display of interest in a young man's garb – after which, I may say, he soon passed on. Though as I write these words it occurs to me for the first time that his coming out of the compartment at all may have been motivated by my presence in the corridor; behaviour prompted by the chance of erotic adventure being as foolish as that prompted by the chance of charismatic encounter.

I was so politically green that though I saw the Labour Party might not be best pleased at the defection of one of its most prominent members, I could not understand the fury of the left opposition to Mosley's New Party. Its dynamic had rapid consequences, however. My own disillusionment came when, quite soon, the Party gave birth to sections with joined abbreviations or, perhaps, acronyms: ORGACT (as it might be: I forget the actuality – though Nicolson's book reminds me that the Party itself came to call itself NUPA). My objection was initially almost an aesthetic one, not seeing the fascist parallel; simply feeling that this patent medicine nomenclature and quasi-militarism would not do for me, nor for the English generally. No doubt the proper penny dropped quickly thereafter: certainly in a year or so NUPA had become BUF, the British Union of Fascists, and when I was in London in 1933, once again at Gibson and Weldon, the comparatively moderate heckling of the Conway Hall (or wherever that meeting I attended was) had turned into the protesting crowds outside the Mosley Rally at the Albert Hall, the hooves of the police horses sliding on the polished pavements, the fresh horse droppings bright against the dark grey. Was I with Marston on this occasion, or had he already joined commercial forces with the Councillor? Someone was with me, perhaps Waller. It was possible, to avoid the police break-up of the mob, to go farther up Kensington Gore, board a bus, and ride past the Albert Hall; the slow progress through the disorder enabling anti-fascist protestations to be shouted through the windows of the upper deck – a cowardly procedure that suited my fear of being bonked, or ridden down, by the Cossacks.

In Blackpool, between my two London sojourns, I became active in local left-wing politics, such as they were. I recall being with both Marston and Waller when I said that for my part I was ready to join the Communist Party of Great Britain. That was after Marston's return to the family house, though perhaps the cause merely his temporary ill-health. With typical enterprise he had made contact with a small discussion group that at that time met weekly in some upper room, I think of a pub. As at J. Isaacs' seminar, I actually spoke on my first attendance – some mainly D. H. Lawrentian tripe about righting social injustice by personal integrity. A man called Warnock gave out some ideas about class rule through the apparatus of police and army from Lenin's *State and Revolution.* I was immediately profoundly convinced by this theory of the State (as I was, probably a little later, about the Oedipus Complex), and started to read the Marxist classics. It shows the strength of the tide that one was in left-wing politics before one had read them to any appreciable extent.

Terry Warnock was one of the few men I have known whose views and proposals for action almost invariably seemed correct, or at any rate hard to controvert; smallish, lean, strong nose, weathered face, wide, turned-down mouth, straight black hair starting to be grey-streaked, in his forties – not utterly unlike the actor Claude Rains – he had come from the North-East, at that time blighted by unemployment. He was really an engineering fitter, but in Blackpool had to work as a labourer in the Corporation gas department. I was haunted by what he casually told me, that a day of digging trenches left him so exhausted that mental work after it was virtually impossible. He had a small socialist library on the dresser top in the kitchen, including a book by the Italian Labriola, who I suppose later in the Stalinist epoch would have been considered heretical; but most of Terry's books had come from America, cheap editions of Wobbly days. Amazing works – of Victorian confidence and *fin de siècle* sedition.

Mrs Terry (as Marston always referred to her, exercising his charm as ever in female company, most finding it agreeable) took in the odd visitor during the summer season, probably just for bed and breakfast, proving beyond doubt the advantage of their having migrated from Tyneside. She was pale, energetic, quite a match for her husband, sang in the premier local choral society. A picture returns of her arriving home after a rehearsal, dropping her score of *The Creation* (or whatever) on the kitchen table; making tea for the two or three of us who had been gassing and smoking with Terry round the aforesaid table; providing a plate of biscuits. The ambience was undoubtedly working-class, yet not far from some atmosphere of ancient days of my own – for instance, my great-aunt Polly's household, touched on in *Souvenirs*. Still, there is (or was) a gap between the petty bourgeoisie (however impoverished) and the working-class (however cultivated); made even more apparent to me in the Navy during the war.

The home of at least one other Blackpool CPGB member was

nearer to those mean dwellings glimpsed in Garside Fold in the Oldham of my boyhood – that of a hulking, slapdash young woman, with small children, where meetings sometimes took place. This must have been the setting of a poem from the notebook to be described later (in self-defence I quote no more than three lines):

> The small, crowded room, the wallpaper
> burgeoning faded roses and the table groaning
> with elbows, DAILY WORKERS, cigarette ends . . .

I was easier with the petty bourgeoisie than with the proletariat; mainly a matter of shared culture, for, man to man, personal inhibitions held sway. I wonder whether a good deal of the working-class culture celebrated by Richard Hoggart in *The Uses of Literacy* (a work of illusion, anyway) is not properly petty bourgeois culture. After the war, when the working class became relatively prosperous, it showed itself remarkably vulnerable to culture of an imposed, commercial, Tin Pan Alley kind; a result the Thirties did not anticipate.

A knotty problem of political tactics, or more enduring political attitude, was often decided by Terry cutting across argument by beginning a succinct account of the issues involved and action needed with a Lenin-like: "What is the situation, comrades?" – a phrase that removed from his awesome presence came to be used in more trivial areas of life. There was little call for demagoguery in the tiny parties of the town to the left of the Labour Party but I doubt if Terry would in any event have been effective as a rabble-rouser. Such few and faint opportunities for exercising that role were best left to the local leader of the CPGB, Ben Goodman. He was a big, dark, friendly, fluent man, working-class like Terry; attractive to women; not old, though balding; said to settle matters of party tactics not with Terry's ratiocination but as a fraction of two, in bed with a woman comrade. Ben was always solicitous (no wonder he appealed to the ladies) about the tasks I could possibly handle, given my status as embryo solicitor. I stood in the street on a few Saturdays, selling "Dailies" (*The Daily Worker*, now *The Morning Star*), but Ben was happier when I was writing for the paper, which I did once or twice about the problems of the seasonal worker, particularly as to unemployment benefit, law being much involved.

There seemed no incongruity between the large aims that had

led one into politics (internationalism, anti-fascism, protection of the Soviet Union against a renewal of the post-Revolution interventionist war, distributing work, wealth and art more equitably) and the chores and arguments of local affairs – though even that phrase is a bit too grandiose for the preoccupations then of small provincial left-wing parties. The day to day detail and atmosphere of such activities are wonderfully recaptured in Edward Upward's trilogy, *The Spiral Ascent*, though I myself lacked the sensitivity and dedication of Upward's hero, Alan Sebrill, and so never felt as truly excruciating the conflict between political work and the poetic life, virtually dropping out of politics (one cannot say painlessly, but without sleepless nights) after a few years of pretty close involvement. Moving from Blackpool, I moved also from political friends and routines, and failed to re-acquire them. Then the war came, with the inevitability of being called up, and that seemed a substitute for political action, or at any rate a salve for one's guilt at political inactivity. I suppose in a sense I suffered from the Sebrill syndrome, but it was rather subsumed in what much later I would have tagged the Wallace Stevens syndrome. The life of contemplation (a phrase, a notion, which then I shouldn't have been able even to formulate about myself; indeed, I think I picked it up from something John Lehmann wrote long afterwards) was what I was best suited for. Day to day life in society (inescapable even in a "life of contemplation", unless one takes the veil!) was, of course, dominated by my continuing occupation as a lawyer. Progress in that, like my political side, suffered from pusillanimity, weakness, lack of real interest in making a name or even money on that side of life. Eventually I found a legal job that suited such talents as I possessed, and rather late in my career I blossomed with the job – the lateness being lucky, for earlier success would have left me with even less time and élan for writing. I really recognized almost from the start that I should never abandon a "job" in favour of "writing", for I never felt the least confidence in being able to attract an audience, even for a book review. Besides, there was my native indolence, already sufficiently indicated.

About the simplest political matters I was at first totally ignorant. The mechanics of chairing a meeting – such as the proper way of putting a resolution and its amendments – caused some worry, even apropos the small friendly meeting it might befall me to have the conduct of. It would have been more to the point if L. Crispin Warmington had expatiated on these matters instead of the rule in *Rylands v. Fletcher*. What was the Trades Council, often mentioned? What were the full names of the trades unions referred to by various initials and acronyms? Classes and publications and media courses on such things then scarcely existed. I could not avoid being brought on by all I was involved in.

By the time of the General Election of 1935 I was able with outward sangfroid to chair a large meeting in the Co-operative Hall under the auspices of the local branch of the "Peace Council", a popular front organization which might have been invented for a left-winger leading a respectable bourgeois existence; in a sense was! All three candidates for the Blackpool constituency – Conservative, Liberal, Labour – had been invited by the Peace Council to come on a common platform to put their views on keeping the peace (or, rather, restoring it, for it was the time of Mussolini's invasion of Abyssinia). In the end none had dared refuse. The audience was preponderantly left. The turn-out, the heckling, the publicity, presumably advanced the cause of peace; the cause of the Peace Council, at any rate. When the proceedings terminated there was a moment of farce. The Conservative candidate, J. Roland Robinson, barrister son of a local solicitor, next to me on the platform, asked me to lead the meeting in the singing of the National Anthem. I was horrified. Such manifestation of nationalism would be a negation of the meeting's purpose; besides, what on earth would such as Terry Warnock (no doubt among the audience) think of my being involved in the patriotic cliché? On the spur of the moment I made a stilted riposte: rather characteristic, I see now – "That is not on the meeting's agenda." I wanted to imply that the other candidates might have scruples, as well as myself: it had been quite a triumph of negotiation to get them all three to appear simultaneously and to agree a procedure. Though the legal touch to this reply might be thought to have held some appeal for him, Mr Robinson did not bandy words further, but raised his voice in song, in which he was quickly joined by a sufficient number. I stood in agonized silent embarrassment.

As expected, Mr Robinson got in, and in fact represented the town until 1964 when he was appointed Governor of Bermuda, and ennobled as Lord Martonmere. One sometimes saw his by then substantial figure, surmounted by tropical-breeze-blown white plumes, in newsreels or newspaper photographs.

Contemporaneously with writing these occasionally facetious words, I have been reading Thomas Okey's *A Basketful of Memories*, published in 1930. In this autobiographical sketch, Okey looks back to the ideological side of his youth:

> It is difficult to convey to the present age the enthusiasm of the 'sixties and 'seventies of the last century for the new gospel heralded by the names of Darwin and Herbert Spencer – a feeling akin to that of religious emotion – a feeling expressed in lyric form by Thomas Hardy:
>
> In the 'seventies I was bearing in my breast,
> Penned tight,
> Certain starry thoughts that threw a magic light
> On the workhouse and the soundless hours of rest,
> In the 'seventies, aye! I bore them in my heart
> Penned tight.
>
> We felt that we were working for a "something" not ourselves that made for right thinking, a *Vita Nuova* for humanity.

This, or something like it, could be said of the early nineteen-thirties. Later in the decade spots of doubt appeared – not about internationalism or equal social opportunity, nor requiring from believers coverups or hypocrisy. It was mainly the sense that the Wordsworthian bliss had gone, that the world would have to be re-made by fallible men, rather than ideas and ideals transforming the individual as well as society.

Poems of mine began to appear in periodicals in 1934, but I think the only piece containing any straightforward political idealism is the "sections from a longer work" published in the Spring 1937 number of *New Writing*, which refers to the "smiling moustaches" of Stalin and of the then leader of the American Communist Party, Earl Browder (later in trouble, and disgraced). The phrase sticks in the mind as something one would prefer not to be on record, but there may be other, forgotten, embarrassments. Parts of the poem were influenced by Stephen Spender's long poem, *Vienna*, so may have been written in 1934 or 1935. In my first book of verse, published in January 1939 (I let this date stand for the moment) political notions are masked

– undeliberately – by surrealism, Gravesian (perhaps I should say Ridingesque) anecdote, and general obfuscation. (When printing the smiling moustaches poem, John Lehmann – I blame him not – left out what may have been the best part of the thing: some prose rather like Section III of Auden's *The Orators*).

The discussion group to which Marston took me was not utterly removed from the *mise-en-scène* of the short story, "Sunday", by Edward Upward, which appeared in the then dazzling, still fascinating, anthology *New Country* (1933). At my suggestion, my brother requested this as one of the books for a book prize he won in his last year at school in the Isle of Man. My first reading of the book may well have been of his copy, the arms of the school in gilt on the front binding, like *Fanny Hill* in brown-paper covers. The Upward story, however, ends with a prognostication rather too solemn to correspond to the Blackpool step forward. The first person narration of the story's start changes to "you" for a discussion of the force of history, and then, for the commitment to left-wing action, to the third person; the famous key sentence being: "He will go to the small club behind the Geisha Café." Quite soon the Blackpool group grew and broadened, and met in premises less conspiratorial than the original upper room.

I believe the notion of the "loose group" has its origin in the tactics of the Socialist Party of Great Britain (SPGB), to be used where political consciousness is rudimentary or ill-spread. In all events, the phrase was first heard on the lips of John Hill who, with an older man, Sammy – amazingly the passage of time has deleted his surname from remembrance – were the two sole Blackpool members of that tiny and simon-pure Marxist party. Sammy owned a snack-bar (as it may well have been called even in those days) in the part of the town patronized by the humblest visitors, hot pies and mushy peas being the kinds of item available, edible enough though the quality would probably have been deplored by Hoggart. Sammy was benevolent but unremarkable save for his beliefs. I never knew him well: I think he was rather a slave of the snack bar. John Hill became, perhaps always was, chairman of the group. The snack-bar seemed not to prevent *his* assiduous attendance. Perhaps he only helped there in the "season", or attended the group on his night off. It was an odd sensation (in spite of his theoretical association with dinners, shortly to be mentioned), going to the snack bar for the first time, to see John in professional white apron taking pies and peas to the untableclothed tables, bringing one's own order, in fact, since he was a youngish, attractive, middle-class intellectual. Alas, his day was already over, maybe had never properly dawned. In indifferent health, separated from his wife, he lived alone in mediocre digs. Because he applied his Marxism to cultural as well as economic and political matters all he had to say interested me. In early days I was struck and convinced by his delineation of the labour theory of value, using "dinner" as the unit of wages – a dinner per day being sufficient to sustain a worker and allow him to reproduce himself. "A man earns ten dinners a week . . ." It should be said that the General Election of 1935 cast him in a new, rather impressive part – temporary assistant Labour Party agent. Going into the committee rooms to address envelopes, one found him at a desk, in authority – as odd a sensation as originally discovering him as a waiter.

But really my sense of what he was, in calibre and character, has faded to a shade with the years. He was strongest in the field of music, may possibly have been a professional in some aspect of it, though his views might seem quaint if accurately recalled now. I myself often uttered the simplistic notion that *Gurrelieder* was symptomatic of bourgeois cultural decline, on the grounds of its gargantuan scale, and forces required to perform it, including an iron chain. The notion of examining the later, twelve-tone Schoenberg from some such standpoint did not occur, mainly through ignorance but also because of the unsubtlety of Marxist cultural criticism, which in those days so rarely got down to details, often wasting space by rehearsing, in true religious fashion, the fundamental dogmas of Marxism itself. John Strachey's *The Coming Struggle for Power* exerted, on its publiction in 1932, great influence on intellectuals both by putting the Marxist economic and political case with persuasive clarity, and analysing, in equally attractive style, the "decay of capitalist culture", particularly literature. Looking at the latter pages nearly fifty years later, one smiles at their closure to the human spirit's perennial creative capability, their refusal to admit the possibility of the appearance still, under the old order, of an Auden or a *Music of Time*.

As I have said, the iron chain theory of culture had only a short-lived effect on my verse. It was more lasting in such criticism as I wrote (exceedingly sparse, mainly book reviews). My prose fiction was disabled more through lack of maturity and application than ideology. After the war I contemplated casting the loose group into fictive form, may even have written a few pages of a story, but my talent and memory were not up to it. I had kept no journal, so conversations and ideas would have needed re-creation; I felt, too, invented characters would have fallen short of the originals. I think particularly of a waitress called Rose, well into her thirties, if not older; stringy, small, intense; almost always when addressing the group liable to make a fool of herself through losing her thread or through emotion or both – to me embarrassing rather than comic, probably so to all. It comes to me now, remembering her features and black hair, that she may have been Jewish; certainly she was tenaciously left-wing, I think more left than CPGB, perhaps Trotskyist, a Rosa Luxemburg of the Blackpool cafés. Poor, dear Rose – poor, dear so many of them, selfless in their passion to ameliorate mankind; the noblest, surely, Maurice Stott, a gentle, stoutish young man, CP member, in comfortable petty bourgeois circumstances who volunteered for the International Brigade and was swiftly thereafter killed in Spain.

The CP approved (or did not disapprove) of the loose group in Blackpool's peculiar circumstances – industry thin on the ground, seasonal employment, the widespread conservatism of those in the holiday trade and also among the retired come to end their days by the sea. The group was certainly an arena for Marxist proselytization (and as it grew there were increasing candidates for that purpose), but really it was more an enjoyable indulgence than a serious political activity, unless, like John and Sammy, you believed in the necessarily slow capture of sufficient of men's minds by Marxist truth. Rather significant that Marston was an effective performer, inheriting his father's talent for oratory (which I never witnessed publicly displayed, however). Some speaker appeared to present the theories of Major Douglas – economic notions dear to the heart of Ezra Pound. Marston waited till the fools and bores had had their say, then made a brief, annihilating speech, ending with: "What we want is not Social Credit but social revolution." I am sure Marston would have been effective under a revolutionary régime; in the early stages, at any rate. Far from being put to any such test, as he might then have imagined to be on the cards, by staying in Blackpool he prospered in the Councillor's capitalist enterprise.

Even judged from the SPGB standpoint, the loose group undoubtedly became too loose – and transformed into an end in itself – the process, as I heard, even accelerating after I had left the town. Fellows, sockless, wearing sandals, appeared at its meetings, and other crankish types so detested by the pre-war Orwell (not that one holds any brief for Orwell's views in those or, for that matter, any other days). As often happens in such situations, too few of the working class were involved.

I do not recall Waller ever turning up at the loose group. In any case, his appearances in Blackpool at that epoch were relatively fleeting. I would have said I was still an articled clerk when during the course of a week or so he took me on several visits to a sideshow on Central Promenade. This stretch, between Central Station and Central Pier (where, as related in *Souvenirs*, I had met the writer John Davenport, future collaborator with Dylan Thomas) was – is – known as the Golden Mile because of its favoured position for extracting cash from holiday-makers. Waller had become acquainted with Harold Davidson, ex-Rector of Stiffkey, who at that time was showing himself to the public in a barrel on the Golden Mile. For some now, perhaps then, obscure reason, barrels were fashionable for exhibition purposes, one having been made famous by a man called, or calling himself, Sacco, who offered for a fee to "fast unto death" therein, and I rather think fulfilling his side of the bargain. It may have been the barrel left untenanted by Sacco that came to be occupied by the Reverend Harold Davidson (as he still let himself be known, not accepting his unfrocking for immoral conduct by the Consistory Court, or whatever). An ordinary barrel must not be envisaged: what the filing public saw was a quite commodious affair, with room for a chair and a camp-bed, rather below eye-level. I say "filing public" but there was time and opportunity for the articulate, if they wished, to have a few words with the ex-Rector, the exchange on his side being characteristically fluent, of the hearty, "modern" padre kind, then not so common as it became, though physically he was far from hearty, being thin, slight, nervy, on the border of old age.

It must have been that Waller had some journalistic project in mind vis-à-vis the ex-Rector, who still proclaimed his innocence when questioned by his customers. I cannot recall anything

Waller got out of him in our private conversations. I was struck by the fact that his hair was dyed, and that he was wearing brown make-up which had come off on the inside of the clerical collar, just as such make-up was to be seen discolouring the white ruffs of the pierrot troupe in Happy Valley years before. He had the self-awareness, gave the sense of permanent performance and of a life lived quite far from reality, of one who had been for some time in the public eye, like the politicians and other "celebrities" I met in fair numbers in later years as a governor of the BBC.

Consequentially enough, in the same sideshow were to be seen living tableaux or artistic poses or however described, though these did not take place in the, or a, barrel, but on a tiny velvet-hung stage in a small room, and a separate entrance fee had to be paid. The sole cast was a quite pretty girl called Eve, no doubt a stage name, though I may be confusing the name with the title of one of her tableaux. These were announced by the fellow who drew the proscenium curtains back and forth. The pictures briefly revealed were decorously erotic, Eve wearing what today would be called a body stocking as well as holding fruit, flowers and the like, as relevant and strategically apposite. The white, tight, over-all garment, one realizes now, must have been available from theatrical costumiers, had probably been in supply since the days of Adah Isaacs Menken, perhaps before. Needless to say, Waller had also got to know Eve and we had private converse with her, too, a dressing gown further concealing her charms, as the presenter of the entertainment might have described her anatomy. She was a nice girl, and I think Waller took her out a couple of times, though I guess what he most enjoyed was demonstrating to me his entrée to this esoteric department of show biz.

The sideshow episode was typically Wallerian: a wonder it did not somehow come to involve ourselves appearing in a barrel. But it also reveals an ambience that, though in Waller's absence one was not an active part of, nevertheless became more and more uncongenial as boyhood was left behind. The incomprehensions and awakenings of early childhood perhaps made my Oldham years seem in retrospect richer than they were in fact, yet without the least hindsight some Blackpool scenes and society were just about as unrewarding as could be for one who yearned to write well, and for mankind to live well.

3 *Unemployed*

Like the striking girl I eventually sat next to as a common occurrence at the Marston bridge table, Mrs Spence-Ormerod was a Blackpool figure who eventually became, if not everyday, less than legendary. The name was euphonious (as, in other contexts, Seymour Mead's and Corny Kershaw, mentioned in *Souvenirs*) but the hyphen added a good deal more, to say nothing of its possessor's fashionable, exceedingly stately appearance. I was impressed when my mother got to know her, probably through their both drinking coffee in the mornings in Booth's Café, a large establishment providing good fare, situate above Booth's, a high-class and equally large grocer's.

It could be said that a somewhat classier clientèle was to be found in the café for morning coffee than for afternoon tea, for the latter merged into high tea of plaice and chips substantiality, which one could not imagine Mrs Spence-Ormerod being surrounded by, let alone partaking of. For two of our dwelling-places, the private hotel *Seacliffe* and the flat overlooking the Hotel Metropole, Booth's Café was absurdly convenient, in the same block as the flat, between the Metropole and the North Pier. It had pretensions to fashionableness as well as respectability, and at coffee time, particularly in the holiday season, it was a place where one might expect to see Greeks. This was a term applied by us to anyone of outré looks or dress, through my brother as a young boy once mishearing my mother referring to a group of such figures as "freaks" – the word a typical expression of my mother's detestation of the unconventional.

A decade or so later than my mother's initial acquaintance with Mrs Spence-Ormerod, Booth's Café again came into my life, for my wife and small son, during their wartime exile in Blackpool, sometimes went there to take coffee with my mother, as did I when on leave. Mrs Spence-Ormerod was still an habitué, and the two epochs of my (very slight) knowledge of her have coalesced in my mind, rather like my two visits to Gibson and Weldon. But it was my infant son and not my mother, my wife assures me, who once when addressed by Mrs Spence-Ormerod told her in plain terms to vamoose – highly uncharacteristic, for even at that age he was agreeable, stoical and beautifully behaved. Possibly he was over-reacting to a residual awe inherited from his father.

Mrs Spence-Ormerod had a boyfriend (let the inappropriate nomenclature stand) of a distinction equalling, if not exceeding, her own: Colonel Harold Parker, DSO, a solicitor and County Coroner, often reported in the local press adjudicating on the drowned, etc. He was in practice with his brother in nearby Preston, but they had a branch office in Blackpool – the south end of the town, between Seafolde House and the semi-bungalow of Mrs Sidey where we once had "rooms". A vacancy arose to manage this office, and my mother must simultaneously have been talking about my future with Mrs Spence-Ormerod in Booth's: after an interview with Colonel Parker's brother (far less imposing than his sibling) I was appointed to the post.

Why being a salaried solicitor at one end of the town should be more attractive than at the other I cannot now give reasons for. As soon as I had qualified, Wylie Kay's started paying me £3 a week. It was *ex gratia*, for until my articles expired I had no salary entitlement. With Parker and Parker I was paid £4 10s. a week, but surely I could have jacked Wylie Kay's up to that figure in due course. Or perhaps not. I was keen to get married, so a salary that brought that state closer would have made the new job less like a mere exchange of provincial servitudes than in retrospect it seems.

The Parker and Parker branch consisted of two rooms over a bank, with a staff of one stenographer-office-boy, and a meagre practice. Possibly my predecessor had taken some clients with him. The room I sat in was inappropriately large – the building being of late-Victorian amplitude. The boy was quite good but underworked: when things were slow I feebly let him go home early. Such business as there was benefited me, at least: I had to do myself what would have been done at Wylie Kay's by minions such as Docking or the cashier or even lesser fry; for instance, issuing a County Court summons, stamping a conveyance. And I had to appear in court under my own steam. In my last days at Wylie Kay's I had done this in the County Court, but only in undefended debt cases before the Registrar, and then my hand was held by the experienced Docking. The fundamentally nervous can never bring themselves to realize that they, too, will in the end master the mechanics of life, however initially strange or enigmatic. Only the other week I came back home with a broken fingernail, having unconsciously attacked demonically an unfamiliar system of self-service petrol.

I learnt a bit at Parker and Parker: nevertheless was not in the least successful. Hard to say whether at the time I admitted this to myself: certainly I took no steps to change my job, though it is true there proved not to be much time for this. I did not feel hugely ambitious as a solicitor, though not averse to "getting on"; aware that a certain quickness of brain and restless energy distinguished me from the ruck. I would have worked at Parker and Parker's had there been work to do: as it was, the days held time for studying racing form and playing bridge had there been others to share such occupations, as at Wylie Kay's. Whether I wrote verse there, pulling an abstract of title or Inland Revenue Affidavit over the lines if the clerk came in, I fail to recall. But it has just occurred to me that in the summer or autumn of 1934, part of the Parker and Parker epoch, I must have written one of my first published poems, a short piece that appeared in Geoffrey Grigson's *New Verse* in December 1934. (The emotion felt receiving a copy of the magazine with the breakfast post in the house overlooking Stanley Park is recapturable still.) It was a freakish turn-up for the sort of poem that might be classed as just passable for its time (*New Verse* did not take another poem of mine for more than a year), not reprinted until James Gibson, in the early Seventies, asked me to contribute to his enterprising book *Let the Poet Choose* (an anthology made by the contributing poets themselves), where in a note to my poem I said that "For an unknown provincial young man, to achieve publication in a first-class avant-garde magazine . . . came as an excitement and encouragement scarcely to be experienced again." The poem begins:

> In a normal rainfall the channel was adequate,
> but all that summer under dripping trees,
> I waited watching pyrotechnics on macadam.

The absence of political moralizing and the presence of comparative concreteness are notable compared with my other verse of the time. Why didn't I see the advantage in this? The poem goes on to tell of the disasters of excessive rainfall. One is reminded of the rather well-worn story of John Piper's water-colours of Windsor Castle, done with his usual dramatic cloudy skies and lurid light. George VI, looking through them, having given permission for the artist to be there – perhaps commissioned him – remarked: "Pity about the weather."

Further as to success in the law: in a few years time, after Parker and Parker, I was on the way to modest achievement. The process continued after the War. Yet I felt comparatively unmoved about the thing until at the age of forty-six, as well as being solicitor to the Woolwich Building Society, I became legal advisor to the Building Societies Association, and a little later on sat on a Law Society committee working on conveyancing law reform. Perhaps such activities revived my old taste for action: quite suddenly I was able to influence legislation, pull the legs of quite distinguished colleagues; in Reithian terms, be more "stretched". I enjoyed it, but was rescued, if that is the word, from its constricting more and more the literary side of things, by being given the opportunity to retire prematurely from the law, which I did.

How far such a future from the solitary and rather run-down office above the Bank! A few existing and loyal clients came in, and I may have introduced one or two new ones, at best family friends with wills to make, in those days a simple and cheap job. I don't recall doing any work for the comrades, in any case mostly propertyless by definition – and if Sammy ever had problems over foreign bodies found in meat pies, and the like, he did not consult me. What a contrast, forty-five years later, when many radical solicitors make a very decent living through subsidized barrackroom lawyerdom!

The bulk of the callers at Parker and Parker's Blackpool branch wanted to take, not confer, business – insurance inspectors, stationery salesmen, *et al.* Some semi-scroungers also appeared, as in a comedy by Ben Jonson, the word presumably having got round that a new green manager was to be found at the top of the stairs beside the Bank. The most persistent of these was a small crippled man who had, or said he had, invented a hospital bed, and was looking for capital to manufacture or otherwise exploit it. Eventually he prevailed on me to visit his house, where a prototype of the bed was to be seen. I expect he realized I would never provide any trusting clients with cash to spare, but he probably saw in myself a source of funds. With his rubber-tipped stick he pointed out the bed's novel features, chief of which was a facility for tilting head and foot separately, appropriate to the patient's needs. It was an iron bedstead, painted white; the colour lending authenticity. Whether the bed was really a prototype, the winding mechanism novel, I do not know. No money was extracted from me; not that I had any to extract. A good bit afterwards I read a newspaper paragraph about the conviction of the inventor for fraud involving the bed, but this may not necessarily have extended to the originality of the device. I used the figure of the cripple in a short story published in *Folios of New Writing* in 1941; and the atmosphere of the affair was somehow revived when, much later, I read the pages about Peter Doyle in Nathanael West's *Miss Lonelyhearts*. Why certain episodes in life of apparent triviality make such an effect, particularly vis-à-vis creativity, is somewhat mysterious; though in this case my taste for the grotesque and the criminal was clearly being appealed to. I ought to add, what now forcibly strikes me, that my four-year-old son for some time amiably mocked me by calling me "Roy Fuller the pig." The title of the story ("The Pig") appeared in *Folios of New Writing* below my name, set without punctuation. His humorous precocity was also illustrated when, on the coming into being a few years later of John Lehmann's *New Writing and Daylight*, he a trifle cruelly referred to it as *Old Writing and Moonlight*.

When, after Parker and Parker days, I was applying for jobs, I was able to put a plausible gloss of success on my managership of the branch by prefacing mention of it with the strictly accurate rubric "1934–35", as though it were a rung in my career, but I doubt if the experience lasted a full twelve months. Not long after I arrived, Arthur Parker suddenly died, and not long after that his brother merged his practice with that of a firm that had a branch in Preston and its main office in Blackpool. The Preston office of W. and B. Blackhurst was to be closed; likewise the Blackpool office of Parker and Parker. It may well have been that the latter action had not been finally decided upon before a visit one day by Colonel Parker and the two Blackhursts to the offices above the Bank.

Colonel Parker had been a Territorial, perhaps still was: with his clipped grey moustache and soldierly bearing could have come from the pages of Agatha Christie, the friendship with Mrs

Spence-Ormerod (also an Agathan name and character) affording the necessary tinge of suspicion (though to have the Coroner himself guilty would have been quite a supreme stroke, even for that author). I knew the Blackhursts, by sight at least. William was a dark, stout, forceful man in his forties, well known in the Courts; his brother much milder, on the conveyancing side. I don't suppose I relished this encounter in the least: indeed, my inability to recapture now its feeling-tone may imply chagrin, even shame. The fact was the office just about failed to break even (as I well knew, having had to learn to keep the books as well as grapple with the clerks, sometimes of Kafkaesque superciliousness, at the County Court offices). "How would you set about building up the practice?" W. Blackhurst asked me. I said something about joining the golf club, what I imagined to be received wisdom. Had I specified the Masons it would have been no farther from my inclinations or intentions. Though W. Blackhurst refrained from enquiring why then I remained a non-golfer, I realized only too well how little he must have been impressed with that and my other observations. He was precisely the type of human to succeed in those departments of life where I would be found to be most lacking, and I expect I was not much surprised that the closure of the branch was unaccompanied by the offer of a post in the main Blackpool office. The further irony probably failed to occur to me that a social life that included membership of the Loose Group was fundamentally a negative asset in the career of a solicitor of those days, though had W. Blackhurst been aware of it he might have thought it some evidence of character at least in one, from his viewpoint, so apparently feeble.

So in 1935 I was unemployed, could rightfully have joined a procession of the kind organized by the National Unemployed Workers Movement that I had watched with compassion a few years before from the articled clerks' room at Wylie Kay's. It was hard to get another job. My application letters necessarily revealed a brief and quite commonplace start to a career; and when called to an interview I see now I was far too self-denigratory about lack of experience. Such kind of honesty is no doubt a species of self-regard, but it did me no good at the time, unless preserving me for an appointment that proved to suit me as well as anything could by way of legal destiny. I had some near misses. For an assistant solicitorship in the West End I went for an interview to the principal's house in Ealing, he being indisposed – though I began to doubt this when he kept introducing the topic of corporal punishment into the conversation, a form of advance I was by then able to recognize and more or less adroitly parry. Should I have taken the post, if offered, and like the narrator in Proust moved unperverted into a perverted world? After the war I used to see the solicitor's letter-heads among the vast legal correspondence coming into the Woolwich Equitable solicitor's department: the principal had by then acquired a few junior partners; whether he kept them in order by strict means I used to wonder. At an interview in the legal department of the Post Office I harped on my lack of practice in registered conveyancing (as though that demanded years of study and practice). What a nitwit! The appointment would have brought me to London and into an organization where I could have scarcely failed to get on.

Quite soon I was prepared to go anywhere, certainly to continue in Blackpool where, in fact, an opportunity or two arose, including a partnership with a youngish solicitor who not much later went to prison for fraudulent conversion. The Parcae, though shilly-shallying about me in this area, were favourable on the whole. When it became clear I wasn't going to walk into a job I ordered a sign and had it affixed to one of the garden gate posts of the house (the house we had moved to after leaving the house overlooking Stanley Park, the latter being found by my mother, in one of her troughs of health, too large to be easily managed):

R. B. FULLER
SOLICITOR

Strangely enough, a little higher up, across the road, was the house occupied by Mrs Spence-Ormerod. Did Colonel Parker, on his visits, guiltily observe this feeble evidence of his former employee's struggle to re-establish himself in the law? Our house was miles away from the town's commercial hub, though quite near the North Shore Golf Club, which the Colonel may have imagined I had belatedly joined.

A few passers-by were actually enticed in by the sign, not of the Peter Doyle variety but neither of the substance to enable me to make a living. I wonder now quite how I passed the abundant time available. There were Party activities and the Loose Group.

I liked watching association football and county cricket. I was a member of Boots' Booklovers Library (a great boon of those days and after) as well as of the Public Library: my reading was non-stop but desultory. My wife-to-be and I had friends in addition to those already touched on. There was the Metropole pianist and his wife, and the organist whose acceptable wedding-present was to play at our wedding, held in church not only to prevent my mother's grief but also to please my wife's parents. He duly married his fiancée of those days, also a friend, but later divorced her, whereupon she married Marston, whose first wife, introduced to him in London by Waller and known to me on my London sojourns, was by then dead. Since I greatly admired books like *The Old Wives' Tale*, I suppose I saw, even before reading Proust, that a vast area of fictional interest lay in the amatory gyrations among small groups in society, time and propinquity bringing about the unlikeliest permutations and combinations. But I would never have thought to treat such matters in my fiction, even had I found power to do so. The minutiae of life, often of what I have called the nose-picking variety, and later crime, absorbed me. For as well as writing verse, I continued to make attempts at prose fiction, ambition of my schooldays. But even at prose I worked as Dr Kettle (reported by Aubrey) said Seneca wrote – "as a Boare doth pisse, *scilicet* by jirkes."

4 *A Phantom Voice*

Since Sir William Jenner was not impossibly tardy in 1871 in recognizing the symptoms of Graves' Disease in Christina Rossetti, it seems astonishing that in the Thirties my mother went undiagnosed for so long. Indeed, one piece of advice she received savoured very much of the faith-healing side of Victorian medicine: she was told she ought to take a prolonged sea voyage. I am not sure if the doctor himself did not suggest a practical and reasonably inexpensive way of doing this, viz. to buy a season ticket for the steamers that plied between Fleetwood, a little way up the Fylde coast, and Douglas in the Isle of Man. Anyway, this is what my mother did, making the trip perhaps two or three times a week, sometimes having to endure boisterous weather, I think seldom if ever disembarking, simply waiting for the boat to back out from the quay at Douglas – an episode in her life like a story by Kafka, or, perhaps, more accurately, that play by Sutton Vane where the characters are mysteriously condemned to shipboard life, without possibility (in most cases) of return – a play that as will be seen later had its application to my own experiences. Inevitably she came to know other season ticket holders, who were mostly dedicated boozers, for the ship's bars opened as soon as the vessel cast off, whatever the time of day. An entirely sober couple, however, who I believe took to sea simply to fill in an otherwise rather empty turn to their lives, became particular friends, the relationship continuing when sailing days were done.

Mr and Mrs Parslew were in latish middle age. He had made his modest pile, was virtually retired, though retaining some undemanding business interest, probably a non-executive directorship. His personality was dominating, not to say domineering; geniality sometimes showing an edge of irascibility undoubtedly alarming to anyone dependent on his money, or obliged by ties of duty or blood to stick with him, or even to friends and acquaintances of mild temperament. His face and bald head (the latter fringed by cropped grey hair) were beaten by the weather of the Irish Sea; later, when, like Ulysses, he had given up his voyagings, the effect was sustained by the sun striking through the sliding roof of his Armstrong Siddeley motor car, quite a novel feature in those days, as was the car's pre-selective gears, with lever on the steering wheel. He said more than once he had lost his hair in early youth through washing it in ammonia, the motive for this drastic absterging never being made utterly clear, though the action very much in character. The toilet fluid he preferred when we knew him was "Larola", a complexion milk. The label on the bottle depicted the head of a girl with windswept hair, rather old-fashioned, the use of the preparation being indicated by a phrase in inverted commas, as though a quotation from a poem, which it may have been – "In summer's heat and winter's cold." The Isle of Man steamers and the Armstrong Siddeley roof had given Larola a good testing, and it scarcely needed the urging of Mr Parslew (always ready to commend his own habits) for me to use it myself. Moreover, there was always the chance it would do my pimples good: hope unfulfilled.

Mrs Parslew, stouter than her husband, was placid and uncomplaining, though had a good deal to put up with. Should she be injudicious enough to yawn during the evening, and be spotted by her husband, he would say Quilpishly: "You're tired, Mother. Go to bed." If the hour were not ridiculously early she might well depart; hardship alleviated by her taking "supper" with her, always in the form of cheese. My mother used to report her eating as much as half a pound on such occasions, but as I have said elsewhere my mother laid it on thick about traits she considered eccentric. Some nocturnal trouble of Mrs Parslew's was ascribed by my mother to this caseous habit – not nightmare, that would have been too obvious; possibly snoring. Another confidence imparted to us by Mr Parslew was that what had originally attracted him to Mrs Parslew, impelled him to marry her, was her ugliness. It should be said that the cognomen "Mother", used by Mr Parslew, resulted from their having a nubile daughter, who frequently sang to herself a popular song of the day:

> I'm on a see-saw.
> You throw me up and you throw me down,
> I don't know whether I'm here or there.

Why my brother should find this funny, and make me laugh about it, too, is now unclear.

Mr Parslew's energy was excessive for the occupations of retirement. "Get on the job right away" was an admonition he urged on others as well as himself. Deciding on even a modest trip required him to resolve to have the Armstrong Siddeley "oiled and greased" forthwith. These two phrases my brother and I began to use interchangeably to express an intention to act, getting "oiled and greased" being applied by us to the human preliminaries. I have no doubt Mr Parslew had observations to make about my joblessness; probably commanded that I put that sign on the gatepost. He specified £1000 a year as an indication of success in life: no further comment from him was needed to bring home to me how far I was from that goal, even before I was unemployed.

He actually determined the general future of my brother's life. He was convinced that the hotel world offered a future for the smart, decently educated young person of respectable family (that such a notion, as novel then as the pre-selective gear, is now a commonplace is due to a considerable extent to my brother's work in the field of hotel and catering education). It may be Mr Parslew had contacts in that world. Certainly my brother was quite expeditiously oiled and greased and interviewed in London by one of the Salmons, the family that ran Joe Lyons, who accepted him as an apprentice. Soon after, he was sweating in the kitchens of the Regent Palace Hotel, getting up at four to go to Smithfield with the meat-buyer for Lyons' London hotels; the shabby but leisurely gentility of the usher's life vanished. Perhaps any resistance to this arduous and unknown world had been undermined by his admiration for Arnold Bennett's novel about a hotel, *Imperial Palace*, then not long published.

It occurs to me not to leave too depressed an impression of my workless days.

> Your pockets gape with wry dismay,
> Turned inside-out we find them funny:
> Strange, now I cannot laugh again
> For fear my tears should fall like rain.

Stephen Spender's poem (subsequently rather spoiled by being made less specific, as explained later) addressed to a member of the unemployed, familiar from *Oxford Poetry 1930*, was not at all apropos. I think my mother gave me ten shillings a week. There would be a few meagre fees from my few clients. Out of her wages my wife-to-be paid her whack. We continued with our entertainments, modest, but that nevertheless might put us cheek by jowl with Blackpool's élite – in seats booked for the Sunday evening showing of the film *Queen Christina*, say, or for a concert by Duke Ellington and his band. In a sense, and even in actuality, we knew some of the promoters of the annual Spinsters' Ball, of the members of the North Shore Golf Culb; though our social life was passed with the Loose Group and its denizens.

It must have been the late winter of 1935–36 that in answer to my application I was asked to go – what seemed a really immense trek – to Ashford in Kent to be interviewed for an assistant solicitorship with a firm called Kingsford, Flower and Pain. By that time I had devised what now seems a very ordinary, not to say egregious formula, but which I then considered fresh and keen-seeming, for the start of my application letters: "I am extremely interested in your advertisement" etc. I do believe this plunging more or less *in medias res* may have secured more response than my near-minimal experience and qualifications warranted. Another phrase used, picked up from somewhere or another, and striking me as a modest way of commending in advance my looks and turn-out, was: "I am of good appearance and address." I see now that both these ploys may have specially appealed to Frank Flower, the senior partner in Kingsford, Flower and Pain.

Probably guilt has caused me to disremember the effect on my mother of the prospect of my leaving her and my brother, presumably for good, but I think she was stoical. In the event my brother never returned to Blackpool to live, either, and she gave up the house, went to stay with friends – not the Parslews, that relationship somehow dying away. Mr Parslew may have thought somewhat better of me for quitting the ranks of the unemployed, though still far from his criterion of success in life, my starting salary being £286 a year.

Writing these last few pages, I have been struck by the contrast between them and what has come down the years as the atmosphere and aspirations of the Thirties (I say nothing of the almost unrecapturable density of life – people, objects, sensations, in their actuality, not simply as traditions or half-memories or impossibly difficult exercises in the literary commonplace). One thing there is no need to labour is the despairing sense then possessed of a succession of wrong decisions taken by authority, decisions that could never be remedied, that brought us nearer doom. This period inculcated a pessimism that lasted far beyond the period itself: I recall being amazed, post-war, at the welcome collapse of the Central African Federation, which I imagined would inevitably impose the injustices of what was then Southern Rhodesia on states more appropriately black-ruled (though whether such collapse has in fact added to the sum of African happiness is an elderly buffer's query *ex post facto*). In the Thirties the prime exemplar of gloom was the so-called non-interventionist policy over the Spanish Civil War. At that time, too, the long-feared anticipation of general war bringing with it the aerial bombardment of civilians, was given concrete form.

I think not until well into the Second World War did one lose the sense that one oneself might yet see a social revolution conducted, to a degree at least, in the terms of armed conflict (an English storming of the Winter Palace, as it were) – the old sense, though much modified by the decade's amazing historical tergiversations, of the closeness of great change, ushered in by the events that followed the Wall Street crash. More or less vague anxieties about a possible capitalist war against the Soviet Union – a continuation of the post-1918 war of intervention – had hardened with fascism's taking of power in Germany. The idea that democratic capitalism might, against the odds, almost against its own interests, join with the Soviet Union to oppose the fascist powers, was unsupported by most of the evidence going, and too much of a happy ending to be plausibly historical in apocalyptic days. Moreover, it seemed simply self-deluding to conceive that mere alliance would deter the fascists making war – an ingredient of fascism's role, by definition. And despair about conventional political leaders in the democracies did not wholly stem from Marxist convictions: they seemed, in Auden's phrase, irredeemably "Holders of one position, wrong for years."

The phrase (from the 1930 *Poems*) represents a side of Auden immediately congenial. His influence continued in various ways. I have found and brought down some trunk-in-the-loft poems not seen for many years. I had envisaged a ring-file of typescripts, but the object in question proved to be a twelve-inch by seven-and-a-half "Memoranda or Minute Book" (as entitled on the stout cover). Surely I must have bought this in imitation of a notebook used by the young Auden, and described as a butcher's ledger, though I can find no reference to that romantically anti-romantic article in either the Auden double number of *New Verse* or *Lions and Shadows*, so the source of my knowledge stays mysterious somewhat. I started in March 1935 to copy poems into my book, sometimes feebly working on them, up to the autumn of 1937. Not all my output is there, but I guess a substantial tranche of it is. A few more poems unsystematically appear in the book right up into the early months of 1939.

The proletcult poems at the beginning of the notebook are, to adopt Poirot's phrase, "bad, but bad, and of a badness" – versification of the crudest left ideas. Some of the idiocies, like those in Wordsworth and moralistic Victorian verse, may be the result of an intention to write poetry the masses could understand and be influenced by; that could be printed in the *Daily* alongside prose about injustice to seasonal workers. I will not give any specimen of these, for the temptation is too strong to mislead by choosing passages that some fact of the times, or some word-concatenation, has slightly enlivened. The smiling moustaches poem is not complete, but some of it seems to date from early 1936, too late for present comfort. Incidentally, Valentine Cunningham's remarkable *Penguin Book of Spanish Civil War Verse*, published at the time I wrote the foregoing words, confirms how the political poetry of the period could in fact move non-intellectual audiences (though such audiences, it is true, were usually as predominantly Left as that which heckled the future Lord Martonmere).

In the autumn of 1935 – with more certainty in the spring of 1936 – an improvement may be detected in the Minute Book poems, though probably only by those reading with extreme sympathy. Elements of Marxism are replaced to some degree by Gravesian fables; and a few observations of nature appear:

> From what far country blow the winds that rattle
> The old ivy on those trees?

That line and a half dates from my arrival in Ashford; the aural phenomenon (commonplace enough) noted on an early solitary walk. Looking through my poems of this period I am surprised how transparent they are. I had imagined far more obfuscation and pseudo-reference, particularly in verse rejected by the editors of those days, but there is a fairly uniform mix of naïveté, propaganda, and unprofound poetic "plotting", not at all hard at any point to comprehend, or so it seems to me now. Within the conventions of the period (which dominate in a strange way, not easy to explain, the feebler poets knocking about), Ashford and its environs may be recognized in some of the pieces. In a ballad (not included in the Minute Book, however), the phrase "blunt, proper knives for scraping scab" was derived from the agricultural window of the Ashford "Boots the Chemists", where such implements were displayed for sale, an enterprising side of the chain never before encountered. The epithets were added by me, "proper" being in the neutral mode then rather favoured by poets.

I recognize the origin of another poem in some visits I had to make to a client of Kingsford, Flower and Pain incarcerated in a lunatic asylum. The business made a considerable impression on me. Hard to say whether dottiness was a period obsession or something of more personal interest; though perhaps any form of the irrational has its appeal, even to the most cerebral of poets. At any rate, I was wholly engaged by the madman's youth and the virtual impossibility of communicating with him; by his inimitably mad letters, not least their handwriting and layout; and the bleak austerity and routine of the institution itself. Almost none of this appears in the poem: pretty well everything is elevated, abstract, stiff.

> The insane are not crafty, they are great
> With smiles that turn conventional gestures
> To blows against pathetic power.

Today such a poem (the "confessional" tradition lively), even from a mediocre poet, would be personal and circumstantial – more interesting and less daft, but whether better, in the sense of being at all readable by posterity, than the fifth-rate in the earlier mode, who knows?

I was primarily taken on by Kingsford's to relieve Frank Flower from the burden of going into court. He was weary of the duty; besides, despite having fixed the minimum fee for appearing in the Police Court at three guineas (then a respectable sum, as my starting salary implies), he could occupy his time far more remuneratively. Conveyancing and non-contentious work would also fall to my lot. On that afternoon of my interview it so happened that Frank Flower had been delayed somewhere away from the office, so I saw the junior partner, Harold E. Pain, and then waited for Frank Flower in the latter's office on the first floor back, a pleasant room (with white-painted shelves holding a good library, including the Law Reports) though looking out merely at and over commercial Ashford.

I suppose the two partners were much of an age. Harold Pain had been a "ten year man" – serving only three years' articles, having already had ten years in the law as a solicitor's clerk. He was a bachelor, lived with his sister, a spinster: tallish, slim, he turned himself out in a manner that even then seemed old-fashioned. I daresay some venerable Ashford tailor made – perhaps had always made – his suits. They were invariably (but can that really have been so?) clerical grey, cut high in the lapel, narrow in the trouser, in a fashion that, after the war, astonishingly made some sort of come-back. His collars were starched, spectacles gold-rimmed, moustache so abundant that when his cigarette had burned down (he smoked by letting the weed burn between his lips) he had to withdraw it from his mouth by inserting his finger and thumb *below* the grizzled whisker. The hair was slightly grizzled, too, and fine, brushed close to a small, rather elegant head, and finished off with an unexaggerated quiff. Really the style was not tremendously far from that later affected by Dick Van Dyke, another unlikely come-back. Harold Pain's competency as a lawyer was great; his kindness and geniality unvarying – though a tone of sad reproof might briefly come over his voice on his discovery of incompetence, even to the extent of a "tck", approaching actual annoyance. About the ordinary affairs of humanity (moving house, say, or dying) with which his professional work was pretty well exclusively concerned, he spoke with a committed enjoyment almost gastronomic at moments of greatest enthusiasm, when one detected a faint slushing of saliva under some of his words – words that seemed to come from an accumulation of speech at the front of his mouth, perhaps impeded in their emergence by the moustache.

He taught me a lot; some I should have already known had I been made to serve my articles more conscientiously. "I am accustomed to working without supervision," I used to write, accurately but rather misleadingly, when applying for jobs, but with Kingsford's much of my work was overseen, certainly at first, mainly by the partners, though also by the extremely efficient conveyancing and litigation managing clerks. Probably from the outset I had given indication of professional deficiencies. I once took to Mr Pain a conveyance I had drafted – of part of Sir Charles Igglesden's ample garden, surplus to requirements, Sir Charles being a local newspaper proprietor, chairman of the Ashford magistrates. I sat at Mr Pain's side while he wrote in, with fluent hand and brain, the grant and reservation of those rights and easements (we were acting for both parties) I had omitted, a fairly elementary but comprehensive lesson in visualizing the practical use of property I never forgot – getting down to the classic case of Blackacre and Whiteacre, as it were, instead of being dilettante about Purpleacre and Puceacre.

Frank Flower was a less patient taskmaster. He had a habit, particularly when standing, of holding a document by the stapled or paper-clipped corner between his right thumb and forefinger, the document supported for his eye by the right wrist and forearm, turning the sheets back with his left hand. No doubt that was how he viewed a draft lease I once submitted for his approval, though only the perusal of a leaf or two was necessary before he tossed the thing back to me, saying: "That's not a full repairing lease." I was chagrinned as much by his withering tone as by my failure to carry out instructions (perhaps at that date not even grasping the implications of the phrase "full repairing"). I went off burning with a resentment damped down by guilt.

I myself acquired the document-holding trick, found myself still occasionally doing it when I came back into the law after war service. It was not the only habit I copied from Frank Flower. He had a brief loud laugh, throwing back his head to emit it. In moments of concentration he compressed his lips and, since his countenance was florid, I used fancifully to think the tightness of mouth was to prevent an outflow of blood. Why I should imitate these two idiosyncrasies I do not know, though Frank Flower impressed me from the moment he came late into his office where I was waiting – I think passing the time by reading a volume of the Law Reports, always containing something fresh and good – that first afternoon. He was wearing his navy-blue overcoat and bowler hat (an indication, I came to know later, of some expedition out of the usual), and with his Savile Row suit his invariable bow tie. As to the suit, Jack Clark told me that Frank Flower, in the days I am writing of, once said of him: "Feel that, my lad," putting Jack's fingers on the coat of his suit, and adding with only superficial inconsequence: "Who gets the furcoats in Russia, the *moujiks* or Mrs Stalin?"

I inherited from Frank Flower, too, to a degree, an emphatic, articulated way of speaking; though this may have resulted anyway from my initial endeavour to bring my style of speech up to educated southern standards, for friends made in Ashford brought home to me that the injunctions from the Boss at school as to not mumbling, to say nothing of correct "u" and "a" sounds, and the hard and soft "g", had in my case been incompletely mastered. I suppose it must be admitted that the fundamental motive for altering one's accent is snobbish, yet self-improvement in other spheres is considered worthy. What I evolved, as heard by me in BBC recordings and the like, was a neutral, quite passable and I believe not bogus mode, which often inclined (as did my grandfather's speech in olden days) to the more demotic within the family or on encountering some friend whose origins had been in the north, such as Richard Hoggart or Anthony Thwaite. A strange thing is – and the penny didn't drop about this until late in life – that I am sure the accent I converted over the years was more Yorkshire than Lancashire. Though I have gone through life reckoning myself a Professor Higgins in identifying Lancashire and Yorkshire accents, in fact in true Thirties fashion I was a frontier figure myself, I'm sure never possessing the soft tones and exaggerated "r" sounds of typical industrial Lancashire (in an Oldham programme on the radio not long ago I noticed "purr-ents" ("parents"), taking me back, but not to my own habits), let alone the esoteric tones of more rural districts, as exemplified in the speech of George Woodcock, say, the trade unionist. When I fall into proletarian speech, I believe it has a Yorkshire tincture – perhaps now influenced by northern comedians rather than the natural ways of my boyhood. On the other hand, I may be underestimating how far the East Lancashire accent familiar in early boyhood was overlaid in memory and familiarity by that of the Fylde coast.

To go back to Frank Flower, whatever he came to think of my legal ability, it strikes me now that the initial favourable impression was mutual, because though he asked Mr Pain to come into his room before the decision was actually made, it was he who engaged me. Kingsford's occupied the middle position of the three substantial firms in the town (there was a one-man band that scarcely counted). Below it was a firm also with a title in the metre of Matthew Arnold's "elegiacs": Poncia, Swann and Carter – though I think Arnold would not have admitted the feminine ending. Poncia, like Kingsford, was dead: his lingering name, suggestive of the Mafia, or Maltese undesirables, lent the firm a faintly sinister air, to some extent borne out by Swann, Carter and the managing clerk all having crooked noses. The fault was a common one in that the nose did not grow straight out of the face, though the side to which it inclined differed in two of the cases, I forget which; but that is scarcely of importance.

Hallett, Creery and Co., the town's premier firm, spoilt the metre by eventually shortening themselves to Hallett and Co. Hallett and Creery were both goners, and such was the size, class and prestige of the firm there had been no need to promote even the most senior on the quite long list of partners to the firm name. Last on the list was Mervyn Bompas, fairly recently recruited. I first ran across him in the Ashford County Court, where he was welcoming and agreeable; made the first move towards meeting non-professionally. He was blond, broad, not tall; open countenance, small nose; scion of a legal family – I believe it was his great-grandfather who had been Dickens' model for Sergeant Buzfuz.

From Mervyn, always correct but quite without side, I quickly learnt a bit of *comme il faut*. Soon after I arrived in Ashford he moved out of digs into a flat, where his way of life was less trammelled. A half-loaf of bread, brown and not pristine, on a bread-board on the luncheon table, with a bread-knife to help oneself, was far from what my mother or grandmother would have thought proper or even edible. Yet I recognized in the careless austerity – as in the flat's sparse furniture and occasional *objet* – a positive good, as might reside in the Spartan lavatorial facilities of some establishment of great learning. Mervyn drove me one Sunday to London to visit his mother and step-father. They lived in a flat in the region of Westminster Cathedral, the sort of place where the Widmerpools and Leonard Short were to live. Proper (the scab-knife epithet comes readily to the pen) cultivated trappings were there even more in evidence; the mother good-looking, intelligent, sharp; the step-father big, elderly, maybe to be addressed as "Colonel", I am not sure.

We were friends with Mervyn all through our Ashford days: his influence continued. He conferred on my wife the shortened name "Kate", still used; had a habit of standing after a meal, to let (as he said) gravity aid digestion – still referred to. What he made of my political views I do not recall, if I ever knew.

I suppose Kate and I would have married on any salary paid by a job of prospective permanency, adjusting life-style to cash available. Flats to rent were available in Ashford, even at our notional maximum mark of twenty-five shillings a week – though at such a price always possessing some bizarre feature, like the bath (covered with a bath-shaped board) being in the kitchen, or (in the case of a flat over a warehouse) the sitting-room being of grotesque amplitude. We settled on one in a village called Kennington (now virtually a suburb) two or three miles outside the town, above a sweet-shop, on offer at seventeen shillings and sixpence a week, rates inclusive. The bizarre feature here was the kitchen, so tiny it seemed doubtful whether there would be room for more than one person to stand in it when a cooker had been installed. A good job my mother saw the premises only as a *fait accompli*. By relinquishing their offer to redecorate the interior, I beat the landlords down to sixteen shillings.

Thus two townees came to live, if not quite in the country, as close to it as they ever would. Did I try to observe and learn about natural phenomena, as I would, however feebly, today? The answer cannot be deduced from my verse of the time. We were not far from Eastwell Park, a beauteous estate then owned by Viscount Dunsford, and once the home of the excellent early eighteenth-century poet Anne Finch, Countess of Winchilsea. One could walk through the park, past the great house, to the little church, where there was an elaborate monument to the Countess. It seems I was less interested as a poet in landscape and wild creatures than a literary and anachronistic version of aristocratic life – weak heirs, mouldering peers' robes, and so forth:

Inside the topmost room
The wellfed spectre
The corpulent ancestor
The vampire sector.

We knew a good few residents of Kennington, particularly after our son's birth, when his pram was benignly overlooked by the elderly and offered to be pushed by admiring schoolgirls. Though we anatomized their peculiarities (and our own, such as Kate's asking in vain for donkey-stone at the village general shop, wanting in her early enthusiasm to tart up the step leading to the sixteen-shilling flat), I think I never regarded the place in imaginative terms, even as the hierarchical setting for a whodunnit. I see now how lightly I took the prospect of being both a writer and a lawyer, letting the former occupation almost take care of itself, relying on the arrival of inspiration, such as it was. It could be argued that this was so until fairly recent times, when, my lawyering days over, time could scarcely be passed without some slightly more systematic ordering of literary activity.

When I began to publish poetry and fiction regularly after the war, surprise expressed at this accompanying a nine to five job did nothing to remove a sense of guilt about my indolence. I expect some people thought my grandfather's life (Superintendent Registrar, Alderman, Magistrate) one of dutiful assiduity, but I felt myself growing more and more like him, success merely some unwilled trick; the double man, indeed, being just as interested, if not more so, in a third existence – in my grandfather's case, playing bridge, buying prize cheese, and such domestic eccentricities as playing "golf" (cherished trivialities paralleled in my own life).

Knowing one Kennington family, the Clarks, had long perspectives. They lived, as we did, on the main Ashford to Faversham road, but in a roomy Edwardian or late-Victorian house. The mother and father were in their middle years, and there were three daughters, attractive in varying styles, the youngest still a schoolgirl. The one son, Jack, was an Oxford undergraduate, not encountered until a fine evening during a Long Vacation when he came walking up Kennington Lees with a fellow undergraduate called Rodney Phillips, we somehow anticipating him near the step Kate had failed to donkey-stone. He and Rodney (subsequently the founder of a smart highbrow magazine called *Polemic*, and a book publisher) were in some disbelief that close to the Clark family house could actually reside a contributor to *New Writing*, as, in a way that now seems baffling, had been reported to them.

I had thought this was the Long Vacation of 1937, in which case the contribution in question would have been the smiling moustaches piece, inadequate trigger for their mild awe. But on reflection I see it was more likely 1938, when earlier in the year *New Writing* had published a poem of mine dedicated to the dead Maurice Stott. In that event Jack may well have actually just come down from Oxford. In the manner detested by some critics of *Souvenirs*, I leave the matter open, though I could easily ask him, for we became friends, and have remained so; he one of the noble band of close readers who do not compete at all in the creative field. Of course, the question also arises whether his memory would be more reliable than mine.

But if the latter date is right I have rather prematurely reached the summer in whose ghastly maturity came the Munich crisis, which, before being resolved by Chamberlain's piece of paper bearing the worthless (as it turned out) Hitler signature, had led us to decide that Kate and our infant son should go to Blackpool, to her parents, in case war started suddenly and the bombers caught us in the South-East with our pants down. The Spanish Civil War had done nothing to dispel the concept, fostered by such films as *Things to Come* (1936) and so completely depressing in those days, that civilians would be immediately under severe air attack when war arrived. Not long ago I came across a letter, somehow separated from its fellows, that I wrote to Kate in Blackpool during Munich days, saying I had been fitted for a respirator (as gas-masks were officially known) by Mrs "Y-cwt". "The thrill of a lifetime," I commented, with a facetiousness not diminishing over the years. The lady in question, in the Civil Defence organization, was the middle-aged wife of the village headmaster, Mr Exton.

Munich was late in the Ashford era: quite early was the arrival of a leaflet inviting subscriptions for a new "twice quarterly" periodical, *Twentieth Century Verse*. I sent my four shillings (20p) to the address named, 17 The Waldrons, Croydon, though not approving of the brief statement of editorial policy, which I judged poetically eclectic as well as politically uncommitted – to say nothing of the editorial address being unreassuringly non-metropolitan. As I write this, I take from the shelf the first number of the magazine, and see with surprise it is dated as late as January 1937. There must have been a longer gap than I recall between its appearance and the leaflet. Perhaps the editor, Julian Symons, was accumulating financial resources (i.e. saving a few pounds from his wages as secretary in the Victoria Street offices of some engineering companies). He says in his autobiographical *Notes From Another Country* (1972) that the leaflet brought in only nine subscriptions.

That first number did not allay the doubts raised in me by the leaflet. It opened with a poem by Dylan Thomas ("It is the sinners' dust-tongued bell"), a poet already a *bête noir* of mine. A poem by the editor was called "The Romantic Speaking": this, coupled with his name, conveyed some wispy figure more like an ineffectual Nineties poet than someone able to stand up to the rigours of the Thirties and the probably even more rigorous Forties. I was surprised when I met, as I did quite soon, a tough-minded six-footer; subsequent meetings gradually revealing a notable eater and drinker, expert table tennis and snooker player, cricketing days not long over. Even his name proved really to be Julius (as was Kingsford's, the founding father of Kingsford, Flower and Pain, always striking me as that of some powerfully astute character), enterprisingly changed by himself; and he had been familiarly known by the sporting youth of Clapham (the place of his family house) by a contraction of his second name, Gus. As to my own name, my few published poems had appeared above the moniker R. B. FULLER. Soon, with his concern for nomenclature, Julian wrote: "Unless it is Reginald, you ought to use your first name." I followed his advice, as I have usually done down to this day, though he is likely to proffer it only infrequently.

Our first meeting was not awfully far from the flat occupied by Mervyn's mother and step-father, though the ambience was sharply contrasted, being a pub close, perhaps next door, to the Victoria Palace. I had been given a lift up, was to be given a lift back, late at night, by Kingsford's cashier, out on some spree with a small party. I rather think Ruthven Todd turned up at the pub; certainly Gavin Ewart came later to Julian's basement room in Pimlico, a locale favoured by him in other epochs, also. I have a feeling I encountered Hugh Gordon Porteus and D. S. Savage on that occasion, but that a meeting with H. B. Mallalieu was postponed till later. All were familiar names, contributors to *Twentieth Century Verse*.

And as I write this, in the late summer of 1980, the whole lot except Ruthven are still alive. Porteus, a man of letters of the highest standards, must now have achieved a tidy age (though in one's own old age one is inclined to exaggerate that of others). Gavin Ewart and H. B. Mallalieu, in those days respectively toughly and darkly handsome, both fell off writing verse, then returned to it in later life, Gavin with widely acknowledged success. Derek Savage abandoned verse for criticism, then more or less abandoned all writing; sustained by disciplines of faith, and perhaps diet, in actual living. Ruthven died not long ago, after years of ill-health brought on by cigarettes, booze and variable, usually insufficient supplies of money. His parrot and jackdaw ways used to offend my Lancastrian puritanism. In the Auden style of the time he turned out many a poem about "history" or some hero of art or letters, like Klee. And soon after the outbreak of war, in the Café Royal, he read a poem I was showing to Julian for possible publication in a pamphlet called "Some Poems in Wartime", a sweeping-up mainly of leftovers from *Twentieth Century Verse*, a war casualty, and plagiarized it in a piece called "Various Ends" (though it must be admitted that the theme – poets' horrid fates – was eventually to some extent embodied by him in actuality; besides, my own poem was suspiciously like J. C. Ransom's "Survey of Literature", which nevertheless I always maintained I had not then read).

However, this rather too practical homage was a natural expression of Ruthven's possessive love for imaginative art and letters, and their practitioners. On the whole his work vacillated between the too hastily produced and the inordinately delayed. I remember seeing decades ago a notebook of his on fungi, with beautiful drawings (he had been trained as an artist), then hearing not long before his death that plans were afoot to publish a book made out of this material, yet to appear. Even earlier, probably at the beginning of the war, I expressed admiration of a large notebook he had, bound in yellow buckram. He said he had found and bought a cache of good but cheap paper, had it bound up into a number of notebooks. He opened the one he was carrying, to demonstrate the paper's quality. His small, shapely handwriting covered the unruled page, save for a generous margin left for addenda and corrigenda, at the foot of which he had entered the running total of words written. How enviable and impressive I found this scrupulous professionalism, and what a contrast to my ugly, commercial "Memoranda and Minute Book"!

Ruthven survived into the epoch of excessively long hair for men, and I saw him two or three times (he lived mainly abroad) with unbecoming grey Lisztian locks, though his image in earlier years is more vivid – hair by no means short and always ruffled, but black, like plumage, matching the rims of his gig-lamps, big even before the fashion for big spectacles came in. He chain-smoked, dragging at his cig in quick snatches so as to retain command of the conversation. His phenomenally narrow visage was rightly emphasized by Julian, as early as the latter's first crime novel, written before the war, where Ruthven is cast as the murderer.

I shouldn't think I adequately showed my gratitude to Julian for his troubling in gathering Ruthven and the others (though encountering my literary peers more or less for the first time made a strong mark), any more than I did to John Lehmann, who about this time also took the initiative in establishing friendship. I review my personality with no more pleasure than my verse.

But thinking back to Ashford days usually brings pictures far removed from jaunts to the London literary underworld – or, what my mind was full of, despite being suddenly out of politics, anxiety over world events and the state of England. I see the limes of Kennington Lees astonishingly holding their golden leaves far into the autumn, utterly unlike Blackpool trees, such few as existed being blasted by the gales of September. I see my son in his "high" chair, probably no more than a year old, insomniac, his restlessness best assuaged by being brought in to overlook the bridge table – where Mervyn would be playing, the fourth probably Jack Clark; if not, as unknown to me now as the "third" to the author of "The Waste Land". And I "see", of the gramophone records bought then, those of the Busch Quartet playing Beethoven's Opus 131, and the young Ella Fitzgerald singing "Deep in the Heart of the South", persisting mélange of taste I never thought unusual. The time there, as measured by the calendar several months less than three years, seems, because of personal and public happenings, of huge amplitude, especially compared with the flickering by of seasons in old age.

My job at Kingsford's was not so arduous that it immediately altered the character I had so far brought to the law. The firm had spilled over the adjoining building, but only on the second floor, where a communicating door had been opened, rather like the dormitories in Seafolde House. My office was the farthermost in the adjoining building, so remote that to save clients a trek I would see them, if it were vacant, in an antediluvian room on the ground floor, nominally used by the Clerk to the West Ashford Rural District Council, whose job, however, seemed even less arduous than mine. On the way to my room I had to pass through one occupied by the cashier and a couple of junior clerks, and here I might linger for a chat or, while the craze lasted, a game of cricket played with an ebony ruler and, much to my timid taste, a crumpled-paper ball. Back in my own room I expect I devoted time to composing the pieces which were eventually a "feature" of the March 1938 number of *Twentieth Century Verse*, though whether more time than to office cricket may be doubted, for when Julian proposed the feature I had to scrape the bottom of the barrel for sufficient poems.

I say "my own room", but I shared it with the articled clerk, Frank Flower's son. That I wrote poetry in his presence seems unlikely – it would have been too conspicuous a demonstration of the firm's money going down the drain. In any event, my period there coincided with his statutory year at law school, possibly also a spell at Gibson and Weldon's, so I saw less of him than might be imagined. He was, or had been, known in the family as "Boy"; old playmates, like the Clark children (I believe our knowing the Clarks was through the Flowers), referred to him as "Bertie". However, his proper name was Richard, and that is what I called him. Even at nineteen or so he had the flair for the law, and for pleasing clients, possessed by his father. I had to represent in the Ashford police court a pilot of the First World War on a drugs charge, to which there was no defence. Richard wrote out the heads of my mitigation plea with such an acute sense of what would properly touch the heartstrings that Sir Charles Igglesden's bench let the defendant off lightly, and Sir Charles's newspaper quite amply reported the proceedings.

When he was free, Richard drove me to the police and county courts of Kent and East Sussex in his father's Triumph Roadster, a fast and dashing soft-top. I marvel now that Frank owned it: he may also have possessed a more sober vehicle, but memory does not report it. I can feel now the wind blowing through the car's side curtains, chilling my neck, already chilled by the stiff wing collar I sometimes did not bother to change out of after a county court appearance; the beautiful countryside, so novel, flying past. I liked Richard: what he made of me, impossible to conjecture. I see him now (a thought I would not have had in those days, taking English virtues for granted, certainly to be carried forward to a communist society) as representative of the best in the solicitors' profession (for he duly qualified, with a rare First Class in the Intermediate Examination). Probably with equal glibness I also took for granted professional independence, and the law's generation of its own idealism, despite cynicism about the apparatus of bourgeois rule implanted by Terry Warnock. In the war to come Richard joined the Royal Marines, was severely wounded, won the M.C. Like Jack Clark, he was a fine cricketer.

The contrast with my own character and career need not be laboured. Why off my own bat hadn't I hit the magistrates and journalists for six in the drugs case? Lack of a true interest, of the common touch, of the energy to avoid the merely routine where the merely routine would serve – all these reasons might be advanced, yet perhaps the truth was vaguer: in fine, the

Vamp Till Ready syndrome once more. Some day I should have a job in the law – or a literary standing – which would allow my selfhood fully to express itself. It was still, however, a blend of the cocky and the shy: the former underwritten by brain power of sorts; the latter made more of a handicap, in business matters at least, by gross diffidence about exercising authority. (It comes to me that this diagnosis was just as applicable in subsequent times).

Nevertheless, in advocacy, as in other sides of a solicitor's life, I couldn't help improving. Did the police court clients get their three guineas' worth? Hard to say. I had a case at Hythe, a small dairy farmer charged with watering his milk, arising out of a routine check by the Ministry inspector. I believed in his innocence, and I don't think I was deceived (as I was about a client accused of careless driving, even though noting his red face: when I pressed a prosecution witness on some point it was plain the defendant was lucky not to have been charged with drunken driving). The line of watered milk cases made it almost impossible to rebut the presumption of guilt if the specific gravity test were positive: phenomenally wet pastures, careless washing of churns, malicious employee – such, as I recall, were about all the defences that had succeeded, and themselves of a fundamental implausibility, needing convincing evidence. The test had not been far on the wrong side, and the farmer made a good witness. But in a sense the very scrupulosity of his procedures with the milk, which I elicited from him, precluded possible defences. What I should have done (I realized, brooding unhappily after the event) was to invite the bench, in the strongest terms, if they believed his denial of dilution, to acquit my client despite the *res ipsa loquitur* line of cases (heavily relied on, of course, by the Ministry prosecution). No doubt if Richard had been writing my heads of submission he would have got me effectively to quote: "when you have eliminated the impossible, whatever remains, *however impossible*, must be the truth" – the reason, though hidden, outside the accused's control or intent. (After I had published the foregoing remark the dictum of Sherlock Holmes in *The Sign of Four* was in fact actually held by the High Court as proper for any tribunal to follow: *Mabanaft GbmH v Consentino Shipping Company SA (The Times*, 15 May 1984).

As one often in the police court, I became known to the Ashford Superintendent of Police, a rather Goering-like figure, fat and jolly but, as one conceived it, not jolly all through. He once gave me a lift back from an outlying magistrates' court where we had both been appearing; at least one stop on the way, at the premises of an obsequious publican, confirming the view of the police taken by *State and Revolution.* I rode in a police-car on another occasion when the Superintendent sent for me at lunchtime at home to bring me to the cells, where a young man charged with rape had asked for a solicitor. There was to be a special sitting of the magistrates that afternoon. The story my new client unfolded seemed one of family fantasy, his accuser being his sister-in-law, senior in years, whose appearance in the witness-box – sallow, nervous, agitated – bore out what the accused had told me. In cross-examination I ploughed on through what without cliché might have been called sordid details, conscious of the woman on the Bench of three, the chairman of which, on that occasion, I think was no less than the owner or tenant-for-life of Eastwell Park, not at all playing the effete role ascribed to such personae in my ballad in that "special feature" of *Twentieth Century Verse.* The magistrates threw the case out, persuaded by my argument that there was insufficient corroboration of the kind required by law. Perhaps the Superintendent prosecuted with only moderate enthusiasm.

Why didn't I use knowledge of this kind in the fiction attempted before the war? And, indeed, after? To advance the Vamp Till Ready syndrome again will hardly do. As a matter of fact I was greatly interested in both crime fiction and true crime cases, but though I eventually wrote a few crime novels they exploited scarcely at all the interesting actualities of the criminal side of things. As I write this, I recall an almost Dostoevskyan scene following an inquest where I had been representing a man whose wife had been killed and his child injured by a motorist who had knocked them down while they were bicycling along a country road. The evidence against the motorist brought out by my questioning proved so damning (among other things, he had not stopped) that the jury returned a verdict of manslaughter against him, though I had had almost entirely in mind my client's claim against the motorist's insurance company. At the end of the winter's afternoon-long hearing, the lights having come on in the courtroom like some *coup de théatre*, the police had to make an arrest on the spot.

I could have soldiered on with Kingsford's. In the long term I may well not have minded the life of a country-town solicitor, probably a partner, early quitting the sixteen-shilling flat, even moving into what Mervyn often pointed out, as we drove with him in his little red sports car, using a phrase my Oldham and Blackpool ears had possibly never heard before, "a lovely old house." But I was still intent on living in London, which I may have seen as a condition precedent to literary achievement – not through metropolitan back-scratching (which anyway I have never found to exist) – but to the young provincial's deep and well-attested, if not entirely rational, desire to be up-to-date and at the heart of cultural action. It could also have been that I wanted to escape from private practice, like (as I learnt much later from his letters, and with whom I do not compare myself in any deep sense) Wallace Stevens, and for the same reasons. I do not remember when I started applying for jobs again – perhaps quite late in Ashford days, even not until after Munich. And I do not think I put in more than two or three applications before success came.

The respirator letter previously referred to also makes naïve yet now enigmatic allusion to my view that England was lined up with the "wrong people" and that it would be necessary to "resist". I shall briefly return to the question of political attitudes to the events of 1938 and 1939, but I pause here to note how mysterious in retrospect seems one's relationship to large contemporary issues, casting doubts on any comparatively simple attitude revealed by these and other memoirs.

The cup of Munich passed, my wife and son soon returned. A memorable feature of the crisis was the house lights coming on one evening in the Odeon cinema – or, perhaps, more dramatically, merely the footlights that illuminated the curtains hiding the blank screen – and the cinema manager appearing from the wings to announce the Ashford Air Raid Precautions Officer. Then entered Swann, of Poncia, Swann and Carter. As a matter of fact, the errant nose was not a great feature of his appearance: he was personable, married to a good-looking girl, and lived in a white stucco house Mervyn might well have put into his approved category. Swann gave a good account of himself in this quite early instance of the disagreeable impingement of world events on cosy English private life.

Quite apart from the poems therein, an unlikable thing about the "Minute Book" is the handwriting, sloping excessively to the right. Not long after, when I had seen and been impressed by the orthography of Julian and of Ruthven, it became a good deal smaller, sometimes comically so. It never achieved Julian's fineness, however, for one thing because I lacked his gift for finding pens with that capacity (at one epoch a *glass* pen). During the war it quite suddenly became almost upright. I used to put that down to having to write legible airgraphs when abroad in the Navy (the airgraph was photographically reduced in size in the country of dispatch, and went through the mails in that form), but I believe now it reflected some psychological change. Cessation of guilt? Expiation? The Nelson touch? Modest literary success? *Quien sabe?* (as D. H. Lawrence, impressively to me in my nonage, used to put in his letters).

Looking back, I realize that as a youth and young man I was never satisfied with my handwriting, though sometimes regarding it with indulgent affection. The attitude was not far from that I had towards my verse. I believe that they continuously improved over the years. I quite see that others may prefer earlier periods, in both departments, but would stick sanguinely to my view.

As stated, I stopped using the "Minute Book" regularly in September 1937. I returned to it early in 1939, starting a satire in couplets, wisely abandoned, and drafting a few other poems. By then we had moved from Kennington to Blackheath, in south-east London. My mother's Graves' disease had at last been diagnosed, and she also came to London, temporarily, to undergo a partial thyroidectomy. The surgeon whose speciality was this then severe operation, held a consultancy at the London Hospital in the Whitechapel Road. I visited there before and after the surgery. Details of the journey have passed from memory, though I must have gone under the Thames by bus through the Blackwall Tunnel, thence by tram. I see the hospital, faintly Grecian, black with dirt – like the Lancastrian public buildings of my boyhood – and my mother sitting up in bed in the lighted ward, wearing a "bed-jacket", probably crocheted by herself. The loss of weight and browning of the skin were so classically symptomatic that to her amusement colour photographs had been taken of her, a technical process not so commonplace then as now. Perhaps they even appeared in some medical journal or textbook. Post-operatively, she was in danger, not conscious during my visit. Later she said she had felt then as though falling into a dark pit, being pulled out again and again.

5 *The Equitable*

A myth that must have gradually formed in my mind as the years rolled by was that my first book of poems came out before the war. In fact, as with slight surprise I recently discovered, it was published in December 1939. Only in the nick of time was I saved from being for ever labelled a Forties poet. I expect I was also sweating on the top line at the prospect of passing yet another birthday (my twenty-eighth on 11 February 1940) without having produced a first collection. With the example before me of Dylan Thomas and a good few others, I felt I was elderly to be gestating still. Publication, even of a fugitive kind, was not easily achieved in that era: it was Julian Symons, ever enterprising and professional, who found a publisher not only for himself but also for his friends – Gavin Ewart, D. S. Savage, me. I expect we had all tried and failed in orthodox channels: what Julian introduced us to was the Fortune Press, hitherto known, if known at all, as publisher of a few scholarly editions, and of more dubious, though one would guess scarcely more readable, works of eroticism and demonology.

Blake Morrison, in his learned book *The Movement*, describes L. Caton as 'head of the Fortune Press', but though strictly correct the words may mislead. I doubt if the Press had any staff at all – except possibly a typist, for I recall once getting a letter from Caton, typed quite well on a machine with strangely large type. On a sole occasion also, I met Caton, in the basement of the Fortune Press premises (or, more likely, the basement that comprised the premises) in the Buckingham Palace Road. Julian was with me: I think Caton had expressed to him a wish to meet the author he had published or was about to. I remember nothing of that encounter except seeing on the basement floor large numbers of unbound copies of the Press' publications; not an auspicious augury, as it strikes me now.

My arrangement with Caton was tacit, and I have never

regarded it as other than reasonable: I paid him nothing and he paid me nothing. Other authors of his, like Kingsley Amis and Philip Larkin, were miffed at not getting money out of him, but theirs was a later epoch and they became writers whose books were popular. I have no idea how many copies were printed or sold of my *Poems* (the foolishly neutral title almost obligatory for a first collection, in light of the example set by Auden and Spender). At some time further copies must have been taken from the basement to the binder, for I have seen the book in a case different from the original biblical black. In either state it is a satisfactorily rare book. The late Cyril Connolly once told me he had tried to get it for his collection of first books, and I promised to send him a copy if I had a spare, but when I searched I seemed to possess only one. (The promise was made on a comparatively genial occasion – after dinner, in John Julius Norwich's house, after I had received the Duff Cooper Memorial Prize for 1968. In lieu of *Poems*, I sent Cyril a copy of the beautiful pamphlet my son and daughter-in-law had printed on their hand press as a surprise for my sixtieth birthday. What was no surprise was that Cyril did not bother to acknowledge it, for he almost always seemed to me difficult and supercilious. Yet I must add that the last time I saw him at his publisher's party in 1973 for his book *The Evening Colonnade*, he took what for him could be called pains to be forthcoming and agreeable. Perhaps he had premonitions of mortality).

I was pleased and excited about the publication of *Poems*, though it was attended by worries that now appear ludicrous. For instance, one had to be content with the poems running-on instead of each starting on a fresh page, seeming a grave aesthetic sin (though now rather favoured by me as keeping the cost down without succumbing to that *minceur* character books of verse often today assume). And when the volume was at last in my hands and I slipped off the dust jacket, I saw to my horror that along the spine, between ROY FULLER and POEMS, was not a dot or asterisk or other printer's device I should have considered satisfactory, but a hyphen.

The time factor may have been even more of an anxiety than previously indicated, for my book was not reviewed with Julian's *Confusions About X*, or Gavin Ewart's *Poems and Songs* or Derek Savage's *The Autumn World*, but with subsequent 'Fortune Poets' (as Caton's slight publicity tagged us) – Glyn Jones and Henry

Treece; uncongenial figures not, so far as I know, promoted by Julian. However, any delay in publication of that kind need only have been of the order of weeks to alter reviewing companions. To speak of reviews at all is a bit misleading, for I doubt if there were as many as half a dozen, the war having put paid to a few little magazines that might have augmented this meagre sum. One of the reviews was in *John o'London's Weekly*, in terms a good deal less encouraging than those in which its editor had once written to me when, as a schoolboy, I used to submit short stories. The reviewer was Herbert E. Palmer, born exactly a hundred years ago, in 1880, not unknown to verse anthologies of a former day. He ended his notice:

> What most of our new poets do not seem to understand is this: If you took all the most curious lines and phrases of Shakespeare and strung them together to make complete poems you would perpetrate metrical monstrosities; and if God took half a dozen pairs of human eyes (even the most lovely) and stuck them all into one human face, everybody would flee from it, and the little children would run screaming in terror down the street.

As a matter of fact, I had recently reviewed a prose work by Herbert Palmer, *Post-Victorian Poetry* – in rude fashion – in *Twentieth Century Verse*, so I could not be heard to complain. Also, I had actually seen him, pointed out to me (or perhaps I recognized him from his photographs) on some occasion I am stumped to identify – for I would have said I never went to literary parties until latish in the war, when John Lehmann began to ask me to his. Palmer seemed aged to me, though then no more than sixty, and indeed his wild hair was quite white; and an aura of irascibility and disappointment seemed to surround his stringy figure.

So no danger of the reviews making me known in the Woolwich Equitable Building Society as the author of a book of verse of (in Palmer's hyperbolic phrase) 'extreme Modernism', with consequent risk to my legal career. I say that not wholly facetiously, though I probably claimed 'literary ability' as a qualification when applying for the job as an assistant solicitor with the society. I think the phrase had become a ploy, like the 'extremely interested' opening of my workless days. The advertisement in the *Law Society's Gazette* to which I responded did not mention 'building society', merely 'large corporate body', and was no more topographically specific than 'south-east London'. The advertisement was of a new post; inserted by A. E. Shrimpton, who six or seven years before had set up the society's own legal department, in origin the hiving-off of the society's business from the practice of a Woolwich firm of solicitors. The society had indeed, during the Twenties and Thirties, grown into a 'large corporate body' – the Solicitor's Department, as it was commonly called, employed a staff of sixty or seventy, representing what in those days would have been a substantial private practice.

Apart from a trivial feature of our first encounter to be mentioned later, I do not know why Fred Shrimpton chose me out of the good few applicants for what looked quite a promising post. He never really came clean when in later years I might joke about his irrationality and my luck, though he once told me of the trouble he had had with another interviewee – just the sort of confrontation under non-Queensberry Rules he detested. This rejected applicant was so irate that he pressed for the decision in my favour to be reversed, and even enlisted the help of an eminent figure known both to him and someone among the society's directors or senior management. Hearing this, thinking of one's own inferior qualifications, one could not but feel guilty, though that emotion Fred was far from intending to induce with his revelation so many years *ex post facto*.

Pressure of the foregoing kind would only have stiffened his resolve, for he also detested dirty work at the crossroads, just as he detested anyone who 'put on the dog'. I worked with him for twenty years, admiration unslackening, never once having even a tiff with him. But I must try not to look forward too much from that pre-National Service period of association with the Equitable, beginning with the day in the autumn of 1938 when I went to Woolwich for my first interview. The journey from Ashford was not arduous. I would simply change at London Bridge or (less cleverly) Charing Cross (both stations of intense familiarity in years to come, neither possessing beauty nor even comfort). A crisis arose when the local train stopped at Woolwich Dockyard. Should I alight? Topographical perspectives, so far as could be seen, seemed inauspicious, and the stomachic worms of anxiety were somewhat allayed by the train soon arriving at Woolwich Arsenal, where I did get out. Equitable House, the society's chief office, quite recently built, its Portland stone still pale, was opposite the station. I had time to spare, wandered by chance into the street market between Equitable House and the Georgian entrance to the Royal Arsenal. I expect I found on that occasion the market's only bookstall for I have always had a nose for such things, even having repeated dreams of bookstalls and bookshops of such circumstantiality that I have sometimes when awake fleetingly wondered if they did not truly exist in some town visited in the past.

On that first walk round the market I certainly found, among the stalls, the public lavatory, where I had a 'wash and brush-up' for 3d or even 2d; the service including a small clean towel in a paper sleeve. The soap was liquid, in a container difficult of access, and strong, pungent, almost redolent of the fluid used to disinfect the bogs at Seafolde House. Nevertheless, I washed my face, improving appearance and morale; a touch, indeed, that would appeal to Fred Shrimpton, as will appear. I was wearing my suit of darkish brown Manx tweed, made by a small gents' outfitter in Ashford. I say "made", but nothing on the Frank Flower or even Harold E. Pain lines is to be envisaged: the operation was not carried out on the premises but by a remoter organization serving such establishments. I had obviously not then come across the dictum that gentlemen do not wear brown suits – as persuasive but perhaps no more reliable than Curzon's saying gentlemen do not have soup at luncheon.

Nevertheless, the suit was a success, not least its material, ordered from a swatch of samples the proprietor had got in after my insistence on a cloth sober but soft – as (it was in my mind) worn by Aldous Huxley in the West End. That the suiting eventually found to fill this bill was Manx tweed conferred an added cachet. Somewhat mysterious why this should be, for neither my mother's voyagings to the Isle of Man nor our holidays there in earlier days had discovered any elegant life, rather the reverse. I still wore the suit after the war, when two or three moth holes had been invisibly mended: amazing art; lost now, I suppose, or priced beyond the thrifty market most requiring it.

I was taken in to Fred Shrimpton by his secretary. On the way we heard the rapid, expressionless voice of one engaged in "examining" an abstract of title. I made some such feeble but amiable comment as the curious sound being a universal feature of solicitors' offices, so that entering Fred's room we were both grinning. I saw later that in the light of Fred's character no better entry could have been made, particularly if that day he had already had a heavily serious interview with the applicant who proved so aggressive eventually. Fred was not in the least lacking in courage (in the First War he had been both a motor-cycle dispatch-rider and a machine-gunner), but preferred life not to include unnecessary clashes of will. One of the lessons my impatient nature did its best to learn from him in the practice of the law was the inherent capacity of a problem to, as he often phrased it, "work itself out" – not that he was in the least a dilatory lawyer. Indeed, I should add that in soundness and accuracy I never knew his equal.

Against the room's light oak panelling (Equitable House was a compendium of Thirties middle-of-the-road styles) I saw a man slightly below medium height, in his early forties, of extreme neatness in dress and hair-style. He was always pretty fit; at this time, after being a fine tennis player, just developing an alternative interest in golf. His questioning would have been measured and methodical, but I think it quite soon became plain that a deal was likely to be on. Superficially, the job seemed mainly concerned with conveyancing (and, of course, building society law) but fairly unpredictable chores arose out of the society's diurnal existence, the full extent of which, of course, I did not discover until I had moved in. Fred was the only solicitor in the department, though in a private practice of that size there would have been several partners. He was never a shirker, but some tasks he found distasteful and wanted help of a kind only a qualified man could provide. He had a number of excellent unadmitted managing clerks in the department, but he plainly felt, in some not entirely obscure way, that it would be an advantage to have a fellow at hand used to defending in cases of rape and watered milk. One example of such usefulness, merely notional, I fear, I will soon give an account of.

It might have been that very afternoon I met the remaining four of the society's senior executives, though more likely an occasion was specially arranged for them to give me the once-over before my appointment was clinched. At that epoch the senior executives had a sit-down tea round a large table in the smaller of the two committee rooms on the boardroom floor. Bread-and-butter and jam, cakes and biscuits, were the order of the day. The amenity impressed me, like others in Equitable House such as the built-in letter-chute running the height of the building, ending in a Post Office controlled postbox on the lower-ground floor, apertures for posting letters conveniently extant on every floor. The communal tea-taking custom survived the war for a spell: it ended just about the time the aforesaid apertures had to be sealed up because of the chute being periodically choked with unsuitable-sized letters. Thus and in other small ways was marked the coming of an era of rotting standards and growing indiscipline.

I joined the executives for tea, whatever the date was. The General Manager and Secretary, T. R. Chandler, was an actuary, of eminence and experience in the building society world, had seen the society grow, helped its evolution. He was then coming up to retirement, grey, distinguished-looking, tallish. He said little, was always courteous but quite awesome. From most men affection and respect can be won: Tommy (not that I ever came to call him that) Chandler won them where possible, in the most natural way. How he fared with awkward bastards I do not know, but have little doubt he would triumph without change of style or tactics on his part. He knew what was going on in the deepest recesses of the society, even in the family lives of its staff. His handwriting was among the most remarkable I have known: modern computer lettering may be envisaged, but executed with idiosyncratic artistic delicacy. The Assistant General Manager was a sweet-natured man called Austin Smith, who had to go prematurely through ill-health, but whose cultivated spirit luckily found compensations in retirement. Alexander Meikle, the Assistant Secretary, was a young Scottish chartered accountant, brought in to mechanize the society's accounting system, which by then he had done. The business-getting side of the organization, including the branches, then quite few, was under the dapper Agency Manager, Harold Codner, who, like Austin Smith, had been a very young aviator in the RFC during the 1914–18 war.

Perhaps even at that testing tea I observed the smoking habits of these four (I would have known something of Fred Shrimpton's from our interview), in those days before the weed had been linked with lung cancer a widespread, almost Dickensian indication of character. Chandler was not averse to a cigarette but preferred a pipe, and greatly enjoyed a cigar on a formal or semi-formal occasion. I have heard of him passing his tobacco-pouch unexpectedly to an underling, and believe its contents were invariably a mixture of Player's Gold Block and Balkan Sobranie. Austin Smith smoked Gold Flake cigarettes, popular during the 1914–18 war and persisting during the Thirties, the buttercup-coloured packet prominent in tobacconists'. The inside of the packet was, of course, white, but Stephen Spender may have come to feel there was some contradiction in the last stanza of his early poem, previously mentioned, about the unemployed friend:

> Nor shall I ever fail to see
> One photographic memory,
> Of how, still leaning on a post,
> You stride the gutter where men spit,
>
> And, laughing loudly, we both look
> Down on a torn and yellow box
> For on my brain I felt impress
> That white, appalling emptiness.

After its publication in *Oxford Poetry 1930*, these last two stanzas of the poem were omitted (and, alas, the impact lessened by other revisions). I think Austin Smith himself gave up Gold Flake, but this would be because of a lung complaint prompting him to give up smoking in general.

Did Sandy Meikle already smoke Du Maurier, a tipped cigarette, in 1938? I am prepared to be contradicted, for Du Maurier, if existent then, must surely have been a new brand. He certainly smoked them solidly after the war (until renouncing smoking late in life), lighting them with matches (preferably non-safety), for he distrusted devices like petrol-lighters, propelling-pencils and pencil-sharpeners. Fred Shrimpton smoked Gold Flake when I first knew him, if not so devotedly as Austin: in any case, he did not inhale, and liked to smoke a cigar. Harold Codner was a Capstan, later a Players Medium man, which eventually Fred became, though I think I am right in saying both went over to Players Gold Leaf when after the war that cigarette was transmogrified by its manufacturers into a tipped cigarette. In his early eighties Fred became skittish about smoking, sometimes on, sometimes off: I believe Harold, who also lived into his eighties, was more faithful. What a pleasure I lost when I myself gave up smoking at the age of sixty-two!

A greater knowledge of those four colleagues of Fred's came after the war – even of T. R. Chandler, who continued as a member of the Board of Directors, and of Austin Smith, whom I saw sometimes after his retirement in 1946. A few all-too-human traits were revealed, not apparent in the briefer encounters of early days, but their standards of work and, above all, of personal dignity and integrity, were extremely high. Moreover, without any apparatus of consumer-protection statutes and organizations, all these senior managers were implicitly convinced of the mutuality of building societies, the equitable balance needing to be struck between the interests of borrowers and investors. It is not without significance that a few years before I arrived it had been decided, on a periodical revision of the society's rules, not to omit the clumsy "Equitable" from its title.

To start with I was gravelled to anatomize the evil role of building socieites in an evil (and inadequate) capitalist economy, analysis not being helped, I suppose, by finding able and honest men running the Equitable. In the novel he wrote at this very time, *Coming Up For Air*, George Orwell faced the same problem, and solved it with his usual disregard for probability and fact. His invention, the Cheerful Credit Building Society, not only lends people money on mortgage: it owns the house-building company, the builders' merchants who supply the materials, and the company in which the freehold of the houses is vested. That these latter activities are contrary to law (as it is for building societies to distribute profits in the ordinary sense) is not taken account of by Orwell, who rampages on about his self-invented scandal in fascist (or at any rate demagogic) fashion.

The answer I came to myself was that building societies served the bourgeoisie by providing funds for speculative builders. There was also a collaborative practice between building society and builder that was soon to be challenged by the Left through the Courts in a quite dramatic way. A society was able to make mortgage advances of an extremely high percentage of the purchase price by taking collateral security on cash deposited with the society by the builder of the houses. The deposits were "pooled" to form security for numbers of mortgages, so that the cash deposit by the builder in any particular case did not need to be the full amount of the "excess" advance in that case.

The Equitable's financial year end was 30 September, so the annual general meeting was held just before Christmas. The first I attended (in the Chartered Insurance Institute in the City) came only a couple of weeks after I joined the Solicitor's Department, and, like much else at the time, made its mark. Once again, the provision of tea came into it. After the meeting this was provided for the big-wigs in a restaurant in the basement. I suppose Fred Shrimpton must have taken me down under his wing on that first occasion. After the war I used to make my own way there, but for years was unsure as to my entitlement, though never challenged. The cloakroom and lavatories were also in the basement: rather stricture-making to find oneself standing, without secure status, beside the Vice-Chairman of the Board, say, or even T. R. Chandler. After my first attendance at the AGM I started a short story in which some demented and out-of-work borrower, who had been evicted from his house by the mortgagee-building society, goes to the society's AGM and shoots the Chairman. Perhaps I am putting the plot in unfavourably stark terms, but could I ever have conceived such a narration seriously? It must be so, though I doubt if I ever finished it. A comic Kafkaesque account of the basement tea-tables and urinal-stalls would not have occurred to me as a more promising concept.

I ought to emphasize that the effects of the economic crisis of the start of the Thirties on building society borrowers was still quite marked. The man in charge of arrears, F. A. Wellman, of infinite compassion and patience, attended on T. R. Chandler first thing every day to report the situation. The department dealing with properties the society had had to take possession of was euphemistically named "Special Securities" and its head "Chief Clerk", mild humbug Orwell would have made much of. It may well have been the then "Chief Clerk" of whom it was first said that he put the "quit" in "Equitable". In some domestic speech after the war the saying drew a slight laugh when I applied it to a subsequent official on the arrears side, but the great days of moustache-twirling mortgagees had already gone. It should be said that the jest comes out better for knowing that the society was called by the local masses "the E*quit*able" (though advertising campaigns may now have succeeded in changing the usage to "the Woolwich") – just as Terry Warnock and Rose and others used to refer to the class enemy as ca*pit*alists. However jarring to those who know better, some justice in both pronunciations must be admitted, the latter seeming to imply a trivial, even disgusting urinatory, quality in the bourgeoisie.

How seriously did I take the role of building societies in sustaining the fabric of a society I regarded as doomed? Was there not much that was ludicrous and cowardly in becoming, with my views, even a junior executive in such an organization; in fact, in being a lawyer at all without professionally helping the underprivileged? Certainly one's spirit was divided, leading a life of outward conformity. The extreme opinions expressed to friends, even acquaintances, seem in retrospect mere parlour pinkism, of the feeblest kind. However, one is perhaps too inclined from this distance in time to play down one's resolution in face of the disasters that threatened, the hopes that glimmered. For instance, though Munich was an enormous relief it seemed clear that the time of testing of one's physical courage and ideology had been only a trifle postponed.

It never struck me with any force in those days that the building society was a characteristic British invention, still with strong elements of mutuality; no doubt benefiting its managers (managers as a new class was a notion just becoming fashionable) and those profiting from house-building, but part of the overwhelmingly well-conducted sector of trade unions and friendly societies. Almost simultaneously with my entry into the building society world came the notorious Borders case (did that prompt Orwell's exaggerations?) and the ensuing reforms and restrictions of the Building Societies Act 1939, the first building society legislation since 1894. The case arose through a combination of bad building, slap-dash legal work, an ill-worded builder's estate brochure, and a mortgage loan by a building society to the wife of a communist taxi-driver. Unlucky for the society involved, but the circumstances were by no means outré, and a fiction founded on them would have compared favourably with Orwell's bosh.

When Mrs Borders was sued by the building society for arrears she denied she had signed the mortgage deed produced. She counterclaimed for damages for fraudulent misrepresentation, alleging that the society and the builder were so closely associated that the society was responsible for statements in the builder's brochure about value for money and good workmanship. She argued that the society had no power to make the loan anyway, because a substantial percentage of it was based on the additional security of the builder's pooled cash deposits, whereas the building societies statutes and the society's rules required the security to be wholly freehold or leasehold property, viz the house. The course of the litigation was complex, but it is roughly true to say that whereas the society prevailed on the points of fraud and the power to make the loan, Mrs Borders was the practical victor. At many of the court hearings she appeared in person, and her eloquence and acumen led her to be compared by the popular press with Portia, the society being tacitly cast in the role of Shylock.

In those days did I truly want Mrs Borders to win? The answer must be yes; greatly in doubt if asked today. I should still feel a similar *Schadenfreude* at seeing another society in the shit (one with standards less rigorous than the Equitable), but also pangs at blows struck at an order established for the people's good. Through his membership of the Legal Advisory Panel of the Building Societies Association, Fred Shrimpton was involved in the legislation following Borders, and collaborated in a book expounding it. A little of the work rubbed off on me (rather a turn up for the "literary ability" qualification) – a taste of something I did much more of twenty years on, and grew fond of; like falling for someone for ages merely grudgingly tolerated, as in a fiction by Charlotte Brontë or Daphne du Maurier.

I did not myself before the war become a mortgagor, though the society made loans to its staff at a privileged rate of interest, and I could have borrowed from my mother the relatively small deposit needed. What an investment a house bought in 1938 would have proved, if not flattened by Goering's men! But in a bohemian way – perhaps a hangover from the red trousers and the like of D. H. Lawrence-reading times – the idea of living in a modest suburban house, perhaps one of a row or pair, was anathema. The emotion may have been reinforced in an odd way by a mild Mervyn-induced lovely-old-house ambition. Our first dwelling in Blackheath was a maisonette, the first and second floors of an undistinguished late-Victorian house in a wide but busy road linking the A2 with the A20. Our Ashford rent was about doubled, but then so was the space, which included an enormous sitting room and a main bedroom scarcely smaller. Heating facilities were minuscule. The winter of 1938–39 was severe, and the pipes froze (fairly rotten, at best). When they thawed, water fell on us in bed, though we were not sleeping on the top floor. I marvel at our youthful hardihood.

In the maisonette below (basement and ground floor) were two elderly sisters and the unmarried daughter of one of them. We put up at the windows of the main bedroom the Ashford curtains made for that purpose there. They were too short, as could be seen from the front garden, and one of the downstairs ladies (all of a certain refinement) could not forbear to remark: "Of course, you'll be getting new curtains." This may not have been the sole reason for tenseness between upper and lower premises, Blackacre and Whiteacre so to speak, for I remember making a grotesque grimace behind the windows of the foreshortened curtains, when one of the ladies was gazing up from the garden with what I took to be continuing criticism; conduct unbecoming a solicitor, particularly one with the nearby Equitable, and not utterly characteristic, though a fanciful recklessness when goaded must be accounted part of my personality.

To the Blackheath maisonette my mother came for a short time to convalesce after her partial thyroidectomy. The place was even less appealing to her than the Ashford flat: her ideas of suitable house property would have coincided with those of the Equitable. Internal doors and window-frames were painted dark green. We saw this as objectionable in the sitting-room at least, and bought some white paint. I made a start on the interior of the door but found it impossible to cover. Letting the paint down with turpentine never occurred to me, so well had cheap labour between the wars insulated even the modestly middle-class from what is now known as "Do It Yourself", and widely practised. We had to call in a decorator, but whether his ameliorations had been effected by the time of my mother's stay I forget. In any case, they were few, and there were plenty of other features to upset one whose attitude to such things was almost certainly stricter even than that of the downstairs ladies to curtains. When she was well enough to get up, and mount to the top floor, she discovered on the landing a disused sink (perhaps a relic of earlier days when that floor had been a separate flat) above a cupboard. The sink was more or less enclosed by timber, the whole affair painted in the formerly ubiquitous dark green. I had used the sink to store old magazines, probably mostly copies of

Left Review. However, my mother's objection to this feature was grounded not in ideology but hygiene, no doubt allied to her strict conception of *comme it faut*.

There may have existed at this date what would also distress her – a moderately dilapidated car belonging to Jack Clark which by a stroke of ill fortune had one day broken down near enough to our house for Kate's help to be enlisted to steer it on to the premises, Jack being on his way to visit us. Who would have thought the car fated never to start again? Weeds and grass grew up in the shelter of its chassis, and in the end Jack had actually to pay to have it towed away to the junkyard. Luckily my mother did not experience the maisonette's fuel crisis in that first winter, when my son's pram had to be used to collect coal from the coal merchant, deliveries being held up. Nor am I sure she closely inspected the half of the back garden that belonged to us, the grass of which on one occasion was attacked by Kate with a pair of scissors.

My mother did, though, get upset in the ideological sphere. It was not long before even optimists saw Munich as merely slightly postponing the inevitable. During my mother's convalescent stay, or possibly somewhat later, my brother visited us. In a discussion about the future war both he and I said we would be conscientious objectors. She was horrified, left the room to shed a tear. The situation was exacerbated by a friend present expressing no such intent, though radical in politics. I can quite understand my mother's anticipation of family disgrace outweighing any wish for the odds against her sons surviving to be reduced. How serious my brother was I do not know: not at all, I should think.

> He only does it to annoy,
> Because he knows it teases.

The lines of the Duchess' lullaby would apply; the trait inherited by us from our grandfather – whom I see, as elsewhere described, rubbing his unshaven chin against my grandmother's cheek at breakfast time, and saying "diddle-diddle" in a loud falsetto. My brother was always appreciative, too, of abrasive conduct on the part of Mr Parslew, not at all rare. "Waiting, pleess!" had become a catch-phrase with us vis-à-vis any sort of delay or command, but as used and originated by Mr Parslew not always to be taken in a genial or lenient sense.

Part of my own expressed intent at that time of opting out of the coming war stemmed from the constant wish to shock, often noted by friends; a more serious part from the sense of the bogusness of the so-called National Government offering to resist fascist Germany. Underlying all this, of course, was the lesson of the 1914–18 war – not to be bamboozled by imperialist motivations masquerading as national defence. But it was quite plain to me that conscientious objection was not legally tenable since I had never worked for pacifism in the moral or religious spheres, nor even expressed purely pacifist views.

As to such matters, why didn't I, in London's greater anonymity and opportunity, return to the political activity suspended during Ashford days? Easy to assign theoretical reasons, any of which may have really existed. I was no longer a simon-pure Stalinist, but did not accept the then anti-Stalinism, from whichever quarter it was expressed. Above all, I did not wish to see the former ruling-classes back in Russia. Some Marxist heresies had grown up among my Marxist orthodoxy, but there was probably no political party to which I could have given whole-hearted allegiance. To support inaction I might even then have advanced the feeble argument that a modern writer lives his politics in the act of writing, with all its difficulties of expression and audience – particularly if the writer concerned to a substantial degree sees life in political terms.

I should add, though, that politics did not come into a novel I wrote at this time, finished before the war, never published. It was inspired by a classic Scottish murder case where the victim took all night to die, in circumstances of some domestic complication and squalor. The notion was a reasonable one, for I also added a classic puzzle element, but the action being confined to one night, I proved to be still wound in Joycean or Woolfish coils, inescapably inside the protagonist's mind; scarcely admitting any gap in the hour by hour account of events. There was, however, an interlude when the hero mercifully dozed off, of surrealist nature and incorporating some features of my contemporaneous reading of Elizabethan and Jacobean dramatists. The latter was a brief salvation from the sin of unsystematic reading I have been guilty of throughout life.

My dubieties about the translation of Marxism into practical politics should not be exaggerated, as I realize apropos of what must have been my next fiction, *The Agents* – an episodic affair in the manner of Stevenson's *New Arabian Nights* or, more accurately, Arthur Machen's *Three Imposters*. The episodes were to be alternately true and false (achieved through varying narrators), the false motivated by a conspiracy for an English fascist *coup d'état*. Part of the conspiracy was a preliminary discrediting of the communist left, and began with an episode that, when I described it to him, greatly appealed to Julian. The hero, wearing a Manx tweed suit, drawn by apparent chance into a communist meeting, is surprised to see so many women among the audience – women, moreover, all wearing mackintoshes, though highly made up. At a certain stroke of a nearby church clock, all the women stand, remove their mackintoshes, and reveal themselves as stark naked – implications, when the thing gets reported, of free love, wives held in community, and so forth, demonstrated practically at a communist rally. Or is there such a plot? The ambiguities were not to be resolved until the end of the book, when truth and falsehood would be identified and explained. However, the ideological sympathies would be no more in doubt than as in the case of a novel like Rex Warner's *The Wild Goose Chase*.

Warner's remarkable work had made quite an impression on me. It was published in 1937, but I see my own copy was not bought until June 1939 and probably re-read then. So it may, as well as Stevenson and Machen, have helped me to achieve the greater distancing and irony of *The Agents*. Certainly the writing indicated some literary progress, and the complicated, predominantly comic, plotting was worked out with ingenuity. Ben Jonson – that quintessentially English, though ever undervalued genius – also must have influenced plot and tone (though I pay tribute to him with due sense of inadequacy). And when I say English, I suppose I mean British, for as I write these words my bedside reading is Walter Scott's journal in which he sometimes quotes from Jonson, particularly from *Every Man in His Humour*, with almost proverbial effect. But though I started *The Agents* after the outbreak of war, I saw I could not go on with the thing after call-up (though opportunities would in fact have existed), for the activity seemed prospectively too irrelevant. Besides, history was rapidly undermining both plot and tone. (Amusing if somewhat macabre to think that nowadays the nude meeting might well be taken as a point not against but in favour of the left).

I mention these piddling literary matters not least as evidence of what progress can be made in matters of art by reflection and application; aiming at a sensible target. My follies in this field went on too long, considering my native wit; and, insofar as they resulted from impulse and indolence, have gone on all my life. Of course, the distance between *The Agents* and one's actual involvement, outside one's volition, in the events of the war, was less than the distance of *The Wild Goose Chase* from such events (or so one would like to think). Rex Warner's novel, though the inspiration of its imaginative machinery lingered on, still holds to a romantic view of class character and destiny I believe I myself was growing out of, even at the time I was most involved in political activity. But such nuances are hard to recapture accurately. The last paragraph of *The Wild Goose Chase* may from the start have seemed too optimistic, for all that further ordeals were promised:

> The crossing of the marshes, the final battle with the king, birth in the desert and the strange customs of some remote tribes – of all this he thought then, and of all this we too have received strange and often self-contradictory information. Yet at this moment the light was clear and it was dead calm. Be the future as it might be, and no doubt that complete success was distant still, he knew that something not unworthy had been achieved already as he stood with the men and women, holding Joan's hand in his hand . . .

Hence the more lasting appeal of the boggarts and ironies and death-preoccupations in the verse of Graves and Riding and Norman Cameron.

6 *The Strongroom*

I joined the Equitable on 1 December 1938. By 1 September of the following year my wife and son had gone to Blackpool to escape the metropolitan dangers of the war in which England became officially involved on 3 September 1939. I have done little to suggest the richness, for us, of what seems now an amazingly short span – a mere gestatory period. It was a time of domestic happiness; of greater comfort and prestige as a lawyer; and of modestly growing literary know-how and friendships. (I see Ruthven Todd somehow elevating himself behind the sitting-room door – still, appropriately, in its dark green paint – to appear with black overcoat over his head, arms in the sleeves: a vampire to gratify my small son's liking to be reasonably frightened). Cutting across all theoretical political desiderata was my wish (no doubt largely covert) that England would rat again, as at Munich, so that peace should persist. This feeling may have been partly rationalized but I doubt much intensified by the belief, already touched on, that in a war against fascist Germany England's participation would be half-hearted, alert for the sell-out, the diverting of Hitler eastward, dirty work at the crossroads generally. I guess my wish would have been the same had England been led by the Archangel Michael.

Uniquely depressing, seeing my wife and son off at Euston; worse for her, not least the retrogression of going back to her parents' home. I have mentioned somewhere else the embarrassing shame felt coming out of the house and passing one's fellow men on the morning the newspapers told of Germany's invasion of Poland, and it was apparent that general hostilities were inevitable. Strange emotion; of a kind a boy might feel seeing his parents arrive drunk on the school's sports day. It was probably on the evening of 1 September, after the office, I swam in the "lido" in Shooters Hill Road, thinking it could well be my last swim. It had been a hot summer: though the sky was overcast, the pool was warm, rather deserted. The sensation returns of swimming up and down, consciously luxuriating in my passage through the tepid medium, a passion even in the absence of war's sharpening.

I cannot recall when I dug the slit-trench in our part of the back garden, penetrating the scissors-trimmed turf. Grisly to have executed the work while my wife and son were still there. A slit-trench was said to be quite good protection against bombs. I do not know why I did not apply for an "Anderson" shelter. I think they were decried by the *Daily Worker* and other leftish voices scornful of the Government's ARP plans. That would have sufficiently put me off.

Blackheath's pebble-rich soil, relic of the glaciation that scooped the Thames valley, resists the spade. I gave up the trench when it merely sheltered one in a recumbent posture. Now I come to think about it, my wife must have been there, for it was surely she who remarked that all I had done was dig a convenient grave. But in this hole I self-consciously went to lie for a few minutes on the Sunday morning when the sirens sounded after Neville Chamberlain's announcement that the country was at war. The sky remained clear.

Later that day I went to see Julian Symons at the Denmark Hill house he then shared with others. Herbert Mallalieu was there, or arrived there, his wife and child also self-evacuated. I accepted his invitation back to his flat in or near Croydon: probably neither of us relished that night alone in our family-denuded dwellings. In the middle of the night the sirens sounded again, wailing that like a chronic pain was to become familiar but never less disagreeable. Herbert and I dressed and went to a nearby public shelter and sat for some time, with a small but varied number of Croydonians, in semi-gloom, on benches against white-washed walls. No bombs fell, but we must have thought them likely to do, for when we returned to the flat before the "all clear" we stayed in the sitting-room, having hoisted a mattress against the window as a protection against flying glass, commonly identified as an air-raid hazard.

I was not due at the office on the Monday morning, which I expect inclined me to go with Herbert to Croydon. Austin Smith had issued instructions that, in the event of war, staff should allow three days to elapse, then report at certain assembly points. Like the rest of us, he was victim of the *Things to Come* complex. I let all Monday go idle and air-raidless by before phoning Mr Shrimpton and finding him and most staff already back at work.

The time that then had to elapse (taking in the Phoney War and Dunkirk and all that) before I was called up for National Service seems, in contrast to the pre-War period with the Equitable, curiously foreshortened. My wife came back to London for a few short visits, and I went up to Blackpool when I could, but for the most part I lived alone in the maisonette until the late autumn of 1940. I must have spent a lot of time at cinemas, and visiting Julian Symons at the Denmark Hill ménage brilliantly sketched in his *Notes From Another Country*. The essential misery of those days is indicated by the sparseness and confusions of the resulting memories. Call-up into the armed forces loomed vaguely but inevitably ahead. I registered with the twenty-eight-years-old age group in the summer of 1940: another step to the grave. The scene was a large, mock-Tudor Eltham pub on a wide, bleak main road, appropriately Orwellian setting for the Orwellian smells emanating, during the medical examination part of the process, from men for the most part in what seemed to me amazingly advanced states of hairlessness, toothlessness and paunchiness. (Even fifteen or so years later, when my son registered for National Service, the medical officer, counting his teeth, arrived with surprise at the total of thirty-two). Being part of a sizable human mass was a strange experience: there were reminiscences of school and of my political past, but really little in life had been a preparation for so thorough-going an assault (however brief) on one's private individuality – as though caught for a crime of which one was not entirely innocent.

Mr Shrimpton, staff already depleted by the disappearance of Territorials and younger men, applied to the Law Society for the deferment of my call-up under a scheme administered by them. A few specious grounds were concocted to bring my case within the scope of the scheme (such as my work in the administration of arrears caused by borrowers' war service) but the application was rightly rejected. In the late Sixties, when I went regularly to the Law Society's Hall in Chancery Lane to sit on a working party concerned with conveyancing law reform, I saw again the little "court room", with its wealth of dark wood (more usually devoted to the appearance of wrong-doing solicitors before the Law Society's Disciplinary Committee), where the application had been heard; and the atmosphere of that war-time day – youth obsessed with time and destiny – came momentarily but sharply back.

Julian has also described, in the work referred to, how on the afternoon of 7 September 1940, a Saturday, he and I watched from the height of Brockwell Park, SE24, neat formations of German bombers, with attendant frisky-puppy fighters, moving overhead to raid the London docks. Soon, slanting cloud-mountains of smoke were seen rising from that area. This was more like *Things To Come*. The raid was renewed at night, which I was spending (or perhaps had decided to spend, in view of the cataclysm) at the house in Denmark Hill. We passed a few hours in a cellar: it seemed wise to do so, not having then acquired the half-divinatory, half-blasé sense of behaviour under such fire that soon came with more experience. When a bomb fell across the road on or close by the King's College Hospital, the coal in the cellar seemed to rise and re-settle itself, one phenomenon of the occasion that particularly struck me.

It must have been after the raids on London that Kate and I began regular (or, at any rate, previously arranged) evening telephone calls. Neither she in Blackpool nor I at the maisonette was on the phone. Did we ring a call box number from a call-box? I certainly see myself in a call box in Rochester Way in the early evening, and saying, in the course of a conversation: "There goes the siren. Can you hear it?" Lowering prospect for us both. On a few occasions, when the raid was especially bad and I was at home, I went to sit in the lower maisonette, where the three ladies would be, plus the fiancé of the daughter (a man of quite mature years), and possibly a neighbour or two. Hours of amazing tedium, scarcely alleviated by games of rummy, for love; modest refreshments. Any resentment about short curtains or vulgar face-pulling had been forgotten or pasted over in the camaraderie induced by the raids. The ladies had even offered sleeping accommodation in a small room on the half-landing between ground floor and basement, adjudged to be safer than our great bedroom on the first floor. I used it a bit, without necessarily taking in rummy or a cup of tea.

I saw much of Julian and his wife-to-be, who was none other than Kathleen, the middle Clark girl. They had come to know each other through us, of course; a consequence of my double life in Ashford. Patiently they put up with a grass widower on the bum for meals and a bed and an interesting social life. I went often to the house in Denmark Hill and, when that became uninhabitable through an unexploded bomb in the garden, to a smaller house in Tierney Road, Streatham; the street memorable through the film star Gene Tierney (then a newcomer, later played the mysterious eponymous heroine of *Laura*), whose beauty I admired. With inexhaustible hospitality they never made me feel *de trop*. There was little on my part I could do for them, though long after the war was over they reminded me I had once dined them at Blackheath, making a hotpot (culinary lore from Hollins Road days); and at Tierney Road cooked a meal of pork chops wearing my raincoat as protection from fat splashes, rather as William Herbert Wallace was thought to have donned his before beating his wife to death with a poker.

A good many hours of that epoch of waiting for call-up were spent playing piquet and snooker with Julian, the latter in a convenient Temperance Billiards Hall. Apart from the few occasions provided by Councillor Marston's half-size table and some games in the basement of the Imperial Hotel with the pianist from the Metropole Hotel band, I was a newcomer to the latter game, but it is as much a tribute to Julian's skill as an indication of my novitiate that he used to give me no fewer than seven blacks.

I think Kathleen would rarely, if ever, come to the billiards hall; such places being as jealously masculine as Pall Mall clubs. I expect we would meet her if we were dining out. I say "dining", but the place that comes to mind in those purlieus is Bicards on the South Side of Clapham Common, one of a smallish chain of "caffs" of those days. A vision arises of the dark street, a few "exhalations whizzing in the air", pushing aside the blackout arrangement at the entrance, and moving into a not large, dazzling, crowded, smoky ambience, rather lower class than even the Joe Lyons emporia of the time. The safest dish on offer was baked beans on toast, but those with hardihood might order a pie.

One morning, in the early hours, I was wakened in the half-landing room by lumps of plaster falling on me in bed – or, more accurately, as I lay on the mattress I had lugged down from upstairs. I cried aloud: "Oh, no!" but without avail. A landmine had descended across the road, a little farther down: outside, in the dawn, were apocalyptic scenes.

With my usual reaction of making light of, even denying, personal disaster, I quite soon set about trying to clear up the chaos in our maisonette. Many of the heavy ceilings had been brought down and windows blown out. Nearly as bad as the ubiquitous plaster and glass was the soot sucked from the chimneys by the blast. I went on working past the start of office hours, and thoughtlessly failed to let the office know what had happened. One of the conveyancing managing clerks, R. J. Edwards, was sent or volunteered to discover my fate. He more than once told the story of that morning – approaching the house, increasing disorder, fire engines and ARP personnel still evident, his car stopped, he proceeding on foot, the house with its windows out, no sign of life. Reg Edwards was convinced I was a goner, yet respectfully pressed the bell of the upper maisonette, though he could have walked in, the door having been blown off its hinges. To his astonishment he was greeted from the bathroom window-space directly above him by a grimy individual wearing a fishing hat. No doubt his surprise was all the greater for his viewing me ordinarily in Manx tweed and the like.

I see now that putting on the hat was like my grandfather putting on eccentric hats when he went "golfing", as he called it: filling the scuttles with coal from the coal-place at 208 Hollins Road, Oldham. The business (described in my novel *The Perfect Fool*) had a rational basis – protection from cold and coal dust – but my grandfather imposed elements of fantasy. The hat in question worn by me was one of a number of memorable possessions that disappeared during the war, not surviving the depredations of air-raid damage repairs men, furniture-removers, custodians of the furniture-store, and, I suppose, genuine accidental loss. I had bought it in some hatters' sale, not to go fishing in but because it closely resembled the hat worn by the model for Van Gogh's *Portrait of a Young Man*, the features of the young man himself very like my own.

Mr Edwards, a man of humour and practical ability, brought sanity into the situation. He was ARP officer at Equitable House, and suggested I slept there for the time being: soberly considered, the maisonette was uninhabitable in its present plight. A couple of blankets and my overnight things were all that was needed to make the transition. With these, he drove me off, and I never went back to live in the maisonette. He must have been able to use his car still because of his ARP role: I expect it was the pale-green immaculate Singer he kept for a good few years after the War, having it resprayed black and cream during the vogue for two-tone bodies.

There was already a small, slightly shifting population of staff sleeping in the basement of Equitable House, in the strongroom where the deeds of the society's mortgage securities had formerly been kept, such deeds having been sent to premises near Westerham bought to house in safety the society's records and accounting organization. In the event, Equitable House was virtually untouched by enemy action: the deeds, stored in a tunnel in the chalk of the North Downs, suffered first from damp, then from an electrical fire caused by the drying machinery consequentially installed. A run of bundles in the S's (initial of the borrowers' surnames) was so badly damaged the titles had to be reconstituted, a task falling to the Solicitor's Department. By the time I returned to the office in 1946 the job had been done save for a hard core of cases resisting efforts to provide secondary evidence of legal ownership. These were passed to me, like some fiendish puzzle grown tedious. (Eventually, with the enlightened co-operation of the Land Registry, I cleared them all up).

As to the wartime race of strongroom dwellers, in some instances it seemed their stay was prompted or prolonged by a wish to escape – not only from quarters more vulnerable to bombs but also from the delays and dangers of commuting travel, even from wives and families. The mode of life offered by the strongroom (not for the last time the war had thrown up a Kafkaesque metaphor for existence), though constricted and monotonous, was not utterly unappealing compared with current alternatives. At the heart of it was a nightly nap "school", playing for small stakes but with proper seriousness, at the close of which orders were taken for fish and chips, volunteers not being lacking to brave blackout and bombs to journey to the nearby fish-and-chip shop. I more or less fell into this routine myself, though tempering time in the nap school with visits to the billiards saloon, also nearby, or a cinema.

The saloon, down an alley off Woolwich New Road, had been in peacetime a place of local disrepute, but I never saw anything untoward there. Freud noticed that obsessional people generally felt better in wartime, since the rest of the population had descended to their level: the former quarrelsome or larcenous frequenters of the saloon had no doubt found, or been drafted to, spheres of greater opportunity. The roof was of glass, so no one was much inclined to linger once the air-raid warning had sounded: it may well be that snooker did not in reality cut far into the evening's cards. A dim picture comes to me of my staying on in my room after office hours, engaged in some literary work, possibly *The Agents*, but I would have been no more steadfast in such a pursuit at that time than any other time of my life.

In the evenings, in strongroom times, I sometimes went to the West End, perhaps fairly often, but memories of that, too, are not sharp. The atmosphere has often been described. The absence of lights, especially on moonlit nights, removed the city to earlier centuries. A measure of my continuing unsophistication about the literary world is that I was greatly impressed to sit, introduced by Julian or possibly Ruthven, at a table in the Café Royal with Bernard Spencer and his wife. Spencer, though he had not then published a book, was a poet I thought well of: a junior member of the Macspaunday group, had edited *Oxford Poetry 1930* with Stephen Spender. He was darkly handsome; his wife, Nora, pretty and chic, wearing one of the small felt hats fashionable at that time which fitted no part of the head. Though not formulating the matter in such terms, I was conscious that he was unlikely ever to be found in Bicards or round a halfpenny nap table. Nora died young, shattering for him, who never quite fulfilled his early promise.

In the strongroom, the most devout nap player was Arthur Pickup. Among the staff Fred Shrimpton had brought from the private firm formerly the Equitable's solicitors were two already elderly conveyancing clerks, rather a different breed from the bright secondary school boys recruited during the society's rapid expansion in the late Twenties. The two in question, Heap and Pickup, were apt to be named together, though not, I think, particular friends. Heap, whom I never knew well, had a nervous disposition, whereas Pickup, philosophically quiescent, seemed unmoved by outside events, even when bringing off, or falling down on, a nap call. Both stayed on after normal retirement age, had reluctantly in the end (after the war) to be asked to go, the one having become jittery, the other somnolent after lunch, neither of "good appearance and address", as I used to put it.

Forty years on, the figure of Pickup at the nap table is clear in my mind (as is his neat handwriting, his methodical way of undertaking a mortgage conveyancing case, established through many thousands having passed through his hands, his papers sometimes coming to me when some difficulty he reckoned beyond his powers, or, more like, what he was paid to carry the can for, arose). He rolled his own cigarettes, making them rather thin, keeping them between his lips as they smouldered away. Fairly frequently a cough would rearrange the liquescence in his lungs, rather as the bomb had rearranged the coal in the Denmark Hill cellar. His grey hair was thick, longish, greased, and parted more or less in the middle: Old Mother Riley without a bun may be envisaged. Deep lines ran from his nose in a colourless face. He had the trick, common in east and south-east

London (and maybe elsewhere) of finishing off a remark with a rhetorical question, e.g.: "Well, I had to come back with another diamond, didn't I?"

Of less than medium height, away from the nap table he moved with modest pace on comfortably-fitting boots; outdoors wearing a large bowler hat that came down low on his grey locks. He lived on the other side of the river: I think had been bombed out, in fact, but was probably unanxious to resume the daily journey in blitz conditions. What his wife was doing as a nap widow I do not recall, if I ever knew. Plainly he had the gift for hitting on the most comfortable existence possible, given an on the whole inimical world – which snowy and fluffy-haired Heap had not.

I must say something of myself as a poet at this period, conceited or self-important though the business may seem. One or two critics have noted that the outbreak of war had a firming effect on my verse: gave me "more to observe", Kenneth Allott remarked. I can't think I was aware of this at the time, though the start of my second book, *The Middle of a War* (1942), with a poem then called "November 1939" does sound a noticeably clear note, especially compared with what had mostly been going on in the Fortune Press *Poems*:

> Cigar-coloured bracken, the gloom between the trees,
> The straight wet by-pass through the shaven clover
> Smell of the war as if already these
>   Were salients or cover.

I remember the occasion of this poem. I was with Jack Clark on the Maidstone road, in the purlieus of Sidcup, the bourne, much later, of Harold Pinter's caretaker. We got out of a car he was driving (perhaps a forced alighting if the car was of the calibre of that previously left in our drive) and the scene at once seemed significant. Even in November, apparently, one's nerves were still sensitive about the changed state of the world.

Undoubtedly, the verse I wrote between the outbreak of war and my call-up is a better record of the world than what had gone before, not that that is claiming a great deal. The rhetoric is ballasted to some extent by observation and an occasional generalization of reasonable insight. But the sum total is meagre of those that could be allowed to be seen by other eyes. The period covered was quite extensive in a sense, and even bombed out and benighted I welcomed the passage of the days as meaning fewer eventually in the disagreeable role of serviceman. No patriotic or even anti-fascist feeling tempered the urging on of time and the war while in moderate control of one's fate. Sometimes, moving well into 1941, a reassuring proportion of the months the war could last seemed already to have gone by; and then, considering German triumphs, British disasters, the weary laps ahead seemed unfairly numerous. There was still ample time in which to be scared, mutilated and killed. Herbert Read's poem of the First World War, "The End of a War", had given me the title for the sonnet I shall mention later, used also as the title of my second book. But I always had an uneasy sense of tempting providence by tagging 1942 as the middle of the business. That might prove to be an early year, the duration of the First War no criterion at all for the length of this.

I must have got my "papers" at the beginning of April 1941. I had to report on the 21st. I cleared up at the office so as to spend the interim with my wife and son in Blackpool, aiming to go straight from there to report. How did I get my blankets from the strongroom back to the maisonette? Or was our furniture already in store and the maisonette boarded up? Was I conscious of my last game of nap, thinking it rather more ultimate than my supposedly last swim? The questions are sufficiently banal, the answers probably only too boringly recoverable from my letters of the time. Fiction would have invented a livelier circumstantial narrative.

7 *The Andrew*

When I was a small boy, perhaps seven, on holiday in Blackpool, I was taken to a show called "The Battle of Zeebrugge". This was held near the place where a dozen or so years later (staggeringly short time for the change in *moeurs* and my own persona) the Reverend Harold Davidson sojourned in a barrel. Entry being proposed by my father, I keenly looked forward to the proceedings, always eager to be entertained. What confronted the audience was a small stage, such as puppets perform on, with a single set throughout – the famous Mole, which even I had heard of, captured during the recently-ended First World War by the Royal Navy (plus, presumably, the service in which Richard Flower served with such distinction) against murderous fire from the German defenders. The thing was within an ace of being a fiasco, but in the end went down a triumph of British seamanship and arms. On Blackpool promenade, the depiction of this affair was effected by model ships (worked from below the stage) sliding up to the Mole, some doubtless sliding back, or disappearing beneath the cardboard waves. Flashes from the guns on both ships and land were ingeniously arranged, the sound of the explosions pretty well continuous and ear-splitting. I was terrified, may have cried and had to be taken out, though the impression remains that much was endured.

I continued not to like loud bangs. A firearm produced on the stage, even by a comic, put me on tenterhooks until the thing was let off or put away. Chekhov's dictum that if a pistol is imported into theatrical proceedings it should sooner or later be let off was too often adhered to for my liking. In later years, caring slightly less what people thought of me, I sometimes put my fingers in my ears during the suspensive period.

I have told of my apprehension as a youth, when embarking on "Uncle" Fred's yacht, that he might command a voyage beyond the calm confines of the Ribble estuary: indeed, even there I would keep a weather eye on the water ahead for signs of "white horses", always glad when Mr Marple turned the wheel to head the vessel away from the open sea. Once, on holiday in Llandudno, my mother had engaged a rowing boat to take us out fishing, probably at my brother's urging, even mine (for children do not always obey their instincts). The experience was disagreeable, cut short; perhaps the origin of my fear of waves, nausea at the smell of stale fish – often seemingly detectable in boats unconnected with piscine activity, usually mingled with the odours of oil and what one imagines to be bilge. Later experiences of the sea were confined to voyages to the Isle of Man, to France once, and to Jersey for our honeymoon: none traumatic but not lessening the sense of Thalassa's power to discomfort, even kill.

In view of all this, why when registering for call-up did I express a preference to serve in the Royal Navy? The sensible thing, as many unbrave realized at the time, would have been to opt for ground duties with the RAF. But in pre-call-up ignorance one wondered if one wouldn't be whisked into the air against one's option, and I feared heights more than the sea (not to mention the dangers of aerial combat). In any case, to go into the RAF with the proviso that one wouldn't fly seemed a contradiction in terms somewhat insane as well as infra dig. (Later, eventually getting by chance into the Fleet Air Arm, a similar guilty sense arose, though in that service there was a reassuring apophthegm: "only fools and birds fly".)

The overriding motivation for my choice of service was certainly the memory of the horrors of 1914–18 trench warfare, perhaps got almost first-hand from such as Issy Gotliffe, undoubtedly revived by the grisly war fiction suddenly popular in the late Twenties. Who could be sure such monstrous conditions would not come again? Besides, if killing and being killed were in question it seemed better for this to be done at a good distance – and here, rather than those of Zeebrugge, the memories of the Battle of Jutland played a part. My surviving brother had been born on the day of that naval action, so it had always interested me. The distance between the rival fleets had been almost reassuringly great. Finally, Rex (I will retain the name Julian gave him in *Notes From Another Country*), of the Denmark Hill ménage, had had no doubt at all that he would put in for the Navy. He said it was the superior as well as the senior service. Why one should have been impressed by the view of an unemployed Trotskyist activist in this realm of knowledge is not now easy to understand, especially as one surmised that Rex's overmastering reason for his preference was that in the Navy he would be able to keep his beard, as blond and virile as Gumbril's false one in *Antic Hay*, and, as an appendage of youth, nothing like as commonplace then as today. As a matter of fact he had initially to shave it off (for whiskers may be worn in the Navy only if grown with permission), and appeared on his first leave with the near-unrecognizable, weak-chinned look later to be noted as common to all the suddenly beard-shorn, whether opisthognathous or not.

On the morning of the day I had to report, my wife came to Blackpool Central Station to see me off. Leave-taking was rendered low-key by our encountering Gilbert Waller, also making for the London train. I imagine his history of tuberculosis, despite the abiding success of the UMKALAOBO treatment, had given him a medical category that exempted him from call-up, though he could already have been London correspondent for the American newspaper which might well have reserved him anyway and certainly at a later date put him into US army officer's uniform – olive drabs, was it called? – as a war correspondent, transmogrification impossible to accept with a generous spirit or straight face. He had probably been visiting his parents in Blackpool.

We had a third-class (as it then was) compartment to ourselves. He had learnt of the reason for my journey with the interest and underlying glee of the journalist encountering the unusual, probably tinged with *Schadenfreude*. He was in no doubt the occasion must be marked with a bottle, and went off up the train to arrange it. At mid-morning, in mid-war, success seemed unlikely. That would have suited me, whose low spirits were not alterable with alcohol: besides, one did not want to go back to days of sneezing powder and like japes, as booze in such circumstances threatened to indicate. However, Waller fairly soon returned with nose twitching and lips pursed more than usual, not long after followed by a steward and a bottle of claret and two glasses. Waller paid with complacency the six shillings or so demanded, taking the money from a purse of the kind he always used – the stiff opening flap held horizontal and a few coins urged into it (for easy extraction) with a slight motion of the wrist.

I seem to think that on arrival at Euston he persuaded me to go to Charley's café in Marchmont Street. Did he have a golden pudding and a cup of tea? Was the pin-table still there and did we play it? Such things savour of fiction, yet may well have occurred. I was already a good way from the character I had presented in London in the early Thirties, yet much remained of the too morbid concern for others that would have kept me to a degree in Waller's thrall.

However the interim was occupied, it must have been late afternoon, more likely early evening, before I was in the train leaving Liverpool Street Station for Harwich. I had to report to a training establishment called HMS *Ganges*. Possibly the train's departure was delayed: certainly there were many hold-ups on the journey itself because of heavy air-raids. Could one read on the train? I think so: it was only the blindless suburban and local rolling stock where the sole illumination was a dim, blue, aquarium-like light. Nevertheless, as the train jerked on, one tired of or exhausted one's reading matter, and sat in excruciating boredom, occasionally squinting past the sides of the blinds at the flat landscape lit fitfully by flashes from anti-aircraft guns. Perhaps, indeed, the lights had been lowered because of the raids. More and more passengers alighted as the various Essex stations were reached until, like the voyagers in Sutton Vane's play *Outward Bound*, who gradually realize they are all dead, one saw preponderantly remaining men of a like age to oneself, obviously en route for *Ganges* – a destination seeming almost as remote as the sacred river itself. Two or three of us got together, compared notes. I was glad of this, my anal-erotic character having made me anxious and guilty about the growing certainty of arriving later than the time specified.

HMS *Ganges* was at Shotley, opposite Harwich on the Orwell-Stour estuary. While there I usually went "ashore" to Ipswich, so Harwich remained largely unknown. That dark night of arrival it was utterly mysterious, not much of it traversed: the train drew up at the harbour and we were soon picked out by someone in authority, perhaps a petty officer, as *Ganges* fodder, and led to the quayside. I have sometimes fancied we were rowed over to Shotley, but I think that is to be too much at the mercy of the Styx parallel: a small ferry boat was probably involved. There was room for the newcomers to be tinctured by naval personnel returning from a night "ashore", their insobriety assorting ill with the prevailing mood.

On the far side of the gloomy river the blackout made *Ganges* equally mysterious: of the initial process of induction all that remains clear is of a petty officer taking a few of us into a galley and offering cocoa, apologizing that it was too late for supper. Though a piece of bread-and-butter may have been also offered. The cocoa was a leftover, tepid, very thick, drawn by the PO with a long-handled ladle from the bottom of a metal vat. Later, the beverage became familiar, the solid chocolate slabs from which it was made sometimes available, through bribery or pilfering, for eating. The shining cleanliness of vat and ladle – indeed, of the whole galley – impressed me much, as it would have even my mother. Also impressive was the service given by the PO, which I soon realized was characteristic of the RN – a rough affection, manifested in countless ways; touching really. The incident may well have taken my mind back to supper times at Seafolde House, though the "coker" brought by the maid there was a vastly inferior brew.

Eventually, one found oneself in a dormitory, also reminiscent of Seafolde House, though much larger than any sleeping accommodation supplied by the Boss. Crowning the fictional coincidences of the day, in the next bed, or preparing to get in it, was a man called Rod Davies, a colleague of my wife's when before marriage she had worked for the *West Lancashire Evening Gazette*. I had known Rod quite well in those Blackpool days of half a dozen years before – solid, fresh-faced, competent, unflappable. He had then been a reporter; since become editor of a local newspaper elsewhere. Immediately the populous setting and, as in a dream, one's getting undressed in the midst of it, seemed somewhat less bizarre.

In my first letters from HMS *Ganges* I described it as resembling a bad boarding school, but this was not accurate. Truer to say it was like an exceptionally good boarding school, certainly of the Thirties. Many of the facilities – billiards tables, cricket tables, gymnasium, and so forth – were first class, and the food was abundant, excellent in its way. The Boss would have been staggered at the size of the helpings. As though on board ship, each mess drew its food from the central galley, and (to take an example) the portion of "figgy duff" (generic term for a pudding the staple of which at *Ganges* was a baked sultana cake) allowed for each man was the dimensions of a half-brick or near them. I was already affected by the dyspepsia later to become a nuisance. It disappeared under the *Ganges* régime of extreme physical effort and low-level mental concerns, and I was not over-faced by the half-bricks, though in early days had a bilious attack through eating a double portion of corned beef, a deadly dish even in moderation. Uniquely at *Ganges*, in all my life, I was conscious of physical fitness; and that sense seemed to make it natural to go along with *Ganges* pursuits – squad drill, PT, swimming, gymnastics, a violent species of football played with a soccer ball one was allowed to handle – most of which would have otherwise struck a non-games-playing solicitor in his thirtieth year as preposterous.

On registration I had been accepted by the Navy as a Writer (the instant conferring of such status, compared with my still unfulfilled yearning to be a writer, an irony not lost on me at the time), but subsequently being overstocked with Writers they called me up as an Ordinary Seaman, so I was issued with "square rig" uniform. One received two sets of blue serge jumper and trousers, best and every day, "Number Ones" and "Number Twos". In my case the jumper of the latter was rather too loose about the hips, but I never took it to a jobbing tailor to have it taken in. Though quite satisfied with my Number Ones, I realized that to the discriminating eye one would always look a sprog in them.

A session was devoted to instruction by a PO on how to put on square rig – strange, on the whole becoming, guise; as historically determined but probably more complicated than any sacerdotal garb. Over a vest, if one wore one (and vests were an issue), went the "cotton 'flannel'" – the two sets of inverted commas needed to delineate the garment itself and its derivation from a like garment made in former days of flannel, not cotton. A. Cecil Hampshire in his *Just an Old Navy Custom* describes the cotton flannel as a precursor of the T-shirt: good point, the thing being short-sleeved and of less than normal shirt length. It was square-necked, however, and thus liable to reveal the shoulder straps of a vest (if worn), as in the case of an unsmart female. On top of the cotton flannel went a blue, white-braided collar, secured by an arrangement of tapes, fastening round the waist. The collar had to be put on before the trousers, which were kept up with a broad, blue, adjustable webbing belt that was fastened before the flap at the front of the trousers was lifted and buttoned – no flies on matelots. The jumper could only be donned by first putting one's arms right into the sleeves (the buttons at the cuffs undone), then manoeuvring the head into the buttonless neck-opening. After the jumper had been persuaded down over the hips, the previously-secured, separate collar had to be pulled out and made to lie over the similarly-shaped serge collar of the jumper. A black "silk", folded narrowly, was then passed under both collars, the ends put together, folded under, and tied down with two blue tapes at the V-opening of the neck of the jumper. A white lanyard was worn only on posh occasions. It should be added that in winter a long-sleeved jersey went over the cotton flannel and under the jumper; and that off duty the separate collar could be untied and slipped off. As to the latter, as I write the words the vision comes pat – not vouchsafed to the outer world – of men collared only by their navy-blue jumpers, drinking pints in the NAAFI, writing letters, and (in establishments like the RNAS, Lee-on-the-Solent) carrying their enamel mugs and "irons" (knife, fork and spoon) to supper.

On kitting-up, there were no trousers matching the jumper of my Number Twos to fit me. In his book *The Prof*, Roy Harrod said that working for Lindemann's "S Branch" he discovered early in 1941 that twenty million pairs of trousers had been produced for an army consisting at that time of only two million men, so that may well have caused a naval shortage. For several days I went about (not alone in my incongruity, for a number of giants and midgets were in similar case) wearing the grey flannel trousers in which I had crossed Lethe's river – under cap and jumper, over pusser's boots. Like Widmerpool's overcoat, the embarrassing trousers marked one off from most of one's fellows (again a reminiscence of boyhood emotion): pleasure and relief came with the delivery of more trousers to the clothing store, and one felt oneself repaired.

Further to the healing business, the question arises how soon I felt that joining the Navy had ended my "divided life". I use the unoriginal, not awfully descriptive phrase to indicate the condition of intellectuals' souls referred to by Matthew Arnold (to go no farther back), and the various alienations of bourgeois existence specified by Marxists. It could not be said that suddenly one's heart was in one's work, unlike being a solicitor; yet since no choice, no possibility of abdicating, existed, there was scarcely a wound that called for being sutured. As a rating, one was pretty effectively proletarianized, even though better off than most (for the Equitable made up my salary). And the business of being a writer, yet with an audience measured merely in hundreds – which so many Thirties writers saw as ludicrous and longed to break out of without compromising their art – seemed to me then likely to be ended as the experience of ordinary mankind became my own experience, and the feeling quickly grew that I wouldn't, as Wilfred Owen had succinctly put it, "want to write anything to which a soldier would say No Compris."

When I moved over from the initiatory "Annexe" to the Main Camp I found myself made Class Leader – a sort of temporary local Leading Hand. We (a class of Ordinary Seamen) shared a mess with a class of Writers, their Class Leader being a Writer to the Signet called Milne, whose Scots conscientiousness and efficiency made up for my own deficiencies as a leader of men. At the end of the course I asked the senior of the two NCOs in charge of the classes why he had chosen me as Class Leader. He said he always chose solicitors, if available: one of few laymen with a good opinion of the profession. Just inside the entrance to the mess was a tiny room containing brooms and cleaning material and the like, but also a table and chair for the use of the Class Leaders in the disposal of such slight paperwork as came their way, and perhaps regarded as a privilege in return for extra responsibilities. It was there I wrote my first poem after joining the Andrew, "ABC of a Naval Trainee". Julian Symons, not yet called up, was editing an anthology of war poetry for Penguin Books and asked me for a poem, so the piece was written to order, in a stanza based on that of the "Epilogue" to Auden's *The Orators*, itself based on a traditional poem. The anthology project (and the excellent way it was fulfilled) was an indication of Julian's coming status as a man of letters of remarkable range, accomplishment, and clarity of mind: for me, it was a chance not to be missed to appear, in however small a way, before a wider public.

I don't believe I finished any other poem at *Ganges*; not even attempting more than two or three. Why the poetic drive should have been so weak in one enjoying robust health, amid fresh scenes, is difficult now to explain (beyond a general charge of poetastry). Some years ago, in a minute, unfilled notebook of the time, I found a few lines whose subject seemed promising, about the old ship's figureheads that stood at the edge of the huge parade ground of the Main Camp, by the dread mast. These garishly-painted images – bearded gods, high-breasted nymphs, staring-eyed young mariners – might surely have been worked up into emblems of one's then present plight, and future traffic with the sea. But probably my mind was still too ideologically rigid for poetic fancy so to function. And as to the non-apocalyptic side of things, somehow I did not see until some months later that what I wanted – was able – to say about my changed life could be done in quite a simple way.

The cupboard-like room was also where I skulked on Sunday mornings, having been told by some mildly exasperated and baffled officer to keep out of sight at such times. This arose through my having said, when asked to state my religion on joining *Ganges*, that I was an atheist, as happened to be so. The

Regulating Petty Officer (or whatever he was, ignorance prevailing in such areas at that juncture) had initially baulked at putting this down, but I provided no alternative and was possibly persuasive in the forensic style valued by the Class Leader-choosing Chief. What a mistake! I have a feeling Rex told me that on joining the Navy he had put himself in the godless category, but I wonder how official the business was in his case. Being classified as "Atheist" almost always caused trouble, starting with that RPO and immediately continuing with the fellow at the Annexe who stamped identity discs with name, rank, number and religion. There was room only for a few letters to indicate the last named, so, after some discussion, my disc read "ATH", which would surely have baffled any RN burial party had the occasion arose, perhaps causing a fruitless search for the funerary ceremonies of, say, some sect calling itself after Athanasius. When I was on a course in Aberdeen, I was told to march the Church of England party to and from the church (or cathedral, as perhaps it was), leaving an awkward hour or so to fill in – the office plainly designed as a punishment on earth for my irreligion. On a few later occasions I feigned to be C of E to avoid any such chores, to say nothing of acrimonious arguments, and when eventually commissioned allowed myself to suffer a nominal conversion (or, rather, return) to that belief.

Almost as mysterious as the gift of religious faith was the acquisition in the Navy of the status of CW Candidate; that is to say, someone who after suitable and successful novitiate service would be put on a course leading to a commission. That I was such a Candidate was intimated to me during training by the Divisional Officer, my spiritual deficiencies apparently no bar. For such Candidates initial training was followed by drafting to a capital ship, and I did not doubt that that would be my next step, reassured rather than otherwise that I should be facing sea and enemy in something of substantial dimensions and armament. But towards the end of my time in *Ganges* a notice appeared outside the Divisional Office inviting volunteers for a course, qualification being School Certificate credits in Mathematics and Physics. The notice was otherwise inexplicit, but a "buzz" went round that a spell at a civilian technical college was involved. The implied amplitude of the thing, to say nothing of the postponement of big ship service, greatly appealed – another opportunity to avoid a crunch in life. Thanks to the demonic teaching of the Boss, I was more than qualified on the Mathematics side, and though I had dropped Physics in favour of Chemistry for Matriculation, I must have had it at School Certificate level, for I was accepted for the course. The Divisional Officer thought it ill-advised to defer or obfuscate normal progress towards an executive commission, but I paid no heed to him, and not until time had removed war's perils safely into the past did I come to think with a tinge of regret that I might have had a more satisfactory and less boring war, if a shorter life, had I let my name be struck off the list. Its going forward (with others I knew) for the unknown training (said to be to do with wireless telegraphy) made no difference to matters at *Ganges*.

The weather on the Suffolk coast had started that April with a wind from the steppes, adding to the discomforts of the much-frequented parade ground. Only belatedly did it become milder, eventually hot; and in my last week an exotic number appeared in Orders of the Day specifying the rig, which being interpreted proved to consist of cotton-flannel and white-duck trousers. By then, the class' skill at squad drill was remarkable, only marred by the ineptitude of one member, a gentle effeminate individual who simply lacked physical co-ordination. When we graduated to rifle drill a fresh PO took over, small and combative, reputation long preceding his actual appearance (though he was nothing of a bully and sometimes inadvertently revealed a kind heart). He once exasperatedly cried out to our awkward member, using a noun seemingly rising unbidden to his lips, for I never heard him use it before or after: "You – you – you cream-puff." Possibly the hesitation was occasioned by his feeling the need to temper in some way the second part of the compound, which would accord with his inner tenderness. It was the same PO who, chiding the class for clumsiness in returning bayonet to scabbard, said of the latter: "You'd find it all right if it had hair round it" – but this was plainly premeditated, probably of ancient lineage.

Despite what is generally held to the contrary, and no doubt except for our cream-puff, we came to enjoy squad drill. Since the class had originally been categorized as one of Writers, all its members were middle-class (using the term to cover some such spectrum as local government clerk to chartered accountant), mainly the same kind of secondary school boys on whose foundation the Equitable's expansion had been grounded, so puritanical work ethic in various aspects would play its part. Similar considerations applied to the gymnasium, where quite soon the instructor was introducing the class to challenging, and thus interesting, skills. It was like the episode in the Paul Newman film *Cool Hand Luke*, where the convict chain gang suddenly find corporate identity and finish a day's road-tarring with two hours to spare. Also it somehow accorded with the notion, still held, that a common effort could productively outdo individual enterprise.

But too bland a picture must not be presented. Usually in the gymnasium – occasionally to be seen throwing off a few press-ups, or evolutions on the parallel bars – was a short figure in white sweater and flannels. One had seen him about the gymnasium purlieus wearing over this garb a naval officer's cap and jacket. His rank was Sub-lieutenant, RNVR, his age a good deal less than mine. In his own eyes he was ruler of the gymnasium (though some superior officer with that responsibility must have existed), not averse to ticking off all and sundry whether challenging his territory or not. It had to be admitted that this chap must by definition have done some big ship service, but it irked me to see him, with his cocky character and pocket Hercules appearance, lording it safely in *Ganges*, building up his already excessive muscle.

The two NCOs in charge of the class have already been mentioned. Both were time-expired men, called back in consequence of the war. The elder, a Chief Petty Officer, big, grey hair, ruddy features, a rather squashed Roman nose like Sir Frank Benson's, had been a deep-sea diver, full of stories of that occupation. He it was who had faith in lawyers. The younger, a Petty Officer, more intelligent in a general way, had gone into the Borstal service after serving his time. When Borstal officers are criticized I always think of him – so quiet, authoritative, lucid, and concerned for those in his charge. He gave me an abiding soft spot for Borstal officers, as did its wartime services for the Salvation Army, often to be found where other amenities were absent. The PO's instructional lectures or talks were particularly good, undeserving of the sleep that fell on many at the theoretical ones, where we were sitting down. Nights were apt to be disturbed, for if the air-raid warning sounded everyone had to get up. As Class Leader I was saved from having to go to the shelters; being on duty in and just outside the mess, on guard for incendiaries, perhaps parachutists. What torture, the business of waking to the siren and putting on trousers and sweater (gaiters excused), after a day of intense physical activity and likely an evening of NAAFI beer. Almost equal torture trying to keep awake during a talk on, say, the Rules Concerning Lights at Sea – though that was a topic less soporific to me than most, since some of its precepts had been reduced to verse, starting in near-metaphysical style:

When both Lights you see ahead,
Starboard wheel and show your Red.

"Wondrous heavy" – Gonzalo's phrase for the magic slumber overcoming him on Prospero's island would rise to mind as I sat on a back-row bench after a half-brick portion of figgy duff.

Being Class Leader also saved me from many menial duties, though I had had a fair share of these in the Annexe, including Captaincy of the Heads. The protected life style before 1939 of even the modestly middle-class male is demonstrated by the recollection that when in the Andrew I initially had to use a broom I simply imitated the grasp and motions I had seen others use (perhaps most closely observed in childhood), rather suprised at their efficaciousness in directing the broom's function. It was the same with darning and ironing, the former possibly now a dying art in days of ubiquitous man-made yarns. As to the latter, I actually sent the bulk of my washing home from *Ganges* (and perhaps later places), but one was always washing and ironing one's square rig collars, in the hope of paling the obdurate navy-blue, tell-tale of a recent recruit. The lessons learnt at *Ganges* were a bizarre mix of the bellicose and the domestic; in that, imitating life, certainly during many periods of history, admittedly mostly primitive. Perhaps the domestic arts were emphasized through the routines remaining, quite a few, of the former boys' establishment. Our class NCOs encouraged us to whip round (or did a modest mess fund for such purposes exist from the start?) to buy a supply of Red Cardinal polish (thereafter kept, I suppose, in the Class Leader's poetry-writing cubbyhole) to incarnadine the stone flags on which stood the cylindrical iron stoves that heated the mess. For weekly Captain's rounds, the mess-tins and so forth were burnished and laid out in prescribed order, as at the foot of each man's bed was his considerable kit, and empty kitbag, the latter presented so as to display its base, on which his name and number had been painted in black at the elaborate and prolonged kit-marking routine in the Annexe (during which, as has been sufficiently said, I was tagged "ATH", which did not excuse me, however, from the hieretical laying-out ceremony).

Were we conscious of the strong lingering force of tradition in all this, the rough, by and large triumphant, tradition of British naval history, of the acerbities and moral standards of the Empire – traditions made fugitive, not to say despised, in the minds of those radicalized by the two decades between the wars? Looking back, the kit-marking routine, the kit itself, seems evidence at once of England's greatness and archaism. I single out almost at random, among that considerable issue of *matèriel*, the substantial japanned tin box for caps; the excellent shoe and clothes brushes, still in good order after forty years; and the dolly-bag made of stout, unbleached linen, for toilet things. As carefully instructed, we marked every item of kit capable of being marked, from long-sleeved woollen vests and quite long-legged woollen pants to hammock. Each man was given a wooden marker, carved with his name, for smaller items. Larger items were stencilled, but the stencils must have been made up *ad hoc* from individual letters, for I do not recall possessing a personal one. Metal punches were available to stamp out one's name on boots and suchlike – even on a brass plate let into the cap box for that purpose.

The "Captain" (he was in rank a Commander) of HMS *Ganges* had been that in the boys' days. Not due wholly to his rank or position, he sent before him a sense of apprehension, like the Boss, the headmaster of Seafolde House. Yet I remember nothing more of him than that he was slim and smallish, penetrating and fearless in the discovery of departures from *Ganges* standards of conduct and cleanliness. This is the more strange since I served as his messenger during my last week in *Ganges*, though the title must not be taken to indicate some close Mercury and Jupiter type relation. Rather, a Kafkaesque element persisted – was even enhanced by this entry, finally, into the headquarters of what had ruled and shaped us during our weeks of training.

I fear I have not given a clear picture of life in *Ganges*. The whole experience must be thought banal by outsiders, even perhaps by the participants, not least because it was so commonplace, especially in comparison with more esoteric situations of war, so that writing about it at all may be considered otiose. Yet that period and place, both with strict limits, startlingly illustrate memory's way with the past. Once, I was master of the topography of *Ganges*: now a few ill-joined features present themselves – the great shed along one side of the parade ground, used for drill when the weather was wet, and always for pay parades (those almost oriental ceremonies where one had to utter – like "Open sesame" – the right formula, while presenting one's cap, so as to receive on its hard, flat surface the prescribed *baksheesh*); the curious covered ways (resembling seaside arcades, and bringing back to me those places where I put pennies in machines in childhood) giving access to the messes on either side; the establishment's own stretch of the Orwell (or was it the Stour?) where nautical training took on slightly more naturalism. Faded, too, the precise sounds: calls on an actual bugle, but mostly heard through the Tannoy, except for "colours"; every day on the parade ground the Marine band playing the RN march past, "Heart of Oak", Boyce's indestructible tune, Garrick's words made almost risible by the disasters of the time. Lore from those days has also survived forty years: cleaning windows by rubbing them with crumpled newspapers, say. In the world outside *Ganges*, the real world, the raids on London continued somewhat worse than in my former experience; Rudolf Hess descended on Scotland; HMS *Hood* was sunk.

Training at last culminated in various tests and displays. One was able to make, if required, a bowline on the bight; and say what was looming up if, in fog, one prolonged siren blast was heard, followed by two short ones. There was an individual *viva voce* conducted by a young RNVR officer. One of his questions, as forecast by our instructor PO, was to ask for the compass to be boxed from one specified point to another. He was visibly taken aback when I said at once, as one reasonable man to another, that I hadn't learnt the compass. "You haven't learnt it?" "No, sir. It was too difficult. I decided to use the time for other things." In the excellent *Manual of Seamanship*, Volume 1, issued as part of one's kit, the pages under the heading "Hints on Learning and Teaching the Compass" were, as a matter of fact, penetrable by the legal mind, even passages such as:

The eight predominant points are selected and the sixteen new points are named after them. As the four cardinal points are predominant to the four half-way cardinals, so the eight cardinals and half-cardinals are predominant to the intermediates. Thus the sixteen points required are named after the eight cardinals and half-cardinal points, two after each point (one on each side).

But I could not see that ratiocination would enable one to talk one's way fluently from one point to a distant point: learning by rote seemed required, a thing I was never good at.

8 *Chatham, Aberdeen, Lee-on-the-Solent*

It must not be supposed that my detachment was as great as this account of service life has so far perhaps made it seem. In particular, though my leftism had gone off the boil during the years between Terry Warnock and call-up, I still longed for a *bouleversement* in society, could not imagine peace or prosperity coming any other way. I believed conditions were ripening for change – probably most of the time thought it would be thwarted by English reactionaries, or defeat in war by the Nazis. When the USSR was attacked by Germany I found it momentarily impossible to believe that Russia and Britain could be on the same side; probably thought muddle-headedly that this would be the signal at last for Britain to sell out by negotiating a separate peace with the Axis powers. It is highly speculative to try to summarize opinions comprehensively in this way, without reference to personal documents of the time. More or less dense detail would have surrounded such views in actuality, and there would be almost day to day inconsistencies. But good evidence of my state of mind is the memory of my pleased approval of a Government propaganda poster of the day (later criticized as foolishly pointing the "we" and "they" division of English society) – YOUR COURAGE, YOUR CHEERFULNESS, YOUR RESOLUTION, WILL BRING US VICTORY – being amended by someone writing underneath: "Uncle Joe will do it on his tod."

It may need explaining to some today that "Uncle Joe" was a by no means unaffectionate nickname for Stalin, used by more than members of the CPGB and fellow travellers. The "smiling moustaches" persona lived still. The belief was not eccentric that Hitler, in invading the Soviet Union – that was in the June of 1941 – had at long last bitten off more than he could chew, though the Russian retreats soon seemed to confirm those who all along considered the Russian armed forces on a par of rotten hollowness with its industrial development and political régime.

It must have been June, too, when the cakewalk that so far had been my Naval life came to a suspension by my going from *Ganges* to Chatham Barracks. Every rating in the RN has a home base, chosen for him on the basis of domestic convenience, insofar as Chatham, Portsmouth and Devonport can be said to be convenient to other than southerners. Mine was Chatham, so, after end-of-course leave, there I went. I have forgotten the figure of the then current overcrowding, and must not make a guess for fear of underestimation. The discomfort and squalor were sensational. It was said some ratings had been there for many months, overlooked among the thousands of changing names, or (more plausibly) their names removed, by bribery or other means, from the filing system; but it is hard to credit that anyone would want so much to avoid the enemy as live there indefinitely without pay, on barrack rations. What did strike me was the apparently slim chance of being found in this ant heap for the long course opted for in *Ganges*: much more likely was the forced resumption of my destiny as a CW candidate and a draft to a big ship. Indeed, is it a mere chimera of memory that I had actually been on a draft to a cruiser when a metaphorical messenger galloped up with a reprieve? Perhaps a dream.

Mercifully there were three watches at Chatham; Red, White and Blue: that meant two nights out of three could be spent "ashore". In barracks, unless one had a night duty, such as fire-watching, it was compulsory to sleep in the tunnel. Once again, topography has become shadowy. My recollection is that the tunnel or tunnels in the chalk of Chatham's geology were not far from the messes, but this may not have been so, some *via dolorosa* bearing one's ammick possibly involved. Whenever I so spent the night – I think it was not more than three or four occasions – I seem to remember slinging my hammock early in the evening, profiting from the experience of the first occasion. For as the evening wore on the tunnel filled up – the hammocks, eventually swollen with their occupants like the larvae of gigantic bugs, thickly dependent from the tunnel walls – and the farther one had to penetrate the worse the fetid miasma grew, one's nostrils smitten by the odour of thousands of feet and farts. The light provided was dim; to read, even to find hammock fixings, an electric torch was almost indispensible.

No wonder the various servicemen's dosshouses in Chatham were well patronized, it being as advisable to go early and book one's accommodation as a place in the tunnel. I seem to think the price asked was no more than sixpence. The amenities offered were only tolerable in comparison with the tunnel. Each man might have a cabin to himself, but the partition walls would not extend to the ceiling, so one heard every sound from adjoining cabins, including, on a weekend night especially, occasional retching, as well as groans and what in a poem I called the "drummings of fluid on enamel", that being the material of the chamber pots provided.

It will seem curious to poets now, as it does to me, that I did not exploit more thoroughly the material life then unfolded, having found one reasonably satisfactory way to do it in the poem referred to, called "Saturday Night in a Sailors' Home". This was a simple sonnet in octosyllabics, further democratized by the introduction of a couple of phrases of what was intended as verisimilitudinous speech, e.g. "Please shake me at five" – "shake" being the Navy word for rouse from sleep, therefore in frequent use because of the perpetual business of going on watch. John Lehmann was at that time choosing the poetry for *Tribune*, and I well recall him objecting to the original two phrases as being insufficiently colloquial. I changed and, however unlikely it may seem, improved them: the superfluous "please" had to be kept because it was a rhyme word – no bold Yeatsian changing of rhyme schemes for me in those days, nor for donkeys' years subsequently. What one was after was a Sassoon-like directness, which lack of skill in my case made difficult to combine with the traditional forms that Auden had, after the experimentalism of the Twenties, rendered pretty well obligatory once more. All the same, I am glad *vers libre* was out of fashion, for the task of being a "war poet" (by no means a conscious aim: rather the problem of continuing, in the role of serviceman, to write verse at all) might then have been too easily, superficially achieved. I could say, indeed, that one aspect of a whole lifetime's poetry has been the effort of trying to make strict forms "natural", using that last word to beg a number of more or less complex questions.

As a matter of fact, on reflection, I am sure the poem at issue, if not its nocturnal experience (though the latter must have been renewed in Portsmouth), came from a later time, when creation was more fluent than in those quite early service days, the period at Seafield Park I am going to come to. So what the three weeks or so of Chatham Barracks offered in the early summer of 1941 I failed to poeticize. In retrospect the days seem to have been varied enough to provide modest reader-interest.

After breakfast all had to parade for duties to be assigned. I rather think skulking was guarded against by "clear lower deck" being piped, but may be wrong about this since such a drastic order, repeated daily, would surely lose its force in time. My first chore was to chip rust off a frigate preparatory to painting it. Some crude tool was provided, and the anti-rust party sent off in an open truck to the quay where the frigate lay alongside. As the truck proceeded through the dockyard another film sequence was unfolded, this anticipating the Ealing comedies that lay seven years ahead. The civilian employees of the dockyard – the dockyard "mateys" – were successively revealed, singly or in groups, on ships and quays, behind sheds and stores, talking, smoking, meditating, just as though the forces of fascism had already been defeated and an epoch of peaceful leisured prosperity ushered in. Did one see hands of cards being played, as in the articled clerks' room at Wylie Kay's? That may be a slight exaggeration of the emancipated idleness everywhere apparent. It was a surprise that all the men were civilians, presumably exempt from call-up through their (non) occupation.

Continuity in the work assigned was at the mercy of chance. There was only one day of frigate-chipping. On another day I was in a party of ratings taken by coach to the Natural History Museum in South Kensington, which had apparently been used as a temporary Government store for semi-perishable foodstuffs, like dried peas and beans, now required to be removed as museum exhibits, loaded up on trucks and taken to some destination undisclosed to the Chatham hands. Sacks of the victuals were ranged along the extensive corridors, and there was a pong in the air reminiscent of the Chatham tunnel. When the sacks were taken up, mice ran out and nests of young mice were revealed, droppings abounding. I could not participate in the mouse mass murder (through both fear and pity); didn't much like even pulling out the sacks. But it was not too difficult to station oneself away from the noisome action; probably a prefiguration of how one would behave in more lethal Naval encounters.

From Chatham I must have gone up to London, when I was watch off, to see Julian and Kathleen, perhaps fitting in a few frames of snooker, but memory does not particularize – though a sensation comes to me of appearing to old friends for the first time moustacheless, with short hair, and sunburnt glow of health, all the more apparent by the *décolleté* cotton-flannel. I would have been accompanied by service respirator, a far different object to that fitted by Mrs "Y-cwt" in Kennington days, and Navy-issue attaché case.

A "buzz" had long had it that one of the "W/T" courses one's name was down for would be held in Aberdeen, and that was where the apparently blind and lumbering machine miraculously despatched me to from Chatham, part of a smallish draft of old *Ganges* faces, plus a few other miscellaneous ratings. Was it for that rather long journey that a packed meal was provided for each man, which included what was ineffably called in the Andrew a "tiddy-oggie"? It may have been so, for however slap-dash the individual messes, the galley at Chatham could well have been resourceful enough to make individual meat-and-potato pasties.

We were the first batch of ratings for the course, to be held in the part of Robert Gordon's College that in peacetime was a boys' day school, the boys having been evacuated or merged elsewhere, some of the staff retained or brought back. Or it may have been that the staff came from the polytechnic establishment in the same place. There was little or no evidence of the Navy's presence. Down near the fish market were the offices of the Port Office i/c (or some such title), a small RN organization, already overburdened, dealing with personnel on armed trawlers and the like. It struggled initially to cope with our pay, but little more. We were spread among civilian digs, mine rather good, in the main street though just beyond the main shops. The atmosphere was not far from that of peacetime summers of the past: modest seaside lodgings occupied by respectable but jolly bachelors, pubs and girls in mind. However, the penny soon dropped among the grass widowers that they might up their status, it being theoretically possible to draw a living-out allowance from the Andrew and, thus supported, move to suitable family accommodation. I was a pioneer in making the moves required to outwit the nay-saying bureaucracy, blend of the Kafkaesque and the Schweikian, and eventually I was joined in excellent lodgings, a little farther out towards Hazlehead, by my wife and son: amazing leniency by the Fates.

Though life took on many of the characteristics of ordinary family life (one of the greatest incongruities, indeed, being seen off by Kate in the mornings not to work but school), service friendships went on, flavoursome, essential, as ever. I have failed to find a way to suggest the richness of such friendships (if that is not too grandiose a term for what could often aptly be compared to ships that pass in the night) – particularly omitting accounts of the personalities revealed, for circumstances often gave little chance for relations to develop.

On the Aberdeen course, some of them sharing those initial digs, were men known from *Ganges* days, a few to be known through future time, one or two becoming close friends. Many were Scots, probably chosen by the roughly affectionate Andrew for Aberdeen rather than for the similar courses held simultaneously elsewhere. In early days re-encounters were multiplied by the premonitory nature of service. Delayed a week or two here and there, one lost some acquaintances, regained others, but the simple design of training imprinted itself quite clearly on the whole mass. Then the Navy was a comparatively small service, inherently amenable to coincidental encounters through the sub-division into home bases – and once in the Fleet Air Arm, a smaller sub-division still, life positively resembled Charles Dickens's schema of repeatedly reintroducing evil or comic characters (indeed, one recalls Dickens's childhood experience of the characteristics of Naval-base life at Chatham Dockyard).

Robert Gordon's College consisted mainly of modest buildings round what was a playground rather than a quadrangle. There, a former life was resurrected. One did not quite expect Waller's twitching specs to come through the entrance gates, but – particularly at first, when one's mathematics were put to the question – the Boss seemed nothing like a dozen years away. In a large classroom, seated at desks, the miscellaneousness of the intake was apparent. Though the bulk of it was of recent entry, there were also those who had seen service, a few hard to imagine possessing the required qualifications. I think all, or almost all, the instructors were from the College: they were excellent. It may be that as in some inflated version of Anstey's *Vice Versa*, they were apprehensive at changing juvenile charges for adults, but they quickly found the required tone, and I guess enjoyed the challenge, certainly in the pioneering days.

Almost at once there was a test, presumably to weed out the hopeless. There may have been some preliminary instruction. For instance, log tables soon appeared. It was as though one had to drive a car after a pedestrian dodecade of years. For a few minutes the apparatus seemed enigmatic; then after a simple enquiry one was away. The few eliminated by the test were augmented by the defection of some not relishing months of what promised to be arduous brain work.

I suppose we were clearly told the scope and purpose of the course, though reliable information in the services was usually preceded by rumour among the lower orders, as in some Shakespearean mob scene before the entry of the lords or tribunes. It was also (if I may yet again educe that writer) akin to what one usually gets in Kafka: knowledge of supreme authority, and of the behaviour it expects, coming from such as ostlers and chambermaids. Moreover, as in Kafka, it was not always clear that supreme authority knew what was wanted, what it was doing even. The Robert Gordon's course began with rapid revision of some mathematics and physics, followed by more detailed study of electricity and wireless, accompanied by practical instruction. All this done, we would go on to a further course in radar at some RN establishment. The idea was to create out of the ignorant job lot assembled in Aberdeen and elsewhere a cadre of radar mechanics, capable of opening up and repairing radar's various boxes of tricks. I do not know that I had any clear notion, even in its simplest terms, of what radar was. Indeed, the term used by the English, if used at all, was not radar but RDF (radio direction finding) or radiolocation. Still, probably some concept of locating and measuring the distance away of objects by bouncing wireless waves off them had been absorbed from popular articles in the press.

As to the theoretical side of the course, no more physics and mathematics were required than the boss had imparted to me –

though that may not be strictly true, for as I write I remember an instructor at Aberdeen using the device of the square root of minus one, which I am sure I had never played with myself, though not ignorant of the concept. The Boss would have loved quietly to acquaint the Fifth Form with it; having no call to carry past the Fourth Form his theatrical – Zulu war-dancing – style of teaching. Possibly the business had not in the Twenties descended to school level; just as I feel our textbooks did not grapple with particles smaller than the atom, and that it was after I left school that I read such exciting things as Eddington's semi-popularizations of the (still-called) new physics.

The few poems that have survived from Aberdeen, meagre sum, are mostly in fairly clotted vein – one, in fact, a versification of themes from Frazer's *Golden Bough*, would not have been out of place in the Fortune Press collection, though its references to war would be taken by the sympathetic reader as having contemporary relevance. Some other pieces bring in natural objects in and around Aberdeen, but without much enterprise; and mention guns and aircraft and other things then much mentioned in everyday life. I was conscious that the sea (so cold all that summer that we never bathed in it, enthusiastic though we were) was the sea my father had seen in his mysterious childhood in Lybster, a town now a mere hundred and fifty miles to the north.

> Where the coast curves the waves' blown smoke
> Blurs with the city's and the pencilled ships
> Lumber like toys. The searchers for coal and driftwood
> Bend; and the beach is littered with stones and leaves,
> Antlers of seaweed, round gulls, to the belt
> Of sand, like macadam, watered by the sea.

Passable as scene-setting, it might be said; but followed merely by a rhetoric and an attempt at generalization that had already been finely brought off by Stephen Spender in the poems that were to be collected in *Ruins and Visions* (1942), about the early disasters of the war. Any notion of adding family perspectives to such données lay even farther in the future.

One Aberdonian piece does reflect the situation (as Terry Warnock would have called it) with reasonable accuracy and sobriety, "Defending the Harbour"; though when I put it in my *Collected Poems* of 1962 I could not forbear to change (apropos my fellow defenders) "the kind and speaking faces" to "the kind and comic faces". Behind the poem lay the Navy's increasing and illogically-resented interference with the lives we were leading of academic days and amatory nights. A petty officer, perhaps a Chief, appeared, to initiate the harbour defence company, pre-class physical jerks, and the church parade before referred to. Nonetheless, existence continued to have strong civilian elements until we left Aberdeen, which incredibly was as late as November 1941, the title given, as a matter of fact, to the poem from which come the six lines I have just quoted.

Pioneering, the course almost inevitably prolonged itself. One of the instructors left to be himself instructed (in a service establishment, or perhaps manufacturer's research department) and returned to communicate, with an excitement shared by most, details of some special radio circuits. Like some bizarre feminine fashion, wavelengths were drastically shortened. The techniques were said to be analogous to those of television, then never even seen as an end product save by a few thousand set-owners. Did we know why we were studying circuits that produced on the oscilloscope a series of pointed or squarish wave-forms? I think not with any confidence. Since there was no "security" at Aberdeen and the teaching staff were civilians, secret material was not used on the course. The instructor to whom details of the "special circuits" had been imparted was cagey, respected confidences, emanated an air of "I could a tale unfold" had he been free to do so.

These matters impinged on my writing no more than had milk-adulteration case law, or building society statutes, in the past. Even wireless of normal wavelengths formed no part of our lives, though in our digs we played a portable gramophone actually bought new in Aberdeen. The make was HMV, like the radiogram that had gone into store with the rest of our furniture, brand fidelity probably stemming from the corniculate machine owned by my grandparents, perhaps even then still playing Harry Lauder and Luigini, though more likely not, for my grandfather was dead, my grandmother to die soon. The shop that sold us the gramophone also sold us records, good relations being established with a cultivated and obliging lady assistant. The apparatus acquired had half gone out of mind until with a slight shock I read the following stanza-and-a-bit in my son's "Epistle to Bryan Kelly" more than thirty years after:

My love for tuneful music dates
From *Figaro* on 78s
At four or five. When I'm in straits
  With *Cage* or *Nono*
I'm glad to know that somewhere waits
  The *dove sono*.

Or the cool clarinet *con brio*
In his incomparable Trio . . .

That trio, and the clarinet trio of Brahms that uses a cello instead of a viola, still arouse, if not precise images other than the appropriately navy-blue label Columbia discs bought in Aberdeen, then certainly a sensation of transient felicity not wholly emanating from the music itself.

At last the Scottish idyll had to end. Farewell to the excellent lecturer whose "er" of hesitation was *in excelsis* the characteristic and imitable Aberdeen "ee", rather saliva-surrounded; to the pubs, unwelcoming to ladies, sometimes confining them with their escorts in waist-high pens, symbolism never quite fathomed; to the delicious species of *croissant*, "buttery rowies", always provided fresh for breakfast by our landlady; to the strong, clean city itself, then supportive of many arts, not least the "varieties", where old favourites were still to be seen. Farewell, above all, to old familiar faces, for at the end of the course some of us were assigned to the Fleet Air Arm, changing our home port to the FAA base at Lee-on-the-Solent. Kate and Johnny and I left Aberdeen together, since I went straight on end-of-course leave. We had to change stations at Glasgow; had time for lunch in some large café, chose haggis from the menu, a good bet in days of even more dubious concoctions. That is all I can bring back of those closing chords, melancholy as Brahms'.

The Royal Naval Air Station, Lee-on-the-Solent (HMS *Daedalus* its pessimistic but not inappropriate cognomen) has become as unfamiliar after forty years as it was initially. There was the main camp and the hutted camp, the latter an addendum, mainly of Nissen huts, occasioned by the war. Naval personnel were slightly diluted by "crabfats", puzzling at first – RAF NCOs, mainly senior, lingering from the days when the Navy lacked its own air arm. Crabfats: I expect at first I was ignorant of the vulgar term, originating in the congruency of the colour of the RAF uniform with that of the ointment prescribed for crab lice, a specific possibly even then superseded by more sophisticated remedies. Quite quickly one got used to the conjunction of elements: air with water; trainee pilots in square rig, differentiated from Ordinary Seamen and ABs by a white capband; the strange aircraft still used by the Navy – the Swordfish and the amphibian Walrus strangest – becoming a commonplace, because training, if not operational squadrons, were about in *Daedalus*:

> Loud fluttering aircraft slope above his head . . .

Some may have found the second epithet, in that line from the eponymous sonnet of my second book of verse, puzzling or inappropriate; and today even harder to imagine, in the absence of analogous experience, must be a biplane of such cautious landing speed. Mention of uniform is a reminder that this was the moment, alas, when one's own was changed to fore-and-aft rig – an ordinary four-button jacket and trousers, with small-peaked cap. The cries of "Taxi!" with which, after kitting-out at *Ganges*, those dressed as seamen had playfully ridiculed the Writers, could now have been directed at all assembled for the Lee-on-the-Solent radar course, re-rated, for want at the time of a new and more accurate category, "Air Fitters (DF)". My glamour had gone, not to be restored until, after years at this dowdy chrysalis stage, sudden emergence as RNVR officer. It was possible to smarten one's appearance in fore-and-aft rig by buying (not from pusser's stores) a tiddley suit, a Number One uniform, made in double-breasted style out of "doeskin", with gold badges. For reasons previously advanced, I never did this; went on suffering the unsatisfactoriness of the issued gear, as years before I had for long suffered the pain of the comedian's Sunday shoes at Seafolde House. One was supposed to fasten all four buttons of the jacket, but this gave what I felt to be an impossible look of the Jutland or Zeebrugge epoch, an effect enhanced by the requirement of returning not just to collar-and-tie but to a collar separate from the shirt, fashion I thought to have liberated myself from for ever more than a decade before, as noted in *Souvenirs*. The Edwardian tone was extended by narrowish trousers, terminating in boots – a look to some degree sanctioned after the war by "Teddy Boy" garb, but then disagreeable to most, if not all. I may say that I had already stopped wearing boots, even my parsimony yielding to the comfort and aestheticism of shoes (allowable, if without toecaps). It was at Lee that both the thrifty and narcissistic sides of my nature were gratified by discovering that for a trifling sum "snobs" (unofficial cobbler) would cut down boots into the simulacra of shoes. I had this done to my better pair of issue boots, and reasonably successful the operation was, though the shoes so formed always needed an effort of will to be worn, if not so great as that required by the comedian's shoes aforementioned.

Come to think of it, I am old enough to have been through the civilian liberation from boots, comparable in emancipatory pleasure with the subsequent liberation from shoelaces. As a very young boy I was photographed in boots, and that was not because, wearing a sailor suit, I had to submit to naval discipline. I remember my mother referring to shoes as "low shoes"; going into a shop (it would be a few years after the photograph) and saying: "May we see some low shoes, for the boy?" In the days of boots it was a great refinement for them to have metal tabs instead of eyeholes for the last few holes, so that the lace could be slipped round the tab, avoiding the trouble of threading. Tabs also avoided the awkwardness of getting a knot through the eyeholes: bootlaces always seemed to be breaking.

Back under the constant care of the Andrew, duties and delays seemed all the more irksome, though as to the latter there was always the compensation of postponed perils. We were Class Number 1 of trainee radar mechanics in the FAA. There was an instruction hut but no equipment; possibly the place had not even been wired up. Some talks on theory were given, of low quality compared with Aberdeen. Two of the lingering RAF Flight Sergeants were involved, I seem to remember, and an RN Schoolmaster. When the equipment at last arrived it was decided by Authority that the hut had to be guarded in its unoccupied hours because of its secret contents. The class members formed the guard, on the Wackford Squeers principle. Torture extreme when one got the morning watch (4 am to 8 am), for one slept and was roused in a nearby wooden shed, unlined, ludicrously cold in that severe winter of 1941–42, heated only by one of those odorous oilstoves that cast patterns of light. Probably the middle watch had to sleep there, too. I wore oilskin over greatcoat, despite the struggle to get webbing over that. By then I had the balaclava and roll-neck sweater knitted by a Blackpool knitting group of ladies, centred on Booth's Café, to which my mother belonged. No doubt in the absence of nepotism the articles in question (perhaps knitted by Mrs Spence-Ormerod herself) would have been in use on more serious naval occasions, such as the Murmansk run.

By the DF Nissen hut was a brick-built air-raid shelter, unused at night, in the entrance to which it was fairly safe for the guard on duty to skulk at times and have a few drags at a cigarette. As to the last, it would almost certainly be made from a tin of "Ticklers", the duty-free, Navy issue tobacco.

No enemy agent ever turned up to penetrate the secrets of the DF hut. I have the feeling the guard was never issued with ammunition, but I could be wrong about this. There is a joke, which I am sure I am not giving the full point of, about the nervous guard who, taught the challenge "Who goes there, friend or foe?" and the ensuing "Advance, friend, and be recognized", on getting the response "Foe", said "Advance, foe." There was this touch of the Fred Karno about the DF hut guard, but if that were the reason for its eventually being quietly dropped, a great many service activities merited dropping also. The experience left its mark: pictures return – of reading or trying to read in a camp bed in the arctic guards' shed (antarctic, rather, for the ambience seemed much akin to that created by Captain Scott, himself RN), only trousers and boots removed, the sole light the pattern of beams from the oilstove.

A constant of service life was shortage of reading material. Sometimes I come across a book on my shelves with Lee-on-Solent and the date under my signature. Such a one would probably have been bought at a quite good secondhand shop in Fareham, a town I usually went to in preference to Portsmouth when I went "ashore", but that source did not satisfy all need. In any case, thrift usually dictated that books bought should primarily be lasting rather than readable – readable in the context of Tannoy music or conditions Captain Oates walked out of, anyway. Yet even at that time (and times thereafter, in fact) I misjudged what I would have found readable, prolonged hangover from the days at school when I preferred Ian Hay to O. Henry. Would I have tackled Walter Scott's Journal in the hutted camp? I doubt it, though was recently held by it with ostensibly more attractive things available. What a bonus that intellectual development never ceases, in the ill-educated at least!

The year turned, the course proceeded in wandering steps and slow. Authority and insight into the business were eventually brought by the young Sub-Lieutenant Gleave, who had worked for Pye and just been commissioned into the RNVR especially to instruct in the function and maintenance of the Pye-made ASV sets. The initials stood for Air Sea Vision: the apparatus, installed in aircraft, enabled targets to be distance-measured, and homed on. The display on the miniature cathode ray tube was a vertical line (measuring distance) on which the target showed as a "blip", a horizontal extension on either side of the vertical line. If the aircraft were navigated so as to equalize the extent of the blip about the vertical, it would *ipso facto* be oriented towards the target.

When I let fall I intended to mention ASV in these pages, my wife was discouraging, saying with truth that what was interesting were people not things, particularly things like radar sets. Yet for some reason scarcely to be uncovered, unless it was the tedium in returning to discipline in a large establishment, details of faces, characters and incidents have largely dropped from my memory of those months. What I summon up is the mess, a Nissen hut, of course, filled with double-decker beds, uncommodious ablutions by the entrance, an obsession with getting heat out of the coke-burning stoves (illegal raids being organized on the camp's coke-piles), and my actually surreptitiously but vainly examining the leads to the loudspeaker for the possibility of arranging a breakdown to give respite from the musical slush, non-stop save for the recorded bugle calls, requests for individuals to report to the RPO's office, and the like. Membership of the mess was not drawn exclusively from the largely middle-class members of the radar class, though the working class would be principally from its skilled echelon, the main body represented by a few Air Mechanics. Of course, these subtleties were not taken account of by the living conditions provided by Authority, which assumed a fairly low proletarian off-duty life.

I still felt, to use Wilfred Owen's phrase, sympathy for the oppressed, often considered myself one of them; and despite turns of revulsion and exasperation this sense continued until the later conditions of my service life made it irrelevant or dormant. Rage would choke me at being wakened by the thoughtless drunks coming late into the mess after an evening ashore, yet at the same time I could write, with sincerity and self-identification, such stanzas as:

> Here in the mess, on beds, on benches, fall
> The blue serge limbs in shapes fantastical:
> The photographs of girls are on the wall
>
> And the songs of the minute walk into our ears;
> Behind the easy words are difficult tears:
> The pain which stabs is dragged out over years.

I see that I was absurdly lenient to the Tannoy music: such poetic soft-pedalling helped to give the Service poetry of the Second World War its pervasive sadness and nostalgia, to choose the two qualities I emphasized when criticizing it at a later date. However, I had forgotten about, and was glad to find, copying out the lines, mention of benches, so characteristic of naval mess-decks, useful (if not the last word in comfort) for card and ludo players, letter writers, make-do-and-menders, even readers. But some features of those ASV sets come back with as much particularity as the humans: valves like little pillar boxes, whose pins, unlike the points of the compass, it was essential to get by heart; or the peculiar awkwardness, due to the interior polythene and the exterior metal braid, of fixing a plug to the co-axial aerial. As to the clip supposed to stop the aerial plug working loose from the aerial socket, this remained a British finger-nipper until American equipment came at a later date to prove their greater regard for comfort even of radar mechanics.

9 *Seafield Park*

Seafield Park, near Fareham, was the overflow establishment for RNAS, Lee-on-the-Solent. It had been a school (not to be confused with my old school, Seafolde House). I do not know at what date boys and masters had left, but when I went there in March 1942 there were signs still of its former function – not merely in the miscellaneousness of its buildings, reflecting the processes of growth and decay so characteristic of prep schools and the like, blossoming in ambitious but institutionalized décor such as timber panelling – seen also in more stable organizations like the Equitable – but also notice and honours boards; well-used upholstered furniture in which might be imagined pipe-smoking beaks of not very far-off days.

When John Lehmann showed me the typescript of his book *Rupert Brooke: His Life and Legend* (1980), I mildly objected to his pretty well wholesale condemnation of the sonnet sequence "1914". I had come to think that those poems not despicably, if vaguely, impugn unserious love and selfish life (to put it banally), and express hope for a future society of true comradeship. Of course, especially in the light of conditions on the Western Front, and the immediately ensuing pacifism of Sassoon and Owen, the notion that such a thing could come directly through war and patriotism will never do. All the same, both 1914 and 1939 had certain saving graces in terms of human relations. Being called up in the second affair gave me a strong sense of *déjà vu*, expressed in several of the poems which at last, at Seafield Park, I started to write (though in extremely modest numbers) about my shared predicament.

I sent practically all the Seafield Park poems to John Lehmann, finding a sympathy and encouragement that did not exclude critical comment very much apropos. After he had given up the literary editorship of *Tribune* (which was in this spring of 1942), he considered the poems for *Penguin New Writing*, passing on one or two surplus to requirements to J. R. Ackerley at *The Listener*. In the second volume of his autobiography, *I Am My Brother*, John actually quotes a poem from Seafield Park in which, as happened, the chaplain comes among naval ratings and speaks of moral matters, to their incomprehension – his concepts of "freedom", "good" and "duty" alien to them in their situation. John's comments on the poem, which follow, are perceptive in a way that now touches me greatly, yet I wonder if I thought at the time (still applying a Warnockian rigour to abstract concepts) I was expressing anything more than a Marxist scepticism.

I rather think one didn't get sent from *Daedalus* to Seafield Park (not awfully far apart) unless waiting to be drafted or otherwise a completely "gash hand". At the end of the radar course – it came eventually to an end – I failed, with a few others, the practical test, and had to stay on for a further week's revision. I was never really any good on the practical side of radar, perhaps too frightened by the lurking presence of 4,000 volts or, more likely, lacking an instinct that allied brain and body, evidenced by my cricket, never learning to play a musical instrument, and (according to my wife) not being able to dance well (though my impressions of soft-shoe and ballet dancers have always seemed to me quite effective). A fellow failure was Willie Robertson who had been at Aberdeen but whom I got to know much better during that extra week. He too came to Seafield Park when we had passed a further practical, and had duly been rated up to "Leading Air Fitter (DF)", and probably had had end-of-course leave. More of him anon.

I see myself among the hands at Seafield Park getting fell in in the mornings for duties to be assigned. I doubt there were nearly enough jobs to go round, even on the Services' labour-intensive system, the unemployment problem aggravated by leading hands being too thick on the ground, deemed to be above utterly menial tasks like shovelling coke, though I am not certain that this proposition was always adhered to. Seafield Park was commanded by a commissioned Warrant Officer, called back into the RN after retirement, promoted to Lieutenant-Commander; quite an elderly man by service standards. It would seem hardly likely to have been his motor car I helped to paint (I think not actually applying the colour, but preparing the surfaces, in which the Chatham rust-chipping experience proved its value). Working on his boat, tied up in a nearby creek, is a task I can be more sure about, though never assigned to it: it was reported a soft option, providing bonuses of cups of tea, even food, from the CO's wife. Nor was I ever given the more dubious job of looking after his monkeys, I think two in number. Whether this was mere guard duty, perhaps including mucking them out, or called for skill in grooming or amusing the pets, again memory fails to reveal.

Such daily duties, so redolent of the preoccupations and eccentricities of those in authority, were again reminiscent of school. Where we fell in was cobbled or partly so, former arena of play for the boys of Seafield Park, and before that, in the premises' private house days, maybe forming an approach or forecourt to the stabling. A drive led through paddocks or former playing fields to a road running parallel to the sea, and so to the then sketchy attractions, as a resort, of Lee, configurations that I drew on for *The Ruined Boys*.

I wrote a few poems in a former common room, quite comfortable in a shabby way, and I fancy not subject to the tyranny of records or radio programmes relayed from the centre. Outside the window was a garden or former garden. Music may well have come from a radio controlled by the common room's users, and thus occasionally classical, if only on account of inertia. This place was the scene of an unfinished poem found recently in a tiny notebook of the time, of which I quote the opening three stanzas, apparently in their first draft:

> In times of parting drums are powerful,
> The probing restless music tears a skin
> From that already raw, sad sensitivity.
>
> And on the floor I see a brilliant square
> With shapes of trees appearing in it and, as though
> It were the drying of a stain, then vanishing.
>
> And should I go outside, across the furrows
> Shadows will be flying with the April clouds
> And all the fields struck into points of light like gems.

Once more, one is gravelled to know why this not wholly impossible start was abandoned – why in general the work of this spring of 1942, evidently a time of a certain openness to experience, and decision about form and tone, was not more ample, more worked on. Physical circumstances might have been more auspicious, but unlike Terry Warnock's job with the Gas Department the chores of Seafield Park could not have absorbed much energy. The poems' dominating theme was separation; a characteristic, indeed, as already noted, of far too much of the verse of the Second World War, particularly in domestic and backward-looking circumstances (though this objection, which even a guilty party like myself held strongly, had to be modified when, after the war, Keith Douglas's collected poems appeared, and later still when Alan Ross collected his revised war poems in *Open Sea*).

When I got to Seafield Park, delay in facing the shooting war – whether deliberate, as in taking up radar at all, or accidental, as by failing the practical – could not be much prolonged, for I was already, or very soon to be, booked for a draft to Ceylon.

Nevertheless, I arranged for Kate and Johnny to come down from Blackpool, and stay nearby. I may well have been influenced in this by the comparatively relaxed atmosphere at the overflow establishment, the general sense that manning overseas air bases and the like had to take second place to simian needs, and also by the conviction (sometimes justified, sometimes not) that the wheels of the Andrew ground exceeding slow. I booked a hotel room in Lee for a night or two, before finding excellent digs nearer Seafield Park. The hotel, scarcely to be dignified by the name, was notable in a series we experienced of more or less scruffy places open for business in wartime; memorable chiefly because the first night the only vacant room was on the ground floor, at the door of which, at intervals during the night, there snuffled and scratched, trying to get at us, what proved to be merely an Alsatian dog. It was no consolation to learn that it was simply, like us, seeking a night's rest, the room normally where its bedding was. My son, patient and uncomplaining as ever, was below par with a heavy cold and ulcerated mouth. Yet the exercise seemed worthwhile.

It turned out we had no more than a week together. The news that the Ceylon draft was to depart from Seafield Park the following morning came on a day when I was duty watch, so Willie Robertson offered to go to the digs and tell Kate. No better messenger could have been found. Though tall, well-made, excellent at tennis and badminton, and fond of a dram, he was a man of supreme uxoriousness and domesticity. And he lacked the usual disadvantage of messengers, that of being themselves unaffected by their bad tidings, for he, too, was on the Ceylon draft. The next morning Kate enterprisingly borrowed a bicycle from one of our two landladies, and rode to Seafield Park in the hope of seeing me – which she did from a distance over the tail of a truck taking the draft and its bags and ammicks to RNAS, Lee, to join those on the draft already there. There was some arrangement that we might meet later in the day at the British Restaurant in Lee, but the draft was mustered with disagreeable rapidity. The British Restaurant (on the whole one of the ghastlier wartime improvisations, possibly later making its mark on Orwell's *Nineteen Eighty-Four*) had been established in the Tower, a modest municipal pleasure-dome, which I passed in another truck the same morning on the way to the troop train, wondering if Kate and Johnny were within, toying with the vegetable pie.

III

HOME AND DRY

1 *Aflatun and Aristu*

When I set off for Ceylon in April 1942 I started a journal, an indication of my sense of the momentous, for I am no diarist, being indolent, and bothered even by the elementary problems of the genre, such as which tense to employ. I kept the thing with moderate conscientiousness for a couple of months, and shall use the material here, having just re-read it, surprised at its moments of interest. I thought I had ransacked it of anything valuable for my novel *The Perfect Fool* (1963), but I see now there may be point in presenting the comparatively brief narrative at greater length.

Questions arise of what memory can add to such a record, and of the rival "truths" of actuality and hindsight. Some things unnoted have stayed vividly in mind. On the other hand, I had forgotten the apparent vehemence of my disillusion with men and ideas. Taking one thing with another, I do not doubt being able truthfully to present this journal with the added perspective of forty years. I say "truthfully" but really the word should be "honestly", for neither pure memory nor memory plus documentation can bring back the "truth". As to this, and the defects of memory, see the fine passages about her early life in *The Swan in the Evening* by Rosamond Lehmann.

The journal was written in the first few pages of a Stationery Office notebook issued to me at Robert Gordon's College, Aberdeen. Sheets of more official guff seem to have been torn out before the journal was started. On the cover I had put my name, number and rating, and the Aberdeen address, but on going thence to Lee-on-the-Solent and being re-rated, I had crossed out the address and substituted "L/AF(DF)" for "Ord/Sea". The "L/" must have been added when promotion to Leading Hand came at the end of the Lee course. "AF(DF)" meant "Air Fitter (Direction Finding)", radar ("radiolocation", the English term still in general use) being considered so secret as not to be bruited in the classification of personnel.

From Lee the Ceylon draft was trucked to RNB, Portsmouth

and entrained at the railway station there. Then ensued an all-night journey to Liverpool, in sharp contrast to the family life recently tasted, a depth of proletarian service existence scarcely plumbed before, not even in Chatham Barracks, where at least frequent escape "ashore" could be envisaged.

I tried to read *The White Cockatoo*, an indifferent whodunnit by Mignon G. Eberhart (I hope I ascribe it rightly, though no fictive talent could have offset the night's debits). But mostly I dozed, or overlooked a game of baccarat at the nearest table in the compartment, played for what seemed notably high stakes by four Air Mechanics. One, red-haired, pimpled, often used an appellation (then a novelty to me) imputing bastardy and a certain homosexual practice, and reasonably enough queried, as a matter of propriety, by the printer's proofreader of the day when I employed it in *The Perfect Fool*. Another of the Air Mechs, for some reason never apparent, was nicknamed Toscanini – usually called Tosca or Toscafuckinini. The amazing extent of the *maestro's* fame thereby revealed did not strike me at the time. Tosca was rather dour, sad at losing. The stooge, as I saw him, of the four was a small, simpler man addressed as Ivan (possibly his real name) or, following a popular song of the day, Ivanskavinski Skavar (authentic spelling not guaranteed). Though derided by the others, he persisted in wagering what were regarded as miserable threepences, though, to put that stake in context, I had played family bridge not many years before for a halfpenny a hundred. Simple stooge or not, Ivan subsequently hopped the troopship before it sailed, after spreading the erroneous information that he was in the sick bay. His absence was not discovered until we had been three days at sea.

The night somehow passed. The high (or low) spot of the ensuing day was disentraining at Aintree station, which could not have been a particularly jolly place even on Grand National Day. There was a bare platform, a footbridge farther up the line. As the Fleet Air Arm draft of 125 men, with bags and ammicks, and an Ordnance Corps draft, with bags and rifles, waited for transport, a few civilians watched from high on the footbridge. An essentially sentimental feeling gripped one, nurtured by the literature and photographs, even memories, of the 1914–18 war, of a doom shared with these fellow servicemen, now separated for ever from ordinary English life.

The Army eventually supplied the transport that took us to a transit camp not far away. Dust blew off the dried mud of the parade ground. As the FAA ate a poor meal in the mess hall, there was the rhythmic sound of approaching boots. Words of command rang out. Some detachment of swaddies burst into the mess and barged about for advantageous places in the food queue. We were astounded, less perhaps at the uncouthness than that men should be marched to their eating place. The experience was a foretaste of what was in store on the troopship, an existence also organized by the Army. The journey and the milieu had induced boredom and pessimism, everyone deeply chokka, hoping, like the terminally ill, that some phenomenon would prevent the looming voyage or at least passage to so remote a destination – "I never did the Japs any harm" a remark heard more than once. My Scottish friend, Willie Robertson, had a catch phrase for the disastrous strokes that fell: "It's no' fair, it's no' right – it's a nigger's left ball."

Rumour soon proved her power. The next day we moved to Liverpool docks, filed aboard the *Capetown Castle*, a steward at the foot of the gangway giving each man a card. This proved to indicate the number of the bunk allotted, in our case in an immense ballroom, panelled in similar style to the boardroom of my late employers, the Woolwich Equitable Building Society. The interior had been filled with bunks on the open wine rack principle. By what I saw at once as an amazing stroke of luck, the number on my card took me to the top bunk of one of a pair, merely two bunks tall, that faced swing doors leading from the deck, the limitations in height and breadth occasioned by the architectural features of the entrance, some slight projection of which afforded a place for a few books and other small items of kit. In the ballroom's interior were crowded alleyways, mass recumbent propinquity. 4,000 were said to be aboard: from the start queues formed for washing, eating, defecating, canteen – the last merely an aperture through which tea, biscuits, fags and nutty could be bought from rapacious merchant navy personnel.

We had embarked on 14 April, at night were pulled into the stream, and set sail at noon the following day. Initially, there were six ships in a very slow convoy; the sea at first dead calm, turning to a modest swell the next day, perhaps as the dread current came into play. The *Capetown Castle* was armed, and I was given the job of look out on the Oerlikon gun on the port side of the bridge. This automatic weapon, oiled, black and slender, not huge, Swiss-made, novel to me, was housed in an iron-framed and concrete-bodied pill box, reached from the deck by a vertical ladder. In time, some perfunctory account of its workings were given by the naval gunners on the spot, but whether one was ever expected, in some emergency, to fire it was doubtful. The Marine CSM started off by muddling the roster, so members of the gun-post crew were uncertain whether they were on watch or off. I did most of the first day, and 9–11.30 of the first night.

This, and the cold as we moved north into the Atlantic, set me against lookout duties (which settled down into the averagely arduous four hours on, eight off), but in retrospect having something to do in comparative isolation, if only to daydream and chat, was another stroke of luck. I am puzzled now as to the point of looking-out during the night watches, but presumably there was a chance of detecting a periscope. I remember being sceptical even vis-à-vis daylight hours, but was reassured by one with experience that it was not unknown for the thing to be spotted by an innocent and unbinoculared eye.

Soon we were sailing into the sunset, the convoy now about twenty ships, escorted by two cruisers and some destroyers. The light sky, blackish-grey sea, white rolls of foam blowing back from the noses of the westward-bound formation – such seemed newsreel clichés, not of interest compared with the miseries of going on watch, sleeping in one's clothes, the rationing of washes to two a day (for those who queued assiduously). Vanished my Wordsworthian interest in natural objects, Spenderian love of fellow men: I squirmed to recall the bullshit I had written about naval life, luckily in letters rather than verse. The even blankness of depression by no means excluded suicidal impulses, as in prisons and concentration camps.

When the swell increased many became ill, increasing the interior miasma. I myself went on eating normally but slept more, talked less, most matters of the mind subordinated to those of the body. I was full of the anxious languor and stuffiness always to some degree lurking at sea, even in "Uncle" Fred Thompson's yacht in the Ribble estuary, to mention one of my previous principal maritime experiences.

We had with us only our personal kit (contents of a sailor's attaché case); kitbags and suitcases still in a hold, though daily promised. Till they came up, all I had left to read was *The Ring and the Book* – Everyman edition, still possessed, with my deck- and bunk-numbers written neatly in ink below my name. Underestimating tactical reading requirements was an error I repeated throughout the war, though the error was compounded by shortage.

The suicidal moods, and sickliness-without-being-sick, passed after a few days. Even at my worst I noted the excellence, even heartening quality, of Browning's poem, which seemed to me then to make Tennyson "look horribly provincial". But for quite a time wind, rain and endless processions of people – all through the facing swing doors – made my bunk virtually uninhabitable during the day, when it was desirable for a certain amount of lost sleep to be recovered. A greater degree of quiet could be had sitting on the broad staircase leading from the ballroom to a sundeck. Others discovered this, too, and after a few days a notice was affixed to a bannister: OFFICERS ONLY. MARINES NOT ALLOWED ON THESE STAIRS. Despite some wag soon deleting "ONLY. MARINES", and a semantic argument about the restrictive connotation of "marines", the refuge was pretty effectively denied. My nerves could not be said to be in good order; and lack of sleep and exercise, and too much tea, and chocolate and biscuit eating, brought dyspepsia.

The journal for 26 April records what I think was not mild paranoia; though I shall have a further instance to recount, and in the light of *The Ordeal of Gilbert Pinfold* one sees that sea voyages are good breeding grounds for the disorder. I complained, without giving examples, that I seemed "to be *distrusted* not to say disliked, by some, the rougher of us. I sense this. Because I am educated? A leading hand? The thing to do is to be precisely myself, not try to adapt myself to these proletarians or artisans. Very difficult – I always try to adapt myself with everyone. 'Negative personality'! And perhaps (when I think about it) I am too amiable – in contrast to the times when I withdraw into my shell of books and abstraction, fearing contact. If I weren't a poet I should be a leader and (most disturbingly) vice versa!"

I reproduce this bit of psychologizing, though not typical of the journal, because the very feebleness of its expression denotes the reality of the hostility; also, it is an early specimen of my self-diagnosis of split personality, a notion I continued to express, even act out, though when echoed by reviewers and others one sees it as far too simplistic. Yes (and I use the journal's language), I loathed the smell of the 4,000 men on the *Capetown Castle*, the way they opened their uncouth mouths – more stupid than animals. I loathed the way they carelessly jostled me. Yet, as will soon be seen, longing for fraternity, admiration for revolt, were still easily roused.

The weather improved. A daily lime-juice ration appeared, and the first flyingfish. At dusk the latter resembled dragonflies; in the morning sun, swallows. The open deck became as crowded as the "flats" had been. The continuous impromptu concert that went on *en plein air* is briefly but not badly evoked in *The Perfect Fool*. It is there characterized as mostly obscene, but I wonder if it was any more so than the entertainments now offered in clubs and pubs, and even on TV. I avoided the Sunday morning church service for naval ratings not by advancing my officially-recorded atheism but by retreating to the gun-post, which in fact overlooked the padre on the foredeck, his breeze-blown vestments surmounted by a khaki topee.

The rig of the day had become khaki shorts and shirts, issued at Lee-on-the-Solent before we left. The shorts were of curious specification, probably dating from the Kipling era. The legs were very wide and reached down to the knee, if not below. They also had extra length in the shape of an absurdly generous species of hem, folded upwards and kept in position by buttons. The idea was that this could be lowered at night and tucked in gaiters or stockings, thus affording protection against mosquitoes. The effect in either position was acutely unbecoming, so much so that the trying on of the issued garb occasioned a painful hilarity, like viewing the humiliation of an Oliver Hardy. Luckily, a fellow existed in one of the huts at Lee who for a trifling sum would remove the folded portions and hem the residue to a reasonable length. What remained was the inordinate width, that made sitting down in the garment, in company where modesty was desirable, as tricky as one imagines a similar operation to be in a short skirt. Unlike the padre, I do not think we ever wore our topees, except in jest. They were white, extremely large, and could only be transported in one's baggage by being saved for the last item in the kitbag, the crown protruding like the top of an egg. The way to the Far East must have been littered with them, but I do not recall when I got shot of mine: because of thrift and respect for authority it was probably one of the last to go.

On the morning of 29 April, through a slight haze, a line of hills came into view ahead, clouds shrouding their tops. Nearer, it could be seen how they stretched backwards, very humped, patched with bottle-green vegetation, sprouting an occasional tree – the convoy floating towards them on a dead calm sea. Already there was an indication of immoderate depth in the landscape, so characteristic of Africa. As Margery Perham noted in one of her remarkable books about the continent, "what a new value the green of earth offers after weeks at sea!" Over and above this was the scalp-crawling sensation conferred by the first sight of Africa itself – part of the modestly nude shoulder of an exciting figure of dreams or literature.

We anchored in Freetown harbour, little of the port discernible from our distance. In the hills were fragile-looking houses half hidden by the green that at the water ended in a brief, paint-box-bright sandy-red cliff of soil. Soon the ship was the focus of activity, a commonplace to tropical voyagers: to us, who but for the war would for ever have been locked in temperate lands, a novelty. A one-seater canoe, like a wood splinter, came far below to the ship's side, the negro guiding it with a closed-umbrella-shaped paddle, singing "Halleluja, I'm a bum" and "Ippy-I", and calling for "Glasgow tanners" and a pipe. Whether his shrewd appeal to nationalist sentiment overcame traditional closeness was not clear. He was the first of a succession of such, prepared to dive for the sixpences, even pennies; bringing bananas for sale. Some on board did business, dubbing the visitors "Charlie", asking what time they signed on at the "Labour", enquiring lasciviously after their wives. The visitors' insolence was not concealed by a mock naïvety, and I reflected ruefully that their idiomatic phrases had been picked up from many boat loads of the only theoretically more civilized and free. A serious exchange, obviously initiated by a socialist like myself, revealed that one canoeist worked on the jetty at Freetown – night duty, 5 p.m. to 5 a.m., wages £2 10s. a month. A persistent memory of the port: a negro in the water, his chip of a boat near him, the green hills behind, calling through a mouthful of pennies: "Any mo'? Any mo'?"

The few days' halt at Freetown seemed to consolidate the decline in fortune and volition, even then not awfully high, initiated by the news of one's drafting to Ceylon. The heat blistered the brow, seized up the bowels: the brilliant light, exhilarating at first, soon produced an acute headache. I told in *The Perfect Fool* of the speeches after an evening concert, when the captain of one of the escorting cruisers earned crashing applause with bloodthirsty anti-Jap sentiments, and the captain of the *Capetown Castle* announced that he would go down with the red ensign flying rather than be captured. More applause, rather less thunderous. This really not surprising manifestation was oddly depressing: a sharper case of the kind exemplified by the future Lord Martonmere starting to sing the National Anthem at my peace meeting in the Thirties. It seemed as though one forgot, until so reminded, that a great part of mankind was engaged in putting its nationalistic and aggressive feelings into practice. The sentiments voiced, however, were far more lowering than the accompanying hints of perils attendant and to come, hints augmented by the thump of depth charges during the night, a German submarine rumoured to have penetrated the harbour defences. Troubled by what in my youth had been called "heat spots" (and soothingly anointed with vinegar), I lay on my bunk scratching, and thinking horribly: "I shall never come back."

Utterly characteristic of the ambivalence in myself about the men (and in the men about the state of the world) was the long political and social discussion in our "flat" quite accurately reported in *The Perfect Fool*, recalling the nobility and pathos of some of the figures of the "loose group", debating arena of my provincial youth. It need hardly be said that in 1942 the widespread desire for change and amelioration, coupled with some uncertainty about methods and results – mood underlying the overwhelming Labour vote in 1945 – was plainly evident. This was greatly to my taste, if insufficiently revolutionary.

We left Freetown on 3 May. The ship's food, never much to write home about, had degenerated vilely a week out of Liverpool. After Freetown it was not merely unpalatable but uneatable. The rich, including myself, lived on issue bread and butter, and sweet stuff from the canteen. No wonder, to harp on the topic, bowels were in indifferent order. Then the canteen ran out of chocolate and later biscuits. Organization was bad, commands stupid; both effected by boorish and bumptious Army and

Marine Sergeants. Distress was all the greater for one trained in the standards of HMS *Ganges*.

Mention in the journal of the bread seems to indicate that its quality was maintained. (Even in those days I was a bread freak, less arduous an enthusiasm even during the war than it became afterwards: much could be written on my post-war metropolitan quest for good bread). Very early in the voyage Willie Robertson had come up to me with serious expression and instructed me to look through a window in an edifice erected on deck. He said: "They're working like niggers in there." When I put my head in I saw a busy bakehouse, staffed mainly by blacks. It was typical of Willie, enhanced by his accent and timing that were characteristic of Scottish music-hall performers like Harry Lauder, Will Fyffe and, in a later day, the marvellous Renée Houston. Willie's presence was a great consolation. Not from him emanated anything spiritually or physically off-putting, though his appearance at times was apt to become bizarre, frequently (as in my grandfather's case) deliberately so (among the photographs to be mentioned later is one of him at what must be Port Reitz, wearing a flying-helmet and gumboots, with a revolver stuck in the belt of his khaki shorts). Many of us had requested and been granted permission to cease shaving, and quite soon Willie's pale, rather large, flat countenance was transformed by a heavy beard much more ginger than his hair, which was in fact strongly inclined to fair, wavy and parted near the middle.

> And Aflatun and Aristu
> Let their Beards grow, and their Beards grew
> Round and about the mainmast tree
> Where they stood still, and watched the sea.

Flecker's stanza was not wholly applicable, for my own whiskers grew patchily, even less comprehensively than those of the tennis star, Borg, and when they came to be inspected by the Lieutenant i/c the Naval draft I had to agree with him that they would never do.

Willie's tall, slightly leaning, shambling figure was not suited – whose was? – to pusser's khaki shirts and shorts. Nor was his appearance improved by his almost always wearing the kapok-filled life jacket issued on boarding, an object that got grubbier as the voyage progressed since it had always to be at hand and was universally in use as a pillow when crashing one's swede on deck. Many naval ratings kept their khaki shorts up with the blue webbing belt in use with serge bell-bottoms: Willie providently carried his enamel mug about, his belt threaded through its handle. Mugs had been issued with the life jackets, and proved to be the more vital equipment. If *The Perfect Fool* is to be believed, my own mug was filched at an early stage, due to assuming the honesty of fellow draftees, typical sentimentality of the bourgeois Marxist of the time. How I replaced it is now mysterious; perhaps theft in my turn.

I have the feeling that Willie also wore the inflatable, motorcycle-tyre-like lifebelt issued to all naval personnel as part of their initial kit, but this may only have been at critical moments or, even, a joke on his part, or the lingering memory of a facetious suggestion by me. His concern for his safety, if mined or torpedoed, and comfort, so far as concerned mugs of tea, was quintessentially characteristic, though that side of his persona, superficially self-centred and unheroic, did not seem dominant in my eyes, or at any rate induced only fond teasings. He was one to whom good jokes were told (though probably he filtered out the dross), and who himself invented many. His sensitivity to harm through warlike action was not paralleled by lack of boldness in his relations with authority. He had actually officially requested to be taken off the Ceylon draft, on the ground that his wife would be upset at his going. (At the time we regarded this as typical Williesque super cool cheek, but years after it came home to me that in truth he was thinking not of himself but his missis). And his calm bearding of a high railway official will be seen later. Like many Scots, certainly then, he had a civilian occupation connected with the sea, so prompting him to opt for the RN, though calling-up as a writer (originally intended, as in my own case) would have made his previous experience more useful, for he had worked behind the counter in a shipping line's passenger division.

One afternoon, three days away from Durban, a couple of explosions, separated by ninety minutes or so, interrupted the solo-whist-playing of an afternoon watch off duty. I did not hear the first, but went on deck to see smoke proceeding from a depot ship that for some time had been on our starboard bow, the vessel already aft, and turning out of the convoy. The second explosion caused a similar happening to a merchant ship, which some said they could see settling down by the bows as we left her behind. The leisurely pace of catastrophe, often remarked on, was noticeable here. After the first explosion everyone grabbed their kapok life jackets, suddenly transformed, like neglected, ugly creatures in fairy tales. On deck I encountered Willie. Surely this was an occasion when he had doubled up in life jackets.

It must be borne in mind that rumour assigned various causes to these events, including mere boiler explosions, though two on the same afternoon seemed excessive. Perhaps it was not until the second that Willie and I arranged that if only one of us survived he would report to the other's wife. The precise nature of the report was not laid down. I would say Willie's nonchalance was less evident than my own, but courage properly so called was not put to any sort of test. On my part, superficial flippancy, the compulsion to joking or facetiousness in the face of the serious (all devices, perhaps, to keep hidden or protected the essential self) still operated. (Mines were almost certainly to blame, one heard later).

As a matter of fact, the moment of greatest unease of the voyage is related more or less verbatim in *The Perfect Fool.* Wandering through the ship, I came across a relatively uncrowded bathroom used by sergeants and the like. I say "wandering", but it sticks in my mind that the exploration was specifically to discover such a wash-place, probably having observed vestiges of it in the shining faces and shirt-sleeved state of certain senior NCOs. The *Capetown Castle* had a strong resemblance to the ship in which Karl Rossman is voyaging at the start of Kafka's *America*, particularly as to the parts cut off from the ordinary experience of passengers in the lowest class. After the war, when I read Brian Aldiss' SF novel *Non-stop*, about an enormous and labyrinthine spaceship, another literary parallel presented itself. In the *Capetown Castle*, the quest for lavatorial facilities was spurred by the water being turned on, in the crude troops' "ablutions" erected on deck (like the bake-house), only for two brief periods *per diem*.

I used the discovered bathroom quite regularly, though never without qualms, relying on the unfamiliarity of Army and Air Force Sergeants with the RN to avoid challenge. The FAA draft was so small that the chance of encountering a suspicious senior naval NCO seemed quite a long shot. My ploy was to go to the bathroom in shirt (collar removed) and trousers, the implication being that I was a Petty Officer, comparative youth accounted for by some technical skill with sonar or the like that had brought early promotion. A few faces actually became familiar enough to nod to. For my rule-respecting nature and fear of disgrace, the peril was substantial, detracting somewhat from the luxury of washes and shaves not queued for and in relatively comfortable surroundings.

After a visit one night, exploring curiously as in that novel does the hero of *Non-stop*, I found a small room, empty, containing a bath. I slipped in, bolted the door. In the linen dolly-bag issued at *Ganges* for toilet articles I had a cake of saltwater soap bought with blind forethought from the ship's canteen. The great taps soon filled the commodious bath with seawater. Lying in it, my nude body seemed already at the mercy of the greater saline element outside the ship. The squeakings and blowings from the timbers and vents round me were far from reassuring; the ambiguous trousers and shirt on the adjacent floor seemed a protection lost. Submarines could be visualized, floating below the ship even as one floated in the itself floating ship. This was before the incident of the mines, otherwise they would have been added to the dangers conjured up, not the least of which were an inability to unbolt the door in case of alarm, and authority hammering on it, demanding an account of my trespass.

The protagonist of *Non-stop* even has my first name:

> Forwards was a region like none Roy Complain had seen before. The Grandeur of Sternstairs, the cosy squalor of Quarters, the hideous wilderness of Deadways, even the spectacle of that macabre sea where the Giants had captured him – none of them prepared him for the *differentness* of Forwards.

A taste of "Sternstairs" came on my way to the concrete and iron tub when I had to pass, even penetrate, the sundeck, where, as soon as weather permitted, stood a comfortable green-canvas chair with the Adjutant's name stencilled on it: MAJOR GORDON-WILSON. More commonplace deckchairs also appeared, for, so far as could be discerned by a denizen of "Deadways", officers and such female supernumeraries as FANYS lived under many of the conditions of a peacetime voyage – charming dining room, cabins, barber's shop, games deck, gramophones, drink. At Freetown, a homosexual RAF officer, previously noted as occasionally wandering, shyly smiling, on the poop deck, actually appeared in chic blue-and-white checked shirt and blue linen trousers. A few close friendships, outwardly discreet, were almost from the voyage's start formed among the troops themselves.

Senses were deranged, dreams all the more amazing, through keeping watch. The journal records an instance – getting only half an hour's sleep before being shaken to keep the middle-watch, and in the gun-post, under the Milky Way, snatches of half-sleep, stream of consciousness active as Mrs Dalloway's. I must have fallen into a deeper doze just before four, because marines roused me at twenty past, coming late on relief watch. I went down, undressed and wrapped myself in my blanket – the weather had cooled, approaching the Cape. I lay facing the wall behind the bunk which, being part of the ballroom, was veneered. Before I fell asleep I observed an ornamental strip of veneering of different grain: in sleep this became a silver cinema screen on which it seemed I could project any image I wished. Girls were running, scene from some mysterious scenario. I willed a more lascivious view but the result was fragmentary and soon faded. I was conscious the whole time of the folds of grey blanket round my shoulders: indeed, I could see them. Then I dreamed I was paralyzed, with such accompanying alarm I decided to wake myself. I did so, or dreamed so, but stayed paralyzed still – only able, cocooned in a blanket, to move my limbs a fraction.

There was a final dream, involving my mother, who confessed to me she had a cancer. I pleaded with her to go to London to see a specialist: "What's the use of money if you die?" Rereading these few lines of the journal still brings unease, for seven years later she did die and from carcinoma. The strange anticipation undoubtedly arose from the long years of her undiagnosed hyperthyroidism – her resultant ill-health an anxiety deeper than my polite uncommunicativeness, even our sharing of jokes, would indicate. (Doubtless, too, in the background of the dream was my father's illness and death, more than twenty years before, from the same disease). So now – I mean in the epoch when I write these words – chronology becomes painfully confused when I dream of her as still alive and suffering, as she grievously did, from that terminal malady, and, waking, I am momentarily unsure whether in truth she is dead or not.

On this voyage I seem to have written only two poems, the last in the collection *The Middle of a War*, one of them actually arising out of the favourable conditions for dreaming, especially gloomily, provided:

> I dreamed of my child's face, all bloody.
> Waking, I heard
> The tortured creak of wood, the whistling
> Like some night-haunting, death-presaging bird . . .

Alun Lewis, making a similar trip later the same year, did rather better, perhaps helped by material conditions, for by then he was commissioned. Though treating of some of the piddling matters mentioned in the foregoing pages, his "A Troopship in the Tropics" achieves a certain detachment, the emotion-recollected-in-tranquillity quality usually requisite for verse of any value. And one of his trooper poems became quite famous: "Song: On seeing dead bodies floating off the Cape." What luck my own was not among them.

2 *The Clique*

As we came into the harbour at Durban there was a stout woman in white on the quay singing patriotic and nostalgic songs to us through a megaphone, though the time was not yet 7 a.m. She was said to be there to greet every troopship; perhaps had done so since the Boer War. The sense returned of being at the mercy of history, history written in a style one strongly disapproved of, even though playing an evidently important role – the pervading sense when lugging hammocks about on Aintree station under the eyes of history's nonentities. Having been denied it at Freetown, everyone expected shore leave here, watch and watch about. But at 9.30 a.m. orders came to pack, and we were all off the *Capetown Castle*, with our kit, by 11 a.m. We entrained at the dock, and in another hour had moved off to a transit camp, Clairwood, by the racecourse, six miles or so out of Durban.

Establishments placarded DUNLOP, LEVER BROS. and STANDARD OIL were passed on the way, confirmation we were here to defend those monopolist interests and only incidentally to defeat the evil Axis powers. My complete lack of patriotic or straight-forwardly anti-fascist sentiment (as confirmed at the ship's concert) was personally characteristic, and possibly others were in like case. I daresay the attitude rose partly from feeling that keeping quiet about disagreeableness might postpone its effect indefinitely – rather as I used to smile with my lips closed as a boy to hide the fact that an eyetooth, growing out like Dracula's, needed dental attention. Even the sparse journal entries show that I still saw the world through innocent left-wing eyes. On the railway line to Clairwood, I noted, on one side were the "suburbanish pretty residences of the well-off: on the other the corrugated hovels of the Indians."

The last word indicates my initial confusion about the different colours of skin. I could not tell which were the country's indigenous inhabitants, which the immigrants (or their descendants) from the Indian sub-continent, the business being further complicated by the "coloureds", a category of mixed breeds and varying complexions. Needless to say, the racial barriers reinforced by the authorities (extending even to the use of the public benches along the seafront) were greatly displeasing, and during all my time in Africa I gained virtuous pleasure by yielding the privilege of using facilities marked "Whites (or Europeans) Only" – or, to put it more accurately, enjoyed mucking in where possible with non-whites. The influx of proletarian or proletarianized servicemen must have been a measurable liberalizing influence in African racial divisions, though without effect in the final crunches. The mere sight of whites engaged in menial tasks was surely an eye-opener to many non-whites.

Clairwood Camp, a town of tents pitched on a gentle hillside, overlooked a landscape through which I might have been driven by Richard Flower on our pre-war circuits of the Kent and East Sussex courts. The first meal eaten was tea: on the tables were newly-broached two-pound tins of preserves. By moving round, in the style of the Mad Hatter's tea party, it was possible to sample half a dozen or so varieties, which I did, greedy after the lousy grub of the *Capetown Castle* – even trying out such dubieties as tomato jam. To South African marmalade, almost invariably excellent, I have stayed faithful to this day.

In Clairwood, the Proustian or Dickensian view of life's

mechanics prevailed: one not only re-encountered men who had been on other drafts at Lee, but also those not seen since *Ganges* days. The final pages of *Copperfield*, say, were brought to mind. There was a strong buzz that the last two Ceylon drafts had been cancelled and made "miscellaneous"; that is, available for any place, any vessel. A survivor from HMS *Hermes* said the Japs "had knocked shit out of" Trincomalee. It occurred to me that Durban might now be the Fleet Air Arm base, instead of a port farther east, but really this seemed mere wishful thinking. One was fervent in one's hope of being saved, after all, from Ceylon – not because of Ceylon's contiguity to Japanese aircraft but simply because Ceylon was about the most distant place from home one was likely to get to. The farther from home, so it seemed, the less the chance of returning before the end of the war. Even moving up the African east coast, as I soon did, was a welcome step in the right direction, though the Mediterranean – Suez Canal route, which would have made it so in reality, was then unusable. How strange it now seems to have measured the sense of separation simply as the crow (or nightingale rather) flies.

There were seven to a tent: agreeable companions in mine, some old acquaintances. But despite the warm sunny days the clayey sand struck chill into the bones at night and got into all one's possessions. Astounding, after three years of the British blackout, to see lights shining under moon and stars. The roadways and alleyways between tents were illuminated by lamps on poles. Crowds of sailors, soldiers and airmen shuffled to and from the canteen, as in some emblematic scene, perhaps from Bunyan. In the long grass at the sides of the road cicadas chirped, loud enough to pain the eardrums. Beer in the canteens was strong and gassy, one shilling (5p) the pint bottle: on that first night we left the canteen quite early to giggle, smoke the dreadful cigarettes available ("Cavalla", one shilling and threepence for thirty-six), and try to achieve comfort and sleep on the cold earth. But apart from the cicadas, the occasional locust or immense flying beetle, strange plant or tree, and a few other oddities, it was really like being in camp in the UK. Among the oddities (so the journal found) was a young Javanese sailor (Royal Netherlands Navy) seen in the showers: skin *café-au-lait*, touches of black where in a "European" would be touches of pink. What one found exotic very much illustrated the insulation during the Twenties and Thirties of the ordinary middle classes not only from "abroad" but also from the extensive visual material now a commonplace – just as one had no notion until the coming of the talkies at the end of the Twenties of the hideousness of American speech.

I think Clairwood was choreless and one was free to go into Durban every afternoon and evening. As in higher South African society, the shitty jobs, e.g. in the godown kitchens, had to be assigned to black labour. With typical enterprise, Willie had brought with him his box-Brownie camera, and several snapshots of the camp survive. One is of Willie and me with such a kitchen in the background, but I am sure we were mere bystanders, without menial or even supervisory duties – indeed, I have a book under my arm. Before sending the snapshot home, I wrote on the back: "SIR THOMAS LIPTON AND FRIEND." Though we are unglamorously garbed in singlets and Number Two trousers, our taxi-drivers' caps are upgraded somewhat by white cap-covers (later to be made familiar in England by their retention by those returning from abroad, not displeased thus to proclaim their foreign service). The cap and his distinguished beard give Willie the fanciful resemblance to the rich, yacht-racing grocer – evidently still remembered though dead a dozen years. It was in Clairwood Willie said: "Come and watch this. They're baffled." He took me over to a few black camp employees, for whom he then performed some simple but adroit trick with coins, the sort of feat he had a useful supply of, like his jokes. Hard to say whether he or his audience were the more amused. The pleasure he took was the kind he would have got from the puzzlement of children. He was not at all left-wing, but always put himself imaginatively into the position of the underdog, uninhibited, for example, about expressing – to whites – his outrage at racial discrimination.

To a puritan lefty from wartime England, Durban seemed a city of overripe and almost embarrassing luxury. Ice cream, fruit, clothes, cigarettes, chocolate – rationed or scarce in England – were plentiful at pre-War prices. All the books, cosmetics, fountain pens, watches and cameras, equally plentiful, seemed to be imported – "a great plantation," I noted, "where the Whites live on the backs of the Indians and natives and drive about in great high-powered American cars." The depth of thought may be measured by the level of the prose. Everything appeared to me, appropriately, in black and white – the head-dresses of the Zulu ricksha drivers, elaborate but shabby, and a frail, diminutive Indian boy selling CP pamphlets in a pub. But one had to accept, as simple bonuses to various senses, brandy (at least that was domestic) at ninepence a nip; the Durban Symphony Orchestra; and the Durban girls, perennially tanned and summer-frocked.

We had docked at Durban on 18 May 1942. The weeks went by, with various buzzes about the eventual fate of the Ceylon draft. We had a "casual" pay parade, but on such occasions the amount doled out was always meagre, the service overanxious to ensure that no man's account was in the red. I must have departed from England with a decent supply of cash, for there was no time for Kate to have arranged bank withdrawal facilities for me in South Africa. Not that I needed, or had the resources for, substantial drawings, and when pay came regularly the fact that I made the minimum allotment to Kate left me better off than most, anyway. Exiguous pay and the availability of Durban brought ruin to some. From Leading Air Fitter Goodbody I bought a cheap watch even cheaper than the price he had paid. I did not really want it for I had myself bought a watch in Durban, despite possessing a perfectly sound one already. It may well have been I envisaged a grotesque future when watches would be effective currency, as indeed happened in the warring nations eventually on the losing side. Goodbody was one of the seven in the tent – smallish, black hair well brilliantined down but still in parts unruly, and possessing a true "tiddley suit" (doeskin, double-breasted, gold badges) which (now I come to think of it) may well have encouraged him to visit Durban more frequently than his current resources warranted. A mild, companionable character, how vivid his appearance and slightly salivated speech still is – yet I cannot recall him after Clairwood.

Even when what seemed definitive news arrived on 10 June that we were to move on the morrow, no destination was named. Kitbags, hammocks, green suitcases, toolboxes, were lugged to the roadway where the cicadas chirped in the sunshine. The end of a summer holiday was the situation evoked. On 11 June, in Durban harbour, we went aboard a nasty, rusty, quite small craft, said to have been condemned before the war, called the *Manela*. With the fraternal instinct seemingly possessed by all of his race, Willie found on the forecastle a fellow Scot, crew member, a fat cook, cleaning baking tins he said had been unused for fifteen years. I wonder whether at the time one saw in this encounter (rather more in the coming Ealing style than that of the war documentary) any connection with the submarine assault and consequent chronic Allied shipping shortage. Willie's business experience enabled him to ask a pertinent question apropos *Manela*: "Is she a guid sailing ship?" "Anything but thaat," said the cook. "It's a wonder she's no moving the noo." We were, of course, still at the quayside.

Our mess deck, a forward hold, was not too horrible, given the *Manela's* outward aspect. What might be deemed a reasonable number was aboard to use the long tables and benches. Theoretical negative features were being on the waterline, and my assigned ammick hooks on the wrong side of the vessel's permanent list. In the corner was a rat-trap: *per contra*, a blanket had been laid on the deck for a fine cat with two charming kittens. We sailed the following day for Mombasa, alone, unescorted. Lieutenant Bailey, the officer in charge of the RN draft, said he would not know our next port of call until we had left Mombasa to go to it, but he thought it would not be in Ceylon. To this touch of Sutton Vane's *Outward Bound* was added a tincture of Conrad. Rolling like Mae West, the *Manela* hugged the coast, mostly high ivory dunes topped with silver-green vegetation, broken occasionally by a flattish piece like a golf-course; of human habitations not a sign. On the after well-deck were a few mangy hens. The crew looked surly and villainous, was said to suffer desertions at every port, and therefore paid well in arrear. There must have been a library of a kind on board, for the journal reports me reading *Henry Esmond* and other works I would never have bought. Thackeray was just the sort of author thrifty patriots took from their shelves to give to the fighting services and merchant navy: I recall elsewhere trying to read *Pendennis*. Print-starved though I was, Thackeray proved a tough nut, has always remained so: a pity I did not come to him through his early works.

Lieutenant Bailey was regular Navy, admirable example of pre-war selection and training: smart, forthcoming, concerned to secure the greatest benefit possible for the ratings in his charge. Would I have put this view in such terms at the time? I had sympathy for non-commissioned regulars, but class prejudice may have made me grudging about others. Also, it must not be forgotten there was a category of officers known as "Naval pigs". After just over a week's voyaging, the *Manela* docked at Mombasa – low green coast, white, red-roofed villas, a concealed harbour containing (*inter alia*) *Indomitable* and *Royal Sovereign*. With commendable speed Lieutenant Bailey announced that, however improbable it seemed for naval personnel, we were bound for Nairobi, where a naval air station was being created. All were greatly chuffed at the prospect of this cushy number, except a dozen or so of sterner stuff – perhaps regulars, like the efficient Bailey – who volunteered for carriers.

The next afternoon, a Sunday, we had shore leave after divisions in whites. If blue fore-and-aft rig made one resemble a taxi-driver (of those days), white fore-and-aft transformed one into a steward or barman, though once ashore one could illegally unhook the jacket's high collar and so make a pretence of more becoming reveres. Walking along a tarmac road from the oil dock where we were berthed to the town, the ambience changed from Conrad to Graham Greene. About that first afternoon in East Africa I made what for me was a quite long journal entry. I am surprised by the prescience that led me to end by noting the "*hopeless* air" hanging over everything: "what one thinks is let's get out and leave the mess for the natives to clear up as best they can." I never lost this puzzlement about British East Africa (as I think it was still commonly called). Surely the white landowners could never be persuaded to give up power in Kenya: indeed, they were demanding more. It seemed inevitable that the astute Asians throughout the territory would continue as an entrepreneurial class at all levels, and that educating, financing and energizing the black to enable him to compete with the other races was certainly very long-term, if not utopian. All seen in Mombasa led to this view.

At first, the local colour seemed merely daubed on something not far from a basic English suburbanization of the inter-war period: concrete, corrugated iron, petrol filling stations. But despite the newness and the colour (red fez, rich vegetation, bright saris) squalor was pervasive. As we had addressed the bum-boat navigators on the other side of the continent, so the Asian owners of the open-fronted wooden shops impudently hailed us as "Charlie". Everything seemed dear, even the carved wooden tourist objects displayed by blacks on the pavements. At the "East" end of the main street was an incredibly decrepit house labelled "Jaurina Hotel", outside which a few patriarchs sipped tea from saucers, an intimation I fear I did not fully exploit when I came to invent the "Hotel Splendide" for my boys' adventure novel, *Savage Gold*. On a few walls were tattered little posters: BE INOCULATED AGAINST YELLOW FEVER – but who could read or act on them, who knows?

Even in the brief time available there were the usual service scares that some were not to go to the sanctuary of the Kenya highlands. What amazing luck it seemed, therefore, when I found myself on the Monday following the Saturday announcement one of the "advance party" of ten detailed to go to the Nairobi Civil Aerodrome. It was said the Fleet Air Arm had taken over the aerodrome as Middle and Far East maintenance depot; scarcely credible panic station following the Japanese bombardment of Trinco – a sort of last-stand eyrie, so it seems now, such as the Nazis planned to make Berchtesgaden. Seats on the ordinary train leaving Mombasa at 4.30 p.m. had been booked for the advance party, its own differences of rank extinguished by the local compulsion for all whites to travel similarly. One played a strange brief charade of pre-call-up life as red-fez'd, white-gowned, bare-footed stewards served dinner in the dining car, thereafter put up couchettes with snowy linen in the compartment. Before the early equatorial night fell the long train could be seen chugging upwards through dramatic forest land; by morning the compartment window framed grassy highland plains with their herds of game and immense skies, soon to become utterly familiar.

The aerodrome seemed merely some tin and wooden huts along a tarmac road leading nowhere. A few hangars subsequently disclosed themselves. The airfield consisted simply of a portion of the Athi Plains, I think already a game reserve. I do not recall a perimeter fence: in any case, such as ostrich and gazelle were quite close at hand. The DF (Direction Finding) and some other fitters were assigned to the "Special W/T Section", cognomen masking, as at Lee, the secrecy of radar. The locale consisted of a hangar, with store, small test-shop and office. The work was not simply repairing aircraft radar sets but also effecting the necessary airframe modifications to enable aircraft actually to be fitted with radar. Such was the novelty of the device in the FAA in June 1942.

Though my journal was soon to peter out, I have a page or

two about the situation and leading personalities in the Special W/T Section.

The following is the record – amazingly feebly written, no wonder the entries soon lapse:

Thursday 24 June. We are sent to the DF place . . . We had not been there a couple of hours before there was a ROW. The place is run by a Lieutenant (apparently a nonentity), a Sergeant, a PO, and two leading hands – one in the hangar, one in the test-shop. The hangar one the type I hate, blond, tiptilted nose, big nostrils, had already made himself fairly objectionable by giving us directions ("two of you will work in the hangar, two in the shop") which he had no authority to give and which proved to be (as I anticipated) all nonsense. Coming back from stand-easy I wandered into the shop and turned-up nose told me to take a ladder back to the hangar. I stared at him. "Why don't you take it back yourself?" He said, "I'm telling you to take it back." I said, "Who are you? A PO?" I had on me my reckless bad-tempered mood – rare but satisfying – my shyness and so on swamped by anger. We had a little argument. "I'm a leading hand – the same as you." "Yes, but when were you rated?" "That has nothing to do with it." At last I wandered off, feignedly intent on some errand. I heard and ignored his voice calling after me. Then the PO, red and wrathful, took a hand. I said, "If you say so that's another matter." I moved the ladder with Barry. A little later we all fell in in the hangar and had a little pep talk by the PO who offensively told us who was who and what was what. He said, "DF ratings are not *proper* leading hands – they are only rated to make their pay up." This was a mistake because when he'd finished I challenged him and asked him what he meant by "not proper leading hands." A long argument and he climbed down. Afterwards in private he was as nice as pie . . .

Wednesday 8th July. Big nostrils is really the best of the hangar's ruling clique and we are now polite and amiable to each other. The PO (tall, insolent, vulnerable) is still offensive. The blond, anaemic workshop killick wears brass buttons and calls himself, entirely without justification, a PO. He is aped by another blond, a cheerful vain extrovert who tries to borrow money. In charge of the whole thing is a Wavy Navy Lieutenant, weak I imagine, white teeth and a minor public school voice – also blond. I think for my truculence I am being *victimized* e.g. a half-day stopped, told off for a job ten minutes before secure. This worries me not at all – lends some interest in fact to the long days with practically f. all to do. But not much interest. I have made myself an elegant paperknife out of aeroplane wire and so has everyone else . . . V. important in midst of real or imaginary "persecution" and clique rivalries to preserve one's normal and proper character. This I find less difficult than I would a few years ago. I have a "character" it seems, even though it consists mainly of intellectual snobbery. No, kindness stiffened by that.

More than thirty years after the persecutory events in the "Special W/T" section, my path through life once more crossed that of the Lieutenant. By that time I had been Oxford's Professor of Poetry, much publicity attending the notorious election, and was currently a Governor of the BBC. I had retired from being the Woolwich Equitable Building Society's solicitor, but was on its Board. One of the Society's Regional Managers told me that at a public dinner in a provincial city he had sat next to a local business tycoon who claimed to know me, had in fact had me under his command in the Navy. The name supplied by the Regional Manager rang no bells. In the light of what happened, it is not easy to recover the dubiety I had initially about the identity of this individual, though suspecting him to be the former supremo of the Special W/T Section. "Is he blond?" I asked the Regional Manager. The answer was equivocal: the hair was sparse and greying.

At the public dinner an open invitation to the Regional Manager to bring me to lunch had been issued by the Lieutenant (if indeed it were he), which I said I would take up if I found myself in the provincial city in question, as might well happen on BBC or building society affairs. Some date thus conveniently occurring had to be cancelled by the Lieutenant, and eventually I made a special journey, less to satisfy curiosity than to oblige the Regional Manager, who hoped for some business to accrue from the Lieutenant's organization.

We were received in a manner befitting the guests of tycoonery, and given lunch in the former Lieutenant's office, buttled by an attractive secretary – though only one pre-lunch drink was achieved, and no more than one bottle of Moselle uncorked. Afterwards, I said to the Regional Manager that this was typical of the Lieutenant (the identity was settled on sight), but it must be conceded that in Nairobi I never tested his hospitality. Our previous relations were only briefly discussed. The Lieutenant said he remembered me sitting on a coil of rope, writing a poem; the locale being a troopship bound for India. I said, as was the case, that I had never been to India. This did not seem to daunt him: in any case he was more interested in establishing the extent of his tycoonery than gassing about the remote past. I see now it is quite interesting that a normal character like the Lieutenant should also have an unreliable memory.

His fallacious recollection brought back to mind that the clique was dispersed, later in that summer of 1942, by being largely drafted to the sub-continent, though its power had earlier been broken by the arrival of a new draft of personnel for the Special W/T Section, headed by two officers. The effect on my own life of this influx I will later relate.

3 *IFF*

Before leaving England I had handed to John Lehmann, in his capacity as a director of the Hogarth Press, the typescript of a collection of poems called *The Middle of a War*. I expect there were sufficient hazards to keep me on tenterhooks until the thing actually came off, but after the poems produced at Lee-on-the-Solent and Seafield Park John was firm in his wish to publish a book. As often happens with collections of verse, *The Middle of a War* struck a new note, such as it was, by containing no pre-war poems, those passing muster having been included in my first book, the 1939 Fortune Press *Poems*. Not to be recaptured now, though the sense must have been acute, is the anticipation of the improvement in status following graduation from a "Fortune Poet" to a "Hogarth Poet".

On delivering the typescript I recall informing John where each poem had previously appeared and his noting the name of the periodical at the foot of the page. This exercise was for the benefit of Leonard Woolf, always cagey about books of verse, I expect particularly so in the case of a virtually unknown poet. Much later, John told me he had had to go through the typescript page by page with Leonard, the fact and status of periodical publication proving a greater allaying of Leonard's suspicions than any merit in the poems. It was agreed I should send John such candidates for the book as might be written after I set out for Ceylon, which I did. They probably only amounted to the last three in the book, one being "The Dream", which John re-christened "On the High Seas", a touching attempt to make me an "active service" poet, in the manner rather of the Lieutenant at a later date. It was also John's idea to divide the book, exiguous enough, into two parts – pre-service poems and service poems. This, however, may have been my compromise with his (or Leonard Woolf's) desire for the service poems to come first, as putting the more saleable goods at the front of the shelf, an arrangement I would have been much against – if nothing else, for offending chronology, one quality at least of any poet's output.

The book, its slenderness accentuated by the scruffy paper of wartime, must have been published in October 1942. The sequence of receiving a copy and seeing the reviews has gone from me, but I do particularly remember Desmond MacCarthy's "World of Books" article in the *Sunday Times* of 24 January 1943. MacCarthy was one of the elderly pundits still dominating the book pages of the heavy Sundays (they were succeeded after the war by a race of young pundits, not such an improvement as might have been anticipated). Most of his article was devoted to *The Middle of a War* in terms essentially friendly, even if very much from the cautious standpoint of a consciously older and wiser generation. The cutting or copy, sent by Kate, came with other mail to the little hut where I was then working. It so excited me I had to go out and walk up and down for a spell. It must be remembered I had just turned thirty-one and that MacCarthy's was virtually my first public recognition in the "world of letters" – a world in which I had been absorbed and tried to compete since boyhood. I should add that Stephen Spender's notice in the *Observer* was equally friendly.

Subsequently, Kate reported a letter she had had from my brother saying how pleased he was I was getting some of the attention I deserved. Of course, my brother knew something of my long strivings and his touching remark struck me as the expression of a tenable view. But I did not quite see the business thus, though discrimination may be difficult to convey in the tricky area of self-evaluation. I desired my verse to be strictly judged, and still not to be found essentially wanting, though all too aware of its deficiencies myself. Such desire has persisted, fulfilled by a mere handful of critics, the bulk merely attacking irrelevancies or following changing fashion. No doubt most indifferently successful artists feel similarly. Even the great are not immune: reading Michael Millgate's excellent biography of Hardy, I was struck once again how many critics in his lifetime pointed out, and objected to, Hardy's "pessimism", though his poetry is full of enjoyment of the world; this business riling Hardy to the end.

MacCarthy's and other notices sent the book into a second impression, but the shortage of reading matter, if not so acute as on the *Manela*, gave every English wartime book a good chance of success. Practically all the "service" poems had been written under training, yet many reviewers commended the book for its novelty in giving a picture of service life – an indication of the pretty wholesale avoidance of the call-up by the better-known Thirties poets. Needless to say, I claim no personal virtue through the working on my particular destiny of the due and common processes of the epoch. They had a generally good effect on my verse; and I suppose on my status with reviewers. I have noted the ire of old Herbert Palmer when reviewing my first book: it would be churlish not to record that he made handsome amends in his notice of *The Middle of a War* in *John o'London's Weekly*. What a pity I never wrote to thank him for a generosity all the more selfless in face of my rudery, in the previous decade, about a book by him.

The hut to which some kind visitant to the Mailing Office had brought the letter with the startling MacCarthy review was a little apart from the hangar housing the Special W/T Section. It may have been specially built for its function, which was the servicing of the IFF (Identification Friend or Foe) radar apparatus housed in naval aircraft. That apparatus was essentially a box of tricks that magnified and returned an incoming radar signal. It was triggered into action by the ASV apparatus also housed on naval aircraft (the ocean "search" radar already referred to), so that friendly aircraft showed up unmistakably on the ASV screen.

With another leading air fitter, Bob Park, I moved into the IFF business in the middle of August. The move coincided with the arrival of the new Special W/T draft, so presumably the former was a consequence of the latter. Bob was a stocky, agreeable, strong-minded but good-humoured Scot, known already, of course, but with whom I became close friends during our IFF days. He was of the breed of Scot that makes a fearless and tenacious wing half-back, to use a now obsolete term. The "iffy hut", as we came to call it, was nearly as incommodious as the class-leaders' cubbyhole at HMS *Ganges*, but in similar manner acting as a refuge. Having the key, Bob and I sometimes used it out of working hours, I for my part writing a few lines of verse as well as letters.

Previous to the IFF move I had scarcely been employed, least of all on the work for which I had been so long and expensively trained. I and my trade were not alone in this. Like the hero of *The Perfect Fool* I had occasionally helped with the ASV mods, crawling into parts of aircraft (mainly Swordfish, with a sprinkling of Albacore and Walrus) difficult of access, for the devisers of the mods had had to use often maniacal ingenuity to accommodate the various bits and pieces. Strange sensation when I first drilled a hole in the fuselage of a Walrus to take a bolt to hold a rack on which to fix an ASV unit. Since the Walrus was amphibian, one almost envisaged it sinking as a result of one's amateur labours. At another juncture some of us had been loaned to the Ordinary W/T Section, not to work on W/T sets (of which in any case we were ignorant) but to provide unskilled labour for the erection of an aerial mast and construction of an aerial frame. And the journal records that at least one day was spent chipping paint off an old car being renovated for the clique to use on shooting trips, work for which I was better fitted through experience at Chatham Dockyard and Seafield Park, as readers of *Vamp* may recall. The idleness among dockyard mateys that had shocked me at Chatham was reproduced among the ratings in Nairobi.

What a relief from the stupifying boredom to get to the iffy hut! Bob and I knew nothing about the IFF equipment, for the Lee radar course had never touched on it, but an IFF test set, perhaps two, had suddenly become available, from which the

IFF circuit diagram could be seen and test procedures gleaned. Perhaps there was even a service manual. With the test set or sets came a good lot of unserviceable IFF equipment, for no one seemed ever to have opened up the latter, either in Nairobi or the entire Eastern theatre. When the apparatus failed, it was simply replaced. We quickly became familiar with the range of common faults and carried out appropriate repairs, the saving in money and *matériel* most agreeable to my thrifty nature.

With the hut came a handcart to convey equipment to and from the aircraft dispersed on the Athi Plains. Pulling this vehicle made Bob and me even more like the working proprietors of some minuscule business, perhaps in the scrap line. However, we were saved from menial duties vis-à-vis the hut by the arrival every morning of an *askari*, probably a mere auxiliary, to sweep it out. He was quite elderly, sang a little melody to the rhythm of his broom. In a lull I whistled it myself, with an effect on him akin to Willie's conjuring, ignorant of my childhood experience of picking up tunes in Blackpool's "Happy Valley". After the momentary surprise he was greatly amused. Though he had no English and I only a few words of Swahili, it was plain that part of the joke was the ruling class adopting a bit of the culture of the oppressed. In Africa I found a good indigenous response to jokes, only a touch of mime or slight facial change being necessary to convey the jesting aspect of any matter in hand.

When we first arrived in Nairobi it was possible to share the services of a native who would launder one's gear, clean shoes, and suchlike, at a price within the means even of leading hands. Willie and I had a stake in a young man called Edward. He spoke, or at any rate understood, some English, and wore a long-sleeved pullover and wristwatch – too sophisticated for Willie to conjure for, though an agreeable relation was established in other ways. It was a disappointment when such servants were outlawed from the air station, probably not long after it was formally taken over by the Navy in the July of 1942. The duties of the *askaris* of the King's African Rifles were confined to official chores. One might be next to such a putteed but bare-footed figure pushing a Walrus out of the hangar, conscious of his faint acrid smell, not disagreeable, far different from the sewer-like aroma emanating from whites with inadequate bathing facilities. Another phenomenon, early noted, was the sun reflected in scores of tiny points of light from the black (or, more properly, brown) skin of an arm, apt matching of climate and species.

It is not to excuse the inadequacy of my response to East Africa that I emphasize now the conviction I had that, despite the activity in Nairobi, any prolonged stay was out of the question. No doubt, as the months crept by, the feeling grew that to be moved from a cushy, if boring, billet would be grossly unfair, but one was always conscious that the war was ludicrously far from the Kenya Highlands. After a time I did buy a booklet of kitchen Swahili but did not work at it, a complete duffer at languages anyway. When I had discovered and joined the public library in Nairobi I read quite a few books on East Africa which had their due effect on my verse and, later, on *Savage Gold*. I realized there must exist a fringe of educated blacks, probably connected with the university, but I never came across it or enquired about it.

Needless to say, I was intensely sympathetic to the blacks, exploited, as seemed obvious, by both whites and Asians. The colour bar was not so blatant as in South Africa but only because the class of urban blacks, potentially pushy, was comparatively small and feeble. Sometimes I used the Nairobi buses; never took advantage of the rear seats being reserved for "Europeans". Such behaviour, not uncommon among servicemen, would be deplored by the white settlers; perhaps did implant in blacks, like the sight of servicemen doing manual jobs, some notion of a more equal order. The big serviceman's canteen in Nairobi, cheap and excellent, was run by Lady Delamere: when three black American GIs entered, she bustled up and told them in Swahili they couldn't be served. "Excuse me, ma'am," said one, "I talk no other language but English." The American presence was fleeting and minute, and caused no other problems that I heard about. Rather odd that one of my first memorable experiences was seeing the all-black band of the KAR playing in the open space in front of the canteen, a selection from Gilbert and Sullivan the first item heard. They were extremely well turned-out, but behind the discipline of their playing could surely be detected some strangeness, as though they might suddenly shift into music with a rhapsodic melody and less metronomic beat, a big-band sound of exciting potential.

Lady Delamere had been the second wife of Lord Delamere, thorn in the flesh of the Colonial Office, able and energetic fighter for the asserted rights of Kenya's white settlers. The tergiversations of East African history, remarkably compressed, will be scarcely known to the ordinary reader of these words, but I have no intention of trying to enlighten, nor am I qualified so to do. White settlement in the Kenya Highlands, a country equatorial but so elevated the climate was non-tropical, had started in the early part of the century, accelerated by restless and jobless officers after the First War. In the Twenties, the place had been a sort of public-school version of the American West, with Asians as the saloon keepers, undertakers, and other small-part players; blacks as extras; whites as heroes with an admitted sprinkling of villains. The salubrious climate, fertile soil and recent colonization marked it off from British possessions run by the Colonial Service for the benefit, with no serious opposition, of the indigenous population. The whites wanted political power commensurate with the work they were doing and the wealth they were creating.

It was not until 1981 that I read *East African Journey* by Margery Perham, seeing it by chance in the local public library, and thinking it might help with this book, then contemplated. The layers of time involved are, in their nature, fictional; I hope worth separating. Dame Margery's book, though first published in 1976, consists of a journal she kept as an Oxford research fellow in 1923–30, journeying in Kenya and Tanganyika. As I read it, in an epoch when the black republics of Kenya and Tanzania had quite long been established, I was amazedly struck that the scene, the life, she depicted I had arrived at myself a mere dozen years after – that all my memories of Kenya, Uganda and Tanganyika were closer by far to her account of things than to contemporary reality. It would be otiose to provide example of the time shifts and parallels that forcefully arose as I read, but one of them has particular point. In Nairobi, the youthful Margery Perham of 1929–30 went on advice

> . . . to the New Stanley Hotel. It was dirty and inefficient and full of white tykes . . . Rowdy groups were always drinking and hanging about the entrance hall . . . As far as I could see Nairobi was largely peopled with young men wearing corduroy plus-fours or shorts, lurid green, orange, blue and purple shirts, and Stetson hats. Some had revolvers in their belts . . . Nairobi . . . is one of the shabbiest and

shoddiest towns I have seen in my travels, which is saying a great deal.

By 1942 the New Stanley had been cleaned up and refurbished, perhaps rebuilt, though a few "white tykes" were still to be seen. Its lounge, convenient of access from the street, was commodious, "modern" of décor, mirrored walls a feature. Attentive black waiters padded over the parquet floor clad in long white gowns and red fez. I was once reprovingly told by not quite a white tyke but certainly an old boy wearing a green shirt and khaki shorts, a tea planter from up-country, apropos of tipping, that copper was "their" currency. But I could never, as did he, bring myself to pass over a single "Kingi Georgi" for services rendered.

I used the New Stanley quite a lot in the early evening, writing a fair number of lines at one of the many small tables. My usually being alone arose naturally rather than deliberately, though I came to welcome it as the afflatus descended. On the air station we worked tropical routine, starting very early, knocking off at 1 p.m. After lunch everyone "crashed his swede". I can scarcely recall being able to sleep at that hour, though not through lack of trying. Constitutional insomnia had already asserted itself, augmented by dyspepsia. Looking back, I see I almost certainly suffered on and off from the peptic ulcers diagnosed some time after the war. Had I reported my symptoms to the MO I might in the end have been discharged with a pension – outcome, strange to say, wholly foreign to my character. For though I have often posed as a hypochondriac (once more, the urge to amuse), privately I never regarded myself a weakling. As I often say in my seventies, if it weren't for my ailments I should be extremely well. Even at that age I sometimes consider my physique (still identifiable with the athleticism of my schooldays) capable of resuscitation – a rejuvenatory process perhaps reminiscent of the delusions of the heroine of Thomas Mann's *The Black Swan*.

Leaving my colleagues slumbering in the mess hut, I would wander a while through the bleached grass of the Athi Plain, hoping to see game at close quarters, then catch the first "shore-leave" lorry into Nairobi. Sometimes, eager for the urban life I was used to and loved, I set out for town before that, hoping to bum a lift on the way. The sensations of those walks on the plains comes back: the wakeful yet stupefied post-lunch condition only slowly wearing off; the grass, tough yet brittle, impeding the shoes; the palms of the hands somehow stiff – rather a zombie-like progress. One never got far enough into the wild: apt symbolism. Under a sun almost too bright and hot for comfort, the blue hills, backed by rotund white clouds, stayed in the far distance; less far, but seemingly not getting much nearer, were a few brown *rondevaals*, each with its small green *shamba*, and mysterious life unexplored. By a still-moist watercourse a secretary bird might be gravely stalking; once I came on a still-recognizable dead hyena.

In Nairobi I would shop, shop-window gaze, visit the library, until it was a respectable time for the lounge of the New Stanley. Sometimes I wrote my daily letter to Kate beforehand, in the reading room of the *Christian-Science Monitor*: good refuge, but lacking the New Stanley's stimulants. Occasionally, of course, I had to have my hair cut, topic dealt with at overgenerous length in the original edition of *Vamp*. I never discovered a satisfactory barber in East Africa, that land of exploration. In the end I patronized an Indian in one of the quieter streets, who was less brutal with scissors and clippers than other Nairobi tonsorial artists, capable of being persuaded to eschew the latter entirely. Notices pertaining to unfamiliar sects, and advertising odd secular events, were exhibited round the mirror, and there must have been additional evidence of a serio-comic life style we would now dub Naipauline, after that novelist's early fiction about Trinidad. When the hair had been cut one's head was subjected to a brief but tremendously vigorous massage, on the first occasion positively alarming, as though one were being scalped. The memory of this also brings Naipaul to mind; namely, his novel *The Mystic Masseur*.

I drank bottled beer in the New Stanley, rather good, brewed by the East African Brewery Company, but digestively ruinous. Why did I not realize this?. Perhaps I did, refused to admit weakness, considered myself still near enough the fit, tough serviceman HMS *Ganges* had made me. But even as an articled clerk I had come to the conclusion beer did not "suit" me, chose another tipple when I could. After a few beers and rhymes I might well dine alone, usually favouring a tiny restaurant, quite chic for Nairobi but at that still early part of the evening almost deserted.

After dinner, on to perhaps one of the two or three cinemas, Indian-owned but usually showing western films, attracting queues and possessing bars, to which many adjourned at the interval, remaining there if the cinematic entertainment was poor, though I was myself prepared to put up with much that was mediocre. By that time I had probably met Bob or Willie by pre-arrangement, more often the former. Asked by the magazine *Poetry* (Chicago) for particulars of my service life for their notes on contributors, I gave some account of these matters, on which they commented that I made darkest Africa sound like Evanston, Illinois.

Presumably a further proximation to provincial America would have been provided had I dilated on the Nairobi society I came to know through Bob, Willie and another classmate in Aberdeen (indeed, in *Ganges*), Tom Duncan, a tall, dark Chartered Accountant, with somewhat of the air of a *boulevardier*, even in the taxi-driver's garb imposed when we were re-rated. These Scots soon established relations with the fellow-countrymen who had preceded them, as civilians, to the colony, mainly through the Presbyterian Church – though Tom Duncan's knowing the manager of the East African Breweries may have been extra-ecclesiastical. That friendship led to the four of us spending a weekend at the brewery, dream of every naval rating. Fatal digestive occasion it must have been. The resultant tennis four (I did not play, had scarcely ever played) was surprisingly skilled, Willie's style tinctured by the sleight of hand previously referred to. Willie was also good at badminton, played at the Presbyterian church hall, where I learnt the game, even improved at it. At the church hall I met the Martins, first visiting their house with other servicemen, then quite often going alone.

Stan Martin was manager, perhaps technically works manager, of the flour mill: smallish, slim, gentle; so far as could be seen, of almost saintly character. He, too, suffered from peptic ulcers, farther advanced down that pitted road. He had literary leanings, wrote a one-act comedy-drama, set in a courtroom and played for some charitable purpose in the church hall. The cast included servicemen, among them me, taking me back to schooldays, when I always figured in the school plays, though lacking my brother's flair, revealed by his senile Apothecary. I foolishly played Phoebe, the maid at Dotheboys Hall, "straight" (in a dramatization from *Nicholas Nickleby*), and I believe as an actor I never properly "let myself go", unless to a degree as Flute in the Boarders' Concert production of the last act of the *Dream*, more notable for Gorill's Hypolita, however.

The single performance of Stan Martin's play may have been the origin of a nightmarish dream, still recurring: I am about to step on the boards and I do not know my lines. In the actuality I had the script out of sight below the top of the jury box and with judicious squinting and some ad-libbing got through the ordeal pretty well. Why did I not learn my part? Fundamental haziness of memory was partly to blame, but I expect I subconsciously thought the whole enterprise *infra dig*. Some deeper significance may inhere. I played the part, a juror putting in his oar more than somewhat, as an elderly blimpish ex-military man, escaping from the restrained Phoebe tradition by a spell beforehand in the New Stanley. Little did I reck that forty years on I should be accused of putting over this character in real life.

In my collection of poems, mainly about Africa, *A Lost Season*, some of the strongest feeling is reserved for mere news about the war, in a piece called "October 1942". When I came to revise it for the *Collected Poems* of 1962 I was going to retitle it "The Defence of Stalingrad", then thought that too pretentious, and simply generalized it a little as "Autumn 1942". Surely the events of the Stalingrad battle, and the subsequent reading of Alexander Werth's remarkable book *The Year of Stalingrad* (1946), prolonged my sympathy for the Soviet Union during the early post-war years.

Stan must have been in his mid-forties, his wife Hilda a few years younger. As I write this she is still alive, still in Kenya, where she stuck it out through all that followed after the war, gaining an MBE for her work in Government service. At the time I speak of, however, she was secretary to the editor of the *East African Standard*: typical of her vigour and enterprise that she arranged for the paper to report my presence in the colony and print in two issues, in well-displayed boxes, poems from *The Middle of a War*. The couple had only one child, a daughter of eighteen, who had inherited her father's character. Strange for a complete outsider temporarily to step into the lives of others and observe the state of play without himself quite becoming involved – a feature of existence that fiction often ignores or exaggerates.

The Martins' hospitality extended to a good many servicemen, but I believe I was specially privileged in their friendship. The ambience offered was similar to that I had been brought up in – utterly unstrained, modest, and informal comfort. It is a mark of the ease of our relations that agreeable trivialities now come to mind – Hilda putting it on the menu when I casually said I liked cold rice pudding; Hazel running me in their car to the lower camp entrance late at night; messing about with a longish poem called "Teba" in their sitting room, alone in the house save for the "houseboy", for an hour or so part of ordinary life once more.

If by some stretch of imagination there could be said to be a white proletariat in Nairobi, it consisted of employees of the railway, I think a quite numerous class, who had their own club. It seems unlikely that honorary membership of the club had been conferred on all servicemen stationed in Nairobi, but that was the status enjoyed by Willie, Bob, Tom and myself. Some Scottish wangling must have been involved, myself a Sassenach beneficiary. I do not recall much social intercourse on my part with the club members, only playing snooker there late in the evenings, a black steward available to bring beer and perform other chores, the members boozing distantly in the bars. A working-man's club with large knobs on may be envisaged.

4 *Green, Black, Brown*

Whether, before the new draft arrived and assumed virtual power in the "Special W/T Section", the clique ever went hunting in the car previously mentioned is lost to history. If the vehicle were not successfully rehabilitated I do not know why they did not use the section's van, for a strict regard for legality in that area seems unlikely. The van was often officially and unofficially driven by a Leading Air Fitter in the electrical branch, yet another Scot, rather good-looking, a genuine tradesman who had worked for British Thompson Houston. I had from Blair a couple of extra-curricular driving lessons, for though my mother owned a car in my latter days at home I never drove it, perhaps still suffused with a D. H. Lawrentian sense of the motor car being impossibly bourgeois and anti-life. I have a clear mental picture of steerng the van along the road from the camp across the plain, and seeing, with increasing anxiety, against the background of the Ngong Hills, another vehicle approaching. Would I miss it? The road was strait.

Blair one afternoon took me and a few others for a spin a little way into those hills. It was really my first venture away from what might be called Africa's beaten tracks. I had written a couple of rather formal poems with Africa as background ("Parabolas of grief, the hills" sort of affair) but suddenly, returning from the Ngong outing, a way to fulfil the wish to write about the country was revealed. It was the business over again of finding myself able to write about service life.

> Can you be much surprised at what the hills
> Contain? The girls run up the slope,
> Their oiled and shaven heads like caramels.
> Behind them is the village, its corrugated
> Iron and, like a wicked habit, the store.
> The villagers cough, the sacking blows from the naked
> Skin of a child, a white scum on his lips.
> The youths come down in feathers from the summit.
> And over them all a gigantic frescoed sky.
>
> (from "The Green Hills of Africa", original version)

This is what was seen on the brief van trip. It may be thought to be laying it on a bit to imply that such simple and direct verse needed some sort of prior revelation. Moreover, the actual poetic achievement probably seems slight today. But however modest the shift in these matters, some not easily achieved, often unwilled augmentation of power must usually be found by the poet. I wrote a few descriptive pieces of "The Green Hills of Africa" kind, comparatively unclogged by the lingering ideology of the Thirties (though as can be seen from line five of the foregoing extract, there was still a touch of what we thought of then as "later" Auden). The landscape of East Africa, let alone its people and fauna, makes a deep impression on travellers.

My reading in East African history and anthropology gave some subsequent poems an extra dimension. Bringing in the war and the question of profound social change was perhaps less successful, though to a few such pieces some contemporary readers responded with sympathy.

> . . . some great faculty
> Like hands, has been eternally lost and all

Our virtues now are the high and horrible
Ones of a streaming wound which heals in evil.

I quote from the Stalingrad poem, mentioned already. Though the outcome of the battle, great hinge of the war, was a sensational German downfall, the news of it, of the sufferings of its participants, came in agonizing instalments, and the poem's last two stanzas do, I see now, to some degree embody a pessimistic yearning about humanity which was renewed and intensified – and persisted – after the atom bombs had been dropped on Japan. I might add, bathetically, that for the 1962 *Collected Poems* I did not alter the end of the poem at all; sensible decision. In general, the revisions I made to *A Lost Season* removed some slapdashery but whether I effected many real improvements I would now think doubtful. What the poems needed was more work on them in the New Stanley lounge and other haunts of the Muse.

Most of the African poems appeared in John Lehmann's *New Writing*, in both its Penguin and hardback forms, Kate acting as typist and literary agent, for anthologies and other periodicals were also involved. The second impression of *The Middle of a War* and the phenomenal circulation of *Penguin New Writing* must have peaked such fame as I've enjoyed to a height not reached thereafter. This had no effect I can recall on my style and output. What did count was John Lehmann's critical support, the constant sense that the best of my work would find its way into print in an ambience of which I wholly approved. As already implied, John's deep desire was to find and encourage writing that would reflect the scale and intensity of the world conflict. Yet being a man of the Thirties he required such writing to be underpinned by observation, by fact. Mere rhetoric was unlikely to get past him. All that was very useful to me. I wonder what he would have said if I had anticipated a side of my verse that showed a few decades later, and dealt ironically with the trivialities of existence. Almost certainly shaking his head a little, he would have chosen the best of that, too, for his romantic nature was balanced by a love of Byron's comic poetry (and his father had, of course, been a notable writer of light verse).

I had rather thought that being a CW candidate at HMS *Ganges* had marked me for an eventual commission even though I had deviated from the executive branch into radar – acquisition of the status, like beatification, inevitably postponed by investigative bureaucracy; that process even more prolonged in such a new technical field. However, looking at the fragmentary journal, I see that in September 1942 I was called out of the iffy hut by one of the officers from the new draft and asked, as though introducing a fresh theme, if I had ever thought about a commission. The following month I was actually set a written test, disconcertingly on wireless telegraphy and general electrics, not thought of since that preliminary course in Aberdeen. It seems I did well; had then to give personal details for completion of the form necessary to activate once more the mysterious CW machinery. I say in the journal I only allowed the recommendation to go forward to gain the chance of returning prematurely to the UK, a statement I see no reason to doubt. Certainly the *animus revetendi* (as the phrase used to go, doing private international law in student days) was intense.

The officer responsible (or jointly so) for this touch on my destiny's tiller possessed the Wodehousian (or, more accurately, early Waughian) name of Peter Lavender, living up to it with somewhat of the voice and manner of a musical-comedy juvenile lead, more likely the second lead, being smallish and humorous rather than tallish and romantic. I expect some Admiralty Fleet Order or other *ukase* had laid on him the duty of sniffing out potential radar officers, but elements existed of a fellow feeling between us, restricted though our contacts were. The journal notes barely that my position in the section had subtly changed, that I was becoming "a sort of personage". Though the "Vamp Till Ready" syndrome was still largely operant, I was, after all, thirty years old and had been established in a quite decent civilian post. But how the "personage" propagated its qualities memory fails to recall (though no effort of will would be involved), except that towards the end of the year I was asked to help with the defence of a rating on some homosexual charge. Probably Peter Lavender's completion of the CW form had apprised him of my profession, and he had gossiped in the wardroom, as schoolmasters gossip in the common room about their pupils. I worked on the submission on behalf of the accused by his "next friend", and did some research in a manual of military law. I expect I missed the talents in this line of Richard Flower, though the result was as good as could be expected.

How incompletely one appreciated in youth – still does, to

some extent – one's effect on others! I remember – the thing out of mind for forty years – that setting out on foot for Nairobi I was once picked up by the station commander in a little open sports car. We chatted, perhaps touched on former days: may have been he who eventually brought the homosexual client. He was in natty khaki, probably off to his exalted version of a "baron". I sometimes saw him with self-evident big wigs in the best seats at the concerts and other entertainments in Nairobi's theatre. But the chic car and the petrol to run it were the most striking symbols of his status in the society among which, like me, he had so unexpectedly and fleetingly descended. To acquire them, how much string-pulling and throwing about of weight was required? Through diffidence, guilt, consideration for others, and a few other disabling traits, I never did enough of that sort of thing during my later career; only as a Governor of the BBC willy-nilly getting some tit bits put on my plate.

The concerts I remember were given by a fine fiddler and pianist, the latter none other than Ivor Keys, later Professor of Music at Birmingham University, whose excellent monograph on Brahms' chamber music happens to lie on one of my loudspeakers as I write. In 1942 he was in the Army, stationed in or near Nairobi, a slim, fair twenty-three-year-old. I used to speculate about the divinatory or driving powers of his parents, who anticipatorily had had him christened thus: indeed, wondering if the name might not be an apt pseudonym adopted for the "showbiz" side of his life, like the tall music-hall comedienne, a favourite of my mother's, Lily Long. However, this latter notion could scarcely be maintained, for no flicker of the least frivolity, in manner or repertoire, disturbed the recitals – which included the Brahms sonatas and much Beethoven (a performance of the latter's op. 96 in G remembered to this day). The duo, as had the Durban Symphony Orchestra, provided an amazing glimpse of the desired life of art which one might return to or, more accurately, come to embrace with more fervour and devotion than heretofore.

At the theatre the local amateur operatic society gave a performance of Gounod's *Faust*. I went with the Martins: whether I should have gone under my own steam is extremely doubtful, at that epoch scorning composers like Gounod (though I knew every note of the ballet music, relic of pier-end days). When the preliminaries (vamp till ready music of supreme effectiveness) to the bass aria "Veau d'or" started up I must have thought of Stanley Birch, one of the "two pianists" at school, for this was an example he educed of great melodies. I could have hummed the initial twiddly bits and launched into the piece itself, so thoroughly had Birch imprinted it on my adolescent memory. What is surprisingly open now is whether the opera was done in costume or as a concert version. Given the presumed scarcity of tights and cloaks and so forth in Central Africa in 1942, one inclines to the latter, in which case the memorable episode of the soprano's underwear may well have occurred during one of Gretchen's arias and not at a concert of individual items.

The singer concerned was a personable local young woman with a good voice. One immediately noticed her carelessness in entering with an inch of white slip showing below her green dress. As the song progressed the whiteness slowly came down, eventually revealing itself as the comparatively voluminous garment called French knickers. For me, hilarity was checked by embarrassment; would have been so even without the presence beside me of the Martin ladies. The soprano courageously continued, chance, or possibly muscular control, bringing the final descent to her feet only at the end of the song, when she stepped out of the crumpled knickers, picked them up, and walked off the stage to applause quite sensational in its warmth. One could not help speculating, when she returned, whether the garment had been restored, the question, if the occasion was indeed *Faust*, having rather more than mere prurient undertones.

In such ways the time wore on. To my surprise (the lenitive scarcely seeming part of service abroad) entitlement to leave arose. Whether a railway warrant came with the entitlement, so to speak, I do not know, but in any event Willie Robertson conceived a grandiose plan for the leave we agreed to take together. Perhaps through contacts at the Railway Club, he procured for us an interview with the Passenger Traffic Superintendent (or title to that effect) of the East African railway (a Scot, it need hardly be said), and put to him the proposition that we should have warrants to Kampala, Uganda, returning to Nairobi via Lake Victoria – the detour itself involving goodness knows how many hundred miles, and aboard a company steamer. Associating myself with this request seemed as outrageous as holding the hat while Gilbert Waller sang in the street, youthful episode familiar to readers of my earlier memoirs. But

Willie conducted the interview with his inimitable blend of the feelingly serious and the jocular, bringing in common Scottish memories, and drawing on the know-how acquired behind the public counter of the shipping line he had served in civvy street. The outcome was that the Superintendent agreed to honour the warrants, with the reasonable proviso that meals on the steamers were not included. He must surely have also provided some chit so as to ensure our warrants being filled in with the amazing route adumbrated – for I see now the responsible character in the RPO's office like one of the barrack stanchions in Alan Ross's poem of that title:

> their complexions, like rinds
> Of bacon, and on their fingers the ring
> Like a knuckleduster that chased the scrawl
> Of their antique penmanship . . .

So I set off on the most considerable unforced journey of my life; a journey I could only recapture, if then, by reading and trying to embroider the letters I wrote to Kate, which I do not intend to do. I know they would be too frail a foundation for anything other than the insubstantial. The makings of a chapter were there at the time, but apart from the letters, essentially perfunctory if sincere and nostalgic, I made no rcord. That deficiency seems the more venal because of my African reading, and the eagerness with which I looked out of the train for the potash lakes of the Kenya Highlands, for example, and the Nile pouring out of the lake's plug hole at Jinja. There were no poems, either, and the uneasy question arises for a writer how much experience loses if not assimilated in a literary way.

We had a night or two at Kampala before catching the lake steamer at Entebbe, Kampala's port, staying at the town's premier hotel, the Imperial, quite luxurious. Willie must have had some baronial introduction, for he took a photograph of me by a swimming pool (probably attached to a club) sitting next to a fellow resembling Alfred Hitchcock who has nevertheless fallen completely from memory. It may have been he who gave me a snapshot of the giant crocodile Lutembe emerging from lake reeds, for this was not taken by Willie: we were driven to the spot, called "Lutembe, Lutembe", as instructed, but the beast failed to respond (unlike Fafner on being similarly called in Act II of *Siegfried*), whether to our disappointment or relief, who knows? Though not extensive at that date, the shops and boulevards of Kampala were attractive to two townees; moreover, Ugandan society was immediately detectable as superior to Kenyan. Absent, the powerful, exploitive, but disgruntled class of white settlers, baronial in a Shakespearean sense: one felt the country was being run entirely for the benefit of the indigenous population – in Kampala, black, tall and stately, the women headgeared and swathed in bright cloth (carrying off even the banal designs of Lancashire mills), a dramatic change from the scurrying brown Kikuyu women of Nairobi and its environs, shaven heads often bent against a strap bearing some back-breaking load. How awful that, as I write, independent Uganda has lapsed into tribal anarchy and atrocities just as bad, one guesses, as before the British arrived. Who could have prognosticated that as the outcome of a further forty years of history?

The lake steamer may be envisaged as resembling the German gunboat more than Humphrey Bogart's *African Queen*, in the eponymous film. It was of substantial Scottish workmanship, greatly pleasing to Willie. The ship's officers were almost equally Scottish: Willie was soon on terms, discovering friends, ancestors and tram routes in common, in Glaswegian fashion. Stepping aboard in the early morning at steamy Entebbe, the quay piled with cargo, in bustling and tuneful process of being loaded by native labour, one suddenly felt part of a Conradian routine, commonplace but fated. Willie and I were carrying not kitbags but the green canvas suitcases available from pusser's stores. One says that, but the Nairobi store had been *non est* or at any rate ill-stocked until recent times, when queuing for its sudden bounties had not unpleasantly passed the best part of a morning. In my case, acquisition of a suitcase had accompanied that of a raincoat (the very raincoat subsequently transmogrified into an officer's garment.)

Wandering round Kampala had included the perennial search for reading matter. But what did I peruse during those hours on deck? Perhaps one day still, a book idly opened will bring back the steamer throbbing through the calm, sometimes out of sight of land in the amazing lake that could sink Wales. The motion made the equatorial sun deceptive. By the time we put in at Masaka, Willie's thighs, where his shorts had ridden up, had been painfully burned, his fair skin reddening, never bronzing.

We walked down the main, perhaps only, street, a small collection of godowns run by Asiatic shopkeepers, Willie in search of a sunburn remedy. A fair range of toilet articles was available – combs, scissors, brilliantine – even, it occurs to me, that hairdressing popular at my school, Anzora Viola, the name in the context taking on a colonial character, as of some former Spanish or Portuguese possession. Hanging cards of powders and phials indicated the pill-peddling assiduity of some African equivalent of Bobby (the manufacturing chemists' commercial traveller who had vainly loved me in my youth, and through whom, as *Souvenirs* tells, had indirectly come the revelation of the Auden school of poets). But since the clientèle in Masaka lacked pale complexions, a specific for Willie's discomfort was not to be found. His tall, raw-boned, sandyish wavy-haired presence, though not now bearded, was given a zombie touch by the white-rimmed sunglasses he often affected, and would not in any event have gone unnoticed: as it was, pretty general interest was roused in his problem, eventually attacked in characteristic Indian fashion by one of the shopkeepers. Unable to bear the absence of business or knowledge of therapy, he confidently recommended the application of *ghee*, the culinary clarified butter which in my experience has never seemed other than rancid, like the butter improbably devoured by the cat in T. S. Eliot's poem. So Willie was duly anointed, whether being sold a supply of *ghee* for future application I do not recollect. What does come back is that his thighs became a target for the numerous Masaka flies.

The food we had to pay for on board was completely unmemorable. The passengers ate in the stateroom with such officers as were off watch. The former were few in number, changing at every port; mostly, it seems to me now, missionaries. The most attractive place called at was Bukoba: a small bay of pale sand we strolled along, the steamer sending up smoke at the jetty at one end. There was time to bathe, which I did, forgetting until afterwards Lutembe's champing tribe. Late in the afternoon a white-habited monk arrived on a motorcycle and sidecar for supplies from the ship, a Greeneish touch to the Conradian picture. Musoma, in what was then Tanganyika, seemed the most African of the ports. In the market there, Willie with his box-Brownie snapped an attractive young girl, bare-breasted, holding a load on her neat head; and an old witch-woman with brass headgear and loaded with charms. Some slight coin passed from Willie on each of these occasions, to the astonishment of the girl, who had to be encouraged by the bystanders to accept it: the witch was blasé – indeed, conceivably got herself up specially for steamer-call days, and chasséd about a bit when the camera was pointed at her. For the literary parallel vis-à-vis the indigenous life, one would have had to go back to the Elizabethans.

We disembarked at Kisumu, back in Kenya, whence we were to return by train to Nairobi: Willie had an introduction to a couple there whose name and very physical presences escape me – unforgivably so, for I stayed with them when Willie went on to Nairobi without me, on some further baronial engagement. But perhaps the Kisumu barons were merely hotel keepers and I duly paid for my accommodation. One of only two surviving Kisumu memories tends to confirm this: seeing from an overlooking room a wild funeral procession along the main street. The other is of spending half a day with an elderly Kisumu solicitor, which included going with him when he appeared before the Registrar of the Court in chambers. I was astonished when fags were offered round by the solicitor and we all lit up before the application, or whatever it was, was made, and smoked through the proceedings. In the solicitor's office the managing clerk was a grave Parsee in frock coat and light trousers, seemingly the type of responsible subordinate I much relied on in the Woolwich Solicitor's Department. The solicitor, whom I took to, said he was in sore need of a younger partner: why didn't I get in touch with him when the war was over? He was quite serious, even mentioned some attractive share of the profits: prospects were good, the Asians were so litigious. Though I saw clearly that Kenya's racial problems were insoluble in any rational way, I gave the proposition fleeting consideration. What a queer turn to life it would have been, perhaps leading down some popular fictional road; Somerset Maugham Avenue, say.

Part of the deal offered by the Navy to those embarking on the career of radar mechanic was promotion to leading hand at the end of the course (so derided by the Petty Office of the clique), and then promotion to Petty Officer a year after that. Would the latter promise be fulfilled; the ponderous machine of the Andrew engage with its remote cogs in Nairobi? There was a good deal of anxiety among those sweating on the top line for this amelioration in pay and conditions, an attendant and almost comparable worry being the securing of the necessary physical indications of higher rank should the promotion come through. In the event, the necessary signal arrived on the dot – signals, rather; for promotion for Willie and me was a week after the others on account of our having had to re-sit the practical test at the end of the Lee-on-the-Solent course. What an emotional week it must have been for us seeing Tom Duncan *et al* ascend to a higher sphere! But all came right in the end. Moreover, Blair (who had been sweating on *his* promotion in the electrical branch), with a generosity that still staggers me, gave me a precious Petty Officer's cap badge, with gold wire, image of a girl's hair in an Elizabethan love poem, at that time unobtainable in pusser's stores. Thus was immediately satisfied the near-mystical need felt in the Services for appearance to correspond to status (and which later I was to observe at the Admiralty in the almost miraculously simultaneous-with-promotion transformation of three stripes to four, even two to two-and-a-half). As a matter of fact, since one had only acting rank until confirmation after a further year, one was strictly not entitled until then to wear a PO's cap badge, merely the crossed hooks on the sleeve.

A small subscription was paid for membership of the POs' mess but the comestible additions thereby facilitated seemed insignificant, mainly the provision of bottles of sauce and pickles for the table. In the bar, however, spirits were not infrequently available: some Australian gin arrived, the brand name of which I remembered for many years, that gave me a two-day hangover. And there were comfortable chairs. It was strange – Madam Verdurin among the aristos, almost – hobnobbing with those who, the very day before promotion, had been set in positions of authority, even control over one's destiny, like the RPO. Did one knock back Australian gin lolling next to the PO of the clique, or had he by then voyaged to India with the Lieutenant?

As with all promotion, there came a sense that the new status was not quite what it had been when longed for from afar, not least because shared with some fellow promotees less worthy in one's own eyes than oneself. Non-technical duties were light: I was faintly apprehensive when my turn came to be PO for the day, but all I remember of that is going round at night with the (black) sergeant of the KAR to inspect the guard posts, which were manned by *askaris*. The experience formed the basis of a poem, "The White Conscript and the Black Conscript", which puts the issues of colonialism, war, multi-racial society, in terms which today seem astonishingly simple, if not simplistic, yet which I would not wish to disown:

> If only I could tell you
> That in my country there
> Are millions as poor as you
> And almost as unfree: if I could share
> Our burdens of despair!

By then I knew a little about the Kenyan tribes, and had been to a remarkable display of tribal dancing at Nairobi's football stadium (or perhaps some entirely different venue, for don't I remember dust rising through the car headlights illuminating the dancers?). So at the guard posts I essayed a bit of chat with the *askaris*, my scullery Swahili barely augmented by the sergeant's similar English; the tribal languages must also have been a barrier. Nevertheless, some communication occurred, as the poem indicates, not least astonishment that I should be able to utter the names of tribes. Moreover, there was a bit of illegal cigarette smoking and the general agreement, previously touched on, about the comic nature of minute to minute existence.

5 *Petty Officer's Mess*

I could not have been a petty officer for very long when it was arranged I should go to RNAS, Tanga, to lecture to aircrews about IFF. The term set was a month, but one had gloomy forebodings that once plucked from the cushy number at Nairobi one would never return. Tanga was on the Tanganyikan coast, somewhat north of Zanzibar. In early April 1943 I went by train to Mombasa, by Naval truck to nearby Port Reitz, and then by air to the naval air station at Tanga. In the outer world the Tunisian invasion would be proceeding, no substitute for the Second Front, though who was I to think it tame? Even after the marvellous triumph of Stalingrad, there would be a sense of unease about the Russian ability to withstand another German summer offensive. One was just as much at the mercy of the news as a civilian.

At that epoch air travel was by no means the commonplace it became soon after the war. For me, apprehensive of heights, it was only to be borne in the line of duty, like climbing the mast at HMS *Ganges*. As a matter of fact I had already been in the air. I went up in a (bombless) Blenheim bomber from the RAF station at Nairobi just to see (or, rather, hear – for the response could be monitored through earphones, the pulse rate having an audio frequency) how the IFF set behaved in action. The Blenheim homed on a beacon (perhaps the ASV test apparatus, but my grasp of technicalities at this distance of time is shaky) set up outside the Special W/T hangar. I also had the opportunity to see the working of the Blenheim's ASV set. One or the other set was in the bubble in the forward belly of the aircraft (the Observer's position), so a certain amount of crawling about in mid-flight was entailed, perhaps the best analogy being the making of a propaganda film illustrative of heroism in the air. Even the staggering sight of the snows of both Kilimanjaro and Mount Kenya, pimple and carnivore's tooth respectively, rising out of the brownish haze, did not alleviate the pretty constant sense of unease, peaking as we banked and dropped down air-pockets – motions all too reminiscent of the Velvet Coaster, on Blackpool's Pleasure Beach, which as a boy I tried to dissuade adults from taking me on. (Later, an even more fearful ride, the Big Dipper, usurped its place, but by then I was old enough to be firm, though still shame-faced, about saying no). My respect for authority on most occasions (undoubtedly allied to timidity) was shown on the pilot's initial appearance in helmet and neutral overalls by my addressing him as "sir", only later realizing he must have been a mere sergeant-pilot, and remorsefully kicking myself. Quite typical of the radar of those days, possibly of all war's apparatus, that so far as I could tell the IFF set was not being triggered; inconclusiveness undissipated by Bob Park, on duty at the beacon, when I returned to the womb of the iffy hut.

At Port Reitz the transporting aircraft proved to be an Albacore, biplane similar to the Swordfish, but enclosing the occupants instead of leaving their busts in the open air. In the early days of the clique I had bostiked the aerial bollards of many an Albacore, skinned my knuckles removing for repair its devilishly situated ASV units. I was not reassured by finding the passenger (normally observer) section rusty, and swimming in tropical rainwater. I shared the flight with a naval medical officer, though not the one quite soon to become a familiar figure. We were airborne for a mere half hour, the element not greatly alarming at this second essay; some emotion to spare for the sight of the green island shapes in the bluest of seas as we flew south down the coast. I got to RNAS, Tanga, a mere clearing in the palm trees, in the null part of the afternoon. The administrative hut was like the sheriff's office in an old western movie. My arrival had not been signalled, or the signal was lost. Some duty messenger was raised to convey me to the Chief Petty Officers' Mess, where the Master-at-Arms (who alone, apparently, could receive me) was still enjoying his siesta. The heat was intense, far different from Nairobi's galvanizing sunshine and rare air.

I have already, more than once, touched on the question of khaki, incongruous colour, it seemed at first, vis-à-vis the Navy. Though in Nairobi I started by going ashore in whites, when it became apparent that an acceptable rig was khaki shirt, and long khaki trousers (shorts in the evenings were banned on account of mosquitos), I adopted it, like many others, as more practical. I had a pair of longs, perhaps two, made at an Indian tailor's. I also got him to make a khaki cap-cover for my taxi-driver's cap. Typical of Indian thrift, even more extreme than my own, that when I came to what should have been the happy moment of putting cap-cover on cap I found it had been tailored too exiguously to fit. The khaki shirts issued at Lee were no more than fairly adequate working shirts, hardly consonant with even an Indian-tailored pair of longs. In the window of a Nairobi men's outfitters I saw a khaki shirt that appealed to me: flannel, dark of hue, expensive. I pondered the textile side of the question, deciding in the end that flannel, though lacking coolness, had the virtue of absorbing sweat. As to cost, I reminded myself the dear old Woolwich was still making up my salary (the burden on its funds somewhat diminished after I had been promoted Petty Officer).

Entering the CPOs' mess at Tanga, cap (whatever colour of cap-cover) politely under my arm, the foregoing shirt was the one I was wearing. Its charisma is the only way I can account for the Master-at-Arms (I let for the moment the term stand without ambiguity) addressing me at once as "sir" when I enquired where I was to go. The Blenheim pilot business was bouleversed. I was profoundly embarrassed, realizing I had long weeks, perhaps months, to live with his damaged *amour propre*. No use my respectfully adding "Chief" to every phrase, for that was exactly what a conscientious officer would do. The misunderstanding was soon cleared up, perhaps by my producing a draft chit if such was in my possession; quite likely, I being the draft's sole member.

I was assigned to a hut among the palms. It was not far from the POs' mess, some of the features of which appear in my eponymous poem, notably the pet monkeys, emblem in the poem for the human condition; reminiscent of the Lieutenant-Commander's hobby at Seafield Park, perhaps some archetypal naval preoccupation.

> The monkeys near the mess (where we all eat
> And dream) I saw tonight select with neat
> And brittle fingers dirty scraps, and fight,
> And then look pensive in the fading light,
> And after pick their feet.
>
> They are secured by straps about their slender
> Waists, and the straps to chains. Most sad and tender,
> They clasp each other and look round with eyes
> Like ours at what their strange captivities
> Invisibly engender.

Mosquito nets I seem to think were optional in Nairobi: here they were strictly insisted on. Getting up in my insomnia, I would see the double row of beds each surmounted by its ghostly box or funnel, as though the inhabitants were dead and strangely immured – or, perhaps, undead, capable like myself of throwing aside their cerements and wandering hungrily into the deep night. Though presumably some drainage had accompanied the felling of palm trees, standing water – breeding ground of the *anopheles* – abounded within mosquito-flight of the mess huts, and a common sight was parties of *askaris* in charge of a naval NCO, setting out with spraying apparatus as though on *safari*. Why RNAS, Tanga, was set up is far from clear to me, perhaps always was. The simulation of conditions likely to be experienced combatting the Japanese was surely rather too verisimilitudinous, though it was, of course, a place for training. My tepid commitment to the locale is indicated by my failure to recall whether more than one squadron was in training at the time of my visit. I must say it seems rather lavish of manpower, even by service standards, to send me to talk on IFF to a single squadron.

The speculation also occurs as to how I spent non-lecturing time, theoretically as lightly worked as a university lecturer without seminars or tutorials. Tropical routine applied, of course, so I was free every afternoon. It was possible to get a lift in a regular truck to Tanga, or slightly beyond to a small bay of silver sand where a diving platform had been erected by some club in the bygone days of peace, an apparatus I brought into a crime novel called *Fantasy and Fugue* after the war. Sometimes I was there alone save for fiddler crabs and the shoals of tiny coloured fish, the shallower water at the bay's edge almost too warm, bathing of a luxuriousness excelling even Durban's.

The truck came to the swimming place for the return journey, but I often walked the few miles along the straight, palm-lined, tarmac strip into the town, and caught the truck, or a later one, from there. Tea, and simple but good home-made cakes (queen cakes come to mind) could be had at a small serviceman's canteen, run by a few devoted patriotic ladies. The premises must have had a long club, or quasi-club, history, for in one room was a shelf or two of books including a number in German, with evidence of their survival from Tanganyika's past as German East Africa, a régime ended by the First World War. Then, that must have seemed an antediluvian era, part of my brother's babyhood, my father reading the newspaper over breakfast on the house in Frederick Street, Oldham. Perhaps he had even mentioned the East African campaign, for I had a vague sense of knowing about it: maybe it had merely figured in an adventure serial in *Chums* or *The Boys' Own Paper*, the bound volumes of which I loved so much, especially the former; or a little later I may have read of it in a poem by Francis Brett Young when, at Seafolde House, I began to voyage out on contemporary literature.

The English books in the canteen (the word is too gross for those bijou and refined premises) were mainly of similar antiquity – volumes of Nelson's red, sevenpenny fiction: the novels of Henry Seton Merriman, William Le Queux, Jeffrey Farnol. I believe I would not have been above pinching any I fancied, for the quest for reading matter had become as arduous as in shipboard experience. One evening I desperately scoured the beds and bedside cupboards of the sleeping-hut, and came up solely, but with gratitude, with a tattered *No Orchids For Miss Blandish*. The satisfaction of physical thirst was also a problem in Tanga's heat. In the town I patronized the garden of the aerated water factory, conveniently near the truck's return point, where the product was available at tables round a fountain. Odd to see at other tables Arabs in robes, daggers in waistbands, for teetotalism allied to mayhem was in those days unfamiliar, to me at any rate. It was an Arab-tinctured coast: sometimes I wandered through Tanga, but the houses were turned inward – courtyards merely glimpsed, no life on the streets.

I do not remember staying in the town after dark. Was there no attractive restaurant, cinema, late truck back to camp? I daresay I could write a bit about evenings in the POs' mess, though monotonous. The insect life at least was varied, amazingly so: the mess kitten scampered over the floor pursuing beetles as big as clockwork toys, which it ate. Nevertheless, it was thin: the life it devoured (one speculated) parasitic, not nourishing. The routine comes back of walking from the sleeping-hut, through the palms, past the monkeys, to the POs' mess, its lights perhaps already on though the sudden dusk still to descend. I might compose a line or two there; more usually read. Boozing came after the evening meal, its extent depending on the variable supply of beer.

It was probably reading and writing that drew Jack Jolly to me. I cannot say that at first I was drawn to him. He was a "crab-fat", a regular RAF Sergeant, at some point in his career seconded to the Fleet Air Arm, a thin line of dark moustache and an air of extreme *savoir faire* seeming to put him outside the range of service characters I might get on with. Nothing could have been wider of the mark than those initial impressions. It eventually turned out that he, too, wrote verse – untutored, but with great feeling, even rhapsodic. We found other things to discuss, including the free play of the mind over mutual acquaintances that is an essential of friendship. In other words, we slipped easily into affectionate and amused relations, one of the few bonuses for me of what was overwhelmingly a fairly disagreeable episode of my service life. On the rarish nights when the beer flowed unrationed in the bar, Jack Jolly revealed an outstanding talent for reciting ballads maybe familiar to regular servicemen but new to me, notably a long piece beginning:

> The sun shone on the village green,
> It shone on poor blind Nell.

Despite the physical handicap referred to, Nell's persona and adventures occupy the whole poem (which, now I come to think of it, may well have mainly consisted of a flashback to her sighted days). A ruthless character, Nell leaves her humble parents at an early age, and prospers illicitly, but

> Did she send them goods and parcels?
> Did she? Did she f – g a – s.

Though recollection seems capable of accounting for a good proportion of leisure activity at Tanga, memory of working life is riddled with gaps. I remember lecturing in a room with a blackboard, which I used; even making a few jokes to try to amuse the aircrew audience. Then some time was spent down at the airfield, presumably servicing the IFF sets, helping with the ASV. When I turn to *The Perfect Fool* I see that there I quite neatly fictionalized the business, using the more interesting parts of actuality, sewing up the ragged ends – but it casts little further light on what really happened in 1943. The five and a half pages devoted to Tanga seem to be among the more successful in the book, mainly through their sketching of the characters of the joss-man, an electrician called Charlie Fowler, and Lieutenant-Commander Theobald.

It may seem difficult to believe, but I do not know – nor do I think have ever known – whether the joss-man (naval slang, like "jaunty", for Master-at-Arms, disciplinary chief petty officer, rank of Melville's dread Claggart), whose exploits are reported in *The Perfect Fool*, was the chief who had mistakenly called me "sir" on my arrival. The misunderstanding would seem to jibe with his reputation, established before my arrival (and who else but the joss-man would I be directed to see?), but I cannot be sure. After that initial encounter, if encounter it was, I don't think I ever saw the joss-man again. An Edgar Kennedy-like figure may be conceived. I refer to the great American film comedian, master of the "slow burn", at one time in a number of Laurel and Hardy shorts; of powerful physique but incomplete mastery of the physical world, particularly of potentially dangerous objects like hammers. It was currently said, when I arrived at Tanga, that a rating had gone to the joss-man and asked for a bar of soap, presumably for his *dhobi*. This episode had corroded in the joss-man's mind, symbolizing for him (and, by reiteration, for others) the collapse of the traditional fear of, and respect for, his office (going back to Billy Budd days and before) and the degenerate nature of RNAS, Tanga, itself. A phrase reported to be frequently on his lips was: "Me, the joss-man, and they ask me for soap."

"Charlie Fowler" is quite closely drawn from life. I was afraid, when I embarked on the business in *The Perfect Fool*, that I should not be able to capture the essence of his anecdotal style, invariably resourceful and funny, but I see I brought it off not too badly. The fantasy he expressed of the joss-man, relegated to civilian life after the war, emptying the cesspit of Fowler Grange, is scarcely too great an enhancement of his everyday manner. Like Jack Jolly, he offset Tanga's debits somewhat, and I wish his real name had not sunk through my porous memory.

In the novel, the hero escapes from the tentacles of the squadron commander, Lieutenant-Commander Theobald, by reporting sick, but as to that the fiction is much more pat. I had been troubled for some time with a discharging ear, that in Tanga worsened, perhaps as a result of so much swimming. I decided to consult the MO, and joined the halt and maimed on an open-sided godown, usually waiting the best part of a morning. Malaria, dysentery, festering insect bites and the like, had turned a large proportion of the station's personnel into casualties, whether more or less had the Fleet remained at Trincomalee, who can say?

"Have you been under gunfire?" asked the MO, a man younger than myself, probing the dubious ear.

"No, sir," I said immediately, guilty at having come thus far from the UK, and into 1943, lacking the experience. Later I recalled that in my lookout tub I had been adjacent to the *Capetown Castle*'s main armament, a three-pounder, when it was fired at practice.

In *The Perfect Fool* I blame the MO's messing about for the ear's worsening, a positive pain and deep tenderness developing, though this could be fiction's simplifying and dramatizing process. But the book's vital dialogue on the subject subsequently took place in actuality.

"What have I got, sir?"

"Tropical ear."

"Is it – serious?"

"No, no. All ears are tropical in the tropics."

Fairly soon the infection moved, and a sore throat developed that more than matched the tonsillitis and quinsies of my youth. As I sat one morning waiting in the godown it was evident that an "ear", even tropical, did not cover the situation. My temperature, when taken at last, was 106°, and the MO dispatched me to the hospital in Tanga. The latter verb is undescriptive of the process. The truck or van waited anyway until the morning's whole hopsital intake had been assembled and then, in the familiar manner of suspect road transport (particularly marked in foreign parts), lingered on while some difference, imperfectly understood by the passengers, about the identity of the driver, even the consumption of his elevenses, was argumentatively resolved. Despite the torrid sunshine, it seemed to me my condition was more bearable if I roamed about rather than sat in the godown. An indifference as to whether I lived or died mercifully stole over me. Perhaps I was the only PO in the party: at any rate, I sat up front with the driver, the others shaken about in the back as the vehicle jolted over the sleepered road of the swamp. Indulgently, I observed the scene, made conversation – both activities as irrelevant as if in a tumbril bound for the guillotine.

The RN had taken over part of Tanga's civilian hospital: in the naval ward the beds were pushed close together, one or two figures known back at camp or in Nairobi lying or tottering about, big-eyed, emaciated ghosts of their former selves, victims of dysentery. Bliss to get undressed and into bed, but I was soon disturbed to have a spinal tap. Later came a massive injection of anti-diphtheria vaccine or serum. Following that, I was told the spinal-fluid test was negative. What I had was presumably merely tropical throat.

I suppose the sensational temperature quite soon went down a few notches, but it did not fall to normal, and the days, even weeks, passed, and I was plainly losing weight. The terracotta tiles of the ward extended to a verandah, its canopy supported by decorative iron pillars. Wounded or malarial servicemen of the East African Campaign of 1916 might well have escaped there, to smoke their meerschaums or Woodbines, from beds as close then as now. Insomniac as ever, I used to wander out during the night, tiles cool to the feet, sometimes thinking that the place might well curiously constitute the scene of my demise. Though staffed by RN doctors and sick berth "tiffies", the naval section was included by the hospital's civilian director in his regular rounds. He was small, shrewd, authoritative, not English, attended by various acolytes. One day he stopped by my bed for a word and I diffidently told him I was making no progress.

"You must stay in bed," he said. "You must not get out of bed for anything."

Someone in his entourage made a note, and following the prescribed routine I began to improve. Had I at that time read Festing Jones's biography of Samuel Butler I would have recognized the redoubtable Miss Savage's sound belief that "the great secret of getting well is not to exert yourself."

6 *Kilimanjaro and Kenya*

After all, I was little more than six weeks in Tanga. Certainly in the result my illness foiled the formidable Lieutenant-Commander Theobald from getting a permanent lien on my services. RNAS Tanga itself would presumably not be keen to retain an enfeebled supernumerary, though it comes to me that I wrote or got a message to the "Special W/T Section" in Nairobi demanding rescue. Or merely contemplated doing so, pacing the hospital balcony. Anyway, towards the end of May 1943 I was once more a naval draft of one, routed to Nairobi entirely by rail, via Moshi. The line went roughly north west from Tanga, and then one changed to the line running east from Arusha, through Moshi, joining the Mombasa-Nairobi line at Voi, really not far from the coast.

The avoidance of rusty Albacores was not the reason I

welcomed this modest official version of a Robertsonian trip: from the map, Moshi seemed almost in the foothills of Kilimanjaro, that once volcanic pimple on great Africa's countenance I longed to see at closer quarters. I could be classed as an anti-traveller, yet much of East Africa allured me. Is the alluring always in the end frustrating, or is that merely the sense of a temperament unable to suck dry the current moment, perhaps especially its visual side? The Martins once drove me out from Nairobi to view the Rift Valley at – but I forget the place. I gazed and gazed: there was even a mountain in the depth of that continental wound. But one had to come away unsatisfied.

I wonder where I read that for the overnight stay at Moshi passengers could remain on the Tanga-Moshi train. Presumably on the ticket, or possibly a notice in the compartment. What I envisaged were fezzed, nightgowned, softly bare-footed stewards making up couchettes, as on that initial journey from Mombasa to Nairobi. On arrival at Moshi in the early evening there was a general exodus (if the phrase can be applied to the few passengers) from the station along the road to an hotel little more attractive than the *Splendide* in *Savage Gold*. I expect that as so often in my life I was playing the thing by ear instead of seeking precise enlightenment. I must have had the hotel dinner – otherwise why should I have entered the place? – but afterwards I made my way back to the station through the nocturnal-noised dark. The unlikelihood of anyone else taking advantage of the railway company's offer of accommodation must by now have been perfectly plain. The train was discovered, I think in a siding or at some subsidiary platform. Encountering a minor Indian railway official, I explained my purpose. He muttered something unintelligible and passed on. The train was empty and unlighted. I selected a compartment at random and stretched out, to sleep if I could, on one of the seats.

Later, someone in Nairobi told me I could have claimed, from the RPO's office, reimbursement of the cost of a hotel room had I produced the bill, but of course my action was not the result of poverty or even parsimony, rather arose from too great a respect for rules and authority, evidenced elsewhere in these memoirs, not least in the tolerance of Stalinism. Shyness, too, played a big part in the business; also an unjustified reliance on mankind behaving rationally, especially when so instructed. It may seem odd that these traits accompany a strong nonconformity of thought, a willingness to be in a minority of one, but so it has been. From a slightly different aspect the persona may be seen as that of the Fool, the gormless but intelligent innocent who only learns about life through his enormous gaffes, and even then repeats them. Such was the representation attempted in *The Perfect Fool.* I think it must have been in conversation rather than a review that Julian Symons said (I put his objection too crudely) that he did not really see the *raison d'être* of that novel; that for him it lacked plot. As always, his criticism – as I came to see – had great point: the failure of the book is that it depicts too short a span of the hero's life to justify itself in the genre of the picaresque, and its repeated illustration of Folly too esoteric an artistic shaping, certainly since the work is utterly naturalistic.

It was possible to have the compartment door-windows open, yet draw up barriers of wire mesh, the material of old-fashioned meat safes, to keep out mosquitos. I did not discover this device at once: in any case, the windows being down, some of the pests were already sharing the accommodation. What with one thing and another the night was troubled. As soon as was decent, in my code of behaviour, I walked back to the hotel for breakfast, no doubt with the air of one staying with friends in the vicinity, but not wishing to impose himself for meals. A mist hung low: nothing of Kilimanjaro was to be seen, though the general direction of its summit could be deduced from the slope of the land. After breakfast I walked farther up the road, hoping the clouds would break before the Voi train left. The poem "Today and Tomorrow" (in *A Lost Season*) tells me I looked across rows of sugar cane (perhaps in reality maize) and encountered boys driving goats (possibly sheep, the African breed ambiguous), the animals belled and the boys with long thin sticks, so familiar in Africa. As another poet has said: "A russet shepherd, his sheep too, russet."

Following the throat, malaria (which duly came) left me enfeebled. During its course I had chatted with the attendant RNVR MO, who turned out to have been in peacetime practice in the south-east London suburb where I too had lived. Like that of "Charlie Fowler", his name has regrettably faded from my mind. He asked me why I had not gone in for a commission. I told him of the vocation conferred on me in HMS *Ganges*, and its later renewal by Sub-Lieutenant Lavender. He said he would do something about it. He also put my name forward to the

Kenya Women's Volunteer Organization for consideration for sick leave at their expense. The hotel they nobly sent me to was in Nyeri, with a celebrated annexe (not in use at that moment of the war) built into a tree, from which during the night animals could be viewed visiting an artificial salt lick. Nyeri was under Mount Kenya as Moshi was under Kilimanjaro, though not so tucked in.

Not awfully long after returning to Nairobi from Nyeri I was told I was to go to Port Reitz, base of the rusty Albacore, to help start a Special W/T Section. At long last RNAS Nairobi was beginning to break up, the shift east affecting even barrack stanchions like myself. One seemed to be able to look back then to the rise and fall of a whole society. Remote indeed seemed the day when the advance party put up a marquee, episode with strong elements of Edgar Kennedy and Laurel and Hardy, to serve as temporary dining hall for the main draft still at Mombasa. At that time, and for some time following, we slept in candle-lit corrugated iron huts, near the guard house, by the roadside ditches where dead rats were sometimes to be seen. Willie, coming back to our hut after an evening ashore and feeling peckish, had searched in the dark in his jacket pocket for a cake saved from the mobile canteen's mid-morning round (another of the KWVO's good works) – and put his hand on a live rat. It being eventually discovered the rats had died from bubonic plague, everyone had to have two, if not three, injections of anti-plague serum, then experimental, perhaps still so. When the frightful effects of the serum had been suffered, the buzz went round it was wholly ineffective. Willie slept opposite me and we discovered that somewhere along the line of our voyagings together our boot-brush polish-applicators had been inadvertently exchanged, as the ineradicable name-marking of HMS *Ganges* showed. We decided not to swap back, and so created a souvenir apiece. My W. E. ROBERTSON brush is still in regular use.

Then Sikh carpenters arrived to build new wooden sleeping-huts farther up the road, squatting on the rafters, white-garbed, white-turbaned. Even in the new huts bedbugs were discovered: they lurked in the folds where the canvas sling met the wooden bed frame. I must have grown enured to the horror of being nocturnally crawled on. Pyrethrum, a local crop, was a pusser's issue, but proved a deficient bugicide. I recall attacking my bed with a blowtorch outside the sleeping-hut door under the afternoon sun; the place where I might in the middle of the night smoke an hour or so of insomnia away, conscious of the vast, starry sky yet getting to know its bodies and constellations no better than the Swahili language, the educated blacks or Happy Valley. As for a medieval peasant, or sutler in a Renaissance war, not only did the great events take place beyond my ken but also some occupational or constitutional blinkering cut down the desirable absorption of life's detail in this place that had become rather more than a wayside halt.

I must have been displeased with the Port Reitz draft. The news was also received glumly by the Martins. Yet it was still an amazingly cushy number compared with what might have befallen. However, I think I had done no more than try to prepare mentally for the move when Sub-Lieutenant Lavender's *confrère* came in the iffy hut and said I should be going not to Port Reitz but the UK. One (or more) of the various efforts to commission me had succeeded, and I had been called home for the status in some way to be conferred. When the news had been imparted I trembled for long minutes. That the frustration of marital and paternal love was to be ended gave a physical shock the like of which I had never experienced before, nor have since.

It must surely have been years later that I learnt that Willie went to Port Reitz in my stead. Probably he told me himself on the occasion I shall later recount. Or I may have heard it from a mutual acquaintance while the war was still on, possibly at HMS *Ariel*. In any case, the knowledge was revived the other day from seeing a snapshot of Willie lying on his bed in his "cabin" at Port Reitz, annotated thus in his hand on the back of the photograph. He is clean-shaven, in white shorts and shirt, well turned-out; family photographs are on the shelf above, comforting soft drink on the side table. The snap being destined for his wife, he explains characteristically in the caption that the bottle on the shelf is merely the bottom half of a lamp. Undoubtedly he would set up whatever organization was required at Port Reitz with far more authority and effectiveness than I could have done myself.

7 *The Road, the House, the Wife*

The penultimate entry in my journal – one of a mere half-dozen for the year 1943 – is for 29 July: "Left Nairobi 5 o'clock train yesterday and landed up here in Mombasa at English Point – tents, flies on the food, forgotten men – a transit camp". I cannot stress too strongly the sense that now constantly nagged of failing to get home – not as a result of torpedoes or other enemy action but simply through a breakdown of bureaucratic machinery; or unforeseen service requirement; or some waylaying, such as suffered by the journeying protagonists of fairy tales. The sense was exacerbated by the "buzzes" preceding any happening to service peronnel. I bathed at English Point, read and even wrote a bit, encountered an old face or two (the camp was less for newcomers from the UK than for those between ships or shore establishments), and then, after a few days, I was actually with my gear on the quayside at Kilindini, awaiting the docking of the transporting vessel. By then I had an extra item of luggage, a japanned tin box bought along the way, proof against the depredations of tropical insect life. I had painted on it in red (the fluid somewhere available, possibly left over from rehabilitating the Clique's hunting car) PO FULLER FAA, letters to be dimly descried to this day, as though part of a medieval fresco.

Where had the ship come from? Massawa? Aden? Lining the rails were many woebegone soldiers' faces, surmounted by those big-brimmed hats one side of which seems to be permanently turned up – antipodean troops, I imagined them to be, but in fact the headgear was not so confined. They had had a rough passage round the Horn of Africa. Those tidings would perturb me somewhat, but the further stage to Durban was unsensational. Part of my luck in the war was that though I spent upwards of three months in troopships I was never sick – no more than occasionally feeling "that queerish sensation", mentioned by Sir Walter Scott in his journal, when "we landsfolk . . .

without being in the least sick . . . are not quite well". I am sure I am not a specially good sailor: simply, the weather was never outrageous. That voyage from Mombasa to Durban was like breaking into a novel or play halfway through, relationships advanced but slightly enigmatic, one's own attention and interest hard to engage. What seemed to me then an elderly nursing sister was cavaliered by a much younger proletarian sergeant, that apparent strangeness of the evidently strongly erotic bond denoting my residual romanticism. One precise image of the voyage has survived:

> Last night between the crowded, stifling decks I saw a man
> Smoking a big curved pipe, who contemplated his great
>   wan
> And dirty feet while minute after tedious minute ran.

The lines are a verse from what I suppose is the best poem I wrote during the war, or at any rate the least spoiled, one of a few written in South Africa on the return journey. As to the African poems in general, some critic has pointed out that the oppressed and beautiful animals and blacks stood in quite well for the proper imagery of "war poetry", but I was never a "war poet", even in the category of John Pudney, who wrote about courage and casualties somewhat at second hand, not that there was basically anything amiss in that. I was struck, just before setting these sentences down, by what Professor Richard Ellmann said in a discussion with the poet Craig Raine, that, to put it baldly, though James Joyce could not be called a political writer "he always retained a political feeling". If the analogy is not too bathetic, I would say politics underlies my African poems, though the political feeling came not from any sort of participation but simply from the wireless and *The East African Standard* and the hangover from Thirties days.

I ought also to take the opportunity here of emphasizing what has already been touched on but may have been forgotten in selective narration, the process of what I called, in an African poem, being "systematically and sickeningly" bored. Donald Davie, in his autobiography *These the Companions*, is excellent about the way newly-trained or newly-arrived naval ratings were during the war excluded from real work, at least in shore establishments. Moreover, I was unused to lavish manpower supply, the Great Pyramid Syndrome it might be named, despite my bridge-playing articled-clerk days, and a season of office cricket as assistant solicitor. The leisurely pace of proletarian work, when continuously available, was also something impossible to become accustomed to. I am now apt to say, with truth, that I am never bored. Though shortage of unexpired life has something to do with this, I suppose the claim is fundamentally arrogant, like Pachmann's, eccentric concert pianist of my youth. "But aren't you bored, M. Pachmann, with all the travelling you have to do?" "No, no. You see I am always with Pachmann." But I was bored during the war.

The "wan and dirty feet" poem I wrote in Durban, the equestrian statue romantically referred to in the first part being some monument on the seafront to a South African pioneer, or perhaps warrior. Almost unbelievably, we went from Durban to Cape Town by train, presumably because of the shortage of shipping: elsewhere, Sicily was being captured, and so forth. The crowded train stopped at stations with household names – Ladysmith, Bloemfontein, Kimberley. We never "did" the Boer War at school, so the names must have been imprinted by stories and reminiscences in the periodicals read in boyhood: after all, when I was born that conflict was only a decade in the past. On the outward journey I had heard Smuts, transmogrified into a great leader of the Empire, speaking in Durban's main square, while here under station boards bearing the old battle names the generous South African ladies had spread trestle tables with free food and drink for the enemies of yore. Little wonder that despite the heroism in the Mediterranean and on the Russian front, the poem feels that in its epoch wan and dirty feet are more enduring than bronze effigies.

By the time Durban had been reached, Petty Officers Pogson and Bridle had well and truly come into my life. In fact, I may have encountered them at English Point. They were two of the solo whist four I was a member of, that played every night of the voyage from Mombasa to Durban. The fourth has gone from recollection, probably through guilt, for he was the least skilful player and consistently lost – sums that even for the small stakes played for added up over the sea miles. The games went on so late I was able, when they were over, to open my hammock on the mess table that had been their arena – long abandoned by other games players and letter writers, disliking the cocooned effect induced by a slung hammock, rather as if one were on the stage to becoming a giant cockroach, like Gregor Samsa. Before turning in I would take the few steps through the blackout baffle into the starlit air of night, amazingly fresh after Pogson's perpetual pipe and our own fags. Probably I would stay no longer than to pee illicitly in the scuppers, though conscious that here, in a sense, was the real world, the world of poetry; certainly a world I should never plumb and be lucky in any great measure to depict.

Pogson was an experienced solo player, and I had long years of bridge behind me. Bridle, though rejoicing at the fleecing of the mysterious Fourth, must also have been a loser in the long run. Pogson and Bridle were Supply Petty Officers. What Pogson had been in Civvy Street I do not recall. He seemed to me quite old – grey haired, plump; with the neat habits and quiet relish of life possessed by many plump men. His being long-married, even perhaps with adolescent children, did not exclude a professed interest in the side of things more appropriate, as I then thought, to a younger fellow – though the amatory was not a trait of his to be emphasized. A strange obscenity was ever on his lips, the syntax of which I sometimes pondered: "You wouldn't f – it, would you?" He would certainly have considered his wisdom in other departments of existence equal to that he displayed playing solo whist: but the erotic knowingness was doubtless to emphasize his more general *savoir faire*.

Bridle was a Lancastrian, in pre-call-up life something to do with publicity – the vagueness now expressed very likely emanating from himself, for he was younger than Pogson, could scarcely have attained much eminence in the realm of advertising or whatever it was. He was short and lean, small teeth giving a sense of toothlessness; assured about all matters, despite any deficiencies of know-how inadvertently revealed; longish brown hair, parted low, quite well-brilliantined. Not seldom he might a trifle flashily overcall Pogson's sound bid of "solo". Pogson would say round his pipe stem: "You wouldn't f – it, would you?" Then at least one knew that what the phrase meant in that context was a sibyllic prognostication of disaster.

The solo winnings went towards a few quite epicurean dinners in Cape Town, when Pogson's carnal relish, Bridle's assumption of vinous discrimination, were well displayed. Which of them chose Van de Hum, the South African liqueur then surely little known outside its country of origin, to go with our coffee after the Cape white and red? The brandy of the country we drank with ginger ale as an apéritif. Despite the sensible restaurant tariffs and the staggering cheapness of the booze (ninepence sticks in my mind as the price of a b. and g.a.), Bridle had fairly soon to cry off such outings, and Pogson may well have been glad to see them end, though never destroying the impression of possessing resources beyond his service pay (and winnings at penny solo).

The transit camp was in a western suburb of Cape Town: wooden huts straggling up a small hill of red earth; parade ground and administrative buildings at the bottom, by a railway siding; not near, but in sight of the moods of Table Mountain. The shifting population was fell in every morning to be assigned daily jobs, of a generally dubious nature. When I first arrived there was much skulking in the huts at this juncture, so that the unusual and peremptory command of "Clear Lower Deck" began regularly to be piped, reinforced by the Jaunty's minions flushing out the huts. Even then, some skulking went on: I remember going up into the hillocks above the camp and playing cards with a few other outlaws (Act III of *Carmen* comes to mind) until the various working parties had been marched off parade and a semblance of quiet had descended. But even this escape route was soon cut off, and one had to parade regularly.

Jobs befitting Petty Officers were rationed out, spread thin. At first it seemed never to occur to authority to enquire about one's trade, so that a little time elapsed before, in my capacity as radar mechanic, I was instructed to walk – and given an approximate bearing – over the hill, where I would find useful temporary employment on some electronic activity there taking place. I should interpolate that just before this, I had encountered in the street in Cape Town a boy known from Lee-on-the-Solent days, if not earlier; good-looking, well-spoken, public school. He was wearing a white ribbon round his cap, indicating officer-cadet status. It turned out he was not only training in South Africa for a commission, and so not to get to the UK on that account, but also, though like me to be a radar and radio officer, his course was the decimating ordeal undergone by potential executive branch officers, even more arduous (he claimed) than its English equivalent. My blood ran cold. Always reticent about the reason for my being on a UK draft, after that encounter I clammed up completely.

Higher even than where the card-playing skulkers lurked was a road that eventually ran along a neck of land with the sea close on one side, the orientation of the route unclear in the absence of a map. Fairly soon I came to a newish concrete building overlooking the water. Stores of some kind were being moved into it by blacks. If RN personnel were evident their nature and numbers have gone from mind. In the building itself I found a naval officer unpacking crates of unfamiliar but obvious ship or shore radar gear. I could easily invent a plausible persona for him – stocky, Yorkshire, unlit pipe clenched in reliable jaw – but the fact is his appearance is just beyond the limits of memory. When I told him my trade and whence I came he was surprisingly, even startlingly, joyous. He told me what he was setting up, showed me round, assuming in me a knowledge of equipment far wider than ASV and IFF. He was chronically short-handed, I was just the man he wanted, a godsend. I explained I was not in some drafting pool, emphasized my transitoriness despite the shortage of shipping, but nothing cooled his warm anticipation of our collaboration. Literary parallels struck me almost at once: the Old Man of the Sea; Tony Last's encounter with Mr Todd.

By the time the explanation, and tour of the building's meagre attractions were over, it was time to return to camp. We worked tropical routine, so the question of the afternoon did not arise. In any case, I never went back. For some time it nagged me that the officer might get in touch with the camp and ask for me, even contrive to get me actually drafted to his radar beacon or training station or what the hell he told me it was. In that event how tragically apt the opening words of the song often sung where matelots gathered at play:

> Oh I wonder, yes I wonder,
> Did the Jaunty make a blunder
> When he made that draft-chit out for me?

On the morning parade I kept mum about technical skills, and soon became petty officer of one of the naval patrols. My half-dozen men, a motley collection, were issued with armbands and batons; I with an armband and whistle. The Fred Karno nature of the force is thus sufficiently indicated, but there was an added factor, never fortunately with material consequences, and that of course was my own unfitness for the assignment. Several members had been on the patrol before, and had strong notions of where it should deploy. We were conveyed by coach to some nearby urban centre where naval personnel might be expected to do mischief, and there I fell in my men, in two's, to march about like a Gilbert and Sullivan chorus, of second touring company class. Some film buff among them directed our steps to an Indian cinema, where we were admitted without question or payment, a prophylactic against the vociferous naval critics doubtless feared by the management. We stood along the barrier at the back of the stalls and watched a film in the genre then (perhaps even now) all the rage with Indians but as incongruous as if the Norse deities should appear among the Canadian Mounties of *Rose Marie*. Another port of call was what may be described as a large sub-post office, a pinball game and soft drinks its attractions – the sale of postage stamps and suchlike presumably having ceased at that time of night, even though it was run by the hard-working Indians. That, too, was an orderly place, despite a few sailors mingling with the more or less exotic customers. Later, one or two of its members led the patrol up an obscure lane to the backs of some houses, which were, however, quite substantial. The purpose of this manoeuvre was to chat up a very good-looking coloured girl, who seemed utterly *comme il faut*; contradicting a few insinuations before we got there. She was a housemaid or nursemaid; offered modest refreshments, which some accepted. Strange insight into the proletarian version of romance, perhaps always lapsing into crude language and desires.

Thus such evenings wore away, my thoughts quite often on their absurd nature, and the preposterous human conduct, from highest to lowest, that had caused and sustained them. Weariness afflicted the patrol before its task was done, the final act being to attend the place where the coaches could be caught back to camp, even more than an Indian musical the likely background of trouble. We did not always wait for the last potential disorderly drunk to depart, but took care to secure coach seats for ourselves in good time – I seem to think slipping armbands off to blend with the other passengers, though concealment of the batons would present a problem. Back at camp, the equipment, such as it was, returned to the guard room, I was free for a couple of nights, duties being no more than one on, two off, if that.

Miraculously, there was a library in the camp, actually

containing a number of readable books. In Nairobi I had been impressed by Karen Blixen's *Out of Africa*, which dealt with the White Highlands at a period which, after all, was no great distance in the past. In the camp library was her pseudonymous *Seven Gothic Tales*, a title I had known since the book came out in the mid-Thirties, but which had never attracted me. Now I read it and was transported. The poetic afflatus of East Africa had not quite left me and the book inspired a poem, "The Emotion of Fiction", for which I used to have a soft spot. The genre – depiction of the enigma of life, no less – in my case usually resulted in clottedness, but here some air seemed to be let in by the Yeatsian three-beat line. The soft spot does not now remain, nor does any real enthusiasm for "Isaak Dinesen" – at least for her later stories, when I dipped into them not long ago.

I should have been surprised, presumably disagreeably so, had I been told in Cape Town that except for a piece or two written in transit, a short sonnet sequence quickly composed after getting back to the UK, and a few small poems as the war ended, my career as "war poet" was over. It was the price paid for becoming "chairborne", as the word was; a sacrifice I was not conscious of making at the time, needless to say. But whatever my eventual fate, I ought to have written more poems in Cape Town. There proved to be plenty of time. The weeks passed and still we did not shift, though buzzes abounded. Then one day a train came into the siding at the foot of the camp for the UK draft. With what energy did one bring one's items of kit down the hill, and pile it up, and help with the loading! By that time my baggage consisted of kitbag, hammock, cap box, toolbox, green suitcase, the PO FULLER FAA tin box, and a substantial cardboard carton. One's personal gear was, of course, in the attaché case issued to naval ratings, and always carried by them outside captivity. The carton was for those "rabbits" that could not be crammed into the other receptacles, and I use the term not in the strict sense of HM's stores or uncustomed goods to be smuggled through dockyard gates but as indicating things likely to be valued by the rationed civilians to whom I was returning.

The laborious stages followed of getting all this gear off the train and into the troopship waiting at the Cape Town quayside. Excitement was tempered by the unsatisfactoriness of the quarters assigned to petty officers; probably other facilities also were below the modest par of a trooper. Whatever protests were made were of no effect, and eventually the floating hell cast off – then, within swimming distance of land, dropped anchor, presumably waiting for a convoy to assemble. There she stayed the night, the next day returning to the quay, where we disembarked. In due course I found myself carrying in relays up the hill of the transit camp – whether to the same hut or not recollection boggles – attaché case, kitbag, hammock, cap box, tool box, green suitcase, tin box and rabbit carton; rather like a practical version of the game of memorising a continuously added-to list of words. Despite a renewal of the helpless and depressing sense that the UK might never be reached, nothing so serious as the Sisyphus myth was invoked; rather *The Music Box*, that film where Laurel and Hardy repeatedly haul a piano up a precipice of steps.

In the end, of course, the gear was loaded on a trooper that actually set sail. Though Pogson and Bridle were of the company I do not recall playing a single game of solo. They had become the Supply POs involved in the ceremonies and mysteries of the daily rum issue. The phrase for the call announcing to the hands that the rum ration was available was "Up Spirits". When these words were uttered, there was usually someone to add (like the *sotto voce* invocation "God Bless Her" from old patriots after the toast "The Queen"; or, perhaps nearer the mark, with inverse piety, as if a response in the Adversary's prayer book) "Stand fast, the Holy Ghost". The elaborate rum regulations were designed to avoid pillage by those in charge, and hoarding and excessive inebriation generally by the recipients. Forbidden, for example, was the practice of sharing one's tot – "Sippers", as colloquially known. "Neaters" (neat spirit) was, like some rare element or particle, designed by Authority not to exist in free form except transitorily, or under conditions of security. In theory, the precise amount of rum to be drawn and watered, and so converted (the word of the miracle at Cana comes readily to the pen) into grog, was calculable from the daily muster sheets (all the easier at sea, where the population remained constant except for any sick or on jankers or fallen overboard) so that there was no cause for an undistributed residue, let alone for any such to be quaffed by the administrators, as properly happens at Holy Communion. Despite all rules and precautions, it was soon apparent, particularly in Bridle's case, that surplus grog, even neaters, was available for the acolytes.

Like the members of my Cape Town patrols, the POs on board were a job lot, including a few tough eggs, notably a submariner stoker, whom I liked but was never exactly easy with. In charge of the naval draft was a rarity at that time of the war (for me, at least), a Commander, RNVR, his wavy stripes like a border round a carpet. The voyage from Cape Town to Glasgow took six weeks: as conditions on board deteriorated, the POs got more bolshie. The crisis arose over morning boat drill. The POs, gathered as in a Shakespearean stage direction, on another part of the deck, refused to attend the daily business of falling-in with life jackets and being counted until some demand – now gone from mind – had been met. A go-between took messages to and fro. At last the Wavy Navy Commander, who had previously shown himself capable of giving a good impersonation of a naval pig, intimated unambiguously that if the POs stayed away they would all, every man jack of them, be on a charge. Of mutiny? Who knows? Most, after some rhubarbing, caved in, including myself. Quite apart from native timorousness, which it would have needed greater ideological involvement in the dispute to overcome, I clearly saw that a disciplinary black mark could dish in my commission. The submariner, for one, would have stuck out, even the possible loss of his hooks seeming to mean little to a man who had descended to the depths of Davy Jones's Locker and returned.

Yet I don't know that being commissioned (given getting back to the UK) meant much to me, except that by now I certainly at times envisaged myself appearing in naval officer's uniform in the odd places where some sensation would be caused: down the Blackpool street where Kate was then still living with her parents, say, or in Booth's Café, which my mother regularly frequented in common with such Blackpool notables as Mrs Spence-Ormerod. Vanity of vanities; all is vanity.

We stood off Libreville, then in French Equatorial Africa, but there was no shore leave. If supplies came aboard they were not seen in the POs' mess. We put in at Gibraltar. In that pre-air-holiday epoch, the Rock was still very much foreign parts, as familiar from photographs as the Sphinx but seeming no nearer home. We had a few hours shore leave, watch and watch about. It was early November, the weather was like a nice English summer's day, and the town seemed a smaller Chatham or Portsmouth, dubious beds and meals available, goods displayed of a kind one could do without. The atmosphere came back a quarter of a century later going into a bar in Sliema on holiday in Malta, where a photogrpah of two POs at a bar table commemorated, according to the inscription, the record number of Blues (the vernacular name for the Maltese bottled beer) consumed at a sitting – a total even Pogson and Bridle I doubt could have approached.

At Gib we joined something of a convoy. After Gib we were soon driving through rain, once again in blue serge and sweaters. The menu for the midday meal was now confined to slices of a tasteless species of large poloney, which one day the POs hung on the hammock-hooks round the mess, bizarre protest of some surrealist mass unconscious. An aircraft appeared, disconcerting for a moment, then seen to be a Sunderland of Coastal Command (or so the identification returns promptly to the mind); next a green rim of Ireland, and in due course Ailsa Craig.

The grey waves rise and splinter:
We voyage into winter.
Beyond the disc of sea
Stretches our northern country.
Our blood made thin by burning
And poison is returning.
Is it too late, too late,
For dreams to approximate?
Will the port be the same,
Or have another name:
The road, the house, the wife,
Only a spectral life?

How far such lines, written as we hit the British November, were poet's play-acting, impossible now to specify. Certainly at first the Glasgow quay had a strange air: uniformly white faces; puddles and shining cobbles; a squalid wooden hut with a slatternly girl serving rotten food to the dockyard mateys. As to the last-named, following my earlier unflattering description of them, Lady Violet Powell reminded me of their classic embodiment in song, though even between us we may not have got the words quite right, the rude ones worsened by me:

The dockyard mateys' children
Sit on the dockyard wall
Watching their bastard fathers
Doing, it seems, f – all.

And when those children grow up
What will those children do?
Why, sit on their great fat arses
And just do f – all, too.

Though I had been out of England less than two years, on my internal timescale the present dockyard mateys could easily have been the offspring of those observed in the Chatham of 1941. During the interminable wait on the quayside I telephoned my mother: Kate's parents were not on the telephone. The ensuing procedure was that everyone would have to return to his home base before going on foreign-service leave, so I was faced with a journey to Lee-on-the-Solent and back up to Blackpool, the mileage daunting enough but less so than the possibilities of bureaucratic sloth and whim attending the process, as though one were serving a vacillating and malicious emperor of Rome's decline, not the agreeable George VI. There were hours of anguish, but it was really not overlong before I was travelling from Lee to Lancashire with Fred Bridle.

It strikes me now as curious that he, too, was from the relatively small FAA branch. But thus it was; and I have observed elsewhere in these memoirs that even the entire RN provided a society like that of a Powell or Proust, where coincidence was an ever-surprising commonplace. When we reached London, some hours remained before the departure of the Blackpool train. There was time to dine, but instead of making for Soho, several of whose restaurants I knew from pre-call-up times (though the most familiar, the excellent and astoundingly cheap Chez Durand in Dean Street, had perished in the Blitz), I took Bridle to the Regent Palace grillroom – if, indeed, his provincial feet might not have found it of their own accord. We probably both had the urge to discover in ration-bound London an echo of our Cape Town dinners, which had tended towards hotels; also Piccadilly Circus would be an easy taking off point for two disoriented boys in blue later on.

My brother, whose first step in his hotel training was to serve as what he called a scullion in the Regent Palace kitchens, used to emphasize the scrupulosity and know-how of the meat buyer for the J. Lyons & Co. hotels (among which the Regent Palace was numbered), evidenced when he went with him to Smithfield in the dawn. On family visits to London we always used to have bed and breakfast at the Regent Palace, dining in the grillroom, pricier and said to be superior to the dining room, where a long *table d'hôte* repast was served. It was a grillroom meal that my schoolfriend Leslie and I sacrificed for the promenade concert the night my mother and Leslie's were baffled by the film *The Cocoanuts*, at which my brother's falling into the aisle with merriment was probably helped by his being well-lined with steak and chips and pêche-melba – typical choice; improvement on the sausage and chips and vanilla ice of the Blackpool Hotel Metropole grillroom, Hobson's choice of our boyhood. Once when I was at the Regent Palace with my wife-to-be, articled clerk days I suspect, for enthusiasm for the Turf still burned, we went to Alexandra Park, a course now no more, on a chill and rainy afternoon at the fag end of the Flat. In the penultimate race, following the principle of the 220 System, I backed Taj Ud Din, a horse that had won last time, or last time but one, out. It won again at the generous odds of 10–1 (perhaps even 100–8), my half-crown each way paying the expenses of the outing, with cash to spare. Afterwards, bathed and changed, with what zest did one descend to the grillroom, where even the cabbage seemed delicious, a dish I used furtively to transport in envelopes from Seafolde House Sunday lunches.

Surely memories such as these were revived as Bridle and I dumped our luggage in the mahoganied cloakroom. Puzzling, what my impedimenta consisted of at that moment. When going on leave ("leaf", as always pronounced in the Andrew) hammocks could be left in the hammock store, and similar facilities existed for tool boxes. I must have likewise deposited my kitbag and the red-lettered tin box, for I could not have carried more than attaché case, green suitcase and the heavy cardboard carton of rabbits. Actually, it was from Bridle's rabbits that a couple of oranges were produced for the grillroom waitress who had served us – fruit then as rare as that guarded by the Hesperides. More than one motherly figure (waiters and younger waitresses all doing National Service) looked fondly after us as we left, convinced we were home after enemy-destroying voyagings, Bridle not discouraging the illusion. What wartime restaurant makeshifts did we eat? More to the point, what did we drink? Details have gone, but I associate the struggle to Euston in the blackout with euphoria, and in the train we took charge of an empty first-class compartment, pulling down the blinds, tying together with a scarf the handles of the centre-opening doors that gave on to the corridor. Before the train departed, a few individuals (whether first-class ticket holders or frauds like ourselves, who knows?) challenged this uncanny reservation of accommodation, but the scarf held, and no official appeared. We stretched out opposite each other on the seating, and slept. Blackpool was reached in the early morning, Bridle having departed a station or two before. Miraculously, there was a workman's tram outside the station. Anticipation sustained the carrying of the unwieldy baggage the tidy step from the nearest tram stop to the house overlooking Happy Valley. My mother-in-law, not yet dressed, let me in. Kate and Johnny were still in their beds, so I went up to them.

8 ASVX

In my absence my wife and son had been having a thin time. Tonsillectomies were still fashionable, and my mother (perhaps forgetting the operation on me had been twice unsuccessful) persuaded Kate to follow medical advice and submit Johnny to the knife – not, as in my latter case, on the friendly dining table but in the strangeness of a nursing home. A far, far worse subsequent ordeal was the poisoning of his whole system immediately following the extraction of a tooth under gas. For a week he subsisted on glucose and water, his life at issue.

These events, rationing, the strain of being a lodger in the house she had been brought up in and grown out of, told on Kate's health. On my foreign-service leave we had little notion of what my movements were to be. Presumably I should have to do a course as a commissioned officer or probationary such, but where I knew not. In the way of the Services, things were not much clearer to me then than they are now, forty years after. Plainly, for safety and convenience Kate and Johnny would have to soldier on in Blackpool, though we talked about looking for accommodation of their own, extremely hard to come by in a town where the RAF was trained and to which Ministries had been evacuated. At least Johnny was happy at the kindergarten

I myself (and my brother, and, indeed, Marston) had attended twenty years before. Though the headmistress of my time, the powerfully refined Miss Moorhouse, was dead, the school was run (an odd effect of time, it now seems) by two mistresses who had taught me – Miss Proctor and Miss Arnott, both sterling characters, whose visages and physique I can clearly summon up as in the days, not merely of my son's wearing the white blouse and horizontally striped black and white tie, but also of my own. Miss Proctor had been music mistress when I attended; as joint proprietor took in more general things. She said to Kate, of my son, aged five or six, that he was almost *too* bright, merited the best possible education; not the only memory of her insight.

Returning to Lee after foreign-service leave, I went straight on to an overflow camp at nearby Bedhampton, presumably the overflow established at Seafield Park having itself overflowed. The war had changed from a somewhat amateur affair on Britain's part – the spirit of the game, good losers, and all that – to an affair she was going to help to win. The transformation had been brought home one day by the appearance in the Cape Town transit camp of a body of Commandos (term then quite novel and strange), lumpen-proletarian barbarians, as they seemed, actually carrying knives. Even the standards of war could deteriorate over the years – or so I had thought, as their great boots and loud voices, and red, boily faces arrived in the mess, and dominated it. Despite such experiences, I suppose I never entirely lost the sense that the frightful transit camp at Liverpool, troopships themselves, mines, killing and maiming one's fellow men, were aberrations; that the war could be won or outlasted simply through endurance. Of course, my verse reflects the hopelessness and horrors of armed conflict: the nine sonnets I wrote in that December of 1943 at Bedhampton – a new camp of Nissen huts along a bleak road out of Portsmouth – are still evidence of that, perhaps too much so. When I reprinted the sonnets in my *Collected Poems* of 1962 I made some revisions that I see now are not all beneficial, though whether that is of the slightest interest I do not know, finding the sequence difficult to judge. It is full of notions that went on preoccupying me (such as the feeling in and behind the more sordid departments of existence) but previous Marxist beliefs (such as the inevitable though painful birth of a new society) have ceased to be presented in any simple or straightforward way, or so it seems to me.

Characteristic life at Bedhampton is indicated in the sonnets by references to stoves in the mess, a ramshackle canteen, lights coming on in a shabby cinema, and my working party hacking with rusty sickles the grass and withered weeds of summer. Though *infra dig* for a PO, I did some hacking myself to alleviate boredom, keep myself warm, and doubtless to demonstrate human equality, despite the sequence taking a pretty cool view of humanity. The camp had not yet developed the size or tradition for daily duties to include interesting items like the servicing of boats or monkeys. But I was not there long, being soon sent on a course, with other PO radar mechanics, to HMS *Ariel*, a shore establishment near Warrington in Lancashire. Apropos my commission, I am not sure whether it was from Bedhampton or Warrington I travelled to London for a Board. I saw a civilian, Mr Brundritt, quite a famous name in his field, who had come up from the Royal Aircraft Establishment at Farnborough. It seemed to me I did not pass through his questioning very well, or at all. Even those better than I at the craft or mystery of radar might have been hard put to it to discuss theoretical matters so long after passing out as a Leading Hand, and with the limited experience subsequently gained. I would have emerged better from a test on the history of East African exploration, even on tropical disease. I believe Mr Brundritt gave no indication either of success or failure, and that I joined, or returned to, HMS *Ariel* still speculative as to destiny.

At any rate, it was as a PO I first went to *Ariel*. The place was remarkable evidence of what could be achieved by an organization that had not hitherto impressed with its alacrity. In November 1941, as Class 1 of FAA trainee radar mechanics, we sat in a Nissen hut at HMS *Daedalus* twiddling our thumbs till the equipment arrived. Now, two years later, a whole establishment existed for the purpose. *Ariel* (one imagines the name chosen by him who chose *Daedalus*, some littérateur of the Admiralty) had been a remand centre, the huts of which had presumably been greatly added to, and brick edifices built. Swarms of young PO instructors, by appearance all grammar school swots, had been bred to train the greater swarms of erks, from whose ranks most of the POs had emerged without their setting a foot outside *Ariel*. Above the POs were numbers of "schoolies", RN schoolmasters, who had got up the theory of radio and radar equipment as though it were some traditional intellectual discipline. At the apex of this pyramid, the Commander Training, was none other than Gleave, whom I had seen arrive as a brand-new sub-lieutenant RNVR at *Daedalus*, and who had put on weight with his extra stripes, even a touch of premature greyness adding to the new dignity.

There was at once an antagonism between the class of POs arrived to start their course, perhaps the first such class, certainly an early one, of POs who had seen service at sea or abroad, and the barrack stanchions of *Ariel*. Even their uniforms differed: as in my own case, POs returned from service had put up gold cap-badges and brass buttons without waiting for their year of acting rank to expire; the resident POs correctly retained their red cap-badges and black buttons. Trouble blew up the first morning. After breakfast, one of the *Ariel* POs (perhaps PO of the day) arrived at the hut where the newly arrived POs were lodged, and ordered it to be swept by the occupants. Shock horror! When had POs ever in naval history wielded a broom? As soon as it was plain the order was going to be ignored, the PO disappeared, and there subsequently entered some officer, probably officer of the day, to whom the PO had evidently sneaked, in the traditional manner of swots. A longish argument ensued, but it was quickly seen that, quite apart from the question of any individual blotting his CW candidature, the position was untenable, for *Ariel* was so stuffed with POs menial tasks were bound to fall to them.

Two strange memories remain of that quite large hut full of POs. The first is of the most persistent and outré snoring I have ever heard, beside which Mrs Parslew's cheese-induced rhoncal sounds (not that I ever heard them), celebrated enough, would have surely been insignificant. The *Ariel* perpetrator was a small, weedy fellow, unnoticeable by day. He was a good sleeper and retired early, so that the initially alarming spluttering and gasping, pretty well continuous, disturbed the first part as well as the dead of night. At the start, one could rely on his neighbours shouting or shaking him out of sleep, for some relief to ensue. But eventually these, better sleepers than I, dropped off, and one was reduced to throwing shoes and paperbacks and suchlike at his bed when exasperation rose too high to be choked back, missiles of limited availability and which had to be searched for next morning. Two or three had been shipmates of his; confirmed the notoriety of his habit. A complaint was put in and I seem to recall acted on, though where solitary, snore-proof accommodation could have been found is mysterious.

The other memory is of lying on my bed (the top one of a two-tier affair, always the better bet) cutting and reading the pages of *The Golden Bowl.* The two volumes of the second impression of the 1923 Macmillan edition, new, pages unopened, had been given to me for my birthday by Kate's brother, Colin. They had probably been obtained by the conscientious Blackpool bookshop, Sweeten's, from the publisher's stock; days of the availability and procurement of serious books of the past not yet vanished. My immediate pre-war enthusiasm for Henry James was by no means exhausted, but I marvel now at the pertinacity that drove me through those tough pages in surroundings so inimical. In the process of writing this I get down the very volumes from the shelf and blow the dust off the tops (for I never re-read them, nor surely ever shall) and open the first at the first page of Henry's preface:

> Among many matters thrown into relief by a refreshed acquaintance with *The Golden Bowl* what perhaps most stands out for me is the still marked inveteracy of a certain indirect and oblique view of my presented action; unless indeed I make up my mind to call this mode of treatment, on the contrary, any superficial appearance notwithstanding, the very straightest and closest possible.

Then follow the often-quoted words about seeing a story "through the opportunity and the sensibility of some more or less detached, . . . though thoroughly interested and intelligent, witness." How the thing brings back my ancient fictive ambitions! Why did I never attempt narration through the sensibility of a detached observer? It might have offset several disadvantages I had as a novelist. And how far indeed is the "story" of the present work told thus! Disturbed by the thought of these memoirs falling abysmally short of Jamesian technique (to specify merely one aspect of the business), I take from another shelf his unfinished book, *The Middle Years* (which the flyleaf says I bought in July 1940), and open that to remind myself of the way the Master tackled *his* autobiography:

> If the author of this meandering record has noted elsewhere [*Notes of a Son and Brother*] that an event occurring early in 1870 was to mark the end of his youth, he is moved here at once to qualify in one or two respects that emphasis.

> Everything depends in such a view on what one means by one's youth – so shifting a consciousness is this, and so related at the same time to many different matters. We are never old, that is we never cease easily to be young, for *all* life at the same time: youth is an army, the whole battalion of our faculties and our freshnesses, our passions and our illusions, on a considerably reluctant march into the enemy's country, the country of the general lost freshness; and I think it throws out at least as many stragglers behind as skirmishers ahead . . .

One might add, to give Henry's metaphor a literal connotation, that when I first visited her parents' house, Kate's brother was little more than an infant. Before I left *Ariel*, he was to arrive there as a National Serviceman of youngest age, opting on his call-up for the path I had taken, clearer than most in promising promotion and intellectual activity of a kind. He is now an eminent City Chartered Accountant, CBE, transformation achieved through mere talent and hard work. Our skirmishing in *Ariel* days would surely have seen dignities of such a kind falling only to the *ci-devant* Sub-Lieutenant Gleave and the like, men of visibly increasing ponderability; our straggling still in bijou Happy Valley – view of life perhaps little changed.

Besides the multiplicity of buildings and personnel constituting HMS *Ariel*, it also offered a new version of ASV – "ASVX" – the mysteries of which I think I am right in saying constituted the main feature of the POs' course I was on. Wavelengths had got still shorter: moreover, cybernetic principles had been ingeniously applied to enable radar to "lock on" to a target, device commonplace now, then a remarkable novelty. The best of the schoolies lectured on this latter development: his description was lucid, gradually unfolding the secret of the electronic machinery that without human intervention enabled the directional wireless waves to track a moving object. When suspense was at its height, I cried out: "I can't bear it!" – characteristic desire, in and out of season, to amuse. Neither cathartic laughter nor my implied tribute left the schoolie best pleased, but he recaptured his audience in brilliant style, so no harm was done.

Ariel was midway between Warrington and Leigh. The former I never grew to care for in any way: set in the great Gromboolian plain of south-east Lancashire, its air seemingly perpetually gritty, it did not satisfy any nostalgia for the industrial north I then possessed, remote in aspect as it was from the green moorland roped with walls glimpsed from Oldham streets, or (the reverse view) red factory chimneys hazing built-up valleys. I preferred Leigh, usually went there on shore leave, though it was only a small, dark, colliery town. The Salvation Army had added to the sparse amenities by opening a canteen in a tin chapel or church hall at the end of an alley; modest in size and comfort but offering some unusually good delicacy, I think sausages. In both towns I patronized any cinema showing a film not positively awful, and sniffed out emporiums with books to sell.

No more than sleeping ashore, watch off, was possible, so to give us more time together Kate and Johnny sometimes came for a Saturday night in Warrington, conveniently on the Blackpool to London main line. We stayed at a non-licensed hotel in the suburbs of Warrington, perhaps becaue of its readily available accommodation, how discovered now mysterious. Memorable, the linoleum on the dining room floor; high tea in the early evening, normally boiled ham (more likely spam, an American import by then despised, subject of comedians' jests, but to me a novelty, thought not bad at all, dried egg in the same category). After that, the patient Johnny would be put to bed, and Kate and I depart for the local pub until the evening ration of short drinks ran out, a period more prolonged than in the central Warrington pubs handy for the thirsty circumadjacent American Army and RAF bases. One marvels at the hope and affection sustaining such crude amusements, so far from one's ideals of domesticity and absorption in art. Even large and superficially quite efficient organizations reveal, when well-known, improvisatory and fallible parts. The sketchy and tenuous nature of small hotels in wartime was almost immediately apparent, but in the end one was always duly thankful for the shelter and sustenance, however odd, that facilitated continuation of private life, however caricatured, when existence was dominated by the State.

A photograph exists, taken by a street photographer near the Charing Cross station of the Southern Railway (as it then was), of Kate, Johnny and me striding along in winter garb. I am still wearing a PO's cap (with gold badge) and pusser's greatcoat. The folder under my arm indicates the occasion: I am off to deliver the typescript of my third book of poems, *A Lost Season*, to the Hogarth Press in the person of John Lehmann at his flat in Carrington House, Shepherd's Market. Plainly I was on leave of some sort, Kate and Johnny down from Blackpool; I would conjecture all of us staying with the ever-hospitable Kathleen and Julian Symons in St George's Square, Pimlico, at the very top of stairs always surprising by their prolongation of flights, as in a work by Piranesi. In his *Notes From Another Country*, Julian dates their moving into the St George's Square flat as January 1944, he by then invalided out of the Army. Emerging from the Strand seems a bit of jigsaw crammed into the wrong place: fitted properly, I expect other parts of the picture might have to be slightly altered.

While I was in Africa, Kate had been in constant touch by letter with John, sending him typed versions of poems and so forth, but on one memorable occasion he arrived by taxi at her parents' house and subsequently took her to the Blackpool Opera House (where there was a week's ballet) to see Beryl Gray and Alexis Rassine in *Swan Lake*. "Built like a carthorse," said John approvingly of the young Beryl Gray. What he said of Blackpool has not come down. His taxi would have driven along the road that divided Sparrow Park and Happy Valley, but getting on for forty years were to elapse before my memoirs enshrined them. Very tall and handsome, his light brown hair little if at all touched with grey, marked features, pale blue eyes that would narrow less from the smoke of his holdered cigarette clenched in strong jaws than a silent questioning of artistic or other opinions, John was a figure in several aspects quite formidable, scarcely to be envisaged in Blackpool at all, incongruous there through both character and personal history. His ancestry went deep into Victorian letters; his early youth was associated with both Bloomsbury and the Auden School; his sisters were already ornaments of the contemporary theatre and novel. Yet no apparent barrier of class or milieu ever stood in the way of his editorial quest for new imaginative art and literature, or of the bestowal of his friendship. Now I have known him so long, I would want particularly to emphasize his sense of comedy – never, alas, quite to find an adequate outlet in his works (though in recent years he has written well about Lear's and other nonsense) – always lurking, ready to break out into laughter and comment about political, literary and human folly. Such a strong sense, of course, presupposes sharp judgements.

He had written to Kate that he must hold a party for me when I returned from abroad. The portage of *The Lost Season* typescript may well have been to that very function. I wonder now whether I had gained, during the half-dozen years that separated this party from the rather more haphazard one, also in my honour, organized by the editor of *Twentieth Century Verse*, increased know-how in expressing gratitude. I doubt it, but on the second occasion I expect Kate would cover deficiencies, for both she and Johnny attended, the latter making a quiet hit.

Could the proceedings have started with tea, merged into early evening drinks? I would like to see a roster of the guests: it might restore one of those set pieces of past life in which one was too involved, however, to have brought away more than an odd room corner or piece of anatomy. Three men I feel sure were there. Stephen Spender was one, his poetry loved by me, his political attitudes more or less reviled, for upwards of a dozen years. This must have been our first meeting, but not for me the surprise expressed by another "war poet", Timothy Corsellis:

> I had expected
> That your body would have been small
> Indeed it was necessary for you to be small
> Stature in contrast with ability.

Though as in another existence, it was only a few years since I had absorbed Isherwood's *Lions and Shadows*, where he is unforgettably portrayed as Stephen Savage, "immensely tall". What made the most impression in actuality was the voice, as for me it has continued to do, the marked sibilants perhaps stemming from his maternal German ancestry. Philip Toynbee was another guest. I admired his novel *A School in Private*, may have told him so. For a few years thereafter, without being "friends", we knew each other, would speak, accidentally meeting in bars or bus queues, but even that slight relationship faded, as faded – or, rather, changed into something quite bizarre, so it seemed to me – the talent that had produced the early novels. My relationship with him was fairly typical of relations with a good few whose background and *modus vivendi* were on a higher social (and intellectual, come to that) level than my own, though shyness and my indolence about personal relations (and much else in life) enter the matter just as much. In one sense, the situation was not unlike the difficulties I found in getting on with the working class in political days of the early Thirties, and, in fact, in the Andrew – as witness encounters with such as Toscanini and Ivanskavinski Skavar. Between more or less high falutin small talk and the expletive-studded account of mere events, there is (or at any rate used to be) an area of communication occupied by the lower middle classes characterized by irony, decency and unpretentiousness, and that was what I was used to by birth and upbringing. But I should add, about Stephen, that from then on we met at irregular intervals, sometimes of literary collaboration or social intimacy, without, to our mutual regret, ever really becoming close friends; all the worse for me since few, with a phrase from tongue or pen, can amuse me more.

The third remembered figure at the flat in Carrington House, and seen on subsequent similar occasions, puzzled me for quite a time: a sturdy middle-aged man not above medium height; noticeable spectacles, large head made to look even larger by the thick, straight, grey-streaked hair, despite its being well parted and brilliantined down. Major Morris was the name I eventually correctly attached to him, wondering if he wasn't a financial backer of the Hogarth Press or character from the printing world. In the end, I saw quite a bit of him, for he turned out to work for the BBC, then, or soon, head of its Far Eastern Service, for which I used to broadcast at the fag end of the war and for some time thereafter. He had been in the First War, served afterwards in India as a regular soldier: dress and manner, as well as age, marked him off from the Spenders and Toynbees, but between us was little more than the gentle bantering established with BBC figures seen regularly in the way of business. When I read his *Living With Leptchas* I greatly admired it, but whether I told him so is even more doubtful than in the case of *A School in Private*.

A Lost Season (its title came from Donne's Elegie XII: "His Parting From Her") must have been published no more than six months or so after the party, timescale commercial publishers should ponder today. Following the modest but surprising success of *The Middle of a War*, its reception disappointed me, an emotion of publication often to be repeated. Even in the New Stanley lounge, better stuff seemed to be emerging, and at the time of its going through the press it struck me as a stronger book than its predecessor, though the extent of the revisions I made in some of the pieces for my 1962 *Collected Poems* indicated the depth of later dissatisfaction; again, a common sequence of events.

However, when I look in my old cuttings book I see that the reviews of *A Lost Season* were almost without exception friendly, some remarkably generous. As so often, the remark applies that was made by Arnold Bennett in a letter to J. B. Priestley: "Like all authors, I feel deeply convinced that I am not understood as completely as my amazing merits deserve." Perhaps disappointment stemmed mainly, if not solely, from a notice, one of the first, by C. Day Lewis, which began with a kind word but failed to keep going in that vein, much preferring Laurie Lee's *The Sun My Monument*, published by the Hogarth Press at the same time as *A Lost Season* and with which the latter was usually reviewed. I may well have known then that Day Lewis and Laurie Lee were colleagues at the Ministry of Information, and so suspected favouritism. I had biffed Day Lewis in one or two pre-war reviews, thus may have been lucky to get the kind word, for some littérateurs have long memories. Both Laurie and Cecil may have been at the Carrington House party: the former I soon came to know quite well, the latter not until long after the war, when he and his wife, Jill Balcon, became neighbours. By that time I was able to judge his work freed from period and theoretical prejudice: for his part, he had established himself more comfortably in the intervening years as, in a sense, a pre-Auden poet – certainly using his own clear voice, without Audenesque ventriloquial turns, probably aided in this by Jill's own clear voice, too.

I was a fair way into the POs' course at *Ariel* before my promotion to Sub-Lieutenant (A) RNVR arrived, with instructions to report to Portsmouth a week or two hence. Another PO was involved in a similar transaction. We were sent on leave instantly, as though the solecism of officers in lower deck uniform and conditions could not be borne by the Andrew. Indeed, the change in status had been marked from the start by the matter being dealt with not by the Jaunty's office but the Captain's – our summoning there effected by the Captain's Messenger, blend of classical and Kafkaesque rolé I myself had once played. On this occasion it inclined towards resembling a supernumerary of the gods (in benign mood), impression augmented by an office complement of white-shirted Wrens amiably serving up railway warrants, advice, etc.

The pieces of paper they handed out embodying our instructions emphasized in terms a nitwit could not misunderstand that if officer's uniform was not by then possessed, one must report to Portsmouth in plain clothes. My leave was spent in Blackpool, and it never occurred to me to try to get uniform off the peg or even find a tailor who might run the essential items up in the few days available. I knew, probably from their advertisement in the preliminary pages of Volume 1 of the *Manual of Seamanship*, issued to all ratings on joining, that Gieves, the ancient naval tailors, had an emporium in Portsmouth, and that was where I intended to go.

Some of the officer entry at Portsmouth were complete sprogs – Gleaves of the day, brought in straight from university or industry to stiffen up the technical side of the Andrew. Others had gone through basic general training, but little more, their commissions having caught up with them betimes. Still others were old sweats, or relatively so, among whom I counted myself. Immediately, one was back on the parade ground, in the gymnasium, the swimming bath, as in *Ganges*. My experience of squad drill stood me in good stead at Portsmouth, since the emphasis of the short course was on the inculcation of the power of command. I was not displeased with my parade ground performance, but one day, momentarily halted as we marched round in single file (possibly in that order for some such manoeuvre, needing no practice in my case, as saluting, eyes right or left), the officer drilling us came irritably up to me: "Haven't you got your uniform yet?"

"No."

"At least you've no need to wear that hat."

"I thought it would be appropriate, for the salute and so forth."

"Not at all."

I am not sure that the reason given for wearing a headdress was entirely honest. Since I could not swank in uniform, there was an urge to appear as incongruous as possible, disguising, too, previous parade-ground experience – a sort of hustler instinct. Besides, I had inherited from my maternal grandfather a strong habit of wearing hats, funny ones included. I should say, however, that on the parade ground I refrained from wearing the poetic-lawyer's overcoat. Kipling almost had the appropriate words in his "Back to the Army Again":

> I'm 'ere in a ticky ulster an' a broken billycock 'at,
> A-layin' on to the sergeant I don't know a gun from a bat;
> My shirt's doin' duty for jacket, my sock's stickin' out o'
> my boots,
> An' I'm learnin' the damned old goose-step along o' the
> new recruits!

I had been measured at Gieves on The Hard by a tailor of the old school who may well have so served those engaged in the action off the Mole at Zeebrugge, the sideshow representation of which had so terrified me as a child. "Watch-coat or greatcoat, sir?" I hesitated only fractionally: "Greatcoat." I was in doubt whether a watch-coat (a shorter affair, cut on the lines of a British "warm") would satisfy every sartorial demand of the Andrew – an Admiral's visit, say, or an Armistice Day parade. On the other hand, if one could get away with the garment on all occasions, it would, with a substitution of buttons and removal of epaulettes, serve quite well for the eventual return to civilian life. But thrift of that kind, even with a nature inclined to parsimony, was outweighed by the desire to make the maximum impression in naval officer's uniform, and that, to my then way of thinking, required the half-belt and pleat at the back, the mid-calf length, the general Erich Von Stroheim effect, of the greatcoat.

I transferred to the hero of *The Perfect Fool* some of my preoccupation and anxiety about the greatcoat and other items of uniform, when actually acquired. Tempting to go into the matter again, but I can hardly expect from others an interest approaching my own. Gieves made me two uniform suits: a "working" suit in serge, and a "best" in more expensive material, probably barathea. Oddly enough, like the jumper of the square rig Number Twos issued to me at *Ganges*, the working jacket was cut somewhat too loosely at the waist and hips, but somehow the opportunity never came to have it altered, and it nagged me slightly till the end. (Yet as I write this it occurs to me that the generosity of cut in the working jacket may have been deliberate, a Gieves tradition to allow greater freedom of movement in such activities as scrambling on to the Zeebrugge Mole.) Another regret was the gold braid round the cuffs. One says "round", but that was the botheration: regulations had been made that, to save braid, stripes (in my case, one) should go only half-way round. Those commissioned before the regulations had satisfactory full circles; a few had illicitly acquired the same: I had to put up with what always seemed an indication of rank more appropriate to a banana republic navy than the Andrew.

Like Chatham had been, Portsmouth was, of course, grossly overcrowded. I slept in a former hotel on the front at Southsea, requisitioned by the RN, atmosphere of former modest comfort, present near-subsistence existence, familiar to everyone doomed to such places during the war, most aspects brilliantly recaptured fictionally by Waugh and Powell. Fortunately, meals were taken in the splendid Portsmouth wardroom, resembling a great provincial club. The building was red-brick, perhaps Edwardian, opposite the main gates of the barracks: holding one's pink gin in the anteroom, the various forms of lower-deck life could be seen swarming out on errands of pleasure and duty, bringing back one's Chatham days in a mist of *Schadenfreude*. The food was excellent. On entering the dining room one asked a steward on charge of a bank of pigeonholes for one's napkin, giving the number of the napkin ring (the same as its pigeonhole) assigned to one on joining the mess – alliance of gentlemanliness and catering-check possibly dating back even before Zeebrugge. Though there was a choice of pudding as of every other course, always on the menu at lunch time were cold prunes and rice: the former plump, in an exiguous but flavoursome juice; the latter not a traditional rice pudding, the grains more articulated, though tender. As I thought about the Portsmouth course, just preparatory to writing about it here, the foregoing delicacy came to mind and, quite moved, I worked it into a sonnet sequence then being composed:

The creamy rice, the prune juice rich as blood.

Even breakfast was taken in the wardroom. I remember dressing in the little hotel bedroom the morning after I had picked up or (I rather think) Gieves had efficiently delivered the final garment enabling me to appear in the role of naval officer. There was difficulty with the stiff, double collar, an item not worn since as a boy at Seafolde House I had graduated from the Eton jacket that had involved an Eton collar (with black bow tie on a stud) to a Marlborough jacket accompanied by stiff, double collar and ordinary black tie – Sunday wear for boarders. The most effective sequence of operations (opening the collar, affixing it to the back stud in the shirt collar, laying the tie along it, closing the collar while it was horizontally extended, etc) came back like riding a bicycle, initial clumsiness soon wearing off. The trouble was getting the knot of the tie to stay in the apex where the collar ends met. I had acquired the collars in the officers' section of pusser's stores, where they were dramatically cheaper than in the shops, but they proved to be cut too high, with non-existent tie-apertures – another Zeebrugge hangover. Once again, parsimony was shown not to pay in the long run. I fairly quickly bought some collars more conveniently and fashionably cut away, but not until I was able to go to Simpson's in Piccadilly was the problem satisfactorily solved: that excellent shop sold stiff collars cut low at the front with long points, very tony, and with an aperture of perhaps as much as three-quarters of an inch into which the tie knot would slide and be retained.

That winter's morning, walking in the dark from the hotel to the stop where a trolley bus could be caught to the wardroom, one felt like a waxwork rather than the juvenile star of a West End naval comedy previously envisaged. The pristine rigidity of the cap, the deficient collar's chill accentuated by the sea air, the embrace of two double-breasted garments, the general hollow insubstantiality of going unbreakfasted into the world – these had most to do with the disappointing first entry in costume, not that such egotistical pleasures can ever come up to expectation.

I was certainly in uniform, maybe just as well to be out of a green overcoat and brown trilby, however dark, when after a session in the swimming bath the members of the course were hanging about, waiting for the laggards in dressing to join them so that all could go together to the locale of the next item on the programme. At the other end of the bath there appeared, half inevitably, half surprisingly, like some minor Dickens character, the familiar figure of the short, dark, muscular young officer who almost two years before I had noted with jealous displeasure lording it over the gymnasium at *Ganges*. In the interim he had put up another stripe. With him were some foreign officers, plainly on a tour of inspection. Quite soon (though after a lapse of time sufficient for him to have made a farewell, most likely a temporary one, to his party) he came along the side of the bath and confronted us.

"Who is in charge of you officers?"

One of us (juvenile, mild, deputed to see us on time for – perhaps march us to – our ensuing engagement) spoke up: "I am."

"Haven't you been told yet to say 'Sir' when addressing a superior officer?"

Even to a sprog, the novelty of one stripe sirring two would have been extreme.

"Yes, sir."

Lieutenant Hercules, I dare say encouraged by imagining us all to be newly joined, and by the easy technical back door, then proceeded to administer a thorough ballocking. We had been lounging about, hands in pockets, chattering, implanting in representatives of the Allied Powers doubts as to the smartness and efficiency of the Royal Navy, not least about the quality of its new recruits. He was minded to report our behaviour to the proper quarters. How pleasing to me the evidence that the shit in manner was a shit in action! Afterwards, I commiserated with our temporary class leader, disclosing Hercules's cockiness of yore.

Since writing the foregoing I have turned up a booklet which for years I have known lurked near the bottom of a perennially uncleared letter tray in my study. It is the Pamphlet on Officers' Divisional Course handed to us on arrival at what I see is identified as "St John's School, RN Barracks, Portsmouth". I am tempted to reproduce the five aims of the course, printed at the start, but perhaps they can be sufficiently imagined. After them are the following sentences:

> To implement the above, lectures are given, brief summaries of which are found in the pages following.
> Squad Drill, Physical Training, Swimming Lessons to Non-Swimmers, and ARP duties also find their places in the course.

The swimming bath visit may well have been merely for the purpose of the instructors there identifying any non-swimmers.

Judging by the length of the pamphlet, we must have heard a good few lectures during the fortnight. The atmosphere was less that of *Ganges* than of Gibson & Weldon, the law crammers I attended when an articled clerk – those lecturers aspiring to humour being sophisticated performers, like L. Crispin Warmington at Gibson's, their jokes far from those perpetrated by, say, the rifle drill PO at *Ganges*. One of them (a tall, dark RNVR Lieutenant, said to have been in advertising) was good enough for the stage, as they say. I see him, for instance, freezing in the middle of a rhetorical gesture to observe his upraised arm with surprise, and pulling it down to modest normality with the other hand.

One page of the pamphlet consists solely of these words:

Handling, loading, working and sighting of following arms is explained:-

Revolver
Thompson Sub MG
Lanchester
Sten Gun
Description of Mark 36 grenade and sticky bomb

The entry brings back what I had completely forgotten – the day spent at the Gunnery School on Whale Island, a place of desolation surely in the best weather, on that drizzling day piercingly cold. A packed lunch was involved, eaten in some milieu of discomfort, if not the open air. As in all arms training, there was more hanging about than firing weapons. I recall shooting off a .303 revolver and lobbing a grenade, but guess the other items unavailable or not reached in the time; again, a common enough situation. It strikes me (maybe struck me then) how preposterous the notion behind the day – that I should use the implements against a living target. The preposterousness would have been increased had the more gangsterish guns been in my hands. I had never been a pacifist, but of course by then it was unlikely I should be called on to fire a weapon in anger. I suppose now, if I were still of an age to be called up, I would declare a conscientious objection to killing, and sweat that position out – though the question arises, in a not dissimilar realm, why one is not a practising vegetarian. To return, after all, to those "aims" of the course, perhaps they may be thought remarkable in never mentioning aggressiveness or the like. Naval customs and a sense of comradeship; good discipline and welfare; powers of command and leadership, and (most remarkable of all) encouraging an "ideal" (inverted commas *sic*) in life and the ambition to live up to it – these are what are hoped to be taught during the fortnight. Again, some lines of Kipling – staggering poet – are not too wide of the mark:

> The Doorkeepers of Zion,
> They do not always stand
> In helmet and whole armour,
> With halberds in their hand;
> But, being sure of Zion,
> And all her mysteries,
> They rest awhile in Zion,
> Sit down and smile in Zion,
> Ay, even jest in Zion,
> In Zion, at their ease.

Soon I was back at *Ariel*, embarked on the officers' course, even longer than the POs' course left uncompleted, since it comprised every radar and radio set used in the Fleet Air Arm. Among our numbers now were Wren officers, as novel as undergraduettes in olden days; also, Wodehousian style mingling with Dickensian coincidence, Peter Lavender, with a second stripe up like the pocket Hercules. Initially it was odd to encounter him again on equal social terms, just as it was to move in the heights of *Ariel*, such as they were, after serving below stairs. No risk, even as a mere Temporary Sub-Lieutenant, to be required to sweep the mess deck; indeed, I had a tiny cabin to myself, though on the whole slept no better.

9 *DAE*

Like Dr Johnson's Rasselas, my wife longed to escape from Happy Valley. Or, rather, as already indicated, from her parents' house that overlooked the former concave haunt of the pierrots of our childhood. During the Blitz any old port in a storm was endurable. Then, for the first part of my National Service, being mobile with a firm base worked out not too badly. But during my time abroad a place of her own grew to be the sole desideratum: in Blackpool such accommodation was almost as scarce as bananas, for the reasons given. As in many facets of tolerable wartime existence, some illegality had to be embarked on, and Kate enlisted the help of the wife of Rod Davies, her former colleague on the local newspaper, encountered by me with full coincidental force at *Ganges*. Rod's wife had also been a colleague, still worked as telephonist, and she undertook to tell Kate, before the paper appeared, of any likely accommodation offered in the small ads section. At once, by lucky chance, Kate secured a furnished flat. Strangely, the house of which it was a part also overlooked Happy Valley, the longer side of its rectangular shape, so the municipal putting course and garden, of which it now tamely consisted, once again began to live up to their ancient name.

The accommodation had been described as a flat, but in fact was scattered throughout a house by no means large. Of course, Kate and Johnny were soon familiar with its tenantry and topography, but to me, a not too frequent visitor, some mystery always remained. The house was owned by Mrs Rosewell, a quite elderly widow: plumpish, white-haired, agreeable, a certain air of scattiness; perhaps had been pretty in her youth. Also in the house, on what terms I know not, was her younger sister, Mrs Slate, also a widow, whether true or grass perhaps in doubt. Mrs Slate could never have been pretty: she came from a bigger and coarser mould than her sister, gave a hint of a man in drag, a pantomime dame. As so often in sisterly relationships (Joan Crawford and Bette Davies in *Whatever Happened to Baby Jane?* come to mind), the underdog, so to speak, dominated. Mrs Slate's dependence on her sister's bounty did not inhibit her from throwing her weight about, and argumentative exchanges were even sometimes heard from those parts of the house retained for the sisters' use (exiguous parts, it must be said, for Mrs Rosewell slept in their kitchen and Mrs Slate in a, or the, bathroom).

On the first floor was the apartment rented by Mrs Cartwright; sometimes with her, presumably when he could get leave, a member of the Polish forces in England whose name was not, of course, Cartwright. As a matter of fact, the consonantal excesses of East European nomenclature often led to anonymity, certainly among Blackpudlians, never noted for articulation – a deficiency particularly deplored by my old headmaster, the Boss. "Mrs (or Miss) So-and-so's Pole" might be the only identity given, as though an inanimate object were in question. Mrs

Cartwright was nice, industrious, rose early, gave Kate and Johnny a knock, and was out working all day.

The rest of the house's accommodation was occupied by Mr and Mrs Denton and their small child. A good deal older than his wife, he was the type of *rentier* perhaps even then dying out. He was plainly able to afford the price of a furnished flat, a lavish supply of gin, and a habit of eating out. He seemed to have no occupation or hobby beyond this odd version of family life, though procuring sufficient gin in those austere days may have passed much of his time. Boozing led to detectable marital disharmony, or *vice versa* – voices and sounds heard from behind closed doors, tappings on which and pleas to be admitted sometimes taking place in the night. When, more than twenty-five years later, I wanted in *The Carnal Island* to suggest marriage's hidden strangeness I remembered the Dentons' bedroom door.

Mrs Slate may have had some sort of job – she would have made a good barmaid in the rougher sort of pub – but Mrs Rosewell simply lived on the income from her house, as though it were an oil well. A good part of her mornings was occupied with studying the runners and riders, and preparing her betting slip for the day, items of which might be as modest as a sixpenny treble. I came as much as I did into the life of the house – a life suitable for depiction in one of those stage sets where the removal of an exterior wall reveals incongruous though occasionally related activity – because now I was commissioned I usually found it possible to get away from *Ariel* early on Saturday and return on Sunday evening. The manoeuvre was illegal, for sleeping out was not permitted, but of course no pass or watch-card was demanded of officers at the gate, so it was simply a question of walking in and out. The ostensible innocence of that operation I maintained by keeping a set of shaving things, pyjamas, and the like, at the flat, and going through the gate simply with a book under my arm. The latter part of Saturday morning instruction conveniently consisted of an inspection of the radio and radar actually installed in various specimen aircraft ranged round the parade ground, the demonstrator a mere NCO. Tearing myself from the spectacle of black-stockinged Wren legs, revealed by the necessary scrambling in and out of the crates, I would walk purposefully away from the group, as though taken short or keeping an appointment with the Chief Writer about income tax. Success made my departure get more brazenly early. But one is inclined to forget the toil and anxiety attending wartime journeyings. A bus had to be caught into Warrington, other military establishments fortunately farther down the road – the full bus passing disconsolate airmen. The fast train to Blackpool usually meant standing in the corridor; the slow train was abysmally slow, I believe involved a change. Coming back, the Sunday late train missed the last bus; unreliable and much sought after, the taxi that might take one to the camp if one waited long enough outside Warrington's squalid and dimly-lit railway station.

One morning at breakfast time – it must have been 7 June 1944 – I heard the wireless in the anteroom speaking of successful Allied landings in Normandy. It was the long-awaited Second Front, thought by some, probably including me, to have been delayed unduly while Uncle Joe consumed his men and *matériel*. Did one feel guilty that the end of the war in Europe was apparently going to come while one putted at weekends in Happy Valley? Perhaps the *Ariel* course itself, interminable, a real grind, provided any absolution required. Against security regulations, I retained on demobilization a "Sketch Book", so called by the Stationery Office, one of a number used up during the course – a substantial notebook, broader than long, notes on the plain pages, circuit-diagrams and the like on the facing graph pages. I suppose I thought I might one day want to distil it for literary purposes, which indeed I did for the brief lovers' dialogue about the radio altimeter in *The Perfect Fool*. The sketch book contains descriptions of, and setting-up and servicing instructions for, much ordinary radio equipment. As has been seen, I never had anything to do with such equipment as a rating, and on the course found it boring in content and confusing in multiplicity. How could any officer hope to be usefully familiar with its whole range? His practical role would be to consult his notes or the instruction manual should his specialist subordinates ever be up a gum tree. Nevertheless, I see my notes and drawings are surprisingly clear and neat, and of course I had to pass tests on the sets. Radar interested me much more, appealing to the side of my mind that apart from some layman's reading in various sciences had been unexercised since, as sufficiently bragged about in an earlier volume, I left Seafolde House with distinctions in matriculation Mathematics and Additional Mathematics.

In the second part of his autobiography, *I Am My Brother*, John

Lehmann says I returned from East Africa "indefinably suggesting that some inspirational ghost of himself had been left behind." Though it does not do to discount anything said by him about human beings, I never took that remark seriously until this moment, when I wonder why I failed to write anything, or anything that has survived, during that *Ariel* time. However, I must immediately add that however solipsistic these writings make me out to be, I have always considered generalities about one's spiritual state from time to time of little validity, most epochs of one's life requiring one simply to soldier on, anything less landing one in a state utterly foreign to one's being. As to the passage of the many *Ariel* weeks, some account could be constructed by taking thought, but in unprompted memory they are curiously neutral and blank. Most evenings in camp I played bridge, always with the same partner, in civilian life a builder from Macclesfield: short, broad, bespectacled, pipe-smoking. We got on well, but he drew atrocious cards with a regularity that smacked of the paranormal, and we were usually a few shillings down the Swanee; rather like being disconcertingly on the wrong end of the solo school on the voyage from Mombasa. Afterwards, bad sleep – not through worry about bridge losses but the result of several psychosomatic factors, actual or incipient ailments already overmuch dwelt on in these memoirs. In my mind's eye I see through my cabin window the dawn coming up beyond the more or less featureless South Lancashire plain.

Jack Beeching – poet, novelist, historian, Petty Officer – claims to have visited me in my cabin at that epoch, but only by pure imagination do I remember the occasion. We met again after the war and despite his living abroad have kept up a friendship. Why I have not asked him if he retains any non-imaginative details of me at *Ariel* is a question perhaps characteristic of those raised by this narrative in the reflective mind. I went once, to play a few rubbers of bridge, into my young brother-in-law's mess of sprogs, taking off my cap at the entrance to indicate an informal visit; gesture doubtless inculcated by my recent *alma mater*, St John's School, though possibly archetypal, stemming from serials in *Chums* or the *BOP*. Colin told my wife he was greatly impressed by my authoritarian bearing and command at morning Divisions. That provides another glimpse into the *Ariel* emptiness, though since the role was confined to calling a Division to attention and reporting it to the Officer of the Day, the encomium was modest – unless arising from an occasion when I *was* OOD, a slightly larger part.

The course closed with written and practical examinations, the latter puzzling not only to me. Peter Lavender told of his great fortune on finding an imposed *recherché* fault: "I just prodded about with a screwdriver and a piece of wire came up 'boing!'" Soon after, an officer arrived from the Admiralty to interview us about appointments. A first and second choice could be expressed. As so often in the war, I was dead lucky: my first horse, the Admiralty, came home; my alternative, a British-based carrier, never ran – though I think London had already the disadvantage of raids by V-1s, the pilotless jets. With me, when I took up residence in the Paddington Grande Hotel, was the other Admiralty appointee, the Macclesfield builder.

The hotel was in the purlieus of Praed Street, as indicated by the first and only strictly accurate part of its name. I cannot remember the address, nor could I lead anyone to the spot, and the hotel may well have been redeveloped, for no such name appears in the current telephone directory. How we came to choose it is as mysterious as its location. One would have thought arriving from the North, and with my Gibson & Weldon days, we would have fixed on Bloomsbury, also more convenient for Lower Regent Street (we were not assigned to the Admiralty building proper), but some unknown force had drawn us to W2, and to an establishment whose general unsatisfactoriness is exemplified in my memory by American military personnel late at night in the corridors, and a condom floating in a lavatory pan. The Macclesfield builder departed swiftly, finding some serviceman's hostel. (Indeed, he also hated the appointment; soon engineered his return to *Ariel*, where he took charge of a specialist mobile repair unit to which my brother-in-law was eventually drafted, in the incestuous manner of Fleet Air Arm encounters.)

Yet even as I write the foregoing paragraph another memory, prompted by the phrase "some serviceman's hostel", comes vividly to mind – a window open in the summer night looking out over the unbrageousness of Green Park, a high window of Piccadilly premises taken over for the duration as an officers' club, where it was possible to stay quite cheaply for a maximum of a couple of days. It may have been that I had come there from post-course leave in Blackpool, and that the Paddington Grande

Hotel advertised its attractions, with other such places, on the noticeboard. Against this version of history is that I was seemingly not with the Macclesfield builder.

For at the officers' club, bedrooms were shared, and when I went alone to mine in the early evening I saw that the other bed was in use, occupation being most strikingly evidenced by the books on the bedside locker, which included *Penguin New Writing* and more esoteric items of contemporary literature I cannot now put a name to. Some spare clothing or perhaps a mere green suitcase indicated that my fellow occupant was in the Navy, and I actually divined in a matter of moments who he must be, so rigorous were the sieves of literary sophistication and the Andrew. We came in at different times to settle down and sleep, so did not speak until the morning. Typically, I failed to let on that I had guessed his identity until sufficient conversation had elapsed about the things that concerned us both – good poetry, good poets and, with equal discrimination, bad ditto.

My vis-à-vis was then just twenty-two. I suppose in those days one knew the name, had made an assessment, of every contributor to approved (and, indeed, disapproved) magazines, but at that moment there must have been little work of Alan Ross to go on, perhaps only a few poems in *PNW*. I am sure he did not appear in any OK mental list of mine. I probably thought that as well as having still to prove himself he might be, as a member of the next (or even next but one) generation of poets, infected by Neo-Romanticism – to use an omnibus term for all new poetry that disobeyed Geoffrey Grigson's Thirties summation of 1939, and failed to take "notice, for ends not purely individual, of the universe of objects and events." I expect I was to a degree guarded in those preliminary exchanges above Piccadilly, little envisaging the long years of friendship that followed, down to this day. Alan Ross, however romantic his appearance and beginnings, soon showed himself as someone who made me laugh; wise in judgements; staunch in loyalties; and who followed Sassoon's dictum to "sweat your guts out" writing poetry.

I wonder if even in Paddington Grande Hotel days I had not already met, either at that first Lehmann party or through J. R. Ackerley, William Plomer, for I moved from the hotel's sleaziness to accommodation not strikingly better in Linden Gardens (now apparently called Linden Mews) off the Bayswater Road. William lived either in that square or the next, and it seems too much of a coincidence that I should have chosen the district, hitherto unknown, utterly at random. My room, though pleasantly overlooking the Square garden, was hamperingly narrow, formed from a larger room by a partition that admitted dubious sounds; furnishing, ambience and denizens of the quarter reminiscent of my Bloomsbury digs of more than a decade earlier, and which would have offended my mother's keen liking for cleanliness, respectability and comfort scarcely the less. No meals were supplied, so I usually called at Lyons' Coventry Street "Corner House" for breakfast before proceeding to Lower Regent Street.

I can still summon up the atmosphere in 1944 of the ground-floor restaurant, the only part of the large, multi-floored establishment serving breakfasts, but who can it interest save the relatively few surviving customers of those years? – a substantial number of the population being now with dim notions, or none, of what a Corner House was. One passed through the shopping foyer (the stalls of bread, chocolates, and the like, not yet stocked and open for business) to the restaurant at the rear, windowless and thus always in artificial light, "orange-rosy lamps" (to use Arthur Symons's phrase), an affair of marble and mahogany veneers. There was usually some anxiety about securing a place at one of the many small tables, wartime shortage of *maîtres-d'hôtel* allowing separate pockets of waiting customers and queue-jumping, perhaps other anarchies. A similar feeling-tone attached itself to ordering from the hard-worked waitresses – as to when the previous breakfaster's debris would be cleared, not mistaken for one's own; what might remain available on the menu, and so forth. The tension pending the actual arrival of the food and beverage was not really alleviated by the exiguous morning newspaper, already sucked fairly dry on the way. Bacon and tomato comes to mind as one of the superior dishes, not always available. The portion of preserve allotted failed adequately to cover what was left of one's two slices of faintly buttered toast after the main dish had been consumed. Because of one's uniform, favoured treatment seemed to come from the waitresses (the eternal feminine throbbing under their black and white garb), but in what this resided is now difficult to specify. Further anxiety about waiting for the bill was avoided by asking for it when the order was delivered. By the time one emerged, the shop stalls were in business, and could be scanned for any rare delicacy available, either on or off rationing "points" or coupons.

Rex House, my destination in Lower Regent Street, was a modern office building partly taken over to house Admiralty departments. The Directorate of Naval Air Radio (DNAR) was where *Ariel*-trained Admiralty appointees normally went, but my appointment was to the Directorate of Air Equipment (DAE), the logic being to have someone there who could see that a naval aircraft's other equipment harmonized with its radio and radar sets, and also to look after items to do with radio and radar whose supply and fitting were the responsibility of DAE rather than DNAR. I was in a not-large room with four other officers, initially five, for I had a brief overlapping period with the officer I was to succeed. We sat at tables, three facing three, nearness to the window depending on seniority. Diagonally opposite me, by the window, only partly visible behind accumulated files, volumes of Admiralty Fleet Orders (AFOs) and other technical works, sat Cornish-Bowden, a Commander in the Supply Branch. Above a dark-eyed, sallow face, his thin black hair was brilliantined close to his head. I would sometimes out of earshot refer to him as Cornish-Pasty, the puerile vulgarism not unapt having regard to his complexion. Of all the room's occupants it was he who took things most seriously, writing as relentlessly as Sir Walter Scott, calling subordinates over the coals, not infrequently going next door to confer with the Director. One saw that for him the Admiralty appointment was a vital stage in his career, next job, promotion even, dependent on his performance. When I first joined DAE the man on his left was also regular Navy, a Commander with pilot's wings – good-looking, with the traditional slightly too-posh, but attractive, naval officer's accent. He was my immediate superior; once asked me to go to the Hungaria restaurant a few doors away and book a table for two for supper, which I did – the morning ambience of a smart place where one danced between courses so strange that I noted it as a possible background in future fiction.

The officer opposite Cornish-Bowden has virtually gone from memory. Next to me was a tall, thin RNR officer wearing the general service ribbons of the First War – except for that indication, of indeterminate age. Though perfectly agreeable, he was unforthcoming to all and sundry, occupying himself, in a way that always seemed difficult to account for, with but a single category of equipment – though that, admittedly, expensive and complicated: Link Trainers. It was a job he was said to have had since the start of the War. At first, in my ignorance, I thought "Link" stood for some continuing process in the training of pilots, perhaps in an undefined manner even embracing group psychology, not realizing it was the inventor's name. Quite strange that he and others, far from the stereotypes of literature, should have come down the years in sketchable form, not precluding greater depth of depiction.

We all had numbers: E5, the Lieutenant I was to inherit this title from, as in some secret society, sat opposite me for the few days of our ambiguous duplication. E5 was a cheerful, extravert young man, with pilot's wings. It soon appeared he had crashed an aircraft, I think in the course of some ferrying job; perhaps had displayed other less sensational disadvantages for the pilot's profession, and been sent to DAE to be "lost". I would have said myself he was less fitted for an office than for the occupation he had just left. One of the first files (or dockets, as perhaps they were known) to arrive from the Registry (the central filing and recording system, staffed by civil servants) concerned the provision of flying helmets for the Fleet Air Arm. It was marked to E5, who (though sequent markings would ensure its passage to the Hungarian Commander and, through Cornish-Bowden, probably to DAE himself) was plainly expected to name a figure. The problem was reminiscent of those tricky ones about water running into cisterns with outlets, encountered at school, but E5 tackled it with the confidence that must have got him his wings. "Let's put 30,000," he said, as I momentarily sat next to him, the better to observe his craft.

Memory may have got the figure wrong, but surely it was of that order. At first I imagined that in his noddle E5 had information about the rate of flow, but, on questioning, he never convinced me that more than guesswork was involved. Though the figure seemed to me more appropriate to the RAF than the FAA, I weakly allowed the minute to embody it, and the docket to pass on. It is no defence to recall that some of the more commonplace aspects of the appointment still held mystery – the proper form of minutes ("I propose the following minute" was the opening for an underling), meaning of initials and acronyms, whereabouts of liaison officers, departmental sections, other Government and service departments – for having worked in a large organization the pennies quickly dropped. One more-abiding puzzle was the bottle of apparent lighter fluid among the paperclips and ashtrays on most officers' desks. With a poet's blend of gormlessness and over-ingenious subtlety (or maybe the mix was merely constitutional), I thought there might be a gin issue to compensate for absence of wardroom facilities, kept by the recipients in a form handy for a quick nip – rather like Pogson and Bridle with superfluous rum. Of course, the bottles proved in truth to contain lighter fluid, displayed because officers sat not at desks but drawerless tables.

I got a second chance at the flying-helmets problem. Whether the docket was returned by E2 (or whatever the Hungarian officer's number was) or I rescued it when E5 had gone, I do not recall. In any case, because of my own dubieties the question became part of a much larger one; namely, the provison of earphones and microphones to go, as it were, with the flying helmets. It was a business pretty far removed from any gen acquired at *Ariel*, even such fundamental knowledge needing research as to whether every earphone jack would fit into the relevant radio-set socket. For when one looked at the massive loose-leaf catalogue of Fleet Air Arm stores (borrowed from the barricade round Cornish-Bowden), types of earphones and microphones (and even of flying helmets) were revealed in considerable number. Which was compatible with which was not specified, nor whether some were merely historical: the conscientious stores officer, in carrier or base, would see he was stocked with all types, in common use or not. The position was complicated by the then new-fangled throat-microphones. My thrifty temperament, sharpened by the solicitor's training that instils logicality and tidiness of thought, was appalled, and I was drawn into a one-man enquiry as to obsolete, obsolescent and currently used helmets, earphones and microphones in the FAA. Some of this consisted of interrogation of individual officers in DAE. For instance, there was the big, jolly, but responsible pilot in the section – perhaps *was* the section – that liaised with Staff in the Admiralty proper. In the fascinating room in DAE whose walls depicted the changing global patterns of FAA squadrons, their whereabouts, aircraft types and numbers, and equipment state, I found Lieutenant Kingsmill, young survivor of the heroic Swordfish attack on the *Scharnhorst* and *Gneisenau*, recovered from his wounds, and witty and intelligent, though plainly still a shadow of his former self: he was another whose microphone lore I listened to.

When, quite recently, I belatedly read the biographical book by R. F. Harrod about Lindemann, *The Prof*, I was greatly pleased to come across the following:

> They [the Fleet Air Arm] had a professional statistician, a highly efficient one as I was to find, Mr R. E. Beard of the Prudential Assurance Company. When asked some question on the telephone, such as how many new propellors were still needed for Swordfish aircraft, he could make calculations from complicated basic data by playing lightly on the calculating machine with one hand while he held the receiver with the other, and give the correct answer almost without any delay.

Plainly, the solution of the problem originally posed to E5 depended on the prognosticated entry to the FAA of aircrew, and their rate of wastage. Someone must surely have a notion of these figures. I made enquiries, I believe of the directorate's civil servants, and was put on to Mr Beard. I went to see him in his modest office: found him broad, blond, youngish, genial; head large, in the manner Wodehouse conceived his brainy characters to be cast. As in Roy Harrod's experience, he seemed quite prepared to give me an answer on the spot, but I think in the end said he would put it on paper. I consulted him a few times on that and other business, reassured to find such a chap involved in the conduct of the war.

It turned out that a number of items of the equipment in question were of a certainty no longer in use; other items needed coordinating. That section of the stores book required drastic emendation. I drafted the necessary AFO, and even Cornish-Pasty found little wrong with it. I give, of course, a truncated version of the action, for the minute proposing the AFO must have made the rounds of other directorates before their Lordships passed it into law. I have gone on about the matter, low-tone and tedious though most will find it, because it was my greatest contribution to what was commonly called "the war effort", eclipsing the work with Bob Park in and from the iffy hut.

In my time in DAE there was only one item of radio or radar equipment for which DAE rather than DNAR was responsible, and which therefore fell to my lot. It had been pretty well fully developed before I arrived, may already have been in process of manufacture. I have tried and failed to recall its codename, once as familiar as my own. If ever brought to the mind's surface it would probably at once betray its Freudian guiltiness. The item in question was a battery-powered radar beacon that sent out a signal on the ASV frequency. Its components had been "miniaturized" (term and process still novel at that time) so that it was no larger than a large electric torch, and could be accommodated in an aircrew member's "Mae West". If he were forced to ditch he would switch on the beacon and thus indicate his whereabouts on the screen of a rescuing aircraft, enabling it to home on him. The great crux when I came into the story was where the thing could be stowed in the already overcrowded Mae West. One of the competing objects was a bakelite box containing such essentials for survival as boiled sweets and a fishing line. At a joint meeting of departments concerned, some specimens of these boxes were produced by the representative of MI9, and I secured one for my son's amusement, risking a foreign agent seeing him playing with it in Mrs Rosewell's house. The MI9 man was another character from Wodehouse – Sub-Lieutenant the Lord Holden: slight, with a gingerish beard; could be envisaged clean-shaven in the Drones Club.

In the account thus far of life in an Admiralty department, perhaps too many trivialities have been particularized. Yet writing, I have a constant sense of the insufficiently factual, though working detail in, so to speak, is almost as much an effort of technique as of memory. Every day at Rex House a mass of incident must be envisaged, much of it of period character. There was the appearance of a Parker 51 in the hands of an officer who had served in or visited the United States, the first time a fountain-pen nib had been hooded, the cap-retention device on the barrel also surely novel in giving an almost perfectly smooth grip. Such an implement seemed one of the most desirable possessions in the world, but I was not able to buy one until on holiday in Switzerland in 1947.

There were the perennial problems of eating, over and above the breakfasts already lingered over. In the basement of Rex House was an odorous canteen, cafeteria style, not much used by me, reminiscent of the British Restaurant. Higher up the street, in what is now the Ceylon Tea Centre, was the Canadian

Officers' Club, not really a club nor restricted to Canadians, consequently always crowded, the food as I recall it quite passable, slightly transatlantic. Once a week, perhaps more frequently, I lunched with J. R. Ackerley and William Plomer at Shearn's, the vegetarian shop and restaurant in Tottenham Court Road, now no more. Nut rissole with a thick brown gravy, and syrup-sponge pudding, is the sort of menu that sticks in the memory (as doubtless it stuck in my digestive tracts), though salads must also have been on offer. I had got to know Joe Ackerley through sending poems to *The Listener*, of which he was literary editor. He had taken a poem as early as 1940, but I did not meet him until 1944. Looking at my file of his letters, which I assembled when Neville Braybrooke, editing Joe's letters for publication, asked to see them, I note that a letter of 16 December 1943 says he was "sorry not to be able to come and meet you at Lehmann's the other day." That more or less dates the Lehmann party and confirms my recollection of first seeing Joe at Broadcasting House.

In reviewing the flurry of books by and concerning Joe of recent years, I have brought in some memories and descriptions of him which I do not feel like repeating here, so will try to say something fresh. It may well be the revelations about his life by himself and others have left a disagreeable impression in many readers' minds, so I ought to emphasize that I liked him a lot, as did my wife, and that apart from making me go a bit red a time or two in those early Shearn days, through his occasional frankness about physical matters, nothing a heterosexual petty bourgeois might find untoward emanated from him. In 1944 he was forty-eight. He was thought extremely handsome as a young man, and some photographs confirm this. In middle age he wore very ordinary spectacles, and tweed-jacket-grey-slacks sort of clothes, with a beret in inclement weather: these contributed to the lack of distinction that had crept over him, perhaps were its source, for though he merged easily into saloon bar surroundings there was nothing shabby or commonplace about his voice, manner, hands, management of a cigarette. (Lack of distinction is rather too harsh a phrase, any way.) By publishing *Hindoo Holiday* in 1932 he had just about sustained the youthful fame brought by his play *Prisoners of War*, but since then no book by him had appeared. When I met him I had not read *Hindoo Holiday*, though aware of it. Like *Seven Gothic Tales*, its reputation had made it seem a book I would not particularly care for, but when I repaired my omission after getting to know Joe I thought it, as many did, a classic, an opinion I have had no reason to change.

At the Admiralty I had only one or two little poems to let Joe look at for *The Listener*, but I see from the old cuttings book, previously consulted, that I began reviewing for him in September 1944, provoking kerfuffles almost immediately. *Listener* reviewing was then anonymous, so obloquy tended to be piled on the literary editor by any of the reviewed who were offended, unable otherwise to siphon off their wrath. Joe asked me to review Edith Sitwell's *Green Song and Other Poems*, which foolishly I did. I believe my original notice was quite short and that Joe suggested I extend it by including more illustrative quotation. Considering the *Listener*'s limited space, the result was an ample review, and I see in it evidence of what I have rarely done as a reviewer, that is to lean backwards to perceive virtue, and to have some regard for the paper's position in relation to the author. Briefly, my thesis was that Edith Sitwell had made a great effort to rise to the poetic demands of the war after "a lifetime's verse which can hardly be said to be other than minor verse of a limited kind", but that judging *Green Songs* by the highest standards its imagery "is for the most part monotonous and unclear, and of very unequal significance." No need to go on: some words of praise do not affect the firm thumbs-down for the notion, then being canvassed, that Edith Sitwell's wartime verse was of Yeatsian calibre.

It may be thought there was not much pulling of punches in these remarks, but my inclination was to be a good deal sharper, convinced that Edith Sitwell's reputation was growing out of hand and ought to be slashed. (Oddly enough, today I would want to be more generous to the pre-war verse, for its fantasy and original technique has weathered well.) Publishing the review, it was said, got Joe struck off the list of house guests for Renishaw Hall, the Sitwell country mansion. I knew from him that Edith was outraged but he never disclosed the extent of the sanctions imposed, nor did he utter a word of complaint. Indeed, six weeks later he printed a review of mine of *New Writing and Daylight* in which I said that an Edith Sitwell essay about the Greek poet and critic Demetrios Capetanakis, recently dead at a tragically early age, was "quite remarkable for its overstatement, and rather predisposes one against" the other essays on Capetanakis. These included pieces by William Plomer and John Lehmann. The publication of this second review was, according to Victoria Glendinning's biography of Edith Sitwell, one of the causes of her writing to John Lehmann: "The dregs of the literary population have risen as one worm to insult me." Capetanakis had been a close friend of John Lehmann (and Edith Sitwell was, to a degree), so I thought it right to tell John I was the author of words that might rankle with him, especially if not carefully read. He was very cross; I righteous but perturbed: we were estranged for some months – the only such episode in a friendship as old as my son; forty-six years, as I write these words.

I do not think Edith Sitwell herself was aware of the perpetrator of these heinous crimes, for I feel sure it was later I was presented to her at a Lehmann party and exchanged courtesies, the occasion (surely written about by me elsewhere) when her likeness to Max Miller in features and headgear was pointed out to me by William Plomer. William, at the era of the Shearn's lunches, was also in the Admiralty, a temporary civil servant in some intelligence department, possibly Sub-Lieutenant the Lord Holden's. I liked William but never knew him well. He had by this date effected the change from dissident colonial to Establishment man of letters noted by Laurens van der Post in his recent book *Yet Being Someone Other*, describing it as effected "with conscious determination and against the stream of natural instincts". William and Joe and John Morris were reported in the stalls of the Camberwell Green Empire at a travelling revue of the day, *Soldiers in Skirts*, but this may possibly have been a joke and in any event does not much detract from the sober and respectable persona William presented – English accent, voice sensationally deep; hair neatly *en brosse*; spectacles and tweed jacket and flannel trousers, a nuttier version of Joe's.

Thinking about these matters, it strikes me what a dull dog I must have been at the Shearn's lunches, not able to contribute much to the gossip about people, nor educe anything amusing from my own life. It would never have occurred to me to go on about Mrs Slate, say, though both William and Joe had a great interest in the nominally ordinary. I cannot say I was awed: simply by temperament and rearing unable to summon up the light garrulity known as "small talk", though I daresay I more than held my own with friends like Willie Robertson and Jack Jolly; trait I have touched on before. No, I was not awed, but the Sleuthing Aldous Huxley syndrome still to a degree persisted: it was a notable occasion for me when John and Myfanwy Piper joined us at Shearn's: he with premature white hair and bright blue shirt, she with uncurled hair and no make-up – a respectable Bohemianism that part of my apprehension might well have been storing away for unflattering use. I admit to being awed when the party joining us was E. M. Forster (the venue being changed to the Akropolis or perhaps the White Tower, Percy Street restaurants), but again what enured was the incongruous, the potentially comic – the eminent novelist's brown-suited insignificance, inclining to the shabby. I used elements of the occasion more than twenty-five years later for the first meeting of the old and young poets in my novel *The Carnal Island.*

Shearn's cuisine and the missile of the time came together in William's poem "The Flying Bum: 1944", in which a V-1 or "flying bomb" explodes outside a vegetarian guesthouse and deposits a "lightly roasted rump of horse" on a dining table previously occupied only by "imitation sausage/Made of monkey-nuts and spice." The question never arose of our meeting in or near Linden Gardens; nor, though he gave me the telephone number, did I ever visit Joe's Putney flat, its curiously squalid romanticism now public property through various Ackerleyiana. It was less being sexually not "of their kind" that confined our friendship than my lack of push and (I guess) their domestic constrictions.

Laurie Lee could well have been the informant about intellectual elements in the South London audience for *Soldiers in Skirts.* I used to see quite a bit of him, despite the attention diverted from *A Lost Season* by his *The Sun my Monument.* Though at this epoch the wartime job already mentioned provided a decent reason or excuse, he had already perfected the strategy that served him well during the ensuing peace: that is, enhancing his reputation with a severely limited production, parsimony some other literary figures one might name could better have copied. In those early days he actually passed on to me an assignment that had come his way – to write the commentary for a pictorial history of the war thus far. The pictures were to be shown on a screen of modest size, sections lighting up automatically as the relevant stage of the recorded spoken commentary was reached.

The assignment came from the Hungarian refugee inventor of this device, which was to stand and do its stuff in Ford's motor-car showrooms, then next to or near the Café Royal in Regent Street. The fee offered was £50, substantial for the time, and I felt I could not turn it down. It was my first experience of something foolishly or weakly repeated down to this day – undertaking literary work at the behest and under the control of others, always laborious and jejune in the composition, usually unsatisfactory in the result, sometimes shamefully tinged with falsity. For many years now my motivation has been not money but friendship or too great a concern for the entrepreneurial problems of others, even strangers; curious twist of character. As to the chore Laurie typically attracted and wisely avoided, in due course I stepped up from Rex House one lunch time and heard (with needless embarrassment, for my part was anonymous) the machine speaking my lines. I expect they were disappointingly unpatriotic, non-Churchillian; nevertheless far from the Marxist dubieties of my real views.

When I first knew Laurie I thought his Gloucestershire accent Canadian; the kind of misconception age has not entirely eradicated. I daresay our friendship was helped by congenial encounters at parties or poetry readings, though if asked to specify them I would be gravelled. In fact, the only poetry reading of the time I can recall was a quite grand affair, for charity, including Laurie but also C. Day Lewis and Louis MacNeice. Afterwards, Anthony Panting, an active photographer in those days, known through Jack Clark, said my contribution was unlike the rest, an observation that has stuck in my mind. No doubt being the only performer in uniform (*Soldiers in Skirts* in reverse, so to speak) was a sufficient differentiation, but I think Anthony was referring, approvingly, to the generally non-poetic or non-conventionally-poetic in my performance and material. I expect I read then, as I do now, for sense; hoping not to falter over the rhythm but certainly not adopting a sing song or incantatory manner. When I hear on the wireless a snatch of Dylan Thomas reading his verse I am amazed the business is still taken seriously, so outrageous, even risible, an example is it of pre-war theatrical hamming.

I was still in DAE when I started *Savage Gold*, "a story of adventure", as it was eventually subtitled. A picture coheres of writing it in the same sort of Stationery Office notebook as contained the brief journal previously quoted, sitting on the Cornish-Bowden side of the row of tables for some reason – perhaps during the evening of a duty officer night, a chore that occasionally came round, involving sleeping on the duty officer's bed, keeping an eye on the signals in the signals room, sometimes (as at Tanga) wandering about in search of reading matter if one had miscalculated, in the former tradition of E5, requirements in that line. One thinks now that one would not have dared to work on the thing in office hours, but who knows what schoolboyish masks of blotting paper and dockets might not have been brought into play, even within sight of Cornish-Bowden? The *genre* aimed at in *Savage Gold* was roughly that of *Treasure Island*. Quite apart from the motive of trying to entertain my son, I felt my fictive powers were not up to the adult novel. That conviction was due less to the past history of novels abandoned, and the novel completed but never published, than to a sense that my invention could not engage the mature reader. I was still hung-over with technical problems from the past. I did not want to enter and stay imprisoned *à la* Dalloway in some single consciousness, yet saw no way of escaping except through the juvenile tale of action or the whodunnit, a form I came to immediately after *Savage Gold*. I think even as I embarked on *Savage Gold* I envisaged gradually easing myself into fully felt, and technically flexible, adult fiction. I fear I have touched on this theme before, not least the irony that though in the end my novels would have satisfied many of my schoolboy daydreams thereof, they are now virtually out of print, rapidly becoming forgotten as their original readers die off.

How steeped one had been as an adolescent in the Joycean or Woolfian interior style was shown by the ludicrous difficulty I had, getting going with *Savage Gold*, of straightforwardly describing events. At some early stage I recalled Flaubert's employment of brief, purely factual sentences at critical moments: Hemingway also uses the device. Bathetic and naïve to say so, but I followed them. Though I set the story in the Africa I knew, I imported into it elements of the world the great African explorers found towards the end of the nineteenth century, so that the book must read oddly in the times of Oboto and Mugabwe. On the other hand, the essential character of some present-day régimes is not too far from that of the kingdom of the Wazamba in *Savage Gold*. Perhaps the years will eventually smooth down historical discrepancies, and a few boys read its yellowing pages as gospel.

It was one of the first publications of the firm founded by John Lehman on his break from the Hogarth Press in 1946. Brilliantly illustrated by Robert Medley (designer for Rupert Doone's Group Theatre and an inspired choice of John Lehmann's), it proved my most successful book, appearing before books lost their wartime scarcity and saleability. Later, Puffin Books did it in paperback; and in 1960 there was a new hardback edition by Hutchinson Educational, aimed at schools. I used to say it would keep me in fags in my old age, but fortunately I gave up smoking at the age of sixty-two.

10 *DNAR*

As the Allied invasion of Europe prospered in the summer of 1944, I began to think about *après la guerre*, at least in terms of somewhere to live. It may be that returning to my pre-call-up job as assistant solicitor to the Woolwich Equitable was still a slightly open question, but prudence and convenience indicated a flat in Blackheath, within two or three miles of Woolwich, and locale of our maisonette the landmine wrecked in the Blitz. Plainly, there would be an accommodation famine when the war was over. Nevertheless, an element of daring resided in the taking on even a short lease of a flat at what seemed a substantial rent of £2.15s a week. The Admiralty appointment could by no means be considered a permanency, and any move would almost certainly be towards the Far East, Japan looking like long outlasting Germany.

Journeying to Blackheath, nineteen minutes from Charing Cross, by what was still the Southern Railway, to visit estate agents, resembled biting into a cream cracker sandwich. The Village (so called) seemed strange, like some childhood haunt, but of course not so strange as in 1938 when we were scouting out the ground for the move from Ashford. I needed only to consult one firm of agents, Dyer, Son & Creasey (somewhat

Dickensian name, still extant), quickly settling on the ground-floor flat in a well-converted, mid-nineteenth century, grey-brick house in a quiet tree-lined road of such, called St John's Park. This time I did not make the mistake of choosing a side of the heath remote from Woolwich, again rather confirming acceptance of a return to the law. Somewhat later, I was invited to stay on as a regular officer in the Navy, further promotion dangled before me, but surely I could never have seriously considered this. The only change more than fleetingly contemplated was an occupation in Grub Street that would at once have been more congenial than solicitoring and given me greater time to write prose fiction. But the conviction, so strong in the earlier part of the war, among the air-raids and on the lower-deck, that one's life and self would never again be the same, must by now have ceased to grip. Being at the Admiralty was a novitiate to prepare one for a renewal of strict office life – though further service in a far-flung, even dangerous and rowdy parish was by no means ruled out.

The St John's Park flat consisted of a large sitting room overlooking a commodious neglected garden, mostly grass; two bedrooms, one enormous, with great mahogany mantelpiece and surround, probably the house's dining room; and, made out of the former billiards room annexe, a dining room and kitchen, reached by a spacious corridor lit by two arched windows and glass double-doors giving on to a conservatory. The solid side of the conservatory had a floor-to-ceiling rockery down which it had originally been arranged that water should trickle. As a matter of fact, a cress-like growth still flourished there, sustained by rain, for bombing of various kinds had breached the conservatory's defences. It was the rockery feature that led us to nickname the conservatory the "Reptile House", though the floor of ornamented terracotta tiles (reminding me of the floor of the Tanga hospital, which I had traversed to reach this further point in life) contributed to the zoolike atmosphere. The garden could be reached from both kitchen and Reptile House, in the latter case via a quite elegant iron staircase. In a garden a few doors away Charles Peace had been apprehended in 1878, after wounding P. C. Robinson.

The house was owned by a Mrs Hipkin, who lived with her unmarried adult daughter in Bexleyheath. The rents from the four flats were perhaps the major part of their income. At any rate, my being a naval officer and peacetime solicitor proved insufficient credentials, and through the agents an appointment was made for me to meet Mrs and Miss Hipkin on the premises. Did some pieces of furniture or packing cases linger from the previous tenancy, or did we all stand up during the interview? I clearly recall it taking place in the south-facing sitting room, light filtering through a species of translucent paper often tacked up at blasted windows by war-damage repair contractors in lieu of glass. Discussion ensued about my plans, my family: eventually I was accepted.

An unwritten term of the lease was that I should employ the charlady, Mrs Morris, who had served the former tenant and currently served another tenant in the house. How many mornings a week she was to come to me I forget, but the hourly rate of her three-hour stint was one and fourpence (7p), so on her days on I used to leave a couple of florins (with any Pickwickian message thereunder), for I had departed for Rex House before she arrived. She had a key to let herself in: her utter trustworthiness had been emphasized by the Hipkins. Small, thin, sallow, mildly depressed, limp hats, Chaplinesque feet, she could have played a charlady on the boards – of the effacing kind, though on one topic, her loved daughter, she was dominating in conversation. Occasionally, a day off of mine (perhaps to make up for a Duty Officer night) might coincide with a morning on of hers, and then her maternal monologue would be resumed. But in general our Box and Cox existence was satisfactory. She was a dedicated tidier-up, which was primarily the service I wanted in my initially grass-widowered period. Thoroughness in cleaning was not her *mètier*: traces of old food in pans or between tines draw forth even today family accusations of a "Morrisian" washing-up. Nevertheless, she went on working for us after the war, and for Kathleen and Julian Symons when they eventually came to live in the top flat. Nor was she a great innovator with language, like Proust's Françoise: nothing much in that line has come down, though she did once observe to Kate that "Mrs Symons's Hoover's an Electrolux."

Strange epoch, living by myself at 16 St John's Park; strangeness inaugurated by reception of our goods and chattels from their place of storage. That was another cream-cracker-sandwichlike episode; items miraculously reincarnated, from what seemed a distant past – a few, like a large blue-painted bookcase made by a friend, a neighbouring joiner, recalling Ashford rather than former Blackheath days. In such feelings resided the strangeness; more than the incongruity of, say, establishing permanent relations between my weekly ration card and a local butcher while the final war scenes, with various prolongations and *coups de théâtre*, were being enacted in Europe. That one's life had been disturbed and disrupted, sufficiently countered guilt at one's own piddling activities; besides one was under fire from V weapons.

I must have moved from Bayswater to Blackheath in the not too advanced autumn of 1944, for good weather attended the early days and, looking back, the constriction and comparative squalor of life in Linden Gardens do not seem of awfully long duration. The move preceded my leaving DAE for DNAR. Topographically, the latter shift merely involved another floor of Rex House: essentially, it was a promotion, though my second stripe did not arrive immediately. I became Technical Assistant to the Director of Naval Air Radio, sharing a roomy outer office, protecting the Director's own office, with a Wren secretary. The window at the rear of Rex House, that even Commander Cornish-Bowden had no view from, was exchanged for an interesting panorama of Lower Regent Street.

The Director was Basil Willett who it was said had retired with the rank of Commander before the war, had been brought back with an extra stripe or acquiring one on the way. Presumably he had no detailed knowledge of aircraft radar and radio such as was imparted at *Ariel*; hence the post of Technical Assistant. He was about fifty: a blue-eyed, slightly weather-beaten countenance, what might be romantically thought of as a true sailor's: and with the characteristic naval officer's accent already noted. Behind him was a solid upper middle-class background: he was a son of "Daylight Saving" Willett, the builder. Once, when I had occasion to speak on the telephone to his home or perhaps his family home, a female retainer referred to him as "Master Basil". His enormous "progress" meetings were famous: I had attended some of them in my role as Mae West beacon king. Now, part of my job was to sit at his side on such occasions, though he betrayed no weakness in technical grasp or, for that matter, any other kind. In fact, he was extremely able and, though capable of fearless strength, exercised his will through completely unselfconscious charm. The accent belonged to a voice slightly hoarse, as though formed in the days when signals were bawled through the tempest. Somewhere in his smile was a hint of gold. He made a good few jokes, usually about the deficiencies of the bodies involved in his meetings, and the recurring personality traits of those representing them. He was a devoted pipe smoker, getting rid of ash and dottle by inclining his hand, palm up, over an ashtray and knocking the pipe bowl on his signet ring. Soon, our intimacy was marked by his calling me "old" Fuller (I was thirty-two, moustacheless state knocking off a few years in appearance), the adjective as he pronounced it almost a mere "o". I write "intimacy", but I cannot recall my attitude being other than utterly correct. But perhaps I did make a few jokes myself.

A tremendous amount of paper came into the Director's office: dockets for his attention, and appreciations, studies and periodicals of diverse kind, many only marginally connected with naval aircraft radar and radio, some from the United States, some Secret and Most Secret, most Confidential. I flatter myself that getting through this stuff, and selecting and presenting the few nuggets I thought Captain Willett should see, was a task up my street. I was a rapid reader, used to dry and complicated prose, soon became familiar with the sources and nature of the bumf, and kept it in subjection. I suppose I must have drafted or suggested minutes, but that side of things has quite faded. It was a revelation to me that some merely technical information was marked as not disclosable to the Soviet Union, though possibly useful against the Germans. That struck me as unfair to an ally who had suffered so much from the enemy. I am sure I am right in saying that in 1944 or 1945 I had no idea that British Communist Party members and sympathizers, likely to be useful, might be recruited by the Soviet Union as spies. During my brief membership of the party in the early Thirties, when there was talk of "Moscow gold" in the *Daily Mail* and suchlike despised organs of the capitalist press, Marston used to say he wished a bit of it would filter through to Blackpool, where we scraped along with our local share of members' subs (reduced for the unemployed) and an occasional donation from the town's more affluent left-wingers, like Mr Pablo, ice cream manufacturer, prosperous, but always reluctant to cough up, since he was said really to favour the Anarchist movement, and he believed anyway in self-help, quality displayed in his own business life.

It may be thought that during 1945, in an imperceptible way, war for the chair-borne faded into peace. But even the sedentary had their annals. When the V-1 launching sites were overrun by the Allied advance, that seemed to bring very close Kate and Johnny's move from Blackpool to London. There remained the question of V-2s – the rockets that descended and killed unannounced, and which in a paradoxical way I personally found more disagreeable than the V-1s, whose explosions were preceded by the suspenseful cessation of the sound of their jet engines. Recently, I read that prehistoric man may have lived through eras of terror when Earth was subjected to bombardment by cometary tails: some inkling of that state may have been given by V-2s. It is an indication of our longing to live together again that Kate and Johnny returned before they ceased – foolishly, it now seems, but possibly they were judged to be exhausted, had a deathbed revival.

In 1945, as in the days of Sherlock Holmes, a horse-drawn cab stood for hire at the side of Blackheath Station. When we arrived (I had met them along the route or perhaps fetched them from Mrs Rosewell's) we hired this vehicle. The luggage was stowed aloft, the horse walked up to the heath and trotted over it to 16 St John's Park, where the driver did what I had not anticipated – turned without hesitation into the semicircular drive that passed the steps to the front door and led out again into St John's Park. That this manoeuvre was possible because the drive gates had been permanently propped open on account of a degree of decrepitude did not detract from the grandeur of the gesture. This free access led to a poem called "Inaction", sometimes anthologized, where a dog enters and urinates on the mudguard of the poet's car, prompting him to think the very animal kingdom is sneering at his cosy life style. However, the poem was written a fair time later, probably when commitment had ceased even to the Society for Cultural Relations with the USSR. The arrival by cab was Kate and Johnny's first view of the house, and of the flat we were to live in for no less than a decade.

Perhaps not many V-2s fell after their arrival, but for a brief period we all slept in one room to increase the chance of dying together if hit. One day, in my absence at Rex House, a rocket landed a couple of hundred yards away on the heath, blowing out another window or two, setting the ceiling lights madly swinging, the noise heard by me in the West End (as proved by a subsequent time check). Kate and Johnny walked out to view the smoking crater, touch the warm debris (no doubt like those bombarded peoples of yore), and learn of the escape of a child in a perambulator almost on the spot. It was a bomb story better than any I could produce, but exposure to such risks after bearing years of a renewed sentence in the parental home was a folly explicable only in terms of utter exasperation at waiting for normality.

Because of its modest size, electric fire built into the wall, our mausoleum room was the dining room, though not affording much protection since above its plasterboard ceiling was mere empty space, topped by the glazed cupola of the billiards room annexe – pride, no doubt, of some Victorian equivalent of Councillor Marston.

In the mausoleum room was the HMV portable gramophone acquired in Aberdeen, the historic Menuhin/Elgar fiddle concerto best remembered of the discs played in those days, days perhaps too strange, too uncertain, to be wholly felicitous. The substantial radiogramophone we had spent most of our meagre pre-marriage savings on came out of store U/S, and, as might have been forecast from my Service record in practical matters, I failed to repair it, despite changing a suspect component, the scarce replacement acquired only after much trouble. Some of our possessions were, in fact, like England (and, it could be said, ourselves), rather decrepit.

Even before the German war ended, my former principal at the Woolwich, A. E. Shrimpton, took me to lunch at Scotts by Piccadilly Circus, a venue as impressive as the Hungaria. His war (carrying on the department with meagre forces, serving spare time on the Observer Corps, a wife and three sons to try to keep out of the bombs' way) had been no cakewalk, and he was keen to get me back to the office when peace came; as good a lunch as the wartime West End afforded not without ulterior motive. I should think it was about the same time when Captain Willett told me he had been offered a managing directorship by Marconi's, and wanted to contrive his premature release from the Navy. Whether he judged my literary ability on the draft minutes and so forth I laid before him or, less likely, had heard of, even read, my verse and critical notices, I do not know: however, he asked me for help with the vital letter to their

Lordships of the Admiralty. Something quite persuasive must have been concocted, for the letter worked like a charm, and to celebrate the victory the Captain took me to lunch among the red tabs and thick gold braid (right round the sleeve) at the Senior United Services Club on the corner of Waterloo Place opposite the Athenaeum, now, alas, no more.

Like all organisms, but sooner than most, set-ups in the Services divide, change, and crumble away. Radar training at Lee-on-the-Solent, the special W/T clique at Nairobi, RNAS Nairobi itself – all examples. One day in Rex House a skirl of bag pipes was heard echoing along the carpetless corridors, and soon, at the open door of the office I was then in, Commander Crichton appeared, playing the Scottish instrument, a talent never before suspected. He was in normal naval uniform except that on his head was a bowler hat to which had been affixed a pair of wings, cut out of stiff white paper, presumably symbolic of transference to a different sphere. The Commander was in charge of appointments, had been in fact the man from the Admiralty who had visited *Ariel* at the end of course. He had been "bowler-hatted", unwillingly retired, no post at Marconi's or anywhere else, and the quite prolonged musical marching was his protest, as out of character as his mastery of wild laments: it brought his displeasure shockingly home, though unfortunately out of earshot of their Lordships. He was based in DNAR. Once when I was alone in his outer office I pulled open a cabinet and had the quickest of squints at my own file. "An extremely smart officer," I had time to read, "who scored 98% in one of his passing-out papers." The first phrase is authentic: I am reconstructing the second, though the percentage was sensational, the paper being on recent radar equipment of outstanding ingenuity, the answers including descriptions of the journeying of current round the circuits.

Why did I not get on better in life? The glimpse from the outside afforded by Commander Crichton's records raises again the question previously posed in these memoirs, and probably sufficiently answered by the mild adventures described. But such as Lieutenant Hercules demonstrated that great arenas were not essential for effective exercise of the will. When sufficiently goaded (rare event) I was capable of behaving quite as bossily as Hercules: mostly, however, fatally fitted merely to describe him.

I served Willett's successor as TA for a spell, but then, in circumstances beyond recall, part of the metamorphotic process referred to, I was moved elsewhere in DNAR. The buzz was that the Department would be set up in Australia the better to conduct its part in the Japanese war, still continuing. Some preliminary shift of the kind may already have taken place: certainly I was underemployed, without a clear role; once more, as in DAE, in a room with officers better equipped than I to make work spin out – the room from which I had seen Commander Crichton, enviably sacked. I doubt I was there very long before one day, in August 1945, buying an early *Evening Standard* to read over lunch, I saw a short item in the stop press that seemed to signal a Japanese surrender. Amazing that doubt now exists as to whether it concerned the first or second atomic bomb, fearful events that were to haunt life thereafter, though conviction about the decisiveness of the news item indicates the destruction of Nagasaki. Also, though I write "to read over lunch", more likely I was as parsimonious about buying evening newspapers as I had been as a law student in London a dozen years before, and only interested in the *Standard* because, warned by Hiroshima, surrender was in the offing. Whether self-interest allowed any feeling for the victims, I wonder.

Relief at the prospect of all hostilities ending was undoubtedly heightened by the virtual escape from the risks of service in the Far East, or at any rate whatever spiritual malaise Australia might have induced. Whether this was happiness, who knows? Before I returned to Rex House I had a few whiskies in Soho, a solitary mini-pub-crawl, for unofficial spirits-rationing compelled one to move on from bar to bar. In my mind's eye I see myself standing in a public barroom, almost deserted as closing time came up, drink on a scrubbed table (for many Soho pubs still had a village simplicity), gazing out into Dean Street or Frith Street (thoroughfares then quite free of parked cars, dubious emporiums, and vulgar displays), in some kind of historical meditation. Plainly, one longed to be happy. But I had noted as a feature of "VE Day", the previous May, the absence of the abandon, familiar from photographs and film, of the Armistice of 1918 – in which, indeed, I myself could have participated as a child of six, though whether I should have been moved to behave with excess even on that occasion is unlikely.

How on earth did I occupy my time from the August Japanese surrender to my release from naval service on the 3 December? I see from the scrapbook I was writing a bit during this period for *Tribune* and *Our Time*, as well as *The Listener*, and there is evidence of other literary chores. Rex House may have been the illegal arena for some of this modest activity. Mention of the first two periodicals leads to other recesses of memory, these especially dim. Julian Symons had introduced me as a reviewer to *Tribune* and the left-wing literary magazine *Our Time*. I used occasionally to go into the *Tribune* office in the Strand, where I saw the literary editor, Tosco Fyvel, and (though this may have been slightly later) his assistant, the youthful Bruce Bain (who eventually turned entirely into his dramatic critic *nom-de-plume*, Richard Findlater). Tosco must be numbered among the generous and patient editors who encouraged me. I never encountered the famous politicos behind *Tribune* in those days. The *Our Time* office, more squalid, was not far away, in Southampton Street. The editor was Edgell Rickword, poetic hero of my youth and ever after. His assistant, the poet Arnold Rattenbury, youthful as Bruce Bain, fairly soon drifted out of my life, reappearing suddenly so much later that momentarily I scarcely knew who he was. Alas, Edgell died in 1982, at a great age, but Arnold, as devout a Rickword fan as I, is still in touch.

Surely my emotion on encountering Edgell must have exceeded that on lunching in Percy Street with E. M. Forster, though my pre-meeting image is now subsumed in the later actuality – the ragged, drooping moustache, the spectacles with one opaque lens (masking the loss of an eye in the 1914–18 War), the almost inaudible voice, an absence of small talk, comparable with the spectacular deficiencies of Attlee and Arthur Waley, not precluding a sudden succinct and acute literary judgement. The Southampton Street premises had no attractions of their own, but their association in my memory with a general movement towards a pub would have arisen in any case from Edgell's own inclination. I never knew him the worse for drink, but the saloon bar was very much his habitat, perhaps stemming, like his earliest verse, from the pub poets of the Nineties.

These fiction-like *tempi* and links raise considerations not only about the autobiographical art but also about its subject. Reading a biography, though carried along by the sequence of incident, one may pause to wonder what the plot is or is to be. The reflection must be followed immediately by the conclusion – more or less obvious or banal – that the plot of every such volume is the progress towards death. What a phenomenally prolonged preparation for the final few pages, the most compelling and moving! By comparison, an autobiography is plotless: in fact, usually resembles the experimental novel (mentioned in *Souvenirs*) I conceived as an adolescent but fortunately made little progress with, a novel beginning normally but gradually getting more and more boring – for childhood has the plot of growing-up as well as incidental freshness and sharpness, whereas (to bring in another art) adulthood is usually mere, and more weakly orchestrated, recapitulation. However, the war, preceded by the threat of war, seems to me to have donated a further plot to the "growing-up" plot of my life, and the *dénouement* of that further plot – the coming of peace – is, of course, containable in autobiographical form, unlike death.

Autobiography, it may be added, is not the story told about oneself in one's own thoughts. That, for all its distortion and partiality, would involve a detail, a frankness, a truth, a *naiveté* – indeed, a talent – hard to conceive possible. The naturalistic successes and failed artificialities of *Ulysses* indicate the parameters of the problem, and that was fictive.

One's place in the demobilization queue was determined by certain rules. Some temporary officers, however, were in no hurry to go: with two stripes one needed to have quite a decent job to return to in Civvy Street to equal one's pay and allowances. I myself failed to get the Woolwich to come up to scratch. All the same, I was eager to get out of uniform, and with some in the queue willing to be bypassed, and by chatting up the office formerly controlled by Commander Crichton, I was able to some extent to beat the rules. With demobilization leave added on, my service just extended into 1946: almost a lustre.

Even for those who never had the experience, the business of getting a "demob outfit" at Olympia will have been made familiar by the marvellous little scene at the end of Anthony Powell's *The Military Philosophers*. There in the vast arena, on open stalls that one wandered through and chose from, were all the items of clothing necessary to turn servicemen back to civilians. The assumption was that over the years of war civilian clothes had succumbed to moth or theft or enemy action – or that one had grown out of them through middle-aged spread or muscular development or figgy duff – or even that captivity or dysentery or malaria had caused one to shrink within them. The clothing on display and the mixture of service personnel strolling about gave the sense that already one's uniform was meaningless – the gold stripes on the sleeves, whose acquisition and semi-circularity had caused such concern, of no account, drawing no salutation. In the background, music played but, unlike the ubiquitous barracks Tannoy, muted, sweet, never to be interrupted by a summons to the RPO's office or the like. In *The Military Philosophers* the narrator encounters, with timeous effect, a figure from his pre-war youth. It comes to me that I myself went along the stalls with someone I knew, accidentally encountered.

If uniform was suddenly of the past, the clothing acquired was, of course, very much an accompaniment of the future, in the case of some garments a future quite prolonged. I speak in terms of life, not fashion. A painstaking search had to be made for items one could imagine vanity allowing one to wear. I took away the best of the trilby hats simply through thrift, but was never seen out in it – dark blue-grey, with a hard predetermined shape that included the indentation of the crown. Nick Jenkins in *The Military Philosophers* rejected the underclothes, understandable in a possible patron of Jermyn Street, but for the true skinflint they were acceptable. The shoes reposed in tangled heaps, as in a sale, but I dug into them with determination and came out with a brown pair made by James White & Co., in style not bad, in terms of wear proving simply phenomenal. The riding mackintosh (was it so dubbed by one of the acolytes at Olympia or did I confer the name ironically thereafter?) was also longevous. Its material was as substantial as that remembered from distant days, stuff turned out by the Windsor Mill, where my father had made his career in rubber-proofing, cut short by untimely death. And it strikes me now for the first time that the material may indeed have been proofed there, the factory continuing its tradition, for its fortune had been founded in Government contracts during the First War. The mackintosh had a single vent at the back, to drape conveniently either side of one's mount, but whether the hacking jacket I selected had one or two (bugger's delight or bugger's puzzle, as the styles were vulgarly known) I cannot recall, though I liked the greenish garment and wore it through countless weekends. The grey "slacks" (name still matching the cut) were inferior; not flannel but a material difficult to wear out – though with perseverance I was at last able justifiably to cast them aside, like a long, boring book one is determined to get through.

In *The Military Philosophers*, Jenkins notes the many grey chalk-stripe suits on offer (an alternative to the tweed coat and slacks). The grey was pallid, its sickliness added to by the paler stripe. For a few years it was the uniform of a ghostly army, as it were; its scattered members sitting at office desks, serving in shops, calling for the laundry.

11 *Aftermath*

Writing "Aftermath" at the head of this chapter, the title of Harold Owen's remarkable addendum to his autobiography, makes me more conscious than ever of the unarduous life that followed what could not be described as an arduous war. Though I addressed envelopes for Alderman Reeves, the local Labour candidate in the 1945 General Election, I never contemplated returning to the political activity of the early Thirties. The simple chore, the ambience of the working class off duty, the gathering of old stalwarts, brought back the previous General Election (of 1935!): the intimation was of an anterior incarnation. Ideological questions presented no agonies of choice or renunciation: I believed in live and let live, depressed by the monstrous growth of foolish nationalism, astonishing after the defeat of the fascist powers. If my human equipment was tested it was mainly in the area of health, but none of my complaints precluded a fair amount of nervous and physical energy. Perhaps, indeed, my wonky physical side had some roots in my longing that "all manner of things shall be well", too cosy an attitude at any historical epoch I have lived through.

A reviewer in the *TLS* (Peter Sedgwick) recently came out with a clever summation that made me grin – the objections of

Marcuse and others to the "deplorable loss of subversiveness once the lustful libido is downgraded in favour of that more reasonable moderator, the ego". The revolutionaries were actually contemplating a change of emphasis in Freudian theory, but one could substitute the factor of increasing age. Moreover, at seventy one is inclined to job backwards, though as already hinted, after the war one may have been bolshie in the old way for a longer period than now seems plausible. For example, I doubt I would have unquestionably accepted in those post-war days such a notion as Mr Sedgwick characterizes in the same review – Freud's theory "that human aggression is a drive in its own right, not merely a reaction to the frustration of libido". I must have gone on believing for some time in human goodness; goodness frustrated only by a society that denied adequate love and power to its most numerous class.

Bob Park, companion of the iffy hut, was one who changed his life after the war, returning to Kenya to work and live despite having displayed absolutely no enthusiasm for the country as a serviceman. I have never seen or communicated with him since our Steptoe and Son life, though can clearly summon up his face and speech as they were forty years ago. Willie Robertson's metamorphosis was perhaps even more surprising: he returned to his Glasgow shipping company, but eventually, starting with the purchase of the building in which his own apartment was situate, profited by the post-war property boom, and became simply a "property-owner". He told me about this when we met in the late Forties by appointment "under the clock" in Charing Cross Station, the first time since Nairobi days. By ill luck it was the moment when x-rays had first confirmed a duodenal ulcer, and I was devoutly obeying a medical injunction not to drink.

We adjourned to a pub in Craven Street where, though disconcerted by my temperance, Willie ordered a Scotch and a beer chaser, perhaps planned in advance, anticipating a serious if brief session (for the whole evening was not free, he or I with some other engagement). The reunion was thus blighted from the outset, though ease and affection were not precluded. But, as is common in such circumstances, neither of us (he less than I) could quite come to terms with the fact that even during the war a great deal had happened to us after we had parted company, symbolized by his having part of a finger missing, the result of a wartime accident. He was, of course, by then habituated to this, but I could not help imagining his original concern, an infinitely worse case than that of the Sunburned Thighs. Characters, too, I but dimly recalled had evidentally subsequently assumed importance in his life: my uninterest in them must have seemed odd.

We never met again. Only through coincidence did I hear of his premature death in the Sixties from a heart attack. Captain Willett passed out of my life on his translation to Marconi's. He died in 1966. Some time after the latter date, the opportunity of dining with his son was thwarted because of illness or some such chance. The opportunity arose not at all because of my former connection with the father, but through an invitation from a mutual friend of mine and the son's. By fictional standards the coincidence would have been accounted strange, for our worlds were far apart. Commander William Willett was regular RN, like his father, and at the time Private Secretary to the Duke of Edinburgh. Alas, his death was even more untimely than Willie's, and we never met – myself to stay for ever ignorant of the more intimate side of "Master Basil", and whether he was happy with Marconi's.

Another post-war non-meeting or, strictly, non-reunion, was between Alan Ross and an old destroyer shipmate of lower-deck days, Butcher. Here, I was the mutual friend, for Butcher had worked for the Woolwich before the war, and returned thereafter. He was at branch offices in urban Essex, so I myself saw him only rarely. Whenever I came across him he was sure to say: "How's old Alan?" – using the adjective *à la* Captain Willett. In later years, when Alan had taken over editorship of the *London Magazine* from John Lehmann and acquired an office, Butch would add: "One day I'm going to call on old Alan", and get from me confirmation of the magazine's address. In earlier post-war times Butch was perhaps not in the best of odours with the Woolwich, apt at our business conferences to get on his feet too promptly, and speak agin the government. Rebelliousness may also have been expressed on less formal occasions. Whenever I told Alan I had seen Butch, passing on his regards and threat of calling, Alan would recall some incident of their service together, perhaps Butch coming down into the mess off watch from Arctic weather; diminutive, somewhat rotund figure enveloped in a dufflecoat, *New Statesman* protruding from pocket, voluble in barrack-room lawyer style about a grievance or injustice. When Butch retired from the Woolwich he had even more time to call at 30 Thurloe Place, SW7, but he never did. The last time I saw him, at one of the dinners for long-serving staff already mentioned, he was looking far from well, had had heart trouble. Not long after that he died. One misses him, no doubt about it.

A poem Alan wrote for my seventieth birthday contains the phrase: "You bequeathed me/A uniform". This surely must have been the better of the two, not the somewhat wide-in-the-hips serge. Younger than I, and unmarried, Alan's Order of Release came after mine; in fact, he was kept on for a while to interpret, and do intelligence work, in occupied Germany, possibly with Sub-Lieutenant the Lord Holden, so required another uniform. Taller than I, he would have needed to lengthen his braces. Later still, there was a further bequest, of my greatcoat, which I had worn for a bit in Civvy Street, having had the epaulettes removed and the brass buttons changed for ordinary black ones, useful when he came to watch Charlton Athletic, standing with us on the great exposed south slope at the Valley. During this further sartorial history I must have regretted not opting originally for the more disguisable watch coat.

Alan's post-war spiritual uncertainty seemed evident despite his respectable occupations on demobilization – at first with the British Council, then with the *Observer*. In my case, the war's upsets were perhaps indicated by the length of time between *A Lost Season* and my next book of poems, *Epitaphs and Occasions* (1949). By that time I had eased myself into writing fiction for adults by producing, after *Savage Gold*, a crime story for teenagers, *With My Little Eye* (1948), which was actually published in the United States as an adult novel.

After quitting the army, Julian Symons had become an advertising copywriter. He inherited from George Orwell a weekly book page in the *Manchester Evening News*, and in 1947 took up the life of a man of letters. Through unremitting industry, jealously noted before in these memoirs, he succeeded; greatly to his credit retaining the critical standards of the old days and never entirely giving up poetry. After a few years he and Kathleen moved into the country from the top flat in 16 St John's Park (and continued to oscillate between Kent and South London), but we stayed close friends, and with Kathleen's brother, Jack Clark. In 1945 the myriad events and changes of middle years lay enigmatically ahead, less complex in one's own hacking-jacketed and riding-mackintoshed case than in that of most of one's friends.

Also by Roy Fuller and published by Collins Harvill

AVAILABLE FOR DREAMS

Roy Fuller's pleasure in ordinary things, caught with a bright and compassionate eye, has delighted readers of his many volumes of poetry, his novels and autobiographical writing. He has, in the words of Christopher Hope, "a great gift for venturing into unquiet waters and writes so well about war, dreams, distance, exile and music". *Available for Dreams*, which has been received with acclaim, continues his remarkable late flowering. Here, a lifetime's thought and feeling, and a delight in the infinitely variable sonnet form, establish the Fuller world of music and science, birds and history and suburbia. Located on the margins of illness and the end of age, his is as openly and unsentimentally its own world as that of any other writer.

"He's a very fine poet who potentially could have two po-
ems or more in any anthology or inventory
of the best English poems of this century . . ."

GAVIN EWART, *Times Literary Supplement*

"Lovely . . . erudite, a human book . . . Poets in their seventies appear to experience a kind of second adolescence in relation to the Muse, bounding roguishly across to it with a drink each hand and life in the old doggerel yet" CAROL ANN DUFFY, *Guardian*

"The poetry of Roy Fuller as he has aged has been the most interesting literary event of the last 20 years. He is like some Chinese sage who can write a poem in one line which satisfies every demand of poetry and which lingers resonantly in the mind. [The sonnets] are gritty, real, so intimate as to seem casual: I find them profoundly satisfying" PETER LEVI, *Independent*

"*Available for Dreams* is a very distinguished collection indeed"

MICHAEL O'NEILL, *Times Literary Supplement*

"One of the most technically accomplished, wryly entertaining English poets of the century, and one of the most durable"

JAMES AITCHISON, *Glasgow Herald*

Harvill Paperbacks

Alan Ross

BLINDFOLD GAMES

Alan Ross, poet, former cricket correspondent for the *Observer*, and editor of the *London Magazine* since 1960, was born in Bengal, in the last days of the Raj. This unusual and stimulating first volume of autobiography is an indelible portrait of pre-Second World War days in England and of the war itself, during which Ross served in the Royal Navy on Arctic Convoy duty. He survived, but very many of his friends were killed. *Blindfold Games* is also a fascinating portrait of the development of a writer who, by the end of that war, had become one of its leading poets.

"This is, from every angle, an exceptional autobiography, beautifully written, and with a poetic unity far more subtle and expansive than a review can show"
JOHN CAREY, *Sunday Times*

"Ross has a painterly eye for the suprising detail as well as the detachment of a working painter . . . a brilliant performance"
ANTHONY CURTIS, *Financial Times*

COASTWISE LIGHTS

Coastwise Lights takes up the story of Alan Ross's life and enthusiasms where *Blindfold Games* left off. Demobilized in 1946, we see him with John Minton in Corsica; with Agatha Christie, Gavin Maxwell and Wilfred Thesiger in Bagdad; with Terence Rattigan in Ischia; in Tunis during the Algerian crisis; covering Test Matches in Australia for the *Observer*; and racing his own horses at Plumpton. But the real, unstated subjects of *Coastwise Lights* are his commitment to contemporary writing and art, and his great gift for friendship.

"There are marvellous portraits of, among others, Cyril Connolly, Henry Green, Keith Vaughan, William Plomer and Bill Sansom"
FRANCES SPALDING, *Listener*

"His obvious affection for the friends who flit through this beautifully written sketchbook is masked by a writer's curiosity and detached amusement"
EUAN CAMERON, *Independent*

"A true celebration of friendship and talent as well as the sports – football, cricket horse-racing – which have engaged him for the last four decades"
PHILIP OAKES, *New Statesman*

Alan Ross

TIME WAS AWAY

A Journey through Corsica

In 1947 Alan Ross and John Minton travelled to Corsica. The result is an exceptional travel book, a collaboration between a gifted poet and the most romantic artist of his generation. As Ross describes and Minton sketches the mountain villages, pine forests and empty bays, we meet black marketeers and political agitators, heroic bus drivers and saintly priests. Corsica may have changed in recent years, but in essence it remains the same enchanted island as the one that emerges from this now classic account.

"A book of real intelligence and beauty" *Daily Telegraph*

"Evocative and splendid . . . alert, fresh and sensuous" *Times Literary Supplement*

"Splashed with bold strokes and burning colours . . . We are made to see and smell, hear and feel the place. That is the test of a good travel book" *Observer*

THE BANDIT ON THE BILLIARD TABLE

A Journey through Sardinia

In this account of a summer journey through Sardinia in the early 1950s, Alan Ross alternates the past and present of a strange and, as far as the interior is concerned, rarely visited island. His descriptions of the Sardinian landscape are interspersed with stories of people who might have come out of Boccaccio, like the billiard-playing bandit or the Firbankian cardinals. The result is a memorable evocation of Sardinia as revealed equally by its art and architecture, its costumes and customs.

"An alert and sensitive travel book . . . Alan Ross has an exceptional descriptive gift" *Listener*

"An exceptionally good book by any standard" *Times Literary Supplement*

"A work of art and imagination" *The Times*

Jonathan Raban

SOFT CITY

The city as we imagine it is real, or maybe more real, than the hard city we can locate in maps or statistics. The soft city of the mind is a private place; everyone lives in his or her own soft city.

In this now classic account, Jonathan Raban vividly documents the experience of carving one's own path through the tangle and sprawl of urban metropolitan life. Like no book in recent years, it recreates the city in its teeming, unknowable variety; it gives to the city, to any city, a vibrant imaginative life quite independent of the millions who inhabit it. Part fact, part fiction, it holds up a mirror to the modern city and finds there a stage for a unique, and sometimes frightening, personal drama.

"A psychological handbook for urban survival" *Sunday Telegraph*

"His impressions are sensitive and informed and worth any amount of meaningless statistics and academic jargon" *Washington Post*

"An absorbing book" ANGUS WILSON

"A highly intelligent enquiry" AUBERON WAUGH

ANTÆUS

JOURNALS, NOTEBOOKS AND DIARIES

Since 1970 *Antæus* has established itself as one of the most successful and distinguished international literary magazines in the world. Now, special issues of the magazine will be published as substantial paperbacks. The first of these celebrates the journal as prose genre: V. S. Naipaul's "Congo River Journal" gets its first British publication; Paul Bowles sends despatches from Tangier; Tess Gallagher and Raymond Carver meet Edmund White in Paris; Oliver Sacks blows the dust off his youth; Edna O'Brien goes to a cockfight in Mexico; and Edward Hoagland learns to eat soup. Other contributors include Annie Dillard, Mary Gordon, M. F. K. Fisher, Jim Harrison, Ursula Le Guin, Norman Mailer, Stephen J. Pyne, Mordecai Richler, Charles Simic and Stephen Spender.

"A gallery for the best imaginative writers in the USA and abroad"
TOBIAS WOLFF

"The touchstone of the highest standard in new literature"
NADINE GORDIMER

ANTÆUS

ON NATURE

"We shall never fully understand nature (or ourselves), and certainly never respect it, until we disocciate the wild from the notion of usability"
JOHN FOWLES

The thirty writers who here discuss man's relationship with the natural world in all its aspects, from the study of nature in the past, through fieldwork, to Western man's sense of alienation from nature, include: Italo Calvino on Pliny's *Natural History*; Edward Hoagland on the great naturalist, John Muir; Annie Dillard on experiencing a total eclipse; Edward O. Wilson on an electrical storm over the Amazon; John Rodman on Dolphins; Keith Basso on the Western Apaches; and John Fowles on the myth of the Green Man of the Woods

"Confirms that today's most exciting work is not being done in fiction but in essays, memoirs and travel writings. *On Nature* presents a feast in four courses . . . and landmark collection of splendid writing"
New York Times Book Review

Harvill Paperbacks are published by Collins Harvill,
a Division of the Collins Publishing Group

1. Giuseppe Tomasi di Lampedusa *The Leopard*
2. Boris Pasternak *Doctor Zhivago*
3. Alexander Solzhenitsyn *The Gulag Archipelago 1918–1956*
4. Jonathan Raban *Soft City*
5. Alan Ross *Blindfold Games*
6. Joy Adamson *Queen of Shaba*
7. Vasily Grossman *Forever Flowering*
8. Peter Levi *The Frontiers of Paradise*
9. Ernst Pawel *The Nightmare of Reason*
10. Patrick O'Brian *Joseph Banks*
11. Mikhail Bulgakov *The Master and Margarita*
12. Leonid Borodin *Partings*
13. Salvatore Satta *The Day of Judgment*
14. Peter Matthiessen *At Play in the Fields of the Lord*
15. Alexander Solzhenitsyn *The First Circle*
16. Homer, translated by Robert Fitzgerald *The Odyssey*
17. George MacDonald Fraser *The Steel Bonnets*
18. Peter Matthiessen *The Cloud Forest*
19. Theodore Zeldin *The French*
20. Georges Perec *Life A User's Manual*
21. Nicholas Gage *Eleni*
22. Eugenia Ginzburg *Into the Whirlwind*
23. Eugenia Ginzburg *Within the Whirlwind*
24. Mikhail Bulgakov *The Heart of a Dog*
25. Vincent Cronin *Louis and Antoinette*
26. Alan Ross *The Bandit on the Billiard Table*
27. Fyodor Dostoyevsky *The Double*
28. Alan Ross *Time Was Away*
29. Peter Matthiessen *Under the Mountain Wall*
30. Peter Matthiessen *The Snow Lepoard*
31. Peter Matthiessen *Far Tortuga*
32. Jorge Amado *Shepherds of the Night*
33. Jorge Amado *The Violent Land*
34. Jorge Amado *Tent of Miracles*
35. Torgny Lindgren *Bathsheba*
36. Antæus *Journals, Notebooks & Diaries*
37. Edmonde Charles-Roux *Chanel*
38. Nadezhda Mandelstam *Hope Against Hope*
39. Nadezhda Mandelstam *Hope Abandoned*
40. Raymond Carver *Elephant and Other Stories*
41. Vincent Cronin *Catherine, Empress of All the Russias*
42. Federico de Roberto *The Viceroys*
43. Yashar Kemal *The Wind from the Plain*
44. Yashar Kemal *Iron Earth, Copper Sky*
45. Yashar Kemal *The Undying Grass*
46. Georges Perec *W or the Memory of Childhood*
47. Antæus *On Nature*
48. Roy Fuller *The Strange and the Good*
49. Anna Akhmatova *Selected Poems*
50. Mikhail Bulgakov *The White Guard*